V

From Catastrophe to Power

Holocaust Survivors and the Emergence of Israel

Idith Zertal

UNIVERSITY OF CALIFORNIA PRESS

Berkeley / Los Angeles / London

This book is an abridged and revised edition of *Zehavam Shel Ha'Yehudim: Ha'Hagira Ha'Yehudit Ha'Machtartit Le'Eretz Israel, 1945-1948* (The Gold of the Jews: The Clandestine Jewish Immigration to Palestine, 1945-1948) (Tel Aviv: Ofakim Books/Am Oved, 1996).

University of California Press
Berkeley and Los Angeles, California
University of California Press, Ltd.
London, England

Zertal, Idith.
    [Zehavam shel Ha'Yehudim. English]
    From catastrophe to power: Holocaust survivors and the emergence of Israel / Idith Zertal.
        p.   cm.
    Includes bibliographical references and index.
    ISBN 0-520-21578-8 (alk. paper)
    1. Jews—Europe—Migrations. 2. Holocaust survivors—Palestine. 3. Immigrants—Palestine. 4. Palestine—Emigration and immigration.
I. Title.
JV8749.P3Z4713   1988
325.5694'09'045—dc21   98-14416
                                                              CIP

Printed in the United States of America

9 8 7 6 5 4 3 2 1

The paper used in this publication meets the minimum requirements of American National Standard for Information Sciences— Permanence of Paper for Printed Library Materials, ANSI Z39.48-1984.

The publisher gratefully acknowledges the contribution provided by the General Endowment Fund, which is supported by generous gifts from the members of the Associates of the University of California Press.

*In memory of my father,
a humanist, and a soldier in the war
against the Nazis*

Contents

Illustrations follow page 212

Acknowledgments

This book was written twice, the first time in Hebrew and the second in its present version. The list of people and institutions to which I owe a debt of gratitude has grown accordingly. I am indebted first and foremost to Saul Friedländer, who assisted with the book since its beginnings, and to the late Yonathan Shapira, who gave it his blessing when it needed it most. Special thanks go to my friend Moshe Zuckerman, who read every word in the Hebrew version and whose wise and learned comments made an essential contribution to the book's writing.

During the long years of research and writing, I was privileged to receive the assistance of many. I am greatly in debt to the Inter-University Project on the Ha'apala Study (in Israel). I owe many thanks to Shlomo Ben-Ami and the Morris E. Curiel Center for International Studies at Tel Aviv University, which he established and headed, for their most generous assistance. The Rich Foundation of Switzerland and Israel gave me critical support while the book was being translated, and I thank them for it. My thanks go also to the Israel Democracy Institute in Jerusalem for its help.

I benefited from working in many archives in Israel and abroad: the Central Zionist Archive and the Joint (AJDC) Archive in Jerusalem; the History of the Haganah Archive and the Labor Archive in Tel Aviv; the Labor Party Archive in Beit Berl; the Ben-Gurion Archive in Sdeh Boker; the Ha'Kibbutz Ha'Meuhad Archive in Efal; the Public Record Office in London; les Archives nationales and les Archives du

Quai d'Orsay in Paris; les Archives de la ville and les Archives departe-mentales in Marseilles; and some other, smaller archives. In these places I found welcoming, professional teams, which turned the taxing te-dium of archival work into a pleasant experience.

In Paris, a very special man, Avraham Polonsky (Pol), one of the leaders of the World War II resistance movement "l'Armée juive," gave me access to his private archive and to the organization's archive, and trusted me with the original operations log of the Mossad from 1947, which he had kept for decades in his Paris apartment. He will not see the English version of the book. He was in his 90s when he died last year. While working on the book I was fortunate to get to know and befriend two central figures of the Mossad, Ada Sereni and Pino Ginsburg. I had long conversations with each, and I learned to admire their dedication, their wisdom, their sober and clear-eyed assessment of the past, and their profound dignity. Both are no longer alive. In a way, this book is a memorial to them and their colleagues.

The translation of the book took longer than anticipated. It was done by two: Chaim Watzman translated the first half, and Gila Svirsky did the other. Both did the difficult work with dedication and care. I owe special thanks to Gila Svirsky, who shouldered this demanding chore in almost impossible circumstances and handled it with the ut-most grace. My friend Ben Frankel, who moves freely between these two languages and their intricacies, invested his own unique flair in the final polishing of the text, making it more truly "my own." I also wish to thank David Mason, the manuscript editor, for his meticulousness and good judgment.

I have spent the last year at the United States Institute of Peace in Washington, D.C., working on my next project. While there, I devoted innumerable hours to this English edition. I wish to express my deep-est gratitude to the Institute and its staff, especially to my direct hosts at the JR Program for Senior Fellows, Joe Klaits, its director, and Sally Blair. I cannot imagine a more hospitable and generous place—both materially and intellectually—in which to work. My research assistant at the Institute, Guy Ben-Porat, was very helpful indeed, and has my most sincere thanks.

My work with the University of California Press, especially with its Sponsoring Editor Douglas Abrams Arava, has been a source of con-tinuing pleasure. It is not possible to exaggerate the praise for the pro-fessionalism and care that Arava invested in my book. I am grateful to him, to Reed Malcolm, and to the entire team for their faith in my book and for their kindness.

I am grateful to my friend, the Israeli painter Yosl Bergner, for his kind permission to use his powerful artwork for the jacket of the book. My thanks go also to Bracha Eshel, Yaron Ezrachi, and Pnina Lahav for their help.

Finally, very special and abiding thanks go to O.Z. for his contagious love for books, for Alterman—although our ways of reading his poems have since long diverged—and for being there for me.

All those mentioned here made this book possible. The responsibility for the book being what it is, is entirely my own.

Introduction

Few events in the period preceding the establishment of the State of Israel have received as much attention or have assumed as much symbolic significance as the clandestine Jewish immigration organized by the Zionists in Palestine. It has become a kind of cult theme in Zionist history, central to the story of the new Jewish redemption. The covert transfer of some eighty thousand people—including women and children, the elderly, and the ill, most of them survivors of the massacre of European Jewry—during the short span of three and one-half years (1945–48) between the Holocaust, the ultimate human catastrophe, and the establishment of the State of Israel, perceived by Zionists as the ultimate national *G'eula* (redemption)—was a project of epic dimensions. Some of its episodes became famous worldwide, inspiring prose and poetry, international press coverage, and films. Soon after the establishment of the state, a major, semi-official Israeli history book defined the immigration campaign as "a central experience" in the life of the pre-state Jewish community in Palestine. It thus became a major element in the Israeli mythology of origin.

Was it a narrative of love and redemption, of "great mercies will I gather thee"? Was it indeed a "central experience" in the life of the embryonic Israel? Or was it mostly an ingenious political endeavor effectively implemented against the backdrop of the chaos in post-war Europe, aimed at achieving, through the unique power of the helpless Holocaust survivors, the higher goal of the Zionist leadership—the establishment of a sovereign Jewish state in Palestine?

1

The purpose of this book is to go beyond the powerful and colorful Zionist rhetoric of rescue and redemption traditionally applied to the immigration enterprise and to analyze it from different points of view in terms of perspective, accumulated knowledge, and new historiographical conceptualizations. The focus of the book is a small Zionist group that organized the clandestine immigration, *Ha'mossad Le'aliya Bet,* known as the Mossad, during 1945–48. The declared goal of the Mossad from its inception on the eve of World War II was to bring Jews to Palestine covertly, circumventing the restrictions on Jewish immigration imposed by the British Mandate authorities. From 1946, however, the British navy had effectively prevented Mossad ships carrying Jewish refugees from reaching the shores of Palestine. Beginning in August of that year, the passengers on those ships were sent to British detention camps in Cyprus. The Mossad was thus transferring Jewish refugees from the displaced persons (DP) camps in Europe to British camps in Cyprus, at a very high cost. The Mossad persisted in sending ships, turning their launches and voyages into political demonstrations and dramatic media productions. Even before this, however, there had been a gradual shift in Mossad activities—from rescue actions and the assertion of the fundamental Jewish right to immigrate to Palestine, to political demonstrations aimed at breaking the British quarantine and bringing about the establishment of a Jewish state.

This change in Zionist priorities, reflected in the changes in the Mossad orientation and modes of operation, can be detected in a conversation that David Ben-Gurion had with the British high commissioner upon returning to Palestine in January 1947, after an eight-month absence. The main topic of their discussion was terrorism, which was then on the rise and of great concern to the British authorities. The commissioner, who believed that clandestine Jewish immigration was the major cause of Arab violence, suggested to Ben-Gurion that it would be in the Zionist interest for the leadership of the Yishuv (the Jewish community in Palestine) to voluntarily halt, for a given period, its organized campaign of bringing Jewish immigrants to Palestine. According to the notes the commissioner jotted down after the meeting, Ben-Gurion responded by launching into his well-known emotional tirade on the right of all Jews to settle in their homeland. The British, Ben-Gurion asserted, had no right to ask the Jews to compromise on such a fundamental principle.[1] At that time, however, Ben-Gurion knew a number of things that now cast his words in a different light. Several weeks had passed since the Mossad, for reasons of its own, had sent any ships from Europe, and no

Mossad ship would be launched in the near future. Ben-Gurion even disclosed this to the commissioner. Indeed, Ben-Gurion's top priority at the time was security, not Jewish immigration. The physical defense of the Jewish community in Palestine was more important to him than exercising the fundamental right of every Jew to settle in the homeland. A series of meetings with the foreign and colonial secretaries awaited Ben-Gurion in London, and he knew he was going to discuss the option of partitioning Palestine. He was thus amenable to reducing friction with Britain, including that over clandestine immigration.

Rhetoric may be defined as language that says one thing but means another.[2] Clandestine immigration, *ha'apala* in the Zionist idiom (literally, "summit climbing," a term charged with its own ideological meaning), was over the years always accompanied by powerful, rich, and gushing rhetoric, speech that indoctrinated and mobilized by forging consciousness and symbols. Like the Jewish settlements in the homeland and the "redemption of the land," Jewish immigration to Palestine was considered the vital force of Zionism, without which it had no life. It was the great issue—"the issue of Jewish brotherhood . . . the issue of the spiritual and mental courage of those responsible for the Jewish collective . . . the issue of Zionism's gravitation," as the Zionist leader Berl Katzenelson told the Twenty-first Zionist Congress on the eve of World War II.[3] So what did Ben-Gurion mean by what he said to the high commissioner? Was he saying one thing but already thinking another? Was Ben-Gurion not already taking other courses of action at the time he defended the principle of immigration so vehemently?

A great number of sweeping expressions of support for clandestine immigration may be found in the documented discourse and canonical texts produced in the course of building the new Hebrew nation and the establishment of a sovereign Jewish state in Palestine. Most Zionist leaders considered themselves intellectuals who were continually writing themselves. They not only played a leading part in historical events but also interpreted, labeled, and classified them in terms of importance in such a way as to influence all subsequent thought about them. They were the authors of these events in both meanings of the word. Their generalizations about the conflicts that drove the process of creating the state became accepted truths. In emphasizing some things and remaining silent about others, they have bequeathed their personal biases to the public as well as to historians.

The fact that these history makers had a vested interest in the representation of historical events in which they played a part and had a specific point of view should prompt us to read this inherited framework critically and search for other perspectives. There are, however, additional reasons for examining other frames of reference. The student of history, examining events from a distance of fifty years, necessarily has a perspective different from that of his or her predecessors. This perspective is the result not only of new evidence but also of new historiographical concepts and issues central to the historian's time and place. Such new perspectives can provide a richer array of views that, when placed against the underlying events or against the body of sources on which the account itself is based, may provide a more subtle and sophisticated decoding of those events and offer new insights.

This book is, therefore, an attempt to examine the Zionist political effort, especially the clandestine immigration campaign in the years that separated—or connected—the end of World War II and the establishment of the State of Israel. Because it was written in the 1990s, more than forty years after the establishment of Israel, the supreme political object of the Zionist endeavor, there are certain things this book cannot ignore. Most important, the establishment of the state itself, in the spring of 1948, which postdates the events described and analyzed here, in and of itself proves clandestine immigration to have been a success, a winning story. Such retroactive knowledge cannot but infuse our perception of the events that led up to the establishment of the State of Israel and of the factors that drove the process toward its "predestined" denouement. Since we know how the process ended, we must ask whether there is a causal link—and if so, of what kind—between the clandestine immigration campaign and the success of the Zionist movement's efforts to establish a Jewish state in Palestine. Do the analysis and interpretation of this campaign, when we know the end of the story, cast us into a perspective within which every event constitutes a link in a causal chain that led inevitably to that final result? In other words, does it lead us to conclude that events could not have unfolded in any other way? Or should our knowledge of the outcome of the historical process lead us, on the contrary, to ask about what did not happen, and what was not done or perhaps was missed?

Furthermore, the specific development of the State of Israel during its first fifty years cannot be erased from the consciousness of the citizen-student of history who today attempts to understand and interpret the events of the past; it cannot but color the historian's insights. The kind of society and institutions created in Israel; the uses and abuses of power; the complex relations with the Jewish world outside Israel; the image of the "Jew" and of the Jewish Diaspora that Israeli society has created for its own needs; the collective memory of the pre-state years, encompassing such meaning-laden events as the Holocaust—all these cannot but be part of the historian's consciousness. An analysis that is aware of this, that is more detached and lucid than earlier analyses, allows a reexamination and reexplanation of the role of clandestine immigration that go beyond rhetoric. It also makes it easier to unearth the various unacknowledged uses the Zionist leadership made of that powerful ideological and emotional instrument. I would suggest that this new reading of past events also offers the possibility of understanding what Ben-Gurion meant by what he said to the high commissioner.

This book investigates a project carried out by a distinct group of individuals, members of an organization belonging to the satellite elites surrounding the Yishuv's central political leadership. This body, the Mossad, was charged with bringing the Jews of the Diaspora to Palestine by clandestine means during the period lasting from 1938 until the establishment of the state. The singular collective profile that set the Mossad apart from other, parallel organizations in the Yishuv, a profile which is analyzed in this book, can also cast light on the system as a whole, as well as on the new Israeli society then emerging. The Mossad, which grew out of the Haganah, the Yishuv's defense forces, and which formally remained part of it even though it achieved almost complete independence, was one of the elites orbiting around the Zionist movement's central political elite. As part of its grand strategy for achieving political sovereignty, the state-in-the-making charged these service elites with carrying out various policies. They gathered power, wove their own networks of connections and interests, trained their operatives to manage and control their environment, and in so doing shaped the state's ruling elite in its first decades.

Ronald Syme was suspicious of elites, viewing them as selfish power and interest groups. "In all ages," he wrote, "whatever the form and name of government, an oligarchy lurks behind the facade."[4] He searched for hidden interests that link members of ruling groups and that guide their covert actions behind the scenes. In his investigation of the Roman aristocracy during the Republic's decline, he traced the family and marriage ties, the common social background, and the economic interests of the members of the aristocracy. Louis Namier, like Syme and other thinkers, argued that the subjects of history are not abstract ideas but people, "actual men and women in their relations to one another and to an actual, three-dimensional, environment, empirically experienced,"[5]—those rational beings whose knowledge is seldom sufficient, whose ideas are but distantly related to reality, and who are never moved by reason alone.[6]

The prosopographic paradigm also guides me in tracing the collective profile of the Mossad. Beyond the ideological dimension—a powerful mobilizing factor in and of itself—accompanying the organization's activities, this book also attempts to pinpoint the less obvious motives that impelled the organization's leaders and members and created the special social character of the group. I consider the characteristics—origin, educational, generational, social, and political affiliation—that united its members, their sometimes invisible internal ties, and the types of active influence and authority among them from both the outside and the inside. I then examine the effect of each of these factors on the character of the very special kind of encounter between the Zionist operatives from Palestine and the surviving Jews in the post–World War II Diaspora.

Because what we have here is an encounter. At the base of this large political enterprise was a multidimensional, social, geographical, cultural, and emotional-psychological encounter, one that had a rare kind of political power. It was this one-time yet ongoing encounter between the Jewish catastrophe and the Israeli Zionist collective that produced immense political power precisely from "the collapse of the earth," from the ultimate Jewish catastrophe.[7] Yet another truth lurks behind the creative power of that encounter. That truth, hidden or manifest, may be found in many texts from that period, both those which are part of the transient political activity and especially those constituting the residual representations of the time—basic, canonical texts in prose and in verse, bequeathing, interpreting, and simultaneously shaping the spirit of the time. At the end of this book I analyze two such texts written by two members of the Yishuv elite, constructors of the great epos of the Zionist renewal in Israel—a warrior and a poet—as examples of the multiple meanings and ambiguous speech describing the encounter. I am referring to Nathan Alterman's poem "Michael's Page" and Yitzhak Sadeh's poetic pamphlet "My Sister on the Beach."[8] Written in a major key, as part of the positive and grand Zionist outlook of the Jewish revolution in the making, the two texts are among the most important depictions of the clandestine immigration endeavor. They are of special interest because there is an unexpected leak of meaning within them, a kind of subversion, giving the text a meaning and tone different from what the writers apparently intended and what their contemporaries read into them. This subtext undermines the texts and reveals their inner truth. Both works describe the actual encounter between catastrophe and strength, between the Diaspora and the Land of Israel, in its most concrete and direct form—young men of the Zionist collective carrying the Holocaust survivors on their backs to the shores of the homeland. This image immediately became a cornerstone of the myth of the redeeming, liberating encounter between the Diaspora and the homeland after the Holocaust, between catastrophe and power.

The "nights of disembarkation" depicted in both texts, the actual and symbolic descent—or rather ascent, *aliya*—of the Jewish refugees on the beach, aided by the young men of the Yishuv, the physical contact between the two groups, the one from "there" and the one from "here," were cast in verse and prose, even though historically there were very few such nights. They were meant to be encounters of love and compassion, of unconditional welcome. Into the two texts, however, which set out to glorify the "Exile" arriving "home" at the end of a long and agonizing odyssey, slips another truth—about the horror and the terror that the Exile evokes in the Yishuv native, about the actual danger to the Zionist project inherent in the newcomers. While on the surface there is a homily of love and acceptance, in the deeper, hidden layers of the text, there is stigmatization, even a kind of denunciation, of those who had somehow survived the Holocaust.

A full analysis of the complex, multifaceted statement of Alterman's poem and Sadeh's text is reserved for the end of the book. Here I will just mention that these works contain a powerful and revealing meaning explaining in part the true nature of that encounter between the Jews of Europe and the "reborn Israel," between the bearers and their burdens, and revealing the mysterious, terrifying effect this encounter had on the ostensibly stronger party to the encounter, the people of the Land of Israel.

For what we are speaking about is the return of the repressed, and the unsettling and mysterious unknown contained within it. What, then, is this paradoxical effect that engenders in the Israeli subject, the liberated "new man," this sense of unspeakable fear of the miserable object of the Exile—"my sister . . . filthy, tattered, wild-haired"—

whom he is carrying on his shoulders? What is that frightening un-known that the Jew of the Exile arouses in the strong native on whose shoulders he weighs, threatening him to the point of "a war of two, un-seen and unbridled," a war of life and death?

A 1919 article by Freud, "Das Unheimliche" ("The Uncanny"),[9] will help, at the close of the book, in understanding the politically powerful and emotionally threatening encounter that took place after the Holocaust between the Zionists' new collective and what was left of the Diaspora. Freud discusses the kind of fear and hostility induced by the un-expected emergence of something not entirely new or unknown, some-thing once *heimlich*—intimate, close, homelike, and familiar—which dis-tancing and repression have turned into *unheimlich*—a potential source of unexplained fear and danger. What is the most familiar and intimate thing the Zionist revolution and Israeli Zionism repressed and obliter-ated within themselves in their campaign to "turn the Land of Israel from a dream into a reality"[10] if not the Diaspora, which was the nurs-ery, even the womb or the "mother" of Zionism, according to Gerschom Scholem?[11] What keeps surfacing from the depths of the Holocaust during the period of which I write, imposing itself in all its distress and suffering on the Zionist collective, if not that very same Diaspora, or what remained of it, negated and repressed for decades?

An extensive discussion of the concept and ideology of "negation of the Diaspora" and its translation into action in the Zionist experience of the Yishuv is not within the purview of this book. As others have said, the rejection of the Diaspora, the total rebellion against it and all it repre-sented, was a central, formative ethos of activist revolutionary Zionism.[12] In fact, revolutionary Zionism negated not only the Diaspora's way of life; it intended to utterly obliterate the Diasporic soul of the revolutionary Zionists themselves,[13] and along with it the past, the entire two thou-sand–year history of the Exile. Here is Yudke in Haim Hazaz's "homily," a classic textual product of the Zionist revolution—a hero of Hebrew labor who knows no fear in facing the enemy at night, who overcomes his usual monosyllabic humming in order to appear before some nameless "committee" and speak about the history of the Jewish Diaspora, which is not "our history": "This is why I oppose it, I do not recognize it, and it does not exist for me. . . . I do not accept it . . . not a single bit, not a single line, a single point."[14] For Yudke, Jewish history is synonymous with the Exile, "because from the day we were exiled from our land we were a people without a history." It bores him, holds no interest for him, and elicits from him an almost violent rejection, since "it has no heroes and world-conquerors, no rulers and men of action and masters of all deeds, only a community of misfits and castaways, sighing and crying and pleading for mercy." He therefore calls for a prohibition against having "our" children taught "their" history, Jewish history, the "shame of their forefathers." Yet such literary expressions of the "negation of the Diaspora," which Yosef Haim Yerushalmi believes are the strongest expressions of new Hebrew hostility toward the Jewish past and of the need to forget and destroy it,[15] are but an echo of the ideological and political doctrine of negation of the Diaspora that was present largely from the time of the Second Aliya. Twenty-five years before Hazaz's Yudke, in 1917, Ben-Gurion dismissed the history of two millennia when he wrote that from the time of the Jewish people's last national disaster, the Bar-Kokhba rebellion, "we had no more Jewish history, because the history of a nation is only that which creates the nation as a single whole, as a national unit, and not what happens to individuals and groups within the nation." Ben-Gurion agrees that the Jewish people had "histories"—histories of persecution and legal discrimination, inquisitions and pogroms, scholars and famous people—but they had no history. "For 1,800 years . . . we have been kept out of world history, which is composed of the chronicle of peoples," he concludes.[16] That same year, after the Balfour Declaration, Ben-Gurion wrote that "all that is great and important enough for our new journey we will carry with us; whatever is small and rotten and exilic we will cast aside so that it may disappear with the bad heritage of the dead past, so that it will not cast its shadow on our new soul, and so that it will not desecrate the holiness of the redemption."[17] Another leader of socialist Zionism, Berl Katzenelson, who, like Ben-Gurion, belonged to the Second Aliya, which left its imprint on the history of the Yishuv and the first decades of the state, tried in the middle of the 1930s to provide an explanation of why Zionism had to "reject" the Exile. "There was a time when we were obliged to close our eyes to the Exile. We had to fix our faces on the soil of the homeland, to make reality from the dream of the Land of Israel." The only relief that the Exile then could have, according to Katzenelson, was in going to Palestine "in order to be what we are." It was then permissible to take from the Exile "everything we could take"—"to rob" the Exile. Now, however, different times had come, Katzenelson said, and the Yishuv had to direct its gaze to the Diaspora because "we are strong, established, rich in material and in spiritual assets for the Exile." It should be understood that "today's Diaspora is tomorrow's Israel. Those we speak about today dismissively and disparagingly will be the Israel of tomorrow. The builders will come from them. Out of concern for what happens in Israel tomorrow we must once more hold out a hand to the Exile."[18] The cat is thus out of the bag. The only perspective is that of Zionism. The needs of Israel rather than those of the Diaspora are the determining ones. Zionists consider the needs of the Yishuv, not those of the Diaspora. It was a concern for the future of Israel and its construction that obligated Zionists—after Israel gained strength at the expense of the Diaspora, after it "sapped" the Diaspora's vitality—in their concern for the Diaspora. The Jews of the Diaspora should be helped not for their own sake, for what they are, but because tomorrow they will be Israel. In calling on his compatriots to redirect their gaze at the Diaspora, Katzenelson, considered the most liberal and "humanist" of the Zionist leaders in Palestine, expresses the same instrumental-political attitude toward it that was so characteristic of the pragmatic, political Ben-Gurion.

This is the background to the encounter with the remnants of the Holocaust, which arouses such inexplicable anxiety, such mysterious fear among the children of the Zionist revolution. The return of the remnants of this Exile, with their "Diasporishness," from the abyss of oppression and destruction evokes the Freudian "uncanny" and threatens to overpower, to swallow up the Zionist subject. "It will be hell if all the [DP] camps come [to Palestine] . . . all this filth just as it is," a rescue envoy in Europe blurted out to a visiting Ben-Gurion at the beginning of 1946.[19]

This long "turning away" from the Diaspora and the "missed encounter" that was its result—the encounter of the Zionist collectivity with the physical and psychological reality of the Diaspora after the Holocaust—are there in the depths of Alterman's poem and Sadeh's pamphlet. Both, in describing the historic "nights of disembarkation" in which young Zionists from Palestine helped Jewish refugees to the beach, reveal in their subtext the process of utter estrangement of which the Diaspora was and still is the object. The Diaspora is experienced through its weight—dead weight—on the shoulders of the young Zionist heroes, or through its defilement, the horrifying tattoo on the body of the young refugee woman. The Diaspora is represented by its hoarse, heavy breathing, by its stranglehold on the young Zionists' throats. There is forced contact of bodies between "bearers" and "burdens," but there is no recognition. The refugees were invisible. Alterman's poem registers no eye contact between the Zionist bearer and the Diaspora burden; Sadeh's eye sees a stigma and stereotype. My argument is that precisely this absence of gaze, or the presence of a clichéd one—in either case, Zionist blindness to the Diaspora—led to the suspension of a true mourning for its destruction and that made it possible to turn the Diaspora, in those critical years, into Zionism's most effective tool in its national struggle. I would then suggest that a new and different reading of the clandestine Jewish immigration campaign of 1945–48 is required, one that reveals the campaign's other motives beyond the one great reason for the operation—the realization of the right of all Jews to come to their homeland.

My reading of this enterprise is based largely on the existing historical documentation, particularly the papers of the Mossad itself. For an underground, or semi-underground, organization, the Mossad left voluminous records of all kinds: operation reports, cables, letters, notes from telephone conversations, and written testimonies. In addition, most of the Mossad's major activists left personal letters, diaries, or memoirs, as well as testimonies kept in archives in Israel. Some of the few who were alive when the book was being written shared their recollections with me in person. This impressive body of material, even if partially consisting of later testimony about earlier events, provides important supplementary material for understanding the events, the background against which they took place, and the positions of the protagonists. In analyzing the conceptual framework of the Mossad's work, the party and political context in which it operated, and its ties to similar groups in Yishuv society and the Jewish world (the American-Jewish Joint Distribution Committee in particular) and to central figures in the Yishuv leadership, I have relied on the main bodies of documents of the period. These include the minutes of meetings of the Jewish Agency Executive and other relevant Jewish Agency offices; minutes of meetings of other "national" institutions; relevant records of the major political parties involved in the enterprise; and especially the documents of the official bodies—secretariat, central committee, council, and other forums—of the Ha'Kibbutz Ha'Meuhad movement and of Mapai (the Israel Workers Party, the Yishuv's largest and dominant political movement). The international backdrop to the Mossad's work is presented largely in the first three chapters, which describe events on the Mossad's three chief fronts—Italy, France, and Romania (and eastern Europe as a whole). To demonstrate the triangular (Mossad–local government–British authorities) relationships that arose on each of these fronts, I have used the literature dealing with these times and local archival material.

The book is divided into three parts. The first is devoted to what I call the "Plot." It presents the narrative of the covert immigration movement. The second part, "Organization," is mostly an analysis, along several central dimensions, of the Zionist organization that carried out the operation. Part III, "Consciousness," presents the spirit of the events, the ethical, ideological, and political backdrop to all that was done in the context of this covert activity. Jacques Le Goff defines this in his article "Les mentalités" as that thing in the air that eludes the individual subjects of history because it marks the nonpersonal content of their thought, that thing that the lowest-ranking soldier knows without having received an explicit order, "that which is common to Julius Caesar and to every last soldier in his legions, to St. Louis and the peasant who dwells on his estate, to Christopher Columbus and to the sailor on his ships."[20] Since Julius Caesar, St. Louis, Christopher Columbus, and, in our case, Ben-Gurion, left behind them richer documentation than did their rank and file, more information about what preoccupied and motivated them, about their world and their vision, is available. I have therefore placed Ben-Gurion and his positions about the Holocaust survivors and clandestine immigration at the center of the concluding section of the book, which deals with the zeitgeist, the Zionist *mentalités,* of that time.

The narrative of the first three chapters is not linear. It is, rather, organized around geographic axes, the three theaters in which the Mossad operated in organizing underground immigration. The three stories provide a view of the entire European scene after the end of World War II, with millions of people on the move, utter political and social chaos, porous borders between countries, and the birth of the cold war—all elements that facilitated the extensive work of the Mossad. Each of these chapters is itself organized around a central theme—the most important and dramatic episodes in each theater. I have described the geopolitical circumstances at length in the chapters to illustrate what seems to me to be central in understanding this mass political immigration project—not the mastery of the Mossad, which indeed was impressive, but rather the time and the place in which the Mossad operated and the overwhelming Jewish catastrophe of World War II. The Mossad's skill and astuteness lay largely in its being there to capitalize on these circumstances and forge from them and from the

Jewish catastrophe a powerful Zionist political force, and also in its ability to quickly adapt to changing circumstances and switch to whatever theater promised to be the most productive.

The second part of the work addresses the organization and its methods of operation. The first chapter of this section (Chapter 4) discusses the way the Mossad made the events of the clandestine immigration into media productions to maximize the political propaganda value of its actions. This it did via the organization of resistance by the refugees on the ships, which turned the ships into Zionism's main battlefields of that period. Chapter 5 discusses the Mossad's development from its establishment on the eve of World War II, its organizational structure, its internal hierarchy, its work methods, the decision-making process, its human collective portrait (depicted through short biographical sketches of the central figures), and its ties and relations with other Yishuv institutions and organs, such as the Jewish Agency Executive, the Haganah, the Palmach, the Bricha operation (which directed the movement of Jewish refugees toward the Mossad's gathering points), and the political parties. Chapter 6 discusses the Mossad's ties with the American Joint Distribution Committee (or JDC), which was the major funder (providing more than 75 percent of the budget) of the Mossad's activities during these years. The chapter deals not only with the tangled and problematic financial connections between the two bodies, but also with the stormy love-hate relationship of these two fundamentally different organizations, representing contradictory concepts of how to resolve the "Jewish question," that is, the problem of displaced Jews after the war.

The third and last part of the book, "Consciousness," which contains the concluding chapter and the epilogue, is largely an analysis of Ben-Gurion's complex and changing attitudes and positions toward the remnant of the Jews in Europe, toward clandestine immigration in general, and toward the Mossad in particular. Through an analysis of these positions I explore the broad conceptual, mental, and political contexts in which the Mossad operated and which motivated and conditioned its work during the period under study. I focus on Ben-Gurion's positions because he, more than any other Zionist leader, influenced Mossad activists and instilled in them an ethos and modes of action. For Ben-Gurion the clandestine immigration was always a weapon—a rhetorical weapon, a mobilizing weapon, a weapon for fortifying his power base within the Zionist leadership, and a real political weapon in his battle to achieve Jewish sovereignty in Palestine. He saw the clandestine immigration as a means to his greater ends; his attitudes were in the main pragmatic and rational, always striving for the larger purpose of his actions. These positions were not necessarily revealed in emotional tirades of the sort he voiced to the British high commissioner, but rather in the decisions and the practical moves he made during major events and their implications for history and the lives of thousands of people.

PART I

Plot

CHAPTER 1

Italy: Between Europe and Palestine

Britain's frustration with Italy's role as a staging ground for the Jewish clandestine immigration campaign in the years 1945–48 was summed up by a British official in January 1948: "It seems to me to be monstrous," he wrote in a memorandum, "that when we have virtually stopped all complicity in the traffic by all other nations except the Communists, our old despised and beaten enemy, the Italians, should be allowed to flout us openly like this."[1] The official, whose signature is illegible, had reason to be angry. From August 1945, when the first Mossad ship sailed from Italian shores, to the day he wrote his memorandum, twenty-five secret ships carrying 16,500 Jews had sailed from the ports of "despised and beaten" Italy, a country occupied by the Allies.[2] Many of the Mossad ships were launched not only with the knowledge of the Italian authorities, but with the assistance of senior figures at various levels of the Italian establishment. The Italians, undeterred by British threats and sanctions, actively aided Mossad agents or simply looked the other way. The circumstances of Italy's international policy, internal politics, geography, and society coincided with a unique constellation of Mossad personnel and deployment to make Italy the major European launching point for Mossad ships during these years. This chapter analyzes these circumstances not through a chronological narrative, but by focusing on the most prominent and significant events in order to expose the deeper structures that produced them. The central event in this episode is what Zionist historiography calls the La Spezia affair.

On 4 April 1946, on the outskirts of the small town of La Spezia in northwestern Italy, Italian police and military personnel intercepted a convoy of thirty-eight British army trucks carrying more than one thousand Jewish refugees. The truck convoy, with forged shipping documents, was led by two men from the Jewish Brigade, the British unit composed of men from the Yishuv, which was then stationed in Italy. To save their thousand Jews, who were supposed to sail for Palestine from the little port of La Spezia that same day, the two tried to turn the convoy around and flee, but were stopped immediately by a police roadblock with machine guns aimed at the trucks. In the resulting turmoil, the two Jewish soldiers decided to hand themselves over as hostages to the Italian police and allow the refugees to be transferred under guard to the waiting ship.[3] The unexpected, and almost fortuitous, capture of the convoy was the result of a series of mishaps and errors committed by all involved. Yet it was the starting point of the visible chapter that in one stroke publicized the extensive underground activity of the Zionist movement in Europe in general and Italy in particular. For more than a month, during which the refugees were confined to their ship in the small Italian port and attracted international attention, the displaced Jews and their Zionist organizers from the Yishuv were a major preoccupation of the Italian administration, the British authorities, and the Zionist leadership. This key event not only forced the covert Mossad out of the secrecy of the underground into open activity, but it set an example for further Mossad actions and can be seen as a case study of the way this shrewd, efficient Zionist organization functioned in Europe during the post-war period.

Three historical protagonists were responsible for the form the La Spezia affair took: the British, the Jews/Zionists, and the Italians. The Italians found themselves tangled in this incident and in the thicket of British-Zionist relations through no will of their own. In the spring of 1946 Italy had other problems. The country's social fabric had been ravaged by the war that had ended just one year before. Its infrastructure had been largely destroyed during the Allied invasion: some eight thousand bridges, 60 percent of the roads, 40 percent of the railroad tracks, and 70 percent of the peninsula's port facilities had been irreparably damaged.[4] Cities and towns had been razed by land battles and aerial bombardment. About half of the public facilities in the country—including schools, hospitals, and train stations—could no longer be used, and about 10 percent of the residential housing had been demolished. In La Spezia, a small and picturesque port on the Italian Riviera that had been bombed from the air, only a few streets remained whole. The shipyards were in ruins, and the harbor was peppered with the hulks of sunken vessels.[5]

One of the most difficult problems the Italians faced—unsuccessfully, because of their precarious economic condition and weak international standing—was the tens of thousands of refugees of all nationalities who were inundating the country. The Italian authorities were helpless in the face of this phenomenon, having been denied most of the fundamental powers a sovereign state enjoys, including control over its borders. These responsibilities were in the hands of the Allied Control Committee, which had functioned in the country since Italy's surrender.

The Italians were not, however, particularly disturbed by the Jewish refugees, even though they were flowing in from the north at the rate of about two thousand a month.[6] Out of the total of 160,000 refugees and displaced persons who congregated in Italy, the Jews were but a handful and were generally, thanks to Jewish organizations, better cared for and did not need the Italians to clothe or feed them.[7] For the British, however, this movement of Jewish refugees into Italy overland and then out by sea to Palestine was a major concern. In mid-October 1945, a Criminal Investigation Department (CID) report determined that there were already twenty thousand Jewish refugees in Italy and that there was a clear link between their infiltration into Italy by land and the aspiration of the Jews in the DP camps and in Eastern Europe to reach Palestine in any way they could.[8] In fact, as early as the autumn of 1945, a short time after the first Mossad ship was launched from Italy, the British began exerting pressure on the Italians to halt this movement at both ends—at the northern frontier, where the Jewish refugees entered Italy, and at the ports, from which they set sail under the auspices of the Zionist organizations to Palestine. At the end of December 1945 the British political adviser to the commanding officer of the Allied forces in the Mediterranean reported on the difficulties in sealing the Italian border. The moment one road was blocked, several others opened, he claimed. This movement into Italy, he estimated, "is part of a very large organization which aims at using Italy and Austria as transit camps between Central Europe and Palestine," and he demanded joint action by Allied forces to stop it.[9] In January 1946 the British foreign secretary, Ernest Bevin, stated that the accumulation of Jewish DPs in Italy "is becoming dangerous." In a memorandum to the Cabinet Overseas Reconstruction Committee, Bevin demanded "action . . . both with the Italian Government and with UNRRA [the United Nations Relief and Rehabilitation Administration] if the situation is to be remedied."[10]

Britain was concerned about Italy for a reason. This country had become the center of Mossad operations after the war. Its long coastline had many natural harbors, and it was relatively close to Palestine and centrally located in Europe, proximate to the major concentrations of Jewish refugees. Furthermore, the country's political and social chaos and the fragility of its institutions of government made it an easy place to work covertly.[11] Until April 1946, when the La Spezia affair began, the Mossad had managed to send eleven refugee ships from Europe. Eight of these had sailed from Italian ports (two had sailed from Greece and one from France). The Italian response to Britain's pressure to stop this movement was less than feeble. Both the authorities and the public in post-war Italy were favorably inclined toward the Jewish-Zionist cause and saw no reason to make trouble for these refugees, who had survived the Nazis and had taken temporary sanctuary in Italy on their way to their homeland. In April 1945 Italian prime minister Ivanoe Bonomi told the Jewish Agency representative in his country, Umberto Nahon, that anti-Semitism had always been alien to the character and tradition of the Italian people and that the anti-Jewish measures taken by Italy during the war had been a disastrous outcome of the alliance with Germany. Italy, he said, assented to and would strive to facilitate the Jewish migration to and from its territory.[12] Presumably, this was not just a belated attempt by the Italians to atone for their Fascist period, nor simply a politically pragmatic move to associate themselves with a humanitarian cause that was not controversial at that time. It was also an expression of the Italian establishment's sincere feelings for the Jews, which grew out of the Fascist debacle. Furthermore, the immediate interest of the Italians was to do all they could to help the Jews leave their country and so reduce the size of the refugee problem they were confronting. A less noble but not necessarily less vital motive for the Italians was the trail of money that the organizers of the Jewish clandestine migration in Italy left wherever they went.[13]

In contrast, the Italians had no particular sympathy for the British. The tens of thousands of British soldiers who were, until December 1947, stationed on their soil were a constant reminder to the Italians that their country was occupied and that they had lost their sovereignty. Nor did the conditions offered to the Italians in the peace treaty make the British popular. Italy's prime minister, Alcide de Gasperi, who succeeded Bonomi in December 1945, stated this in very clear terms at the peace conference in Paris.[14] Unlike the Americans, whose inclination was to ease the restrictions imposed on the Italians, the British took a hard line. The British ambassador, for example, recommended that his country reinforce its internal security units in Italy and increase military control over Italian ports (the Italian navy was forbidden to use its remaining vessels to patrol its country's coastline). However, this recommendation was not accepted only because it was opposed to the American position that Italy should be allowed, as the American secretary of state said at the first session of the foreign ministers' meeting in Paris, "the largest possible freedom [to re-build her broken economic and political life] without a formal peace treaty."[15]

An additional reason—perhaps the most important one—for the Italians' unwillingness to cooperate with the British in hunting down Jewish refugees was their assumption that the American president, Congress, and media, not to mention the American Jewish community (whose political power was the object of an almost mystical reverence), were closely following the fate of the Jewish refugees in Europe, in-cluding Italy. The goodwill and aid of the Americans were vital to the Italians both for economic rehabilitation and in advancing their cause in international forums and the peace talks.[16] A British report on clandes-tine Jewish immigration to Palestine issued in the summer of 1946, after the conclusion of the La Spezia affair, stated that the Italians "are fright-ened of the storm of protest that may arise if they stop the Jews sailing." The author of the report added that "we are not very popular in Italy at the moment."[17] The Italians thus were careful not to take any action that might damage their relations with the United States. Moreover, they sought to use the conflicting interests of the Allies, between which they found themselves trapped, as a springboard for improving their bargaining position in the talks on the post-war treaties and arrange-ments to regain their sovereignty and improve their shattered economy. Thus the capture of the Jewish convoy was not the result of a sudden Italian urge to cooperate with the British, as the latter originally thought, but the result of a misjudgment.[18] The Italians had assumed that the refugees were Italian Fascists escaping to Franco's Spain. By the time they realized their error, it was too late. The local police comman-der had already reported the incident to the Allied Control Committee, and the matter was no longer exclusively in Italian hands.

The Italian response to the events at La Spezia took two forms: the public's response and the authorities' response. The public reaction on the local level was largely spontaneous, but it was also handled with great skill by the head of the Mossad's Italian station, Yehuda Arazi, who dis-guised himself as a refugee and functioned on the ship as the refugees' leader. With the help of Aldo Rastani, a young Italian journalist from a

Genoan newspaper who voluntarily became the intermediary between the ship and the outside world, the Palestinian Zionist agent waged his virtuosic propaganda war, setting the pace and tone for the whole affair. He conducted a sophisticated and effective public relations campaign aimed at the local Italians, Rome, and the world as a whole—not excluding the refugees on the ship. Arazi could not, however, have achieved such success in molding public opinion without the Italians' traditional sympathy for the Jews and their post-war guilt feelings. Indeed, from the moment the local Italians learned, through Rastani, that the people imprisoned on the ship were not Fascists on their way to Spain but Jewish survivors of the Nazi horrors on their way to Palestine, the entire population of the city and the surrounding region made numerous gestures of generosity and friendship.[19]

According to Arazi, testifying shortly after the events, the leaders of the anti-Fascist resistance in Liguria and other underground fighters assisted the Jews and Arazi throughout the affair, and even before. They directed him to the port of La Spezia in the first place, where the ships were prepared for sailing. They put him in touch with the Italian district prefect, who promised to spirit the ship away from the port. Through the agency of these partisans, the longshoremen in Genoa threatened to declare a general strike at the port if the ship and its refugees were forced to sail to Genoa so that the British could forcibly take them off the ship and interrogate them.[20] The Italian Socialist Party, which was holding its national convention in Florence at the time of the incident, issued a statement in support of the refugees and called on the authorities to allow them to sail to their chosen destination.[21]

The response of government officials, both local and in Rome, was more complex. For the most part they were embarrassed but powerless, caught between their traditional sympathy for the Jews and their subordination to the Allies. Their actions were thus a response to moves by the British and the Jews and were aimed at achieving a compromise or untangling a predicament, and saving Italy's skin. More than anything else, the Italians feared that the situation in La Spezia would deteriorate into violence. The Jewish threats that they would take desperate measures (for example, collective suicide) and the potential international repercussions of such actions were the Italians' nightmare. This fear was the major motivator of the Italian authorities. They refused to play the role the British expected of them, rebuffing the British demand to interrogate the refugees in an effort to expose the organization behind the activity. Moreover, after the plight of the Jews on the ship was publicized and the Jewish Agency representative met with Italian prime minister de Gasperi,[22] there were even attempts by the Italians to persuade the British government to respond favorably to the Jewish Agency's demands regarding the number of refugees who would be allowed to sail to Palestine, as well as the date of their departure.[23]

British Ambiguity

The episode was a complete surprise for the British. They were in the process of formulating their policy against illegal Jewish immigration throughout the European theater, and capturing Mossad ships at their European points of departure was one of their major goals. However, when the opportunity presented itself at La Spezia, they were unprepared. All in all, the British response was marked by confusion and a lack of coordination. The problem of the Jewish refugees attempting to leave Europe and sail to Palestine required the British to work on several fronts: the north Italian frontier, from which the Jews insinuated themselves into the country at a rate of hundreds, sometimes thousands, a month;[24] the coast and ports of embarkation from which, beginning in August 1945, the Mossad ships sailed;[25] and the refugee camps, which served as the human reservoir for the Mossad's campaign. In addition to the diplomatic pressure (exerted by British ambassador in Rome, Noel Charles) and military pressure to reinforce control of the northern Italian border, the British knew that they had to prevent UNRRA from extending aid, even indirectly, to the illegal immigrants. They also had to increase cooperation between Allied headquarters and the Italian security authorities to control the flow of people into the country and try to get, in exchange for this, Italian assistance in preventing the refugee ships from sailing.

The situation in the field, however, and contradictory interests thwarted a concerted British action. While London was instructing its units in Italy to take all measures to prevent the refugee ships from sailing, the headquarters there retorted that a "majority of Italian ports are no longer under military control and therefore that prevention of embarkation of illegal immigrants to Palestine cannot be guaranteed."[26] While the British military and diplomats in Italy and the Mediterranean argued that Italian cooperation was vital to the effectiveness of these preventative measures and demanded that the Italians be included in the efforts to halt Jewish migration through Italy, London decided against this in order not to restrict its military and naval options and to avoid having to give the Italians information about the ships involved. Their fear was that the information would be leaked to the Jews, allowing them to take "steps to circumvent any measure of control."[27]

By the time the Italians captured the convoy of Jewish refugees on the outskirts of La Spezia, at the beginning of April 1946, however, the British had overcome their reservations about cooperation with the Italians. As Jews continued to stream into the country and sail out of it, the argument for autonomous, exclusive British action became weaker. Thus, upon hearing the first reports of the arrest of the convoy and before learning the truth about the event, the British ambassador was quick to see the capture of the Jews as proof that, in contradiction of his predictions, the Italians were willing to cooperate with the British in their struggle against Jewish migration.[28] He soon faced a double paradox: the first Mossad ship captured in a European port was siezed not by the British, who were not even prepared to cope with the repercussions of such a spectacular achievement, but by the reluctant Italians, who, by mistake, offered the British this troublesome gift.

Paradox and ambivalence characterized all British moves that followed. The British planned first to interrogate the refugees and then return them to their points of origin outside Italy. Obtaining this information was, however, likely to require the use of violence. The Foreign Office, which did not want the British to be involved in such an interrogation, ordered the British delegation in Italy to leave the questioning to the Italians and went so far as to recommend avoidance of any direct British diplomatic connection to the interrogation. So ambivalent and convoluted were the instructions from London that they merit direct quoting: "Any appearance of peremptory interference on our part with the business of the Italian authorities" should be prevented, instructed the Foreign Office, "both on the grounds of general policy and because the Italians might be led to think that their active cooperation would be unnecessary on future occasions." The Foreign Office also suggested that Allied headquarters "should try to come to some local arrangement with the Italian authorities that would continue to associate them as far as possible in any action taken. They will no doubt be glad to enlist our help in disposing of this party if we let them know that it will be forthcoming."[29]

These instructions proved to be mistaken not only because the Italians refused to play the role assigned them by London, but also because the Jewish refugees under Arazi's leadership had their own agenda. Arazi called the shots, and he did so in a way different from what the British had expected. A hunger strike by all the refugees on the ship and threats of setting the ship on fire and engaging in public suicide[30] were the last thing the British needed. So when the chairman of the British Labour Party, Harold Laski, showed up in La Spezia a week after the affair began, the British authorities welcomed him, though they had earlier been less than enthusiastic about the prospect of his visit.[31] Laski, a close associate of Prime Minister Clement Attlee and of Foreign Secretary Ernest Bevin, had come to Italy as a guest of the Twenty-fourth Congress of the Italian Socialist Party. A Jew who never tried to conceal this fact, he now used it in his meeting with the agitated refugees on the ship and managed to contain the crisis. He promised to present the refugees' case to Bevin and do all he could to help them get to Palestine. In exchange, the refugees promised to end their hunger strike, then in its fourth day, and refrain from violence or acts of desperation until Laski met Bevin upon his return to London, no later than 19 April. It was also agreed that during this period the refugees' living conditions on the anchored ships would be improved, that the police would be deployed out of the harbor, and that no attempt would be made to remove them by force. The British also committed themselves to releasing the Italians who had been arrested at the outbreak of the affair on charges of aiding the refugees.[32]

The temporary lull in events at La Spezia shifted the focus of the plot from Italy to Britain and Palestine. The head of the Jewish Agency's Political Department, Moshe Shertok (later Sharett), who was in London at the time, demanded of Colonial Secretary George Hall that the ships be allowed to set sail and bring all one thousand refugees to Palestine at the expense of the monthly quota of certificates (immigration permits) that had not been used in November and December 1945. Shertok, who had stayed abreast of the events at La Spezia—he received daily reports from the Mossad's Geneva agent, who had rushed to La Spezia to handle things on shore—worked on several levels in London. Parallel with his talks at the Colonial Office, he sent instructions to La Spezia and demanded that the refugees make no concessions.[33] The two parties directly involved, the British and the Zionists, ostensibly adhered to unbending positions, but in practice they searched for a compromise that would prevent the deterioration of the situation into violence and death and that also would not excessively embarrass the other side. This unseen balance worked to soften the actions taken by both sides under cover of their tough rhetoric. Both the British and the Jews had been unprepared for the incident, and both were feeling each other out to discern what force they had and their willingness to use it. Both sides also knew that the struggle between them would not end with the resolution of this crisis and that they would be grappling for a long time to come. At first, the colonial secretary categorically rejected Shertok's request for a special quota of immigration certificates for the refugees, arguing that the Jewish Agency should use certificates from its regular monthly quota.[34] A compromise in this affair, he reasoned, was likely to lead to a negative Arab response to the pending recommendations of the Anglo-American Commission on the Jewish refugee problem. He was also concerned that Britain would lose its deterrent power in the fight against clandestine immigration, and he claimed that "if we now deliberately further the voyage, we shall stultify ourselves if we ever ask such [Italian] co-operation in the future." The hunger strike declared by the leaders of the Yishuv in Palestine in sympathy with the strikers in La Spezia was defined by him as a political move meant to force Britain's hand.[35] Nevertheless, in a tone contradicting his inflexible stand, the colonial secretary described to his prime minister the dangers that a tough British policy could bring about. Implicit in this description was a recommendation to seek a compromise in order to prevent parliamentary intervention, above and beyond Laski's lobbying of Foreign Secretary Bevin, and avoid pressures from the Americans.

Other factors played a role. There were reports from Palestine about harsh Zionist rhetoric comparing the La Spezia affair to the traumatic sinking of the ships *Patria* and *Struma,* with their hundreds of casualties,[36] and nervous cables arrived from the different British delegations in Italy concerning the refugees' threats to commit suicide if the ship were not allowed to sail.[37] Furthermore, the American press was evincing a growing interest in the affair. Ambassador Noel Charles called on the government to choose between "the risk of violence and bad publicity on the one hand and some immediate further concessions on the other," recommending the latter course.[38] All this finally impelled the British government, over the opposition of the high commissioner, to allow the La Spezia refugees to sail to Palestine. They were to enter the country in two contingents on the basis of the regular monthly allowance of certificates.

The Zionist side was not united either. On behalf of the refugees, Yehuda Arazi rejected the compromise, claiming that it would undo the gain that had been achieved and that it "diminished" the position of the refugees, the real heroes of the affair.[39] He demanded that the Zionist leadership live up to its rhetoric ("Where is the pride that you preach?").[40] In the end, in a resolution that was a composite of all the compromise proposals made up until then, it was decided that the refugees would not be divided and would sail together, as the Zionists demanded. It was agreed, however, as the British demanded, that the refugees would not reach the Palestinian coast before 17 May, the day the regular immigration quota for that month ran out.[41] For both sides the affair was an instructive lesson in the limited power of force and the great power of weakness. The British learned, for the first time in their war against Jewish clandestine immigration, about the limitations of the force they could use when faced with survivors of Nazism. This first direct confrontation also demonstrated to the British, and even more to the Zionists, the psychological-political and propaganda power embodied by the refugees.

One Person's Signature

On 8 May 1946, five weeks after the thousand Jewish refugees were arrested in La Spezia, two Mossad ships sailed from the small port with the refugees on board. A few days later they reached Palestine, openly and conspicuously.[42] One passenger, however, was missing. Dr. de Paz, a.k.a. Yehuda Arazi, secretly left the ship after it had gone some distance from the Italian coast and returned, in a small boat that awaited him, to La Spezia. He was to continue to head the Mossad station in Italy for almost a year, where he would be part of a network of agents active throughout the world. In the spring of 1946 the Mossad was already fully deployed. Its agents were planted on several continents, and each agent worked in his or her location and within the area of his or her responsibility with a great deal of independence. Arazi was a prime example of this. The La Spezia episode bore not only the imprint of the specific geopolitical circumstances of time and place, but also the signature of Yehuda Arazi. It marked a personal high point in Arazi's long years of tumultuous Zionist clandestine work, which stretched back to the 1920s.

Yehuda Arazi had arrived in Italy nine months previously, in June 1945, under a false identity.[43] The original purpose of his assignment to Italy was to put him out of reach of the British in Palestine, who had been hunting him since 1943 because of his involvement in clandestine arms procurement. After hiding in Palestine for a long time, he was spirited out of the country and held in a safe house in Alexandria.[44] As soon as the war ended, at the beginning of June, Arazi was smuggled, in a Polish air-crew uniform, from Cairo to Bari in Italy.[45] Arazi was not a Mossad man, although he knew the organization's work and members well from joint activities before and during the war. At that time Arazi had been part of the special intelligence department called Special Operations (SO2), which was directly under the command of the British War Office and was assigned to foster underground organizations and help plan sabotage activities in areas likely to fall into Nazi hands. This was part of the cooperation between British intelligence and the Haganah during the war.[46] His area of operations was the Balkan countries, where Mossad agents were also working in a desperate effort to smuggle Jews out before the countries fell under Nazi occupation. That joint work left both sides with unpleasant memories. Arazi criticized the Mossad's way of working, its egalitarian structure, and its decision-making process; he argued that it should function as a "military organization."[47] For their part, Mossad agents had little faith in Arazi because of his "arrogant" and "totalitarian" disposition. At the end of the war, when Mossad headquarters deployed its agents in Europe, Arazi was not among them. It was Haganah commander Eliahu Golomb who sent Arazi, one of his closest and most loyal associates, to Italy.[48] He was thus imposed on the Mossad from above. Formally, he was autonomous in choosing his base of operations and the areas of activities he would engage in, and Golomb also promised him that he could pick the men with whom he would work. Arazi's intent was to initiate some clandestine immigration activities on his own for the period he worked in Italy, although Golomb told him explicitly that there had to be contact with the Mossad. In any event, Arazi believed he was going to Italy for only a short period in order to take a few groups of Jewish survivors out of the country.[49] The reality turned out to be different. Upon his arrival he encountered total chaos. He also found great potential for rescue work, along with two Mossad agents who had spent several months there without sending even one ship and had managed to quarrel with other Zionist agents who were operating in Italy.

Because Arazi was an outsider, not a hostage to routine or standard operating procedures or a prisoner to party or other sectarian loyalties,[50] and because he was an individualist by nature—insubordinate and a nimble improviser—he could maneuver with deftness in a country where work was such a complicated and intricate business. Since he was not formally a Mossad agent, he succeeded in blazing a trail through the tangle of Jewish and Zionist organizations operating there, which had already parceled out among themselves the functions, the territories, and the areas of activity. In addition, Arazi had an aura of personal authority and a unique charisma, and he was an expert at exploiting them. His physical appearance was imposing, and, unlike his Yishuv socialist partners, he stood out as a dapper, worldly man. His daring past adventures (which were known to his colleagues), an inexhaustible store of energy, and a certain aloofness and air of mystery added to his status. His arrival in Italy produced a shake-up in all the Zionist bodies there—the Mossad station, Jewish-British soldiers, the Jewish Agency delegation, the headquarters for the Diaspora—all of which were on bad terms with each other. Boats, money, possible ports of departure, Jewish refugees, Yishuv representatives whom he could work with in his own way, and good Italian contacts were what Arazi was looking for after his arrival.[51]

The most important element were the Jewish refugees—the "human material," according to the Zionist formulation, for the clandestine immigration. In this regard there was a major change concurrent but unconnected with Arazi's arrival. Arazi was sharp enough, however, to recognize this upheaval in the making. "There has been a great change during the last few days," he reported to the Mossad chief at the end of June. "Jews have begun to flow into here with our help and at their own initiative. There are close to a thousand of them and the way we see it in a month or two we will reach many thousands."[52] Like others, he was still not fully aware of the potential of the survivors of the war, who were spontaneously making their way toward Italy in a vast wave of migration.

Immediately after the war, the Jewish Brigade men stationed in Tarvisio, where the Italian, Austrian, and Yugoslavian borders met, set out on unofficial reconnaissance missions on both the Austrian and Yugoslavian sides of the border to look for Jewish survivors in the refugee camps. On 1 June representatives of the Eastern European Survivors Brigade reached the border on their own initiative. The Survivors Brigade had been founded in Romania on 26 April by Abba Kovner and his associates, resistance fighters and survivors of the Jewish ghettoes. On 31 May, ninety-eight Jewish refugees had been found in Villach on the Austrian border, across from Tarvisio. They and members of Kovner's group told of thousands of survivors who were waiting for a signal from the Yishuv.[53] During June 1945 the members of the Jewish Brigade, most of whom wanted to be discharged and return home as quickly as possible, began to grasp the nature of the human challenge they faced in Europe.[54] They did not, however, correctly estimate the scope of the phenomenon, and spoke of only fourteen thousand survivors. Yet the news that a Jewish brigade was stationed in northern Italy did spread over all of Europe and began to attract Jewish survivors from eastern and

central Europe to Italy. Italy thus became the focus for the migration of
Jewish survivors. Reports from the Yishuv representatives, soldiers in the
Jewish Brigade, people from the Diaspora Center, and Mossad agents
suggest that, between June and mid-August 1945, some fifteen thousand
Jews reached Italy over the country's northern border, mostly from
Austria, in every possible way.[55] Refugees sneaked across on foot, in army
trucks, and in trains. The Diaspora Center, founded on 29 October 1944
in Italy, now coordinated and organized the lion's share of this movement, using the Jewish Brigade and the British army's transport units
made up of men from the Yishuv.[56] Every empty truck that returned to
Italy from a military mission in Austria illegally brought back refugees.
Some of the refugees were dressed in army uniforms and provided with
military identity papers.[57] When one of the DP camps in Austria was
slated to be transferred from American to Soviet control, men from the
brigade, aided by an Italian organization for aid to displaced persons,
brought in hundreds of Jewish survivors, disguised as Italians, on a train
from Salzburg to Modena.[58] The work of getting the Jews over the border was done against the clock, with the sense that it was necessary to act
before the British found the refugee parties and their organizers.

This combination of circumstances suddenly flooded the human
reservoir needed to consummate the great migration of Jewish refugees
from Italy to Palestine. Arazi, after deciding to remain in Italy because
"there is a broad field for action here,"[59] attached himself to the immigration enterprise. One of the first things he did, after a lightning
tour across the country to become acquainted with the people and organizations active there, was to arrange a division of labor and responsibility among the different Zionist bodies. With his force of personality and the urgency he projected, he gave them a purpose that was
perhaps more important than any other purpose their work had served
since they came to Italy. To the Mossad agents under his direction he
assigned the job of dealing "[only] with the vessels and their con-
veyance" and with "immigration, and only immigration."[60]

The arrival of Ada Sereni and the departure of the Jewish Brigade
(which the British deliberately transferred north to Belgium) changed
the organization's mode of activity in Italy. Like Arazi, Ada Sereni was
not a typical agent from the Mossad's own ranks. A native of Rome
who had settled on a kibbutz in Palestine in 1927, she was the widow of
the legendary Enzo Sereni, who had parachuted into Nazi-occupied
Europe and died at Dachau. Like her husband, she was the scion of a
highly regarded Roman family—a keen, beautiful, and individualistic

woman with an aristocratic bearing that did not match the stereotype of the Mossad agent, moved more by collective imperative than by private vision and personality. With her bourgeois origin and upbringing, and in her character and personal style, she fit in very well with Arazi.

Arazi thus found in Italian-born Sereni a sister soul and the local connection he so needed. She could provide him with direct contact and closer acquaintance with the Italian way of thinking, the Italian character, and Italian manners. At first she assisted him in weaving a web of deals with merchants, ship and shipyard owners, banks, and Italian Jews whose help he needed. Soon she became his trusted lieutenant with regard to all financial dealings and purchases necessary for the Mossad's work; she also made and handled contacts with the Italian authorities.[61] Her origins and deportment opened every door. When southern Italy became untenable for the Mossad after the exposure of its covert activity by the British, Arazi reorganized the entire system of work. Controlling Zionist activity throughout the Italian peninsula from his headquarters in the northern part of the country, Arazi was now the Mossad chief for all of Italy. His associates were Sereni, some other Mossad agents, and a group of discharged British soldiers from the Yishuv who usually worked disguised as refugees or in British army uniforms.[62] These were supplemented by young Jews from the Yishuv who had been recruited by the Mossad from Palmach units and dispatched to Italy on the returning refugee boats to work as sailors and radio operators.[63] Northern Italy, with the city of Milan at its center, became a vast theater of activity for the Zionist underground and immigration activists. The soldiers organized caches of fuel, food, and equipment. These goods were usually stolen, through the use of forged bills of lading, first from the stores of the soldiers' own units and then from British military general supply depots. Quantities of fuel were purloined in the same way and were stored in subterranean reservoirs on Zionist training farms. This was later used to fuel refugee ships or sold to the Italians in exchange for the cash necessary for the Mossad's ongoing activities. Houses and villas were purchased in the names of Italian Jews who volunteered to help the Zionists, and these houses served as centers of operations, residences, and radio stations for maintaining contact with ships and with headquarters in Palestine. Over time, the soldiers also assembled a large fleet of vehicles stolen from British units and from American army vehicle pools. Other vehicles were assembled from parts that were methodically pilfered from the Allies. A military garage—that is, one with false papers—maintained this fleet of vehicles and supplied a cover for the activity surrounding it.[64] In almost every port city that served Mossad operations a storehouse was established to hold provisions, fuel, equipment, and sleeping bunks for the ship, which were installed by a special team on the eve of sailing.[65]

With Great Mercies

After the first boat, the *Dalin* (which had been given the underground code name of *Eliahu Golomb,* after the Haganah chief who had just died), sailed in mid-August and reached its destination, an almost regular shipping lane opened between Italy and Palestine. From the end of August 1945, when the second ship sailed, through 4 April 1946, the day the La Spezia affair exploded, seven ships carrying steadily increasing numbers of refugees sailed from Italy, bringing a total of some two thousand clandestine immigrants.[66] This was at a time when Mossad agents in other countries still had not managed to arrange a regular series of sailings. While other Mossad stations were still in their embryonic stages, the agents working in Italy had already gained a considerable amount of experience in preparing such boats for travel; they established close relations with the authorities and with various sectors of the population, including political parties and organizations of former resistance fighters, who provided assistance and who proved their commitment at times of crisis, such as the La Spezia affair.

The intensive Zionist underground activity in Italy had a price. Arazi suffered several heart attacks, and his health deteriorated. Many of the trips Mossad agents made through Italy, often in hours of darkness, ended in accidents, which led to police investigations and attracted the attention of the British intelligence services. A "top secret" report written by British intelligence in the Middle East in February 1946, on the involvement of "UNRRA, the Jewish Units, and Jewish relief organizations in illegal immigration to Palestine," was fairly accurate and did a good job of summing up the elements of this activity. Stating that organizations spread over all of Europe were involved in the illegal activity and benefited from official resources, it singled out UNRRA, whose officials, it claimed, had been implicated in the provisioning of illegal immigration vessels and in facilitating black-market transactions from which unofficial funds for illegal immigration were in part derived. UNRRA "camps in the heel of Italy are excellently sited for illegal immigration to Palestine, and five of the seven boats have embarked their passengers in their neighborhood," the report stated. "Clandestine liaison between Palestine and the refugee organizations in Europe is maintained for the most part through Palestinian Jewish personnel in the British Army," it noted, adding that "immigrants and organizers have been provided with false military papers and so passed through military and civil controls with leave parties"; "army addresses have served as P.O.B.s for the illegal immigration organizations; and that military personnel detached to refugee camps have been implicated in preparations for illegal immigration."[67] Another British report on illegal immigration from Italy, dated March 1946, on the eve of the La Spezia affair, also stated that groups of Jews were entering and leaving UNRRA camps in southern Italy without the knowledge of the central office and that it was clear from UNRRA records that many of these refugees had never been registered.[68]

It was at this juncture that Arazi decided to leave his post in Italy. His fragile health and the fact that other Mossad stations had succeeded in dispatching their illegal ships, so that he was no longer indispensable, were among the reasons for his decision. On 1 April he requested that Ben-Gurion visit Italy and meet with him (together with the Haganah's European commander), apparently to transfer the management of the Italian Mossad station to other hands.[69] A day later a more detailed cable was sent from Paris to Palestine: "Alon [Arazi's code name] has announced categorically that on April 14 he is quitting."[70] However, during the very days he was announcing his resignation, Arazi was planning to send from La Spezia 1,500 refugees on two ships he had purchased two months earlier. According to his plan, the *Fede*, with one thousand passengers, was to sail on 4 April, and the *Fenice* was scheduled to leave a few days afterward. In a rendezvous at sea a day before the arrival at the Palestinian shore, the people on the *Fenice*, which was smaller, were to be transferred to the larger ship for the last leg of the trip; the empty ship would return to Italy to continue to serve the Mossad. This maneuver was meant to keep at least one of the vessels from being captured by the British. Undoubtedly, the launching of these two ships was the jewel in the crown of Arazi's work in Italy, and of the Mossad's work in general; there had been no other action so complex, involving the fate of so many people, and with such great operational risks. Arazi wanted to end his term of service in his own special way, with this extravagant display of his organizational and leadership skills. The entangled background traced here, as well as the initial operational failure involving the arrest of the refugees by the Italians and their delivery to the British, help to explain Arazi's actions throughout the La Spezia affair and the way the incident developed. As he set strategy alone, operating as if his life's work was at stake and as if he had nothing to lose, those observing from the sidelines thought Arazi was walking a tightrope and acting like a dangerous adventurer gambling in human lives.

The first move Arazi made after learning of the capture of the refugees, the most important one he made, was to join the refugees under arrest on the ship. It was a key action that affected all the other developments as well as the spirit and meaning of the La Spezia affair. In this spur-of-the-moment decision, made entirely on his own (Ada Sereni, whose advice he generally sought, was on leave in Palestine),[71] the proud operative from the Yishuv decided to become one of the Jewish refugees, to join the victims. Identifying himself as Yosef de Paz,[72] he went to the La Spezia police and turned himself in. He told the police that he also wished to sail to Palestine and demanded to be put on the ship. One of the undercover Mossad agents at the harbor realized what Arazi was doing, and he confirmed to the police that he was a Jewish refugee and got permission to include Arazi among the other refugees on the ship. In retrospect, from a vantage point distant from the event by many years, it is possible to see Arazi's act as an attempt "to turn an operational failure into a political demonstration."[73] The results, both immediate and long range, indeed prove this to be so. It is, however, arguable that already, in that very instant, Arazi had a plan in mind that would turn the fiasco into a political victory. Arazi's deed was, first of all, a spontaneous gesture of humanity and basic decency toward the helpless people who needed him and for whom he saw himself responsible—an act that any decent person would have to take under the circumstances, without thinking of the future outcome. "I have no idea what's awaiting me, or what will happen when all this ends. For the moment I know this; there are sick people and they need curing. Later on, perhaps they'll think things over; and so shall I. But what's wanted now is to make them well. I defend them as best I can, that's all," says Albert Camus's antiheroic hero Doctor Rieux in *The Plague*.[74] Both Arazi and Rieux, in times of calamity, invest their personality, experience, and leadership—and risk their lives—to come to the rescue of the neediest of the victims. Both do this out of the "certitude that a fight must be put up . . . and there must be no bowing down," and that to do this there is "only one resource: to fight the plague"[75]—or, in Arazi's words, quoting Isaiah: "If we are talking about saving lives, so with great mercies will I gather thee."[76]

At a time of extreme crisis, when simple human solidarity was called for, the most unlikely person did not think of utility or expedience but rather mustered his compassion to defend his people and "cure" them. He chose to be not just an outside manipulator of the victims for some external political purpose, but to be with the victims, inside, sharing their state of victimhood. As with all involuntary heroes who see nothing exceptional about their deeds ("There was nothing admirable about this attitude; it was merely logical," as Dr. Rieux says[77]), it was a spontaneous action of great personal courage. Arazi had been hunted by the British for more than three years, and everywhere he went there was a price on his head. Boarding the captured ship as a refugee was likely to lead to the exposure of his real identity and could have resulted in his being handed over to the British. Furthermore, given the state of his health, joining the refugees could endanger his life. No external factor forced Arazi to do it. He was not captured with the refugees. He could have easily escaped unnoticed in the commotion surrounding the capture of the convoy, as did other Mossad agents who were accompanying it. He could have disappeared back into the underground anonymity that had been his way of life, to continue to direct the battle over the refugees' fate from outside, from the position of relative security that he had enjoyed in Italy up until then. He could have ordered someone else to do it. Yet he chose to join the refugees, sharing their fate at risk to his own life.

Arazi's boarding of the ship under the identity of a Jewish refugee bore an additional, symbolic meaning, one much more far reaching. In assuming the identity of a Holocaust survivor and nullifying his own, Yehuda Arazi symbolically bridged with his own body a chasm that had opened with the Holocaust between the Zionist collective in Palestine and the Diaspora. This was the abyss separating the Diaspora, or whatever of it had survived, from the homeland whose dominant collectivist ideology negated the Diaspora and failed to mobilize itself to the fullest extent to save what could be saved of the dying Diaspora in the war years.[78] This was the first time, since the Yishuv sent some thirty paratroopers behind the lines on intelligence and rescue missions in Nazi-occupied Europe, that a person from the Yishuv had assimilated himself so immediately, concretely, and dramatically among the Jews of the Diaspora, linking his fate with theirs. Only after the fact did it become clear that this act of crossing lines and creating this common fate (even if it was only symbolic and short lived) had a decisive effect on the refugees' willingness to endure the long test they faced. Thus, Arazi's spontaneous, humane act also eventually bore great political benefit.

From the moment Yehuda Arazi turned himself in and boarded the ship as a refugee, the activity in Italy split into two domains—on the ship and off it. While Arazi, in the guise of Dr. de Paz, assumed the leadership of events on the ship, the Mossad agents who had not been arrested began working to repair the damage on shore and to reestablish the network so that work would not stop for long. In addition to trying to create discipline and order among the refugees,[79] Arazi's main effort was to get the refugees' voice, as he conceived it, heard by the outside world. He enlisted his influence and his rhetorical and organizational abilities in his public relations campaign, and he stopped short at nothing. His methods were sometimes no different from those the Hebrew national poet Hayyim Nahman Bialik condemned as being typical of the Diaspora, merchandizing death and suffering, crying for the "pity of the nations."[80] The Italian soldiers who came to confirm that the Jewish refugees were not really disguised Italian Fascists trying to flee republican Italy were shown the tattooed numbers on the refugees' arms. When a British intelligence officer and military police wished to search the ship's stores, Arazi castigated them for occupying themselves with silly matters like cookies and cans of meat in the presence of a thousand people, each of whom was a "tragic and shocking story." In his messages from the ship, Arazi spoke about the ill and the handicapped, about the 150 pregnant women and the dozens of small children among the captives. The entire world, he said, was responsible for them—but first and foremost the Italians and the British. In establishing contact with the outside world, Arazi made use of the sympathetic local press. "We are 1,014 Jews from the remnants of the German slaughter and we are headed for the Land of Israel, our natural homeland" was the opening statement of the manifesto Arazi wrote on the day after the arrest. The manifesto was addressed to the Italian prime minister, the minister of the navy, the Pope, the president of the United States, and to "all who have a spark of humanity in their hearts and all those whose souls have not been marred by the Nazi-Fascist scourge." "No power in the world can prevent us from reaching our destination, even if many pay with their lives," it stated.[81] When Arazi learned that the British intended to demand that the Italians take the refugees off the boat and transfer them to the Chiavari refugee camp, he threatened to sink the ship with all on board.

The climax of the worldwide media campaign conducted by Arazi with the refugees' help was the hunger strike declared on 7 April and which was, according to their threats, to continue until they were allowed to sail for Palestine. On the strike's third day, isolated from the world on their ghost ship (whose engines had been removed by the Italians on British orders), Arazi issued a statement to the Italian press and to the British ambassador in Rome in which he reported that many were ill and that "dozens of people are fainting" on the ship; he said that pregnant women were "collapsing from exhaustion." "Are you waiting for us to die?" the statement asked. "If there are any human feelings among you, put an end to this mass suicide. Let us sail for the Land of Israel!" Harold Laski, who believed Arazi was risking too much and gambling with the lives of the refugees, was told by Arazi that the refugees were prepared to take their own lives, publicly if necessary, "at the gate of the port" in protest against their detention. "Because what do we have to lose if we aren't allowed to settle in Palestine—returning to the camp? . . . Can you conceive what your fate would have been had your grandfather not emigrated to England? At the very best, if you were lucky, you would perhaps be one of us. . . . Here we have the representatives of 1,000 families who were slaughtered and murdered. They survived by a miracle and their only hope is to return to their homeland."[82] The sophisticated and manipulative use of the refugees' voice, on the one hand, in tandem with silence or the threat of silencing the voices of the refugees, on the other, thus served Arazi in his shrewd management of the situation. The general hunger strike, the dramatic open and implied threats of suicide, and the enlistment of the rhetoric and images of the Holocaust, as well as the real danger to the refugees' lives, made the world's newspaper headlines. The affair reached the desks of Attlee, Bevin, de Gasperi, and President Truman. Ben-Gurion himself, the theorist and expert practitioner of transforming Jewish agony into Zionist power,[83] could not himself have conceived of such a virtuoso performance. Others, including Arazi's fellow agents, the British, and Harold Laski, considered him an "adventurer and demagogue."[84] The La Spezia affair was Arazi's. He made the decisions and led his fellow refugees in their dramatic demonstrations. Somewhat unconsciously, he designed a new strategy for the Mossad, one that unashamedly used the helpless refugees as its main information weapon.

Meanwhile, on shore, the Mossad rebuilt its organization. The Italian representatives of the Jewish Agency and of the JDC were summoned to La Spezia to make use of their international connections and their organizational influence. Rafael Kantoni, the Jewish and socialist leader (he was president of the Jewish Communities of Italy and a senior member of the Italian Socialist Party), who was at that time participating in his party's convention in Florence, was also mobilized. He had wide-ranging connections in post-war Italian society and with the new socialist establishment, which had grown out of the ranks of the Italian resistance. These made him a key figure in the efforts to rescue Arazi and the refugees. "Immediately assign Kantoni to take care of releasing Alon [Arazi] and his comrades" was the order in one of the first cables the Mossad's central command sent to Italy. "Daniela [Ada Sereni] informs Kantoni that he should act with maximal caution . . . Kantoni should offer a large bribe. Make money available to him," says another cable. Kantoni was also assigned "to act [to ensure] that the press is on our side."[85]

Zionist Lesson

Indeed, the Zionists learned a lesson in the La Spezia episode that would be reinforced by incidents in France and elsewhere. They discovered the power of the media and the indispensability of some well-situated and well-connected Jewish figures on whom the Mossad could depend—Jews such as Kantoni, most of whom had themselves come from the underground[86] and who held senior positions in the socialist parties that came to power throughout Europe after the war. These people wanted to participate in the Zionist enterprise, which at the time was led by the socialist movement, and saw themselves as natural partners of the Mossad, ready for any mission. To a large extent they saw this clandestine work for the establishment of a Jewish state and in aid to the Jewish victims of Nazism, concealed not only from the British but also sometimes from the local authorities, as a continuation of their anti-Nazi resistance activities and as their contribution to the new world. They thus provided the political, economic, and social foundation for the Mossad's covert activities and in time of need served as lobbyists in the corridors of socialist regimes.

At first, Arazi's fate was the main concern of those on shore and in Zionist circles. This was because of his health and the fact that he was the central figure in the immigration campaign in all of Europe, and the only one, so far, who had produced real results—ships loaded with refugees. Losing him was liable to paralyze the entire operation at the worst possible time, just after the Anglo-American Committee had submitted its recommendations and when the Yishuv needed the refugee ships to put pressure on the British Mandate. "Must make supreme effort to free Alon [Arazi]," read the first message cabled from Mossad headquarters in Palestine to Italy. "Did you clean thoroughly Alon's house? . . . Don't destroy [false] IDs, put them in safe place" were the orders that followed.[87]

It was not, however, Mossad headquarters in Palestine or the Zionist central leadership that set the priorities or determined the progress of the affair. The Mossad's chief set out from Palestine to France during the course of the incident and remained distant and cut off from events. Members of the Yishuv's central leadership were scattered through several world capitals, and the capture of the refugees came during an inconvenient time while the leaders were revising the Yishuv policy in the wake of the Anglo-American Committee report.[88] It was the refugee representative Dr. de Paz (Arazi) and the refugees in the La Spezia harbor that made events unfold as they did; they set the tone of the affair, and their moves forced the other parties involved to respond. After ascertaining the endurance of the refugees and persuading them that they had been given the privilege of taking their fate into their own hands, even if the price was high,[89] Arazi decided to lead a political campaign to confront the world. With this single decision he accomplished several things. First, he brought the Mossad's activities in Europe, which had until then been covert, into the open. Even if he himself appeared to the Italians and the British, and at first to the refugees, as a refugee himself, it was impossible not to identify the ship and its passengers with the activities of the underground Zionist organization that the British were already pursuing.[90] Second, he effected an irrevocable transformation of the Mossad's work in Italy. From that point onward, the Mossad was exposed to the Italian authorities and needed their cooperation, whether active or passive. Third, Arazi's actions forced an agenda and a timetable on the Zionist leadership, one that it was not prepared for and about which there was no consensus. The moment he received, as the refugees' leader, permission freely to leave and return to the ship, Arazi took the opportunity to go to Milan. From there he called the head of the Jewish Agency's political department, Moshe Shertok, who was in London at the time, and demanded that the La Spezia episode not be allowed to slip away, that its political and propaganda potential be exploited to the fullest. "Do not concern yourself with me more than with the matter itself," he said. "We are stronger than you think and are continuing our fight . . . all of Italy is on our side. It is my intention to sail the ship at any price. In the meantime we are preparing new *ma'apilim.*"[91] The capture of the refugees and Arazi's subsequent actions created confusion in the Zionist camp. With Ben-Gurion and Shertok out of the country, decision-making procedures were not working. The other members of the Jewish Agency Executive had no real authority and were dragged along by events. They did what they were used to doing in such situations: they made do with demonstrations and the usual ritual of protest, strikes, and fasts. Fifteen members of the National Council (the *Va'ad Le'umi*) launched a hunger strike as a token of identification with the La Spezia refugees. A one-day general strike and a day of fasting were also declared in the Yishuv.[92]

Encouraged by Arazi's message, Shertok took an aggressive stand in London. He demanded of Colonial Secretary George Hall that all the ship's passengers be allowed to sail together to Palestine, undivided, on the basis of the unused certificates out of the monthly quota.[93] The Jewish Agency in Palestine, in contrast, accepted the government's proposal to allow the La Spezia refugees to enter Palestine on the basis of the regular monthly quotas, and in two separate groups—675 in April and the rest during May. Mossad headquarters in Palestine agreed to this arrangement and cabled to Europe: "The engagement on the *Fede* has ended. The battle for *ha'apala* will continue."[94] Arazi strongly repudiated the decision from Palestine and made sure everyone knew it. Claiming that the leadership was failing to rise to this exceptional challenge while the refugees themselves were meeting it honorably and heroically, he maintained that the decision was tantamount to surrender and meant throwing away the great achievement already made in La Spezia. He quickly sent to Ben-Gurion, Shertok, and Mossad headquarters his and the refugees' refusal.

We have launched a serious struggle and have brought the problem of the survivors before a major forum. We have refused to talk about certificates. . . . Every Jew may immigrate to Palestine, and we will strive onward [*na'apil*] in our ships. At the current stage there is [in Italy] full understanding of our cause and we are certain of a total victory. What was the purpose of conducting negotiations in Jerusalem that ended in diminishing our image and weakening us? . . . For your information: any order to concede anything will not be accepted by the people, who consider themselves pioneers for all the others.[95]

From London, Shertok, who was also dissatisfied with the compromise with the British government, sent instructions to Arazi to continue the battle until all the refugees could sail together.[96] Messages from the Yishuv explained to Arazi that the Jewish Agency could not refuse to accept the immigration certificates offered it, when such were on offer, but that this did not mean the struggle at La Spezia should be ended.[97] The Jewish Agency's representative, Nahon, was received by Prime Minister de Gasperi and asked him to intervene with the British. On 19 April he and Kantoni again traveled to La Spezia and met with the official in charge of the port, who promised to offer all necessary assistance in preparing the *Fede* for travel. The official maintained, however, that he could not allow the ship to sail with more than six hundred passengers on board. It was agreed that the second Mossad ship, the *Fenice*, which had originally been slated to sail together with the *Fede*, would be returned to the port and that some of the refugees would be transferred to it. In London Laski met with Foreign Secretary Bevin and then sent a cable to the ship in which he asked the passengers to have patience for another week until he could see whether his efforts were bringing results.[98]

Meanwhile, some Jewish soldiers managed to smuggle the missing engine parts to the ship and prepare the vessel for sailing. Arazi, who would not agree to subordinate himself to compromises with the British, could now threaten to set sail, without permission, with all the refugees on board.[99] However, just as his threat to take the fate of the refugees into his own hands was casting a shadow over the efforts of the statesmen and diplomats to find a way out of the crisis, the negotiations conducted in Jerusalem, London, and Rome were reaching a conclusion. Secretive Mossad chief Shaul Meirov, who had arrived in Europe in mid-April and gone to Italy to supervise the conclusion of the episode, had been directing, from behind the scenes, Nahon's contacts with the British embassy in Rome. Even though the Mossad chief had an aversion to any overt public activity, he realized that nothing could stop Arazi and reluctantly supported Arazi's strategy.[100] Nevertheless, he forced Arazi to accept the principle of immigration by certificates, and to make a gesture toward the British, who were already willing to accept all the refugees into Palestine at once, the Zionist negotiators offered an out according to which all the refugees would arrive after 15 May and be counted in the May quota. The ships thus set sail from La Spezia on 8 May and reached Haifa a few days later.[101]

When the ships sailed, there were sighs of relief from the British, the Italians, and the Zionists.[102] None of them came out of the affair as they had entered. It can be said that all became more experienced, though not necessarily wiser. The amateurish way in which the Italians and the British, and to a certain extent the Mossad, had handled the sailing of the *Wedgewood*, with 1,257 refugees on board, from Vado Ligure just a month and a half after the end of the La Spezia episode is testimony to this.[103] In any case, the burden of the refugees was no longer on Italian shoulders. A thousand trapped Jewish refugees fighting for their future were no longer likely to be detrimental to Italy's standing in the international community, and especially in American public opinion. The British, for their part, tightened their field security in the Riviera ports of northwest Italy. There, they believed, was the most important theater for the Zionist organization responsible for clandestine immigration. In parallel, they quickly demobilized the Jewish units and sent their soldiers back to Palestine.[104] Despite the outcome of the La Spezia affair, the British could point to a gain with regard to their larger interests: the entry of a thousand refugees into Palestine with immigration permits had not broken the certificates regime. Moreover, the affair and its handling by the British had not caused much damage to the basic British interests in Palestine and to the harmony of Anglo-American relations.[105] In Palestine, the Tel Aviv daily *Davar* wrote the following commentary while the ships were still on their way, in a surprising tone of almost philosophical resignation to the Jewish fate and to the world's cruel ways:

It could have been otherwise. The world could have spared the Jewish remnants the final, poisoning bitterness that it has been pouring into their souls daily and hourly for the entire last year. The remnants of the Jewish people can come to settle in their homeland, not despite the wishes of the British authorities, but rather with their consent and assistance. The world would then not look to them like a confederation of murderers and hypocrites, as it does today. It could have been otherwise, but it was not. The world is still hell. The *ma'apilim* of the *Dov Hoz* and the *Eliahu Golomb* [the Hebrew names of the ships] have had to undergo all the trials of oppressed Jews, and then they had to taste the experience of La Spezia, with their hunger strike and their forced stay on their boats, in conditions that normal people could not endure, with the imputation that they were Fascists, with the cheerful promises of the president of the British Labour Party, and with all that came of these promises until the signal to sail was given.[106]

All three administrations—the Italian, the British, and the Zionist-Hebrew state-in-the-making—were shown in this affair to be fragile and internally divided, to be groping their way through their international policy, and to be carefully defining their political image in the post-war period. The ostensibly marginal problem of a ship with a thousand Jewish refugees at a small, out-of-the-way European port was not resolved by lower-level local officials of these governments, but instead reached the offices of the foreign ministers and prime ministers at a time when all of them were busy with much more serious problems. It was not just general political chaos, as new regimes were formed and new international blocs created, that was responsible for the fragility of these governments and for the affair's deep reverberations. The weight of the Palestine question, at least for the British and the Zionists, a question exacerbated by the Jewish catastrophe, had an effect as well. The symbolism of the hounded boat, loaded with refugees, survivors of Nazism who were unable to find a safe port, was too heavy for that historical moment. The Italians and especially the British thus acted only half-heartedly. They failed to use their full power and authority even if this went against their policy and their immediate interests. Furthermore, the interests of the Italians and the British did not coincide; in fact, they were opposed. In this gap between contradictory interests, a goal-oriented, stubborn yet flexible Zionist organization such as the Mossad could, with the help of local Jews and non-Jews and sustained by the guilt feelings and general compassion that the West had for the survivors of Nazism, use its relative advantages with maximal success. This was the major lesson learned from the episode by the Zionists, and it was confirmed in similar episodes that the Mossad would confront during 1947. What can be stated with certainty is that by the conclusion of the La Spezia episode, Italy was no longer the Mossad's only launching point or even its principal one. Another ship had already sailed from France, and the *Smirni* (the *Max Nordau*) had sailed from the Romanian port of Constanta, carrying close to 1,700 refugees. In June and July 1946, the Mossad's ports of sailing were spread over all of Europe, from Piraeus in Greece to Antwerp in Belgium, from Bakar in Yugoslavia to Marseilles in France.[107]

Pending Crisis

What is surprising is not that forty-five days had to pass between the end of the La Spezia episode to the sailing of the Mossad's next ship from an Italian port,[108] but that *only* forty-five days passed. This demonstrated, in addition to the continuation of the Italians' positive attitude despite La Spezia, the organization's powers of regeneration and readjustment. It changed its profile; the three men of the Jewish units in Italy who had been the foundation of the Mossad's efforts left Italy.[109] Other discharged soldiers took their place—as civilians, under identities borrowed from Jewish refugees who had been sent to Palestine with the papers and biographies of the soldiers who remained.[110] These men no longer enjoyed the cover and secure conditions that a British uniform could provide. The Mossad's logistical infrastructure also had to be remade swiftly and practically from scratch. The operational headquarters were transferred from the soldiers' club in

Milan to a downtown apartment and office that were rented and purchased under the names of Italian Jews. The many vehicles that the
Mossad used for its activities now bore the insignia of the American
Joint Distribution Committee (JDC). The refugees for the *Wedgewood*
were already brought to port in civilian vehicles, which meant that their
arrival was conspicuous and very noisy.[111] For a while, Arazi continued
to run the operation.

The worst damage was apparently suffered by the communications
system. Soldiers manned it almost exclusively until their discharge, and
their replacements were late in arriving from Palestine and did not meet
Arazi's requirements. Arazi believed that the unprofessional operation of
communications with Romania—each broadcast lasted for hours—put
the entire network at risk. Nevertheless, he continued to send out ships;
between 31 July and 9 October 1946, six ships sailed from Italy—five from
Bocca di Magra and one from Metaponto.[112] He continued to demand
more people—radio operators, sailors, commanders for the camps, physi-
cians, and accountants to fill the roles needed as a result of the increased
activity.[113] He also wanted more money. In mid-September Arazi notified the Mossad that the debts of the Italian operations had reached
"Fifteen thousand big ones [Palestinian Pounds]" and that if the money
was not sent, work would stop in less than a month.[114] In October he argued that the rate of sailings was declining "just when we need to do
[more]," just when there was a new flow of refugees into Italy ("1,500
have already arrived and they continue to stream in daily")—this at a
time when the refugee centers were in danger of falling apart if the
refugees were not sent to Palestine, "ship after ship."[115]

Paradoxically, the Mossad's relations with the Italian authorities improved after La Spezia to a new, quasi-official level, and this allowed
the organization to work with almost complete freedom for close to a
year. It was Ada Sereni who built and maintained these ties. "The fiasco of La Spezia . . . marked the beginning of the Italian institutions'
assistance to us," she concluded.[116] Sereni represented a humanitarian-
political cause that was very attractive to the Italians, who wanted to
atone for their pro-Nazi past, and this cause enabled her to quickly gain
entry to the highest levels of the Italian establishment. At least until the
peace treaty was signed with Italy in February 1947, requiring Italy, as
its leaders understood it, not to get into overly sharp disagreements
with Britain, the Mossad's agents operated openly in Italy with the protection and help of many people in the government. Among the officials who directly aided Jewish migration were the police inspector-

general, the navy's intelligence commander, the general prefect of the ports, and the director-general of the Ministry of Foreign Affairs. Government ministers knew about the Mossad's activities, and Prime Minister de Gasperi and the foreign and interior ministers had to intervene at various stages.[117] Sereni did more than plead the humanitarian case to Italian officials. Getting as many Jewish refugees out of Italy as fast as possible was in Italy's own interest, she claimed. The country's economy was in shambles, and tens of thousands of refugees and some million repatriates were a burden that could lead to the nation's collapse. By her own account, Sereni told Prime Minister de Gasperi that sending Jewish refugees and arms to the Yishuv served Italian interests, since the future Jewish state would be "one of the factors that would balance Arab power in the Mediterranean." If, on the other hand, the Yishuv were to lose its war with the Arabs, most of the Jewish refugees fleeing Palestine would return to Italy.[118]

The bottom line was that up until the signing of the peace treaty in February 1947, Italy made no special effort to prevent Jewish refugees from making their way across its borders. In response to British and Allied protests, the Italians used several tactics. First, they exaggerated the strength of the Jewish-Zionist organizations working to smuggle Jews into the country. Then they blamed the Allies, claiming that the large number of official and semi-official Allied bodies with authority to grant transit papers created disarray and confusion at the border. In any case, the Italians insisted, the responsibility for preventing Jews from entering the country had been, until May 1946, in the hands of Allied troops, and since then there had not been systematic border crossings by Jews.[119] That the movement of Jews into Italy had not stopped for even a day is demonstrated in a June 1947 Mossad report stating that during 1946 "between 13,000 and 14,000 individuals had infiltrated Benyamin [Italy] via the northern border."[120]

The crisis in the Mossad's work broke out toward the end of 1946, when Yehuda Arazi angrily announced his resignation from the Mossad. The differences in personality, in the conception of the Mossad's mission, and in opinion concerning work methods could apparently no longer be papered over. Despite, or perhaps because of, the proven success of the Italian operation (eleven ships with 8,500 refugees sailed from Italy during 1946[121]), the arguments and clashes between Arazi and Mossad headquarters had become a daily affair. The list of charges this virtuoso soloist sent to the collectivist Mossad reflected the pain of a betrayed autocrat: "I thank you for wanting to educate me, but it is too late. I have tried to find the most polite expression. You can imagine the other expressions. From this point onward I am no longer at work. Ben-Yehuda [Mossad chief Shaul Meirov] will arrive tomorrow and will appoint a temporary replacement. Before parting I want to assure you that it has been a nightmare for me to work with you for such a long period."[122] Indeed, the divorce had been pending for a long time. Arazi was used to having his every word obeyed and viewed himself as a man of lost causes, problems that were insoluble for others and whose solution enabled him to display his ability and uniqueness. Once the Mossad's work became more or less an administrative routine and Mossad ships were sailing in reasonably good order from other ports in other countries, Italy lost its special role, and Arazi, it seems, lost the special interest and the sense of mission that had motivated him since his arrival in Italy.

He left Italy in the latter half of April 1947,[123] although his no-less-intractable replacement, Ada Sereni, had been running the operation formally from the end of 1946. Yet even after his departure, for as long as Sereni commanded the operation, Arazi's spirit was still influential. This meant that the cause of the refugees and the work itself transcended any sectarian, political, or institutional consideration, and the result was constant conflict with the Mossad leadership. During the period from October 1946 to March 1947, when no ships sailed from Italy, the Twenty-second Zionist Congress decided on a campaign to bring 100,000 Jews to Palestine by means of the Mossad. At that time the Mossad's pendulum had swung toward other ports in France, Yugoslavia, and Sweden. A harsh winter made it difficult for Jews to cross the Alps into Italy, although they continued to come. According to the Mossad's reports, 2,200 people entered Italy from Willy [Germany] and Arthur [Austria] in January 1947, 380 in February, and 1,300 in March.[124]

Despite the improving relations between Britain and Italy after February 1947, when Italy joined the Western bloc, the two countries continued to play cat-and-mouse over the entry of Jewish refugees into Italy and their departure from its ports for Palestine. In fact, up until the end of the period under discussion here, the Italian authorities took no clear and comprehensive steps to halt this activity and formed no clear policy about it despite constant British pressure. The Italians squirmed, spoke out angrily against both the Jewish migration and British pressure, closed one crossing point while ignoring another, and generally looked the other way. In the words of a British intelligence report from the summer of 1947, the Italians "closed their eyes" and allowed Jews to both enter and leave Italy.[125] In the spring of 1947 the Italian foreign ministry reported to the British embassy that the Jewish migration had not stopped at all and that it would probably even increase as the weather improved. "These illegal immigrants are not displaced persons but individuals who have freely and spontaneously left places where they were residents with a view to reaching Palestine." Therefore, they were not entitled to UNRRA aid, the foreign ministry maintained.[126] In early June 1947, after a mass exodus from Romania led to concern that Italy would soon be flooded by refugees, the British ambassador stated to the Italian foreign minister, "This is a matter on which the interests of our two governments must obviously coincide, and I have no hesitation therefore in urging that immediate measures be taken."[127] Britain also took advantage of the Italians' interest in being accepted to the United Nations to pressure them into making an official promise to cooperate in this matter. Italian control of the border did increase, but Italy continued to demand in return joint measures by the Allies to prevent border crossings and to return infiltrators to their points of departure.[128] Mossad and Bricha agents reported increasing difficulties in getting refugees over Italy's northern border. "The flow [of refugees] from the north has run into unprecedented obstacles. The local authorities are under constant pressure from the enemies and are giving in to them more and more. Surveillance and spying are very severe and it has reached the point that UNRRA is going to demand that every refugee in its camps be equipped with a residence certificate with a picture and fingerprints. The intention is transparent—control of movement."[129]

Cat and Mouse

Despite this, Jewish infiltration into Italy continued and at times even increased. Both the British and the Zionists were aware of this and received constant up-to-date reports. During July 1947, for example, word reached the Mossad's operations room in Paris that dozens of Jews were entering each day. During that month almost three times as many—nearly two thousand—Jews entered Italy as during the previous month.[130] "The Jewish immigration is of a nature and on a scale which bears little comparison with normal peace time problems," stated a British expert who examined the Italian border controls. "The movement is organized and the organizers use resources superior to those employed by the officials with the cunning and persistency of an underground movement. Ordinary counter-measures are therefore totally inadequate."[131] The effects of British pressure were apparent, however, especially in the attitude of the Italian foreign ministry. The Mossad found it much harder to get assistance from the authorities, and its work had to go underground once more. "There is terrible pressure from the enemy and all work is conducted on the sly," Sereni reported to the operations center in Paris.[132] Elsewhere she stated, "We have returned to completely underground work, with all the complications and difficulties involved."[133]

It was the sweeping negative transformation in the Italian authorities' attitude toward the Mossad's work, beginning in the spring of 1947, that prevented the sailing of the *President Warfield* (later the *Exodus*) from an Italian port, as the Mossad had planned. Instead, the large ship had to sail from Sète in France, bringing the clandestine operation's French link into the headlines and shifting the Mossad's European center of gravity from Italy to other places. In the summer of 1947 and the following winter, Italy no longer had top billing in Mossad activities because of circumstances and conditions not under the Mossad's control. The giant ship (the largest the Mossad had used thus far) kept the Italian Mossad operation busy for two and one-half months until it was transferred to France.[134] While being prepared for sailing there, it attracted the attention of large naval and intelligence forces and, Sereni said, sapped energy and occupied "huge forces."[135] It descended on the Italian station at the least fortuitous time, when British pressure on the Italians was at its height and when Mossad field agents were working at full capacity in ever-worsening conditions. The *President Warfield* reached Italy with, as a Mossad report stated, "a huge stink that had been dragging on since it was with Danny [the United States],"[136] a reference to the media frenzy that brought close British surveillance of its every move. Because of its size, the attention it attracted, the U.S. direct involvement in its cause from the day the ship left that country with an American crew, and its sailing just as Palestine was being discussed by the UN General Assembly, the British considered this ship the climax of their fight against clandestine Jewish immigration and a test case in which they would either fail or succeed in creating a model for future actions. They used all the means at their disposal to stop it. Even before the ship put down anchor at Porto Venere, Foreign Secretary Bevin instructed his ambassador in Rome to take all possible steps to prevent Jews from boarding the ship and to keep the ship from leaving the port of Genoa or any other place.[137] The immense pressure that the British exerted on the Italians bore fruit, as evidenced by the Mossad's work, which was tense and confused at the time.

According to the ship's license, it could only take passengers on coastal cruises, and the Italians found a way to play smart with both the British and the Mossad—to give in to a certain extent to British pressures but without angering the Americans and the Jews too much. The Italians pressured Sereni and her team not to board refugees on the ship and refused to supply fuel, but at the same time refused to hold up the ship for an unlimited period. Later, Foreign Minister Carlo Sforza would admit that he had personally and illegally delayed the ship.[138] At a meeting with the Italian foreign ministry, however, the British learned that the Italians would under no circumstances take control of the ship out of fear that it would cause problems with the U.S. government and powerful American interests.[139]

On 10 May Ada Sereni reported to Paris that the British had surrounded the *President Warfield* with destroyers. She demanded that the Mossad immediately instruct the shipping company under whose papers the ship sailed to telegraph the Italian foreign, interior, and naval ministries to protest this violation of international law and make it clear that they would be responsible for any damage caused to the company.[140] A few days later Sereni reported that the complications were growing, as the Italians themselves now had the ship under constant guard. Work on fitting out the ship was, however, continuing. Until that moment, Sereni and other Mossad agents still believed that the ship could sail from Italy carrying some "4,000 passengers, including babies."[141] Sereni also emphasized that it would not be possible to continue to work in Italy with vessels that had been publicized overseas and that were manned by "garrulous sailors who deal in the black market." She asked that, for the time being, no additional ships be sent to Italy for fear of British surveillance. Although it might be possible to obtain Italian assurances that they would not interfere with such ships, she explained, this would require large payments "under the table" that she doubted would be worthwhile. She also demanded the organization of a campaign in the American press against the illegal detention of the ship by the Italians.[142] On 16 May the Italian pressure on the ship let up a bit, and Sereni reported that practically "there are no more obstacles from the authorities against its sailing." She added, however, that it would be dangerous to load people on the ship because the Italians had issued strict instructions against this and that it could upset the working relationship with the Italians.[143] At the beginning of June it was clear that it would not be possible to board refugees on the ship at an Italian port, and plans were made to use two intermediate ships to carry the passengers outside Italian territorial waters and board them on the *President Warfield* there.[144] On 11 June the Mossad leadership, including its chief, who was then in Italy, decided to return the ship to Marseilles for fueling and then send it back toward Italy to the point where the boarding at sea would be carried out. Should this plan fail, the Mossad chief determined, the ship should be sent to Romania to wait for the execution of "the big project": taking thousands of Jews out of that country at once. On the next day the ship set out for France, and a day later it arrived at Port de Bouc and refueled.[145]

It could be said that when the *President Warfield* sailed from Italian into French territorial waters under close British surveillance, the clandestine immigration operation's center of activity in Europe moved from Italy to France, and so does our narrative. However, this does not mean that work in Italy ceased. Between this time and the establishment of Israel, eleven more refugee ships sailed from Italian ports, sometimes at a rate of two per month. British pressures did not cease and even took a more violent turn, exemplified by the sabotage carried out by British commandos against the Mossad ship *Pan Crescent*, which was undergoing repairs in a Venetian shipyard.[146] The British pressure intensified even more in October 1947, both because the flow of Jewish refugees from the north was growing (in October alone, according to Mossad reports, 1,800 Jews entered Italy in this way)[147] and because at the end of that month Minister of Foreign Affairs Sforza was scheduled to visit London. In a preliminary personal message to Sforza, Bevin expressed the special interest he had in the subject of clandestine immigration. "Italian ports were filled with illegal ships fitting out for Palestine," said Bevin's representative to Sforza, and "even if they embarked Jews elsewhere, there was a risk of a serious incident and it would be particularly unfortunate if such arose at a time when the Minister was preparing to go to London." In reaction to this unsubtle hint, Carlo Sforza promised Bevin that he would do his best.[148] Yet the visit's success and the atmosphere of apparent reconciliation that typified relations between the two countries thereafter did not significantly affect Italian behavior. The Italians continued to play their double or triple game, trying to appease all parties involved. They made efforts to please the British out of political expedience, and they wanted to help the Jews and Zionists because of their traditional sympathy for them and out of a desire to ease the refugee problem. On top of all this, they tried not to annoy the Americans.

The boats continued to sail. Close to fifty thousand Jewish refugees had made their way across Italy's northern border between the end of the war and the end of 1947. Some twenty thousand of them set out on Mossad ships to the southeast. No wonder, then, that the unidentified British official wrote at the beginning of 1948 that "despised and beaten" Italy was the only country continuing to flout Great Britain.

CHAPTER 2

France: A Carefully Organized Zionist Campaign

The tranquil sailing of the *President Warfield* into the waters of the small harbor of Port de Bouc, near the city of Marseilles, marked the beginning of the climactic stage of the Mossad's work in France. It happened on 13 June 1947, at an early evening hour.[1] On that date began the reckoning of the French chapter of what would later be called the *Exodus* affair, which was, in many ways, the high point of the Zionist use of clandestine immigration toward the goal of establishing a Jewish state. When this chapter ended, less than three turbulent months later, France had lost its centrality in the Jewish clandestine immigration campaign.

For two years, from the autumn of 1945 until the autumn of 1947, France played a central political and operational role in the Jewish struggle for an independent state and in the Mossad's work. Ben-Gurion established the European headquarters for his activities in Paris and from that time onward paid extended visits to the city. In the spring of 1946 the Mossad's operations center moved from Palestine to Paris, and the organization's leader, Shaul Meirov, spent a great part of the period there; Marseilles became the Mossad's central maritime base. From March 1946 to the establishment of the state, a total of fourteen ships sailed from France, carrying approximately twenty thousand Jewish refugees. Among the factors that turned the geographical and political space of this country into a focus of the Zionist struggle in Europe were the country's long coastline and numerous ports; its geographical proximity to the Jewish DP camps in Germany,

which were already, in the autumn of 1945, perceived as the main resource of the Zionist movement's power; and, distinguishing it from its
neighbor, Italy, the absence of armies of occupation or Allied forces.
No less important were France's complex and turbulent relations with
Britain; the weakness of French political institutions, which were then
just starting to be rehabilitated and reconstituted after the defeat and
occupation; and a Jewish community that was very much a part of the
new political establishment and familiar to the Zionist leadership.

On the face of it, there could hardly have been a less apt moment
for the giant Mossad ship to make its entry into a French port. Since
American secretary of state George Marshall's speech at Harvard eight
days earlier, it had seemed as if relations between Britain and France
were on the verge of a new era of conciliation. For the Mossad to
launch its largest clandestine ship to date from a French port would risk
these tenuous relations. This ship was especially problematic because,
as Mossad agents themselves noted, it had been the subject of a "great
stink" of publicity and media attention from the instant of its departure
from the United States. The British had doggedly trailed it everywhere
it went, and the British foreign secretary had already decided to make
an example of this ship in his war against illegal Jewish immigration to
Palestine.[2] Marshall's summons to the countries of Europe to establish
a united front for the purpose of rehabilitating and rebuilding the continent with the aid of American capital set in motion joint British and
French moves to immediately convene a conference of European foreign ministers to formulate a comprehensive rehabilitation program
and draft an all-European declaration on the continent's needs. Any
additional friction between France and Britain, above and beyond the
other differences between them, was something the two countries
would gladly have done without.[3] None of the parties involved, however, imagined at that time that the boat would set sail, full with
refugees, from a French port; nor could they anticipate the international maelstrom that this ship would create.

The Mossad agents in France acted as if they had received the ship
for safekeeping until it could be sent back to Italy and sail from there.[4]
In fact, they were busy preparing for the launching of four other boats
anchored in different French ports.[5] The British also believed that in the
end the ship would try to board passengers and sail to Palestine not
from France, but from Italy.[6] Despite this, they took no chances. Even
though the Foreign Office staff estimated earlier that month that illegal

sailings from France would be halted as a result of effective French measures against them,[7] the British foreign secretary promptly, on the ship's entry into French territorial waters, instructed the British ambassador in Paris to make it clear to the French authorities that Britain expected them to prevent or delay its sailing for as long as possible, just as the Italian authorities had done. Bevin further stressed in his cable to his ambassador that he attached special importance to the boat and to preventing it from sailing since it was the largest one so far to take part in what he called "this traffic."[8] The French, for their part, also took action when the ship entered Port de Bouc. Local Mossad agents received, a day after the ship's arrival, a communication from their sources of information in the French administration that the maritime inspection department *(Inspection maritime)* had received an order to search the ship. The stated reason was that its seaworthiness was questionable and that its license limited it to sailing along the coast.[9]

It was actually the British representatives in France, headed by Ambassador Alfred Duff Cooper, who expressed doubts about France's willingness to take serious action to counter the Jewish "traffic" in their territory. Cooper wrote to the foreign secretary, ostensibly quoting a high-placed French source, that whereas Britain could hand down orders to Italy, France was a sovereign and free country. The application of too much pressure about the ship, the ambassador argued, was likely to boomerang and undermine Britain's attempts to enlist France in a comprehensive strategy against illegal Jewish immigration.[10]

For the Mossad in France, and in Europe as a whole, these were days of uncertainty. The British steamroller exerted heavy pressure everywhere and reached every port. The British had been preparing for an especially turbulent spring and summer, during which, they estimated, the Mossad planned to send fifteen thousand refugees to Palestine as part of a display of force timed to coincide with the UN Special Committee on Palestine (UNSCOP).[11] Yet since the sailing of the *Guardian* (or the *Theodor Herzl*, its official Zionist name) from Toulon on 2 April 1947 with 2,650 people on board,[12] no ships had sailed from France. This moratorium had led to optimistic British assessments at the beginning of June that the French authorities, despite their unwillingness to commit themselves, were taking "effective measures against the [Jewish] traffic."[13] It also gave rise to rumors and reports in the news services that the Haganah in Palestine had decided to temporarily suspend the immigration operation because of the difficulties it was encountering and in order not to interfere with UNSCOP and its work. The Haganah in Palestine denied this, claiming that the rumors were part of a disinformation campaign meant "apparently to confuse and to create conflict." "But the fact," it added in internal communications, "that there are no ships makes it possible to continue disseminating reports like this."[14]

Destination—France

It is difficult to identify precisely the day the Mossad decided not to return the ship to Italy or store it in a Romanian port, but instead to launch it, with 4,500 passengers on board, from France itself. Circumstantial evidence indicates that the decision was made about a week after the boat arrived in Port de Bouc. There is support for this supposition in the fact that on 20 June the ship's captain notified Mossad headquarters in Paris, where people were still toying with the idea of sending the ship to one of the small ports in Romania, that "the *President* is not a possibility in the Black Sea in September."[15] In fact, that same day the Mossad's operational telephone communications, as recorded in the operations log, began to include indications of increased activity in Germany in preparation for the swift clandestine transfer of thousands of people from the DP camps to France.[16] Ada Sereni's report from Italy on 22 June that British pressure was making the situation there steadily worse and that "strict orders have been given for them to search every corner"[17] apparently contributed to the removal of Italy from the Mossad's agenda. France thus became the only possible launching ground.

For both British and Jews, this ship was to become the flagship of the Jewish "traffic" in the Mediterranean. For the Mossad, however, time was short—the political clock was ticking. On 12 July the European foreign ministers were scheduled to gather in Paris for a conference under the joint sponsorship of French minister of foreign affairs Georges Bidault and Foreign Secretary Bevin to discuss the Marshall Plan. Even the Zionists' best friends in the French administration sent clear messages that no ship could sail at that time. There was, however, an additional factor that the Mossad could not avoid taking into account, and it dictated that the ship be launched from France before the inaugural day of the conference. UNSCOP was at work and was visiting Palestine in June and July. The political and moral effect of such a huge refugee ship, and the substantive link between such a demonstration of the Jewish immigration movement and the committee's investigation, were evident to all parties involved. British documents indicate, as already noted, that the British expected a special effort by the Mossad to move fifteen thousand Jewish refugees to Palestine during the period of UNSCOP activity.[18] A letter dated 21 June 1947 from the commander of the Palmach to his men in Europe, urging them "to bring a large number" of ships "precisely" during the committee's sojourn in Palestine, is one example from the Zionist side.[19]

The importance of the time factor is evident in the frenetic step-up of the complex logistical effort to transfer thousands of refugees from the camps in Germany to the French Mediterranean coast, which began on 22 June and ended at the beginning of July. The Mossad chief's instructions to Marseilles on 10 July, the day before the ship set sail, to give no consideration to any difficulties or obstacles, to do everything "physically" possible and "without any consideration of cost," "paying as much as necessary" in order to get the boat and its passengers out to sea that same day or night,[20] is evidence that, for the Mossad agents, time had become critical. Messages that Mossad headquarters in the Yishuv sent to the ship at sea and as it approached the shores of Palestine, are another piece of evidence of the importance the Zionists attached to the ship in light of the UNSCOP work. This included precise instructions regarding what the ship was to broadcast to the shore: descriptions of the suffering of the refugees, with an emphasis on their fierce desire to reach their homeland. In particular, the instructions stressed, the ship should broadcast from the high seas a call for UNSCOP to intervene, to board the ship and record living testimony before the commission's members leave the country.[21] Accordingly, the ship messages implored the members of the commission to come see with their own eyes the plight of *Exodus*'s passengers.[22]

Where was the Mossad to get 4,500 human beings, and how were they to be transported in such a short period of time to the French Mediterranean coast? In France itself the Mossad had at that time no more than five hundred to six hundred refugees available.[23] The Italian station was prepared in principle, if necessary, to supply half of the quota of people needed.[24] The natural pool which had until then provisioned the Mossad's sailings from French ports were the DP camps in Germany, and the transfer of thousands of refugees from Germany to southern France in the span of less than ten days was one of the most ambitious and complex operations the Mossad ever attempted. The op-

erations log, which lists the incoming telephone calls at the Paris headquarters, provides an hour-by-hour report on the organization and the
execution of this ambitious project. On 20 June 1947, at 10 P.M., the
Paris headquarters recorded a preliminary report from "Ernst"
(Efrayim Frank), a Zionist agent in Munich, on the situation with regard to French entry certificates and on possibilities for the immediate
retrieval of people from the camps and their transfer through French
territory to southern France.[25] "The French consul will apparently
cause problems," Ernst said during that night call. "[He] demands
identity cards from the army in order to give individual visas." Ernst
added that he was afraid that the French consul had received an order
from higher up and that every effort should be made to ensure that he
would receive an explicit order to provide collective visas. "[Ernst] demands the intervention of the priest," says the log.[26] These cryptic
lines reveal the tangled policy of the French government on the question of Jewish DPs and the great dispute over these questions, which
split the French government and divided leading ministers in the cabinet, especially the foreign and interior ministers. Unremarked in
French historiography of the Fourth Republic,[27] these questions preoccupied the French government beginning in mid-1946 and especially
during 1947, and left behind them rich documentation. They were
bound up with other serious questions that were at the heart of the
complex relations between Britain and France and that grew out of the
issue of the rehabilitation of Europe and the delineation of spheres of
power and influence in the post-war years. The Zionist agent's brief report from Munich testified to the complicated nature of the French position on movement into and out of France and on the temporary residence of refugees on its territory during transit, a problem Mossad
agents had to deal with continually. It was also evidence of the Ministry
of Foreign Affairs' rigid position, which was passed on to the consular
network in those countries from which Jewish refugees were reaching
France. Furthermore, it showed the kinds of connections the Mossad
had in France's corridors of power and its ability to use these connections to arrange for a French consul to receive orders contradicting his
foreign ministry's instructions.

Ernst's demand that "the priest" intervene refers to one of the
Mossad's most important contacts in France at the time, a person with-
out whom any description of Zionist activity in the country is incomplete.
"The priest" was indeed a man of the Church, a Polish-born Jew named

Glasberg who had converted to Catholicism, fought in the French resistance, saved Jewish children during the war, and after the war managed the social direction center for refugees in the French Ministry of the Interior. He was enlisted in the Mossad's work by Marc Jarblum, a prominent member of the French Socialist Party and a resistance man himself, as well as a personal friend of Ben-Gurion. The two were among the many connections the Mossad had made in government circles in France, especially in its socialist wing, with the help of Jewish-French agent-mediators in senior positions in the French establishment. This thick mesh of relations lay at the foundation of the Mossad daring and imagination that was needed to launch a complex project like the *Exodus*. What is interesting, and in a sense paradoxical, is that all this happened during a period of far-reaching improvement in French-British relations. An even greater paradox is that the initiator and leader of this improvement in relations was the French socialist leader Léon Blum, and yet it was Blum's spirit and political beliefs that inspired the socialist ministers to provide their assistance to the Mossad's work in France. Blum's influence was particularly instrumental in the progress of the *Exodus* affair, even though it opposed Blum's own policy of improving relations between the two countries.

Porous Borders

More than a year earlier, in March 1946, the first Mossad ship set out from the port of Sète with some 750 passengers on board, most of them refugees from DP camps in Germany who had been transferred to Belgium and then taken in Jewish Brigade trucks to Marseilles; a minority were Jews from France.[28] It was not until 22 June that the next ship, the *Haganah,* sailed with 999 people on board.[29] The British began putting pressure on the French right after the first ship was intercepted as it drew close to the Palestinian shore. From interrogating the crew, the British discovered that the ship had been openly rebuilt and prepared for sailing, over the space of several months, in Marseilles and that French police had even supervised the boarding of the passengers.[30] In May 1946 the Foreign Office in London instructed the British ambassador in Paris, Duff Cooper, to direct the attention of the French authorities to the illegal sailings from French ports and to demand that they act to prevent them. The British had reason to believe that this

Zionist operation was being commanded from Paris.[31] In response to the British inquiry, the French Ministry of Foreign Affairs promised to do its best to prevent illegal ships from setting out from France, but the British ambassador had doubts about its ability "to entirely prevent further illegal boardings." He stressed the "traditional strength of the Communist Organization in French ports and the tendency of the French government towards Zionist opinion."[32]

In France, as in Italy, the British acted on two fronts. They tried to compel the French to restrict or entirely prevent Jewish refugees from entering French territory over the country's east and north land borders, and they made every effort to block departure by sea from French ports. They soon discovered the reason the land borders were so porous: France's policy toward displaced persons in general and toward the Jews in particular. In the chaos that reigned in post-war Europe, France's borders, like those of other countries, were as permeable as a sieve; nearly anybody could cross them in one way or another. The French authorities recognized a wide assortment of identity papers, including certificates issued by the French police for stateless persons, certificates issued by UNRRA, and military transit visas from Germany. The large variety of acceptable documents made their forgery and exchange easier. Furthermore, the French consulates in various countries almost never checked the validity of the ultimate-destination visas held by the people who presented their transit permits for inspection.[33] In the summer of 1946 the French government went even further and signed, under pressure from Zionist Jewish organizations in France, an agreement with the Polish government granting permits for two thousand Jewish children to travel through France.[34] The French also agreed to provide temporary asylum for five thousand Jews who had not yet left Poland.

This administrative tumult provided fertile ground for the counterfeiting industry run by the organizations smuggling Jews into and out of France. The authorities had no way of knowing how many Jewish refugees were on French soil at any given moment or what their legal status was. "The local authorities are giving transit papers to shipments from the camps in Bavaria, Czechoslovakia, and Austria on the basis of final visas to Ethiopia or to South American countries," reported a Mossad agent in France. "The shipments are openly entering Kasuto [France]. The ships sail officially to those countries listed on the final visas. Before sailing the refugees receive exit visas from the local government and leave legally."[35] The visas of the passengers on Mossad ships were usually prepared and stamped in Mossad laboratories in France, using either forged stamps or authentic ones obtained by the Mossad from foreign consulates through connections or bribes, or in exchange for other services.[36]

When they discovered these methods in August 1946, the British launched a systematic effort to get the French to prevent Jewish refugees from entering France with counterfeit papers. In response to the British pressure, the orders given to French border police were made stricter, and the policemen were ordered to inspect documents carefully and prevent the entry of people whose papers were not in order. Yet the French maintained that they had no legal power to refuse to grant transit visas if the country of ultimate destination declared its willingness to accept the immigrants. The British embassy assessed that the French government "will be as helpful as they can, though they do not want to commit themselves to going beyond the strict terms of the law."[37]

After the elections to the second French constituent assembly in June 1946, a new government was formed by Georges Bidault, who previously had been minister of foreign affairs in a government headed by the Socialist Party. Bidault was a conservative Gaullist who, during the German occupation, had been part of the Catholic group within the resistance movement and who, after the war, was one of the founders and leaders of the Christian Democratic Party (MRP). While heading the Ministry of Foreign Affairs under a series of prime ministers, he represented the ministry's traditional position: concern first and foremost with preserving France's vested interests in the Levant, North Africa, and the Anglo-Saxon world. It was Bidault who tried, throughout this period, to bring France and Britain closer together and who, in the face of opposition from the socialist Ministry of the Interior, continually pressed the French government to restrict the movement of Jews into and out of France in accord with British demands.[38] During his term as prime minister from the end of July 1946 to mid-October of the same year, Paris hosted the peace conference, a meeting of foreign ministers meant to resolve the status of the former non-German enemy states. During this conference, relations between Bevin and Bidault grew closer. Under Bidault, and in accordance with British demands, the French government changed its policy toward the refugees infiltrating into France. Every Jewish immigrant who tried to cross the French border or who was already in France without valid papers would, the government decided, be sent back to the French occupation zone in Germany. An order was also given to prepare temporary refuges for those to be deported.[39]

The struggle within the French government over the policy on Jewish refugees erupted during the month-long government of Léon Blum. Blum's was a homogeneous, all-socialist minority government that bore the old socialist leader's personal imprint. He himself served as both president of the Council of Ministers (prime minister) and minister of foreign affairs. The dispute surfaced on 27 December 1946, when the minister of the interior, Edouard Depreux, received a letter ostensibly written by Blum and signed by the minister in charge in the Ministry of Foreign Affairs, "Perier." The letter contained a report on a thousand Jews in Prague who were planning to cross "our territory" in order to board the ship *Archangelos* at Marseilles, to sail for Santo Domingo. "However," said "Perier's" letter, "according to information handed over to us by the British embassy in Paris, the Santo Domingo government has declared that it has no desire to receive these Jews into its territory. I therefore contacted our consul in Prague as well as the Tripartite office for military documents in that city so that they would refuse to give any transit permits to those immigrants."[40] Depreux was quick to pass this letter on to his friend, the socialist attorney André Blumel, a key Zionist activist in France after the war. This urbane man had a special position in socialist circles. He had served in the second half of the 1930s as chief of Léon Blum's bureau when Blum headed the Popular Front government. Now, as a result of both his status and his many ties to the French socialist elite, along with a new Jewish consciousness that he developed during the war, this assimilated attorney became the major mediator between the Mossad's agents and the socialist administration.[41] Blumel rushed to Blum with the letter, and Blum, in his own hand, wrote that the letter sent in his name was written without his knowledge or consent. In a separate letter to the minister of the interior, Blum stated that "the French position in this category of matters has not changed in any way. It is not our job to check the validity of the visas from the countries of destination that are presented to us."[42]

André Blumel was in France what Rafael Kantoni was in Italy. The two had almost identical biographies. Both were members of their respective countries' anti-Nazi resistance and were prominent activists in the Socialist Party, which was a central component of the new regime after liberation. This is what made them such effective aids to Zionist activity. Their work for the Zionist cause allowed them to participate not only in a national ideological struggle in which they believed, but it also provided them a way of continuing the battles they had fought in their years of underground activity against the Nazi occupier. Furthermore, it helped them assert their Jewish identity and civil identity in countries where there had been attempts to destroy both.[43] As for Blumel, he was one of the founding members of the socialist resistance movement Liberation Nord. On his way to England on a mission to meet with de Gaulle, he was arrested in Portugal, extradited to France, and convicted and imprisoned by the Vichy government. The man who had maintained contact with him while he was in prison, and who rescued him just a few days before he was to be sent to a death camp in Germany, was Edouard Depreux, now minister of the interior.[44]

Immediately after liberation Blumel was put in charge of the bureau of the first socialist minister of the interior, Adrian Tixier, and gained additional contacts in the government and in the Ministry of the Interior. The close contacts that Blumel maintained with the leaders of the Socialist Party, including the man who inherited the prime ministership from Blum, Paul Ramadier, is apparent in the tone of a letter sent by Blumel to Ramadier on the subject of the government's treatment of Jewish migration through France. Using the intimate *tu* form of address, Blumel wrote, "My dear Paul. Your predecessor, Léon Blum, took, with regard to the problem of Jewish migration, the following position: We [France] do not check the veracity of country-of-destination visas presented to us. Is the position of your government different? If not, I would be thankful if your government would remind the officials of the Ministry of Foreign Affairs that they must carry out the government's decisions. I would appreciate it if you could resolve this problem with utmost urgency."[45]

Aware of the special ties between the socialist Ministry of the Interior and the Jewish-Zionist lobby, officials of the Ministry of Foreign Affairs counterattacked. Having failed to block the entry of Jewish migrants at the land borders, they now acted to prevent the illegal departure of the Jews by sea to Palestine and to return them to the places from which they came. They intensified this action after January 1947, since, in the preceding four months, two Mossad ships were launched from French ports. A third ship, which left from Sweden, received along its journey service at the French port of Le Havre, even though Stockholm had reported in advance to the French Ministry of Foreign Affairs that the Cuban visas held by the ship's six hundred passengers were counterfeit, and even though ministry officials had promised the British that they would make every effort to detain the ship.[46] On all these sailings, the British learned, French officials affiliated with the Ministry of the Interior had given active assistance to the Zionist operations.[47]

The British learned of this complicity from French Ministry of Foreign Affairs officials who complained to their British interlocutors about the attitudes of the Ministry of the Interior and its employees, both as an excuse for their ongoing failure and in order to provide the British with a mapping of the structure of power and influence in the French government. In one of his reports the British ambassador wrote that the Ministry of Foreign Affairs was, "as usual," putting the blame on the Ministry of the Interior.[48] A French Ministry of Foreign Affairs official responsible for Jewish migration complained about the lack of coordination between the ministries concerned and dropped hints that there was corruption in the Ministry of the Interior;[49] and in a conversation with the British embassy's chargé d'affaires Ashley Clarke, the director of the Ministry of Foreign Affairs' Division of Administrative Treaties stated explicitly that "as long as there was a Socialist Minister in the Interior it was to be expected that these persons [the Jewish refugees] would receive very benevolent treatment." He also explained to his British colleague that the socialist ministers, acting under the inspiration of Léon Blum, "were not only disposed to give full weight to humanitarian considerations but were much better disposed toward Jewish emigrants from eastern Europe than are the [French] Communists."[50]

The signing of the treaty between Britain and France in March 1947 brought new hope for the British. Prime Minister Attlee said that the British now had "the right to expect active assistance in the prevention of illegal immigration into Palestine from the French government in view of the recently concluded Anglo-French treaty of friendship and alliance."[51] Yet the professional staff in the British Foreign Office was realistic enough to recognize that the situation was grim from the British point of view, "as the Zionists wield considerable political influence and the French Ministry of Interior is proving obstructive."[52]

Realpolitik versus Morality

The countervailing pressures on the French government from the Zionists and the British on the issue of the Jewish refugees, and the diametrically opposed positions within the government, required the prime minister to intervene and to try to set a consensual government policy on the question. A choice had to be made between pursuing realpolitik in a complex political and international situation during a difficult period for France[53] or acting in accordance with the fundamental principles of justice and morality to which post-war France considered itself committed. On 21 April 1947 an interministerial meeting was called at Matignon Palace, the residence of the French prime minister, to determine the government's position and decide how the government's representatives, in its various ministries, should act. The meeting was preceded by lobbying campaigns and intensive organized pressures from both wings. At the Mossad's request, its liaison André Blumel met with both President Vincent Auriol and Prime Minister Ramadier. The sense that emerged from these conversations was that France would continue to support Jewish migration and that there were "serious possibilities for action," as was reported in the Mossad network.[54] The director of the Regulation of Aliens (*Réglementation des étrangers*) department of the Ministry of the Interior, Marcel Pagès, who was previously recruited by Abbé Glasberg to assist the cause of the Jewish migrants, prepared a working paper for the meeting in which he explicitly accused the Ministry of Foreign Affairs of an attempt to "impose on the French government, by every means possible, a position that will adopt the thesis of the British government," in violation of France's traditional principles. He argued that the adoption of the British position would require France to make a "racial distinction" and to check who among "the aliens wishing to leave our country for a country of absorption" was Jewish and who was not. He used the sharpest possible language to criticize the proposal to arrest the refugees with invalid documents who had already managed to enter France and to return them to their camps in Germany and Austria. In the wake of a war in which major deportations of French Jews by the Nazis were aided by the Vichy government, those words stung. "Getting rid [of the refugees] will require the organization, on French territory, of a virtual manhunt (women, children, the elderly), of concentration camps, of well-guarded transports, and as a result it is liable to awaken, in our country, various developments and movements regarding the Jewish question. Such actions will not take long to cause, because of the circumstances of the displaced persons of Jewish origin and their mood, extremely unfortunate incidents throughout France." Regarding the action at the ports that the British were demanding via the French Ministry of Foreign Affairs, Pagès said, "Personally, I am of the opinion that it would be very unfortunate if France were to oppose the sailing of migrants who have French *laissez-passers* and entry visas from their countries of destination, on the grounds that the ships meant to convey them do not meet the criteria for sailing at sea. Parenthetically, we have no information about these ships except the information supplied by the British secret services to our Ministry of Foreign Affairs."[55]

The British, for their part, were not idle either; they amplified their demands. In one of the central documents on this matter, one that reveals the dimensions of the British war against Jewish movement into and out of France and which sums up the state of affairs and makes Britain's demands of France clear, Ambassador Duff Cooper settled accounts with the Zionists and with the French who had not been competent enough to put an end to Zionist activity on their territory. The ambassador wrote to Minister of Foreign Affairs Bidault that the British had much information revealing the intentions of the organizers of the illegal movement to send to Palestine, during the coming two or three months (April–June 1947), some fifteen thousand Jews in an effort to influence the recommendations of UNSCOP. Marseilles, he wrote, was home to the operations center for "this traffic," and there were currently three ships at the port ready to raise anchor at any time. "There is," he claimed, "abundant proof that the illegal Jewish immigration traffic is not a spontaneous exodus of refugees, but a carefully-organized Zionist campaign designed to force the hand of His Majesty's Government and to increase the proportion of Jewish population in Palestine." In allowing this "traffic," the ambassador added, the French government was no doubt moved by humanitarian considerations; however, it was actively supporting the Zionist movement and thus causing severe embarrassment and difficulty for His Majesty's government in its efforts to reach an equitable solution to the Palestine question. The British protest continued with claims that despite the great amount of information the British had passed on to the French, information that representatives of the Ministry of Foreign Affairs had welcomed, the French government had not taken any real steps to halt the movement.[56]

There were further contacts between the two foreign ministries in the wake of Cooper's submission of the document to Bidault. French Ministry of Foreign Affairs officials hinted to their British colleagues that it would be best to directly involve the two ministers themselves, who were at that time in Moscow at a meeting of the foreign ministers of the four Allied powers.[57] The capture along the Palestinian shore of the *Guardian* (*Theodor Herzl*), which had sailed from Toulon with 2,640 people aboard, did not contribute to the atmosphere of reconciliation between the two countries. Information about this ship's presence in a French port before it sailed and its involvement in the clandestine Jewish movement had been sent to France many times. Similarly, the operation in which Bricha and Mossad agents had brought thousands of people destined for the ship from Belgium to France could not have succeeded without the assistance of border police and officials in the French Ministry of the Interior.[58]

This, then, was the background to the high-level interministerial consultation on the question of Jewish migration through French territory that was held in the office, and under the chairmanship, of the French prime minister. The importance France attached to this discussion is evident from the list of participants. In addition to the prime minister, it was attended by the deputy prime minister, the president of the Planning Council, two ministers of state, the minister of transportation and public works, and the top officials in the three relevant ministries. On the agenda was France's reaction to the document submitted by the British ambassador to the French foreign minister the previous month. We do not have a complete transcript of the proceedings; the custom at meetings of the French cabinet is that no minutes are taken, and that, apparently, was followed at this meeting. The document listing the decisions made there, however, is on file at the French National Archive, and it informs us that, on the face of it, the French government acceded to some of Britain's demands. The French, however, conditioned their acquiescence on significant British concessions on other issues that were in serious dispute between the two countries. France's consent was thus a qualified one. In fact, had the British examined the French response more thoroughly at that time, they could have saved themselves the trauma of the *Exodus* two and a half months later. The document included indications presaging the obstinate stand the French would take toward the British during that incident. The deputy prime minister, representing the absent foreign minister, was assigned the task of giving the British ambassador a "firm answer," which included the following statements: "The French government refuses to make any racial distinction among the aliens whom it is responsible for supervising, or to determine whether or not they are Jewish . . . . The French government has difficulty agreeing to entrance visas to Palestine being given only to Jews who are in the British [occupation] zone of Germany. . . . There is a need to find an acceptable formula, so that recipients of these certificates will come also from the French and American occupation zones, and, eventually also from France itself. . . . In order to prove that it is not encouraging covert passage to Palestine, [the French government] will check the validity of entrance permits given to Jews in the form of collective permits." Nevertheless, the French response noted, in one of the document's most important sections, that "only collective visas will be checked, while personal visas will continue to be subject to the same regulations applying to all aliens." It also stated that "Obviously, in practice France will not take any action to deport Jews who entered the country's territory covertly."[59]

And the Ship Sails

This background information makes it easier to interpret the move that began with the cable sent on 20 June 1947 by the Zionist agent in Germany to the Mossad's headquarters in Paris. The next morning the Bricha agents in the American zone in Germany were already organizing the gathering of thousands of refugees from the camps and planning their transfer to southern France. The entire plan was based on an official collective French transit visa for 1,700 people that was to arrive from France any day with the help of Abbé Glasberg's organization. The intention was to divide this visa into six collective visas and to make three copies of each of them. On 24 June a Bricha agent reported that the copies of the visas had been prepared and that they were "almost authentic." The three initial shipments were scheduled to leave on 29 June via Mulhouse and on 30 June and 1 July via Strasbourg. The fourth was to go through Neuf Brisac and to leave Mulhouse on 4 July. The fifth shipment was slated to leave on the night of 5 July.[60] The legal travelers were sent in trains while those carrying the forged papers were smuggled in trucks. On 7 July, after the conclusion of the border-crossing operation, the Mossad agents in France were able to report to headquarters in Palestine that they had brought "from Hanan [Germany] 4,500 people. Of these 1,700 with saplings [visas] and the rest by enema [smuggling]."[61] During the days in which the mass transfer was made from Germany to France, each of the passengers designated for the boat was photographed, and the Mossad's counterfeiting experts used these photos to produce, in a secret laboratory in Lyons, 4,500 personal travel documents.[62]

No details are available about the assistance extended by French officials and citizens at each stage of the transfer operation. It can only be assumed that, as in previous border-crossing operations, the transfer of these 4,500 people from the camps in Germany to the French Mediterranean coast in such a short period of time required good contacts in the government and also some cash ("small losses in cavaliers [Swiss francs] and steffans [dollars]" according to the Mossad operations log in regard to another operation).[63]

Supporting this assumption is the fact that Britain was exerting increasingly heavier pressure on the French to prevent the big ship anchored in Marseilles from sailing. Foreign Secretary Bevin, in a letter sent to Bidault, went so far as to remove the matter from the level of relations between the two countries, arguing that the arrival in Palestine of a boat carrying thousands of Jewish refugees (he cited the number two thousand) was likely to endanger the peace in Palestine and in the Middle East.[64] Anonymous letters were sent to French port officials, and in Marseilles a British destroyer was keeping watch on the ship.[65]

The Marseilles Mossad agent's reports to headquarters in Paris, as recorded in the operations log, make it possible to follow, step by step, the developments that preceded the launch. Sète, from which more Mossad ships had sailed than from any other French port, was the chosen departure point. This small, remote port also held the electoral constituency for the socialist minister of transportation and public works Jules Moch, and most of its public jobs were held by members of the Socialist and Communist parties; Mossad agents had established irreplaceable connections there, including ties with the police.[66] When, on 4 July, Mossad agents in Marseilles received the instruction forbidding them from sailing from Sète, it appeared as if the operation had been thwarted. "There is no other place from which we can work on such a scale," Zameret reported to Paris. When the prohibition on sailing was lifted on 9 July, Zameret could report to Paris: "Everything is ready. One hundred fifty cargo vehicles will take the people. The *President* [the ship] will leave in the afternoon [from Port de Bouc] such that it will arrive in S [Sète] as evening falls, and only then will the people leave Sidney [Marseilles]." Zameret further reported that his plan was to begin boarding the people on the ship in the early morning hours of 10 July and complete it by the afternoon. He requested that communication lines between the Paris center and his headquarters in Marseilles be kept open, so that "we can be in touch at all times."[67] The next report arrived the following morning at

6:35, when Zameret communicated that by that time 300 people had boarded the ship in Sète. A second report stated that by 7:30 A.M. 1,500 had boarded the ship, and at 11 A.M. Zameret reported in English, "No news good news."[68] Then, however, some bad news arrived. This was a period of mass labor union strikes all over France. A truckdrivers' strike had halted the vehicles bringing Jewish passengers and life rafts to the ship; however, good contacts with the local and central workers' organizations helped get the ban lifted so that the convoy could proceed. A decoy maneuver that Zameret planned to carry out with the help of another Mossad ship was aborted because of the mistral and a sea storm.

In addition, the British raised a storm of protest regarding the activities surrounding the ship. The French Ministry of Foreign Affairs hastened to promise that instructions had been given to the port authorities and to the area supervisors to delay the ship. Furthermore, ministry officials affirmed, if people had boarded the ship, they would be forced to get off because the ship was not allowed, according to its license, to carry passengers or sail in bad weather.[69] The British consul in Marseilles alerted the local maritime inspection department, which intervened to prohibit the sailing even though Sète was not within its jurisdiction. According to Mossad documents, the situation at 1 P.M. on 10 July was as follows: "With the completion of the boarding the agent applied to customs to receive an exit permit, but they rejected him in accordance with the orders of maritime safety in Sidney [Marseilles]. They request our intervention. They boarded 4,300–4,400."[70] Following up the news of the prohibition against sailing, Rudi [Zameret] reported to the Paris center that his men had obtained two certificates for the ship from Maritime Safety—one approving the ship's sailing ("the subject of passengers is not mentioned") and the second stating that "everything is in order and that there are life vests for 4,300 people." "The certificates are on the vessel," Zameret further reported, "and it is not clear whether there is a copy of the second certificate and whether it was sent to Sidney [Marseilles]. It was given by the 'friend,' the maritime safety official, and it is a sort of 'private' one. The prohibition against sailing was apparently received by his boss in his absence—because the friend was on the vessel. Since Sidney's intervention is procedurally abnormal, because S [Sète] is not subject to Sidney, there can be no doubt that there has been intervention by the bastards [the British]." The certificate mentioned by the Mossad's agent specified the sailing day—July 8—and its destination—Istanbul. The ship was not authorized to carry any passengers.[71]

During the following hours it became clear to the Mossad agents that their contacts in Paris were of no use. The *Inspection maritime* agent in Sète informed them that he was subject solely to the office in Marseilles and was not permitted to speak directly with the main office in the capital.[72] It also turned out that the required certificate was an "international sailing safety permit," and this regulation could be circumvented only with a special document certifying that the vessel was "a military carrier."[73] The Mossad's friends in the government, headed by ministers Edouard Depreux and Jules Moch, were unable to do anything at that juncture, especially given that the Conference of European Foreign Ministers was to assemble in Paris on July 12 to discuss the Marshall Plan. The Mossad operations log indicates that at 7:30 on the evening of 10 July an order was sent from Paris to Marseilles and Sète to launch the ship in any way possible, and to pay any price necessary—"two, three, and more grand" (meaning, apparently, millions of French francs).[74] Zameret personally traveled with the money from Marseilles to Sète. At 9:15 in the evening the Mossad chief himself called from Paris and spoke with the ship's commander, Yossi Hamburger (Har'el), instructing him "to do everything physically possible for the launch," whatever the cost.[75] That night a navigator was hired; he was to arrive at 2:00 A.M. to take the boat out of the port, but he did not show up. As 4:00 A.M. approached the *President Warfield* started up its engines and began to move on its own out of the port.[76] At 7:30 A.M. on 11 July, the ship commander reported to the shore that the ship had entered the open sea; that despite running into a sand bar on its way out, it had not incurred any serious damage; and that the effort to steal out of the port had been justified, despite the danger. At that very same hour, the Marseilles station called the operations center in Paris and notified them that the ship had left the port and was already in "open waters," and that a British destroyer was trailing it.[77]

The first French report on the launching of the ship was written the same day, 11 July, by the chief of the General Intelligence Services in Sète, Laurent Leboutet. It was intended for the services' director-general in Paris, who was directly subordinate to the minister of the interior. The report stated that with his supervision the services' agents had over the course of 10 July overseen the boarding of 4,052 "Israelite" refugees, "men, women and children" on the steamship *President Warfield,* which flew the flag of Honduras and was under the command of Captain Marx Bernard, of American citizenship. "The migrants, formerly prisoners in the German camps, arrived from the assembly center in Lyons, on rue de la vieille, house number 13b. Each of them bore a valid travel permit, with a photograph, issued by the prefecture of the Rhone district, upon which was written 'approved by the Minister of the Interior on 26 June 1947.' They also bore entry visas to Colombia, issued by the Colombian Republic's consul in Marseilles." The boarding of the ship, the intelligence chief in Sète further reported, was conducted from 4:00 in the morning through 1:00 in the afternoon as the trucks carrying the "Israelites" arrived. "The preliminary visit to the boat, the close supervision of the boarding, and the searches of the passengers' possessions carried out by my agents and customs agents did not produce anything suspicious." The intelligence chief reported that the *President Warfield*, which entered the port on 9 July at 10:00 P.M., had anchored on the spot determined by the port commander, which allowed direct entry into and exit from the port without requiring that the bridge be opened first. The navigation inspector (*Inspection de navigation*) visited the ship and issued a sailing permit. However, during the course of 10 July the *Inspection maritime* in Marseilles, under pressure from the English consul-general, issued orders for "inspection" in Sète, in order to prevent the sailing. Instructions were given by this service to the port navigator and to the tugs to withhold all assistance from the ship. The ship, which was ready to sail at 1 P.M., remained with its engines running. Toward 6 P.M. an *Inspection maritime* agent went on deck to remove part of the engine, but the captain resisted. The *President Warfield* remained anchored at a distance of 20 meters from the wharf, and its only connection with land was a shuttle in the form of a rowboat. Toward 4:00 in the morning the ship's cables were raised. It began to exit the port under its own power, hit a sand bar, freed itself entirely on its own, and sailed out to sea at 6:00. A British vessel— a patrol ship, apparently—which since the morning of 10 July had circled near Sète, followed the ship, which, after a moment's hesitation, set its prow to the southwest.[78]

The next day, on 12 July, the report's author passed on to the General Intelligence Services' director-general a list of the names of the 4,052 Jews who had boarded the ship on 10 July. He noted again that each of the passengers carried a travel permit with a photograph issued by the Rhone prefecture and that the passengers held entry permits to Colombia, issued by the Colombian consul in Marseilles. "All the travel permits were checked by my men at exit," the report concluded.[79] That same day the prefect of Herault, the district that included Sète, reported to the minister of the interior about the series of events at the port leading up to the sailing "in secret" of the ship. The interesting addition to this report, which was written using the very same words used by the general intelligence chief in Sète, appears at its end: it states that as soon as the news of the ship's sailing reached him, he took the initiative to call the British consul-general in Marseilles to report the sailing.[80] These reports by Leboutet and the prefect were recycled in the days to come, almost word for word, in the plethora of correspondence between the French ministries produced by the inquiry into the sailing without permit of the *President Warfield* from Sète. The official inquiry was opened as a result of Prime Minister Ramadier's personal promise to Foreign Secretary Bevin that the entire matter would be thoroughly investigated.[81] Even before this, however, the various bodies that had cooperated with the Mossad launched their own internal inquiry into the moves that preceded the sailing, apparently to create the appearance that it had been an entirely secret, subversive action carried out without the knowledge of the authorities.[82] This use of almost identical language and expressions in all the reports on the incident produced by the various organizations subordinate to the Ministry of the Interior and the Ministry of Transportation and Public Works indicates that a single hand apparently guided the drafting of all of them.

Even more important than the technical and operational details revealed in these documents is the evidence they provide of the depth to which Zionist agents and their French-Jewish collaborators penetrated the very fabric of the French intelligence and security services, as well as the various bodies connected with the French ports authority, labor unions, and political parties of the left—all with the backing of central figures in the French administration. The documents also reveal a deeper phenomenon: authentic compassion for the Jewish refugees shared by common people—policemen, port officials, intelligence and security agents, customs agents, and prefecture officials (most of them members of the Socialist and Communist parties) and former resistance fighters, who found in their assistance to the Jews a way to preserve the spirit of the French underground of the war years.

The news of the ship's sailing came like an explosion under Bevin's seat at the Conference of Foreign Ministers. Early in the morning of 12 July, the day the conference opened, Bevin met with his French counterpart and demanded an explanation for the French assistance to the ship, as well as for how the ship was able to slip out of the port despite the French government's promises and in violation of the sailing permit. Stressing that this was the largest number of illegal immigrants ever to sail from any port on a single vessel, Bevin demanded the punishment of those responsible and informed Bidault that the British intended to make an example of this ship by forcing it to return to a French port with all its passengers. He added that Britain was concerned not only with peace in Palestine and the region, but also and no less so with the welfare of the Jewish refugees: "Jews in all parts of Europe are being encouraged to sell their possessions in order to purchase at extravagant rates a passage to Palestine. When it is too late they discover that those who have taken their money have no means of affording them a safe passage and they are obliged, having no resources left, to undertake the voyage not only in conditions of extreme misery but also faced by considerable dangers."[83]

Dissatisfied by his meeting with the French minister of foreign affairs, Bevin demanded to see Prime Minister Ramadier on the same subject. Ramadier agreed to meet with Bevin that same day, apparently to appease his anger. "What would the French Government say if we connived at the introduction of unauthorized persons and troublemakers into French controlled territory where there was a problem similar to ours?" Bevin asked the prime minister, hinting that he could cause serious problems for France in North Africa in the same way. It was the Jews of New York who pulled the strings in this financial scandal, he added. Ramadier, responding with his own special kind of calmness, said that he had no way of checking the seaworthiness of all the foreign ships that anchored in and sailed from French ports, and that the immigrants to Palestine were hiding their true destination. Nevertheless, he promised Bevin that he would do his best to remove the matter of illegal Jewish immigration from the agenda of the two countries because it was a sensitive matter that was clouding their relations. He also promised to conduct an investigation in the relevant ministries regarding the circumstances of the ship's sailing.[84]

At the end of the internal inquiry into the services linked to the affair, and in response to the French prime minister's 16 July request that the minister of the interior provide an explanation for the ship's secret sailing, Edouard Depreux wrote a detailed letter on 21 July in which he repeated the major points brought before him in the various reports. He added that the French port authorities could do nothing to prevent the "physical exit" of the vessel and that they had immediately alerted the British consul-general in Marseilles. "It is clear from the information presented to me," Depreux wrote to Ramadier, "that the French police services acted completely in accordance with the orders they were given, both in verifying the certificates held by the passengers and in their efforts to prevent the ship from leaving the port of Sète. The exit permit was issued properly by the Lyons prefecture after an examination of the entry permits issued officially by the consul of the destination country. In the wake of this the updated instructions were carried out precisely." Minister of Transportation Jules Moch was even more blunt in the report he submitted to the prime minister: The port authorities had no way of getting the passengers off the ship by force because this would have led to bloodshed, and no one was willing to assume responsibility for such an incident. Once the ship had slipped out of the port there was no point in sending a warship after it because warning shots would not have stopped it; the only way to stop it would be to sink it, and that was not an acceptable alternative.[85] Both ministers thus fully backed their subordinates.

While the politicians in Paris were busy wiping away the Mossad's fingerprints, the *President Warfield* was sailing eastward, accompanied by a British vessel and airplane. On 15 July the ship established contact with the Mossad in Palestine and left the area of radio control by the Mossad's Marseilles station.[86] For a few days the focus of the affair passed to the ship itself, at sea, before it landed on the shores of Palestine. This interval in the historical events, and in the Mossad's work in France, provides an opportunity to flash back to the beginnings of the Mossad's activity in this country, more than two years previously.

Political and Social Chaos

France, where the first operatives from the Yishuv in Palestine, including Mossad agents, arrived at the end of World War II, was a ravaged and hopeless land. The liberation in stages of the country concluded with the cleansing of the last German enclaves in April and May of 1945. This brought France, as one French historian put it, "a great sense of relief but not necessarily an opening to new hopes." "France of the liberation," wrote George Bernanos, "went bankrupt just like the other France [of Petain]. Perhaps because the two were really one."[87] The country had paid a heavy price. Its infrastructure was destroyed, and the French state was unable to raise itself to its former station in the world and control its destiny. Its defeat and immediate surrender to Nazism four years earlier, and the collaboration by the French government and a large part of the population with the occupation authorities, were cause for deep feelings of guilt. All this made the years after liberation one long stretch of political and social chaos. The gradual return of some of the *déportés*, Jews and others who had been sent to the death camps in Germany, were a constant reproof against the heirs of Vichy, and this deepened France's sense of betrayal of its destiny and history.[88]

More than a quarter of France's real estate had been destroyed by the war, and more than a million families were left without homes. The transportation infrastructure was heavily damaged, and entire regions of the country were disconnected from each other. Not a single bridge remained to link Paris with the Atlantic ports; the heavy bombardments and the "battle of the train tracks" fought by the French resistance had destroyed more than half of the 40,000 kilometers of rail that had been in use on the eve of the war. Systems of agriculture, industry, commerce, and the country's economic and financial structure, as well as the food supply system, were no longer functional. The official food rations in Paris at liberation (August 1944) provided only 900 calories a day per adult; this grew to 1,515 calories in May 1945.

In many ways, this France was an ideal place for the Mossad to work. Its geography provided a long coastline with many harbors on the Atlantic and Mediterranean sides, offering an almost infinite variety of ports from which to launch ships. It had relatively good accessibility to Belgium, Holland, and the Scandinavian countries, as well as to the DP camps in Germany and Austria, and it was possible to move people from those countries into France across its long land borders. Furthermore, France's territory was, unlike Italy's, free of the presence of the Allied occupation armies, and this allowed the agents of the Mossad and other Zionist underground groups freedom of action. Of no less importance was the public political space that the country provided. The fragile party regime established at the beginning of 1946, with the end of the period of the interim institutions and after de Gaulle's thundering exit, led to revolving-door coalition governments unable to grapple with the political, economic, and social chaos.[89] This as well as the different, even contrary interests that motivated organizations, institutions, and parties created a comfortable environment for covert or semicovert work in this "party re-public."[90] Moreover, the government ministries relevant to the Mossad's kind of activity were manned at all levels, from the ministers to the offi-cials in the districts and at the borders, by militant members of the Socialist Party, former resistance fighters who, according to the minister of the interior himself, were less interested in the reestablishment of law and order in the republic than in the preservation and application of the spirit of the resistance on the public and state levels after the ejection of the occupier.[91] The mayors of the large port cities such as Marseilles and Bordeaux, as well as of smaller cities and towns, were also socialists.[92]

In contradiction of the forecasts of the Zionist leadership in the Yishuv, however, France itself lacked significant potential for Jewish im-migration to Palestine. "Nowhere else have I met Jews who have suffered so much without learning anything," wrote a Mossad agent after his first meeting with the Jews of France.[93] The first Mossad agent, David Shaltiel, reached Paris at the beginning of 1945. German-born, an officer in the French Foreign Legion, and a man of the world, he was meant to prepare France, which was already undergoing an accelerated process of liberation after the landing of Allied forces at Normandy, to be a center of Yishuv activity in western Europe and North Africa. The plan was to base the Yishuv's activity there, on the Zionist nucleus of the Jewish re-sistance movement—the *Armée juive* (the AJ, or Jewish Army), which had been forged in the underground battle against the Nazis. Prior to that, in May 1944, representatives of the AJ had signed in Barcelona an agreement with the Jewish Agency Executive representative that put all the members of this organization and all its resources at the service of the Jewish Agency Executive and the Haganah for "the common struggle whose central goal was the establishment of a Jewish state in Palestine."[94] A second operative, Ruth Klieger, then the only woman in the Mossad, arrived in France at the end of April 1945, a few days before V-Day.[95] Two additional operatives arrived after a two-month journey through Egypt and Italy and began their work: the organization of training programs for future French activists, the search for ships, and the establishment of con-tact with other European countries.[96] Thus, beginning in June 1945 there was a Mossad team at work in France that was larger than those in other countries in which the organization was active.

Just four days after V-Day, Ben-Gurion paid a quick visit to France. The trip was for the purpose of learning the territory and the tools with which he would be managing the last stage of the war "to open the gates of the Land of Israel to the immigration . . . [of] some one million Jews from Europe and the countries of the East," and to establish "the Land of Israel as a Jewish state." Ben-Gurion considered these goals interdependent and complementary.[97] During the five days he spent in Paris, Ben-Gurion tried to acquaint himself with as many people and organizations as time would allow. He met dozens of men and women representing various Jewish organizations, youth movements, underground groups, aid institutions, Jewish financiers, and French government officials—and, as was his habit, he wrote down every detail he thought might be of assistance in his future work. These entries in his diary (13, 14, and 15 May) are packed with data on the situation of Jewish communities in France, Belgium, and Holland; the numbers of Jews belonging to Jewish, and especially Zionist, political parties; the Jews registered for immigration in the Palestine offices; infighting between different parties and their characteristic factionalism; the toll that assimilation was taking, especially on the Jewish communities in France ("They change names that sound Jewish"); anti-Semitism; the movement of Jews returning from the German camps to their countries of origin; and the political arena and the anticipated changes therein. In meetings with Marc Jarblum and especially with André Blumel, the socialist attorney who was close to Léon Blum, Ben-Gurion tried to obtain information on the possibilities for working within and with the help of the political system. He wrote down detailed information on the situation of survivor children, most of them orphans, on how they were being cared for and the immediate need to ensure that they received a "Zionist" education, as he defined it.[98]

Ben-Gurion devoted a separate chapter to his meetings with the members of the various resistance organizations, with an emphasis on the leaders of the AJ. He carefully wrote down details of their underground activities and operations during the war, as well as their active manpower ("They still have 100 members [40 of them women]: drivers, gunners, radio operators").[99] He also made note of their efforts since liberation to locate children and bring them back to Judaism and to establish a comprehensive card file of all the deportees and victims. The great interest Ben-Gurion displayed in these underground fighters, their operational capacity, and their range of expertise both as members of the resistance and as civilians, makes it possible to state with near certainty that as early as the spring of 1945 Ben-Gurion had already made a decision to base Zionist activity in France, in western Europe, and in North Africa on this group of French Jews. This band of women and men, anti-Nazi underground fighters in France, which had lost many of its members during the war and which still maintained an almost military framework—including a command hierarchy, intelligence compartmentalization, and combat discipline—obviously made a great impression on Ben-Gurion as Zionism was taking stock after the Holocaust.[100] These were the "new" Jews, as he conceived them, who had taken their fate into their own hands and were now also prepared to pay a high price for the Jewish nation and Jewish sovereignty. Both Ben-Gurion and the Zionist operatives in France had high expectations of these resistance fighters, many of whom had been decorated by the French for their heroism during the war. So when, in the fall of 1945, Ben-Gurion decided to activate the "fighting *aliya*," which he said would stand "on its own power . . . at sea or on shore . . . equipped with machines, grenades, and pistols," it was clear that its local organizers and main figures would be the members of the Jewish Army.[101]

The first cooperative effort between the AJ and the Yishuv operatives went well. Thousands of Jewish children were located in France and were gathered and cared for in homes and at a farm purchased for this purpose. Many Jewish children were brought from the camps in Germany, and they too were housed in France before their transfer to Palestine. In fact, the Jewish Agency and Mossad agents could not have organized and functioned in France during these initial stages without the experienced manpower and resources that the AJ put at their disposal.[102] Former underground fighters became instructors, radio operators, messengers, drivers, and logisticians in the service of the Zionist cause in France. The major role played in Italy by soldiers from the Yishuv wearing British uniforms in preparing the ground for the Mossad to work there was played in France by the Jewish Army.

In the fall of 1945, however, it became clear that the mission the Yishuv wished to assign these Jews was heavier than they could bear, and apparently also heavier than they wanted to bear. Unlike the survivors of the death camps, who had nothing to lose and who had no other real choice since the gates of other countries were closed to them, French Jews continued to view their country as their homeland. Dialectically, although their having fought in the ranks of the resistance was the source of the Zionist admiration for them, their resistance experience led them to see themselves, and to be seen by their countrymen, as full members of French society. At the end of December 1945, after having labored for months to find ships, train people, and secure the financial means necessary to fund the sailings, the leaders of the AJ reached a painful conclusion: they could not under their own power and with their own people carry out the ambitious immigration project they had formulated together with Ben-Gurion and the Yishuv opera-tives.[103] Furthermore, it turned out that the group of AJ men and women who had aspired to join the fighting Zionist struggle for a Jewish state in Palestine represented no one but itself; it was not the expression of a popular mass movement among French Jewry toward Zionism and Palestine. As during the war period, though under other circumstances, the AJ remained isolated in its beliefs and actions from the rest of the Jewish community, most of whom did not want to as-sert their uniqueness and Jewish identity and preferred to blend incon-spicuously into the society and life of their liberated country.

The great human potential for clandestine immigration and the most efficient instrument for carrying out the Zionist political design were one and the same, and were located in the DP camps. The Zionist op-eratives to western Europe understood this, as did Ben-Gurion during his first visit to the camps in Germany in October 1945. Ben-Gurion's de-cision at the end of that month to wage a coordinated Zionist struggle against British policy and to turn the European continent into the major theater of this struggle derived from his awareness of the ultimate moral power of those wretched Jews in the camps, who had lost everything but their lives. Contrary to the wishes of his colleagues in Jerusalem, who urged him to return promptly to Palestine and direct the battle from there, Ben-Gurion decided to lengthen his stay in Europe to pre-pare the ground for a large covert Zionist operation, direct it politically and organizationally, and head it during its formative stages.

Theater of Struggle

At the end of 1945 the Mossad's European command was established in Paris, and in January 1946 regular telephone and radio con-tacts were constituted between Paris and Bricha and Mossad agents in Czechoslovakia ("Franz"), Poland ("Ada"), Germany ("Hans"), Austria ("Walter"), and other places. A permanent office in Paris functioned day and night managed by a Hebrew secretary, radio stations were established in all the central countries where the Mossad operated, and internal links were set up for the transfer of funds ("Zehavi").[104] In parallel with this, Marseilles became the maritime operations center for the Mossad, headed by Shmaria Zameret (Rudi), who was to direct the launching of the

Exodus. In the spring of 1946 Mossad chief Shaul Meirov arrived in Paris and began to manage the organization's affairs from there. Yet almost a year had passed from the arrival of the first Mossad agents in France to the sailing of the first ship from a French port, and it seemed even longer because of the intense pressure being exerted both by the refugees in the DP camps and by the Yishuv, which needed the clandestine immigration extravaganzas for its own political purposes. The long and strained birth pangs of the immigration campaign from France were in part evidence of the endless political, logistical, and operational problems that the Mossad agents encountered wherever they located themselves.

The preparation of the first ship from France, like the first stages of the activity in Italy, could not have been accomplished without the help of the soldiers of the Jewish Brigade and the passive assistance of the British army, from whose stockpiles huge quantities of equipment were lifted. The first ship set to sail from Marseilles was fitted out from top to bottom, with everything from fuel to medicines and from blankets to food, all taken from British army reserves and storehouses. A hole secretly drilled in the pipeline that the British laid between England and Holland after the landing at Normandy produced all the fuel needed for the ship to sail. It was the men of the brigade who went out, in British army vehicles, on the first visits to the DP camps and who chose the first candidates for sailing. The Bricha agents arrived afterward and assumed the task of transporting the people via Holland to the training camps in Belgium. These visits by the brigade's soldiers and by the Bricha agents had an importance that went beyond the removal of the first people from the camps. The Bricha routes from Germany to Italy were not yet in use, and the residents of the camps in Germany had almost no chance of reaching the first ships to sail from Italy. The new trail leading to France thus provided additional hope for liberation from the camps. Moreover, from the Zionist point of view, it was important on the eve of the Anglo-American Committee's visit to the camps to demonstrate that Palestine was a real alternative for the DPs.[105]

The refugees were concentrated in Belgium, some in Antwerp, and some at a mansion near Namur purchased by the Jewish soldiers in the British army. The equipment and people were transported to Marseilles in trucks belonging to the 178th transportation company, which had spent the previous several months traveling the roads between Belgium and Marseilles on military missions. Two convoys of brigade trucks set out from Namur and from Tournai a week apart, carrying 550 Jews from the

German camps. The second convoy reached Marseilles on 15 March, two days before the ship was to sail. The trucks' original identification insignias were removed, and their drivers were supplied with forged documents for crossing the Belgian-French border. The passengers were disguised as prisoners being transferred over the border for various labor tasks, and appropriate instructions were given in advance to the border police.[106] The Turkish ship, renamed the *Tel Hai,* a name bearing special connotations in the Zionist mythology of rebirth in Palestine, sailed on 17 March from the port of La Ciotat for Palestine.[107] Both the preparation of the ship and its launching were carried out, as noted, under the supervision and with the assistance of an agent of the French General Intelligence Services (*Renseignements généraux*). There were 743 people on the ship, including 548 Holocaust survivors from the DP camps in Germany. On 27 March at 11 A.M. the ship was captured 120 miles from the Palestinian shore. On the following morning it entered the port, where British soldiers and armored personnel carriers awaited it on the dock. That same day the passengers were taken off the ship and transferred to a detention camp at Atlit.[108]

Three months passed between the first and the second sailings. The Mossad's operations headquarters in Paris grew more powerful and developed political contacts. An intelligence report by the right-wing Revisionist Zionists in Paris, dated March 1946, asserted that there was a large group of some forty "Labor Zionist" agents there, not including UNRRA agents and official Jewish Agency representatives. "From here they are active in all the other countries, here is the transfer center and the heartbeat of Jewish life."[109] The Mossad's central radio communications station was also stationed in Paris in April 1946.[110] In Marseilles, Zameret established a network of suppliers and helpers, Jews and non-Jews, who saw to all the needs of the ships, from equipping and preparing them for sailing to provisioning them with all they needed for the sea journey.[111] This network, along with the political leadership in Paris, made it possible for the Mossad to disconnect itself logistically from the brigade and henceforth run the operation itself. The passengers on the second ship to sail from France had already been brought in from the DP camps in Germany in rented civilian vehicles directly to the previously prepared gathering points in southern France.[112]

Paris was the Mossad's headquarters at the European front. The organization's communications went through it; the reports from the American station and all the European and North African stations were channeled through it, and decisions and instructions were sent out to all the stations from Paris. Beginning in January 1947, in the wake of the organizational and operational decisions made at meetings of the Mossad that took place behind the scenes at the Twenty-second Zionist Congress, the Mossad opened an operations log in Paris in which all the conversations at and reports coming into headquarters were recorded, as well as some of the instructions that were sent out from it.[113] The political safety net that the Mossad established in France through its Jewish mediators was tightened and withstood several tests. At one point, the Mossad's radio communications station in Paris was raided, apparently after the French intelligence services had been listening to it for a long time; four of the station's operators were arrested, and a large number of documents were captured. André Blumel was sent to speak to his French friends and colleagues and was able to smooth over the incident. An agreement was reached with the authorities that the Hebrew cables would be translated into French and handed over to French intelligence, and that the radio operators would then be released. "The government's attitude is friendly and warm," the Mossad's deputy chief reported from Paris.[114] Unofficial agreements were also reached with the authorities on the ways in which the Jewish refugees were to be transported from the DP camps to France and from the French ports onward, and by the end of 1946 a Mossad agent was able to report them in detail: "The local authorities grant a transit visa to shipments from camps in Bavaria, Czechoslovakia, and Austria, on the basis of final visas to Ethiopia or to one of the South American countries. The shipments enter Kasuto [France] legally. The ships sail officially to those countries recorded on the final visas. Before the sailing the refugees receive exit visas from the local government and depart legally."[115] Thus, from the beginning of 1947 to the sailing of the *Exodus* in July, three other ships departed from France.

The Return of the Refugees

Eighteen days after the *President Warfield* slipped away at dawn from the port of Sète, its 4,500 passengers crowded onto three British prison ships appeared again on France's horizon. During the weeks between the ship's sailing from France and its passengers' return in British custody, while the *President Warfield* was still making its way toward Haifa, its name was changed at sea by the Mossad agent on board to the *Exodus 1947*. Its passengers engaged in a bloody battle against the British navy and eight British warships. They were then led to the port at Haifa, taken off their ship, and forced, in view of UNSCOP members, onto three British "prison ships" meant to return them to the port from which they had departed.[116] During this period the issue of the ship and its passengers never left the political agenda of the Zionist leadership, the British, and to a slightly lesser extent the country from whose port they had sailed, France. As in the La Spezia affair fifteen months earlier, there was a three-way international confrontation of interests and forces, with the Italians replaced by the French. As in previous incidents, the Zionist struggle ostensibly fought over the fate of the Jewish refugees was, in fact, aimed higher, directed toward the great, decisive battle for the establishment of a Jewish state. The people who actually showed concern for the immediate fate of the 4,500 human beings thrown at their doorstep were the French, in whose territory the *Exodus* affair reached its climax. They displayed concern even though—or perhaps precisely because—they were the junior, accidental partner in the power triangle; in any case, they were not involved of their own volition. The Zionists had never intended to actually bring the 4,500 refugees onto the shores of Palestine, and such an effort had no chance of success since the *Exodus* was a show project from its inception. The ship's sailing was no secret, except for the moment it made its way, at dawn, out of the port at Sète, and as it set sail, it was under close surveillance by a light British patrol plane and the ships of the British navy. The messages sent from the ship to the Mossad center in Palestine, and from the Mossad to the ship, as well as the Jewish Agency political department's invitation to the members of UNSCOP to be present at Haifa when the refugees were loaded onto the British deportation ships, prove that those involved on the Zionist side were aware of the tremendous political effect of a ship carrying thousands of Holocaust survivors being denied access to the shores of their "national home" through the use of British force.

This does not mean, however, that every step in the *Exodus* affair was planned in advance by the Zionists. The opposite is true. They made intuitive and effective use, as the incident developed, of the "weapon" they had at their disposal—the survivors themselves—and quickly and cleverly exploited the opportunities the British so clumsily presented them during the course of the affair. After the battle on the ship close to the shores of Palestine and the deportation at Haifa had their political effect,[117] the

Zionist leaders and the organizers of the operation continued to derive the most benefit from Britain's mistakes. When it turned out that the British intended to return the refugees to France in the context of their new *refoulement* policy (sending the refugee ships back to their departure ports), the Zionists turned their efforts toward the refugees on the ships and the French authorities in order to prevent the refugees from being taken off the ship in France. Zionism's friends in the French establishment were instructed to exert their influence on the government; the French press, which was already favorable to the Zionist cause, was activated and prominently displayed the Zionist claim that the refugees would refuse to get off the ships and that France, if it tried to respond to British demands, would find itself conducting a war that was not its own—a British war against the Jewish refugees, a manifestly immoral war contradicting France's policy and spirit.[118] At a meeting of the Jewish Agency Executive on 28 July, Moshe Shertok, the director of the political department, declared that the *Exodus* was indeed a test case. He spoke explicitly about the challenge facing the refugees, "whether or not the people debark," but by implication also demanded that the French pass the test.[119] Even before the British deportation ships reached the shore of France, all the Zionist offices in the Western capitals had been mobilized to conduct a coordinated anti-British campaign. In the United States, the Jewish Agency staff was lobbying the American government and the French representatives in that country and organizing public demonstrations in New York. The Mossad's representative there met with former secretary of the treasury Hans Morgenthau, and Morgenthau appealed, in turn, to the secretary of state. The two men, the Mossad's agent reported, intended to go to the president on the matter. Similar efforts were made in London and Rome.[120]

The British, for their part, decided to pursue a dual strategy in the case. For the Zionists, they planned to make this incident into an example of British determination to put an end to illegal immigration. They also intended to teach a lesson to the country from which the ship sailed in the first place—France—and obligate it to bear the consequences, that is, to accept responsibility for the refugees. The British ambassador in France, Alfred Duff Cooper, warned the foreign secretary that returning the refugees to France was likely to arouse a "lurid anti-British propaganda" to which French public opinion might well be receptive in view of its memories of German persecution of Jews under the Nazi occupation. Forced removal of the refugees from the ship would not be ac-

cepted, Cooper added, because the "man in the street" had no interest
in problems in Palestine and saw in these "illicit immigrants survivors of
a persecuted race seeking refuge in their national home."[121] The foreign
secretary replied that the Jews were being returned to France in accordance with an oral agreement reached between him and Minister of
Foreign Affairs Bidault, and that he expected to hear from the French as
to which port they preferred to have the refugees brought to. Yet this
same cable to the ambassador in Paris also implied that the Foreign
Office was not ruling out the possibility that circumstances would require the refugees to be taken off the ship in Cyprus rather than in
France. In fact, from the time the deportation ships began sailing for
France, the British were on course to a predictable disaster. Their intention was to put full responsibility for the fate of the refugees on France.
British colonial secretary Arthur Creech-Jones declared in Parliament
that France was the destination for the passengers from the *Exodus*. In a
meeting at the Colonial Office in London, Jewish Agency officials were
also told that once the ships reached French territorial waters, Britain's
part in the affair would end.[122] France's reaction indicated, however, that
it would refuse to play the part assigned it in the British scenario. For the
British, it was also clear that the refugees would resist any attempt to land
them by force on the French shore, and that it would involve violence.
Still, with eyes wide open, the British strode into this moral debacle.

At first the French toyed with the idea of sending the refugees to
Colombia, the country whose visas the *Exodus* passengers held. A
French Ministry of Foreign Affairs official even raised this issue with
the British ambassador in Paris, saying that the British deportation
ships should continue on to Colombia immediately after refueling on
the French shore.[123] The Colombians, for their part, demanded that
the French investigate how the Colombian visas were issued and bring
to trial the Jewish organizations responsible for this mass forgery; they
refused to accept the DPs.[124]

France's refusal to force anything on the 4,500 Jewish refugees despite
the heavy pressure from Britain was largely the result of the relative and
momentary power of the socialist ministers. After the cabinet meeting of
23 July, the government's youngest minister (and, by custom, government
spokesman), François Mitterand, announced that even though France did
not consider itself responsible for the sailing of the refugees from its territory, it would not close its doors to any of them who wished to land at its
ports. Neither, however, would it force them to disembark.[125] Yet the

sharp and traditional disagreements between the socialist Ministry of the Interior and the Ministry of Foreign Affairs surfaced once more at this meeting. In response to Bidault's insistence, in accordance with Bevin's demand, that the cabinet authorize the port authorities to disembark the refugees in France, Minister of the Interior Edouard Depreux proclaimed that he would refuse to disembark the refugees by force even if the cabinet were to pass a decision instructing him to do so: "You'll have to send your officials in order to greet them [the refugees] at the port," Depreux said to Bidault. "Don't depend on me to give you even a single policeman to disembark them, if they won't do so of their own free will."[126] The minister of the interior also issued instructions in this spirit to his ministry's representatives in the port administration, the police, and the district. These contained explicit orders to prevent the ships from approaching the dock in order not to create even the possibility of the disembarkation of "the aliens who will refuse to descend onto our land." "I am absolutely certain that in the spirit of the human understanding that has always characterized our country you will faithfully interpret the government's intentions and decisions," the minister wrote to the prefect of the Bouches du Rhone district.[127]

The spirit of the aged Léon Blum indeed infused the decisions and actions of the French government in the matter of the *Exodus* deportees, just as the British and the French minister of foreign affairs claimed.[128] The retired statesman was kept informed of the details of the affair and involved himself both in behind-the-scenes political activity and as the author of articles published under his name in his newspaper, *Le Populaire*. The fate of the Jews in the war (he himself had been imprisoned by Vichy France and had been deported to Buchenwald) changed this assimilated urban Jew's perception of the Jews' right to their own country and of the urgency of the Jewish question. Blum put himself at the service of Zionism, and Zionist agents availed themselves of his help through socialist Jewish mediators. Before the *Exodus* affair exploded in French territorial waters, Blum had written an article in his newspaper on the inalienable right of Jewish Holocaust survivors to go to Palestine and build themselves a homeland there. "How can one accept," he wrote, "that the survivors of Lublin and the remnants of the Warsaw ghetto and the orphans of the victims of the gas chambers of Auschwitz not be allowed to alight on the soil of the country in which they wish to find a new homeland?"[129]

When the British prison ships reached the French shore carrying the 4,500 refugees who had been denied entry to Palestine, the Socialist

Party newspaper covered the affair day by day. There were front-page stories, photographs, editorials by Léon Blum and others, and a long series of reports, all motivated by one clear intention: to help the *Exodus* refugees exercise their right to reach Palestine. In response to the British demand that the refugees be disembarked on French soil, by force if necessary, on the grounds that they had sailed from France, Blum wrote, "The conscience of humanity cannot be moved by this hairsplitting concern for the [British] government's honor. It is moved only by considerations of justice and compassion, it sees only one thing, a miserable band of Jews, last remnants of the Hitlerian destruction, for whom victory brought no liberation from the concentration camps in Germany and who are being prohibited by force from the sole refuge they wish for—the land of Palestine that their brothers till. There is something heartbreaking, intolerable, unforgivable in this sight."[130]

The frenetic activity within the French government did not cease for a moment during the incident. The intragovernmental battle was waged over almost every issue, from the wording of the declaration that the French government was to send to the Jewish refugees on board the ships, through the composition of the interministerial delegation that was to serve as liaison between the ships offshore and the various authorities,[131] to the care of the refugees themselves and the question of their immediate future. On 1 August the head of the Aliens Division of the Ministry of the Interior, Marcel Pagès, demanded of the director-general of the national security service *(Sûreté nationale)* that he put an end to the affair because of the state of the refugees and that he demand of the British authorities that within forty-eight hours they remove the ships from French territorial waters. "Letting the situation drag on will raise a storm of public opinion," he stated.[132] Four days later, when it became clear that the majority of the *Exodus*'s passengers—with the exception of the ill and the elderly—did not intend to alight on French soil voluntarily, Minister of the Interior Depreux wrote an official letter to the minister of foreign affairs telling him to demand of the British that they quickly bring their endeavor (to disembark the refugees on the shore) to an end. "This," Depreux wrote, "is in order to prevent serious incidents for both the United Kingdom and for our country."[133] The next morning Bidault rejected the attempt to pressure Britain, arguing that "the entire affair is liable to cause great damage to French-British relations."[134] At the French cabinet meeting of 6 August, Bidault again put the *Exodus* on the agenda and demanded a revision of the decision of 23 July. He spoke of the international situation and of the bad impression the affair was making. The passengers should, Bidault argued, be informed that the choice they were facing was not just France or Palestine, but also "anywhere else on the globe." Depreux informed his colleagues in the cabinet that he refused to convey an ultimatum, but agreed to meet with the leaders of the Zionist organizations and to explain the situation to them.[135]

In the final analysis, it was France's stand that brought the *Exodus* affair to its resolution. The French refusal to accede to the British demands worked together with the refusal of the majority of the refugees to take advantage of the French offer of hospitality and their heroic stamina in enduring, for over a month, the atrocious conditions on the British prison ships in the heat of July and August. The refugees' heroism had already made an impression during their first meeting with the French delegation that boarded the ships during the first two days after their arrival at Port de Bouc. Accounts of their determination were immediately disseminated in the press, as well as in the reports of the relevant British and French Jewish organizations. The Mossad's operations log describes the first meeting with the refugees as follows:

The ships arrived at 8:30 in the morning and the representatives of the prefect and the foreign and interior [ministries], Farhi and the Priest [André Blumel and Abbé Glasberg] boarded the vessel. The two Hanans and Venia [three Mossad agents] also boarded as interpreters. They boarded the *Runneymede*, on which there are 1,700 people . . . they greeted them with *Hatikva* [the Zionist anthem]. The prefect's representative read them the declaration. A young woman came out in the name of all the passengers and announced that they thank France for its consideration but they do not agree to disembark—their destination is the Land of Israel only— there to live and there to die. We will not disembark alive, she said. Afterwards they went through all the storerooms and in each place the same thing happened. The sick people also refuse to disembark. The *ma'apilim* related that during the whole time they were not allowed on deck to breathe fresh air. The people's mood is grim but determined. Farhi [Blumel] left in shock. No one wanted to get off.[136]

The British, in their documents, also admitted after this first meeting that the immediate negative response by the refugee representatives to the French offer reflected the position of the great majority of the immigrants, and that it was clear that the passengers would not disembark from the ships without the use of force.[137] In all, only about 130 people, most of them ill, old, or women in the last months of pregnancy, disembarked during the period that the ships lay at anchor. The estimate of the Yishuv representatives on the shore was that only about 20 of the 4,500 people "defected," that is, chose the French option and disembarked of their own accord.[138] On the ships, the refugees tried to keep up the appearance of normal life; schools were opened for the children, newspapers were published, and there were parties and Sabbath ceremonies, as well as a few weddings.[139]

After twenty days passed, the political and media interest in the Jewish refugees imprisoned on the British deportation ships began to fade. In order "to reawaken the press's and the world's interest in our cause," a hunger strike was organized.[140] The idea of the strike was suggested both from above and from within, that is, on the ships and on the shore. The people on the ship "demand unequivocally that a hunger strike be declared, even if only for a single day," reported the Mossad agent on shore. The refugee leadership on one of the ships even decided to launch a general strike, but it was postponed "because today there are no newspapers and there won't be any publicity."[141] On the evening of that day it was reported that the strike would be declared for the next day and would last about one day, as a warning. It was determined that each of the ships would send a letter to the French prime minister stating that the strike was being declared in protest against the arrest of the boats' passengers in French waters. "We thank France," the letters were to say, "for its generosity and its willingness to receive us, but we repeat that the decision we made three weeks ago not to descend to the European shore has grown even stronger. We are living in inhuman conditions and the rains have made conditions unbearable. And this is after what we endured in the camps. We are convinced that the French government is not interested in having this suffering continue. But the suffering is continuing. We demand that the British remove us from here and return us to Palestine."[142] The strike, which in the end lasted less than a day and was not complete, achieved its purpose even as the British tried to minimize its importance, arguing that it was "bogus."[143] The major news agencies reported it to the world. "The world has conveniently forgotten them," read an article filed by the correspondent of the *New York Herald Tribune*.[144]

The role of the people on shore, headed by the Mossad agents, was secondary in the *Exodus* drama. Aided by various elements in the Jewish community—party representatives and youth movement members, Jewish Army veterans, community aid and welfare institutions—the Yishuv operatives produced the campaign for the *Exodus* refugees and organized from afar the unfolding events. Through the Joint Distribution

Committee and other international organizations they collected food, medicine, and clothing for the people on the ships; they exploited contacts with representatives of the French and world press and orchestrated the events in accordance with the press's presence; and French-Jewish mediators maintained contact with the labor unions, the police, political parties, and the political establishment in the French capital. André Blumel met with French president Vincent Auriol to discuss the fate of the refugees.[145] Yet as the futile stand off the French shore went on, both the people on the ships and those on the shore shared the sense of helplessness and despondency from being caught in a political and human predicament in which any foreseeable outcome appeared to be for the worse. They also shared the sense that, despite the international attention they received, they were standing alone, without any support behind them, on the front of a struggle that was supposed to be that of the entire Jewish people, and especially of the Zionist collective in Palestine. One of the Mossad agents in Port de Bouc wrote to his friends in Palestine that everyone "here" had only one wish: "that the Zionist movement and the Yishuv stand together with them, fight together with them. And we promised. Did we promise the truth? I'm a bit doubtful, because also in Port de Bouc we were only a few comrades who devoted themselves to the work without enough help from the Zionist institutions and leadership."[146] These feelings, experienced by the refugees, those accompanying them, and the agents on the shore, that the "world has conveniently forgotten them" and that the Zionist leadership and the Yishuv had abandoned them and left them to fight alone, were echoed in the leadership itself. "The *ma'apilim* of the *Exodus* will rescue the Zionist struggle before Zionist diplomacy will rescue the *ma'apilim*," stated one of the Haganah commanders in charge of the clandestine immigration operations at the time.[147] At the meeting of the Zionist Executive Committee held in August 1947 in Zurich, at the exact time the deportation ships were sailing from the French coast to Hamburg, Germany, a representative of the left-wing party that launched the clandestine immigration project before the war protested that the Yishuv "is not an active partner in this battle" and that the leadership was placing the entire burden of the struggle on "the weak shoulders of the *ma'apil*," "who is being expected to endure weeks and months in those prison ships."[148]

The speeches at this meeting were paeans to the heroism of the refugees—the *ma'apilim* in Zionist rhetoric—of the *Exodus* and to the clandestine immigration campaign as a whole. In practice, however, this campaign had already lost its primacy in the hierarchy of Zionist policy, and nothing concrete was done by the Zionist leadership to prevent the *Exodus* refugees from being sent from France to Germany. Léon Blum denounced the British in *Le Populaire* after the ships had been sent to Germany, proclaiming that "the passengers from the *Exodus* are not packages that porters pass from hand to hand and unload impassively on one or another wharf at some station; they are human beings, free people."[149] He could have leveled the same charges at the Zionist leadership. From London Chaim Weizmann, the elderly Zionist statesman, tried to join forces with Blum in preventing this outrageous deportation to Hamburg, but he was vehemently rebuffed by Ben-Gurion. In a way, the sending of the refugees to Germany was, for the Zionists, an additional and unexpected—if cruel—propaganda windfall. Not only did the leadership not try to prevent the prison ships from sailing to Germany, but it went so far as to obstruct every possibility of saving the refugees the trip. Additional, more detailed discussion of this incident may be found in Chapter 7.

The *Exodus* affair put French-British relations to a difficult test at a time when the two countries needed to be cooperating closely. It also forced the French government into a state of constant tension between the advocates of realpolitik, who urged France to accede to the demands of its British allies, and those in the government and the public who would base policy on moral and emotional considerations—and who sympathized with the Jewish refugees' plight. In the face of London's pressures, the French minister of foreign affairs defended himself to the British with the claim that the matter was not "a suitable subject for Ministerial crisis, which could only precipitate the end of the present Government by a few weeks." He added that, in any case, the socialist Ramadier government would not last until the fall of 1947, and when it fell, he would be appointed prime minister.[150] He was only partially right. The Ramadier government fell in the autumn; however, the premiership did not go to Bidault but to his colleague Robert Schumann. The socialists lost in the new government the senior position they had in the old one. From the Zionist point of view, however, they had already done their part. As if observing the *Exodus* affair from a distance, Duff Cooper, the British ambassador in France, remarked that he could not remember such a display of bad will and noncooperation from the French government.[151] As the *Exodus* affair waned, France relinquished its leading role in the Jewish clandestine immigration campaign and its serving as a launching center for Mossad ships. The affair had "con-sumed" France's territory and public sphere. From July 1947—when the *President Warfield* sailed—through the end of that year, only two other small ships departed from the French coast (from Bandol), each with fewer than two hundred refugees on board.[152] As the British consul in Marseilles reported at the beginning of October, the main stage for il-legal sailings had moved to the countries of the communist bloc.[153]

CHAPTER 3

Romania: Under the Red Flag

The report of the British consul in Marseilles was at the same time correct and imprecise.[1] It was true that in the last months of 1947 the major effort of this immigration campaign was concentrated in the countries of eastern Europe. However, the Mossad's bases in the area had been active since those countries' liberation from Nazi occupation at the end of World War II and had, by the date of the British consul's report, sent to Palestine eight ships carrying a total of fifteen thousand refugees.[2] More than any other theater of Mossad activity in Europe, the geopolitical space of the eastern part of the continent, and Romania in particular, exposed the weaknesses and limitations of this small Zionist organization, as well as its strengths and relative advantages. The latter lay in its flexibility and nimbleness, in the ability of its people to transcend rigid procedures and swiftly exploit temporary political and operational opportunities.

These strengths, however, were not sufficient to overcome the daunting complexity of circumstances over which the Mossad agents had no control. Neither the local authorities in this theater of Mossad activity nor the vigorous countermeasures of the British affected the Zionists' possibilities for action as strongly as the emerging politics of this region. Metaphorically, it was not the blue and white flag of the Zionist organization that flew over the Jewish refugee ships that sailed from Eastern European ports, but the Soviet red flag. No sailing from this region of the continent was accidental or the product of artful Zionist insinuation across borders, as had been the case in other

Mossad areas of operation. It was the Soviets who forbade or permitted sailings, in line with their own interests and according to their strategy for gradually taking control of the region via the local communist parties. It is against this background that the activities of the Mossad station in Romania and its neighbors, Yugoslavia and Bulgaria, should be examined.

Hugh Seton-Watson has divided into three stages the process by which the communist parties, under Soviet inspiration and navigation, gained dominance over the governments of Eastern Europe following World War II: the "genuine coalition" stage, the "bogus coalition" stage, and the "monolithic regime" stage.[3] The genuine coalition in Romania lasted only seven months. It was set up before the fall of the Fascist regime in August 1944 and was ended by a Soviet coup at the end of February 1945. The three short-lived governments of this stage included all four main political parties, including the communists, whose leaders plotted to overthrow the pro-Nazi Georgeu Antonescu. The bogus coalition, headed by the leader of the National Democratic Front (NDF), Petru Groza, openly rested on Soviet bayonets but still included representatives of noncommunist parties; these, however, were appointees of the Soviet occupation forces. The three Allied powers withdrew their objection to this regime and granted it recognition only a year later, in February 1946, after Groza (and the Soviets) agreed to hold general elections and to guarantee freedom of press, religion, and organization. None of these promises was kept. The elections of November 1946 were a Soviet-organized sham, and the results fit their design perfectly.[4] Any opposition activity encountered insurmountable obstacles.

In 1947 Soviet dominance, through Communist Party rule, stabilized and solidified, and the opposition was liquidated. The signing of the peace treaty between the Allies and Romania, in Paris on 10 February, established the nation's borders and also put an end to any moderating influence that the United States and Great Britain had on the communist government. The culmination of this process was the forced abdication, on 31 December 1947, of King Michael, the last symbol of the old regime, and the formal transformation of Romania into a People's Democracy.[5] The Soviet takeover was deliberate and ruthless. Of the armistice treaty negotiations in Moscow, the American ambassador, W. Averell Harriman, reported to the secretary of state that the "Russians entered upon these negotiations with the determination that the field should largely be theirs and that we [the Americans] should give them pretty much of a free hand in arranging the armistice terms and the subsequent treatment of the Romanians." He noted that the American attitude throughout the negotiations had tended to conform with the Soviets' determination.[6] The Soviet army command in Romania was given active control over the running of the country, including censorship of the media. The Balkan area was divided into spheres of influence between the West and the East; the Soviet Union got 90 percent predominance in Romania against 10 percent for Great Britain. In Bulgaria Russia received 75 percent control, and in Yugoslavia the partition was 50-50.[7] As noted in a Western briefing book prepared for the Potsdam Conference, eastern Europe became, in fact if not in name, a Soviet sphere of influence.[8]

The representatives of the Western Allies in Romania retained the same status they held in the Moscow discussions on the armistice conditions—that of "observers and advisers." Their only real theater of activity was the Allied Control Commission, which was set up during these talks.[9] Yet even here the British and Americans had little influence, as the British in particular learned when they tried to stop the Mossad ships. A section in the agreements stated that all three powers had the right to decide the fate of refugees who wished to return to their countries of origin or leave for elsewhere. This was the only section on whose wording Britain had insisted during the armistice talks.[10]

The first example of Britain's aborted efforts to use the commission to prevent Jewish refugees from sailing on a Mossad ship was the case of the *Smirni*, which sailed in the spring of 1946 after a long Soviet detention on the ship was lifted.[11] The British demanded of the commission, on instructions from the Foreign Office in London (which was informed about the imminent departure), that it exercise its right to oversee the exit of refugees from Romania and act to obstruct the ship's sailing. The Soviets confirmed that the refugees, whoever they were, would be permitted to sail only upon the joint certification by the commission's members of the validity of the exit permits.[12] When the ship sailed anyway, with 1,666 Jews on board,[13] the Soviets' formal answer to Britain's protest was that there was no reason to stop it since the passengers held valid Mexican visas. Indeed, the British high commissioner in Palestine, Sir Alan Cunningham, had already estimated in December 1945 that the Soviets would make it easy for Jews to exit the Balkans, not out of sympathy or support for Zionism but rather to "undermine British influence and embarrass His Majesty's Government."[14] At the end of May 1946, after the *Smirni* had been captured with its passengers by the British, he said almost philosophically, "Possibly this was an example of a tactical mistake . . . which is attributable to Soviet ignorance of the Arab world. . . . Alternatively, the opportunity of causing embarrassment to Great Britain may have proved too tempting to resist."[15] In a cable to the Foreign Office in London the day after the sailing of the *Smirni*, the British chargé d'affaires in Bucharest wrote that the Soviets were "not only conniving at, but assisting this traffic,"[16] and the director of Britain's consular division in Romania wrote in his memorandum, some two months later, that the Soviet policy of assisting Jewish emigration did not derive from political, economic, or humanitarian considerations; its aim was to increase Britain's difficulties in Palestine.[17] In response to the British protest and the demand that the Allied commission prevent the sailing of additional ships carrying Jewish emigrants, the head of the Soviet mission, General Susaikov, denied all responsibility and claimed that it was not within his purview to permit or forbid the sailing of ships from Romania. His role, he insisted, was to certify the departure of people whom the Romanian government wished to allow to leave. As for the sailing of the *Smirni*, Susaikov said that he could not keep track of what the ship's real destination was, nor did he intend to do so. Regarding the general issue of Jewish emigration, the Soviet general directed the British to the Romanian foreign ministry.[18]

The attitudes of the Soviets and the local communists toward the country's large Jewish community, and toward Jewish emigration, were geared largely at obtaining Western recognition of and support for their government, which had been established under the aegis of Soviet military power. The Jews were meant to serve as messengers and intermediaries for the regime in its effort to win legitimacy from the West. When representatives of the Romanian Jewish community first met with Groza, the new communist premier, on 30 May 1945, the hints were not subtle. Groza remarked on the leadership of Dr. Wilhelm Filderman, the historical leader of the Federation of Jewish Communities in Romania, and on the respect and goodwill he enjoyed not only in Romania but also elsewhere, especially in the United States. "Filderman could render great services to the Romanian population through increasing assistance that would be given to the National Democratic Front within and outside Romania," the premier said.[19]

Contradictory ideologies, personal conflicts, and deliberate machinations by the communist government, through the agency of Jewish communists, aimed at intensifying the dissension and division within Romanian Jewry, tore apart Europe's largest remaining Jewish community. Dr. Filderman, the traditional, apolitical leader who had headed the Federation of Jewish Communities in Romania since its founding after World War I, did his best to protect the Jews by intervening with the authorities. However, he had been opposed since the 1930s by Abraham L. Zissu, the leader of the nationalistic Jewish Party and a revisionist Zionist journalist and author, who conducted an aggressive campaign, largely through his newspaper, against Filderman's "assimilationist" tendencies. Only his party, he claimed, represented the ethnic political interests of the Jewish population in Romania;[20] all other Jewish bodies were capitulationist and collaborationist and detrimental to Jewish interests. Filderman's aid and rescue operations during the war and his refusal to cooperate with the "Center of the Jews" (*Centrala Evreilor*), which many considered a symbol of Jewish collaboration with the Nazi regime in Romania,[21] did not change Zissu's opinion of Filderman and his work.[22]

The Jewish communists also played a role in the disintegration of the Jewish community structure, which the party perceived to be, like the organizations of other ethnic minority communities, a power focus to be taken over as part of the overall communization process. From its establishment in 1921 until Soviet occupation in 1944, the Romanian Communist Party played only a marginal role. The small and motivated group of veteran Jewish Communist Party members, which grew steadily as the communists became the real rulers of the country, promised Romanian Jews a socialist utopian future, an equal and just society in which Jews would enjoy all the rights and benefits of full Romanian citizenship.[23] At the beginning of 1945, however, the communists launched a deliberate campaign against the Jewish organizations and leaders who were labeled either anticommunist or noncommunist and Zionist. This attack was conducted both by seemingly legal means and with the use of violence. On 25 March a group of Jewish communists entered one of the offices of the Zionist Organization and demanded its evacuation. When those in the office asked for an explanation, the intruders drew pistols and said that the place was a "den of fascism." In parallel, a government order halted the publication of Zissu's newspaper on the grounds that it expressed "pro-fascist positions." "The skies darken," wrote the Mossad agent in Romania, Moshe Averbuch, to headquarters.[24] Dr. Filderman, the erstwhile ally, was a target of these attacks, accused of past cooperation with "reactionary elements" in the government and of holding conservative opinions.[25] From the spring of 1945 an unofficial forum of Jewish members of the Romanian Communist Party, made up of secondary party activists, defined the party's Jewish policy. As this forum conducted its attacks against those elements deemed likely to frustrate the communist takeover of the Jewish organizations, it also decided "to continue in principle the collaboration with democratic elements from the Jewish scene."[26] Part of this campaign was the establishment, on 7 June 1945, of the Jewish Democratic Committee under the auspices of the ruling National Democratic Front. The committee was an impossible conglomerate of the communists, the socialist Zionist groups, and leftist political parties, as well as Yiddishist organizations.[27] Its true, main purpose was to mobilize support for Groza's government within the Jewish community and to undermine Zionist influence.

As early as November 1945 the director of the British consular division in Romania reported that Zionism was losing ground in the Jewish community as the Jews were coming to realize that the Zionist goal was given precedence above all else, including the immediate interests of the Jews themselves.[28] He indicated that communist influence was increasing in the Jewish community. In the face of growing manifestations of anti-Semitism in Romania in the summer of 1946, British consul A. C. Kendall claimed that it was "only natural that the Jews should collaborate very closely with the Russians who liberated them from the degrading regime to which Romania had subjected them." "The Jews whom they have consistently repudiated and to whom they have never given equality and status, cannot justly be called traitors to a country that has always disowned them," the consul wrote. Yet his report about anti-Semitism also contained derogatory language about the Jews. He wrote, for example, about their lack of "any sense of responsibility" and their "greed [which] drives them remorselessly towards excesses."[29] More than a year later, in his November 1947 report on Jewish affairs in Romania, Kendall noted that the Jewish population enjoyed a privileged situation under the new communist regime: Jews held key positions in the secret police, political police, universities, and the press. The full integration of the Jews into the Communist Party was an established fact.[30]

The activity of the Zionist agents in Romania is to be read against this complex and contradiction-laden background. The first operatives of the Yishuv in Romania, paratroopers in British army uniforms, arrived in the spring and summer of 1944. They made contact with the community's leaders, the heads of the various Jewish organizations, and members of the youth movements even before the end of the war. Later, in October 1944, came Mossad agent Moshe Averbuch and two additional agents representing political parties: Yosef Klarman and David Zimend. This tiny delegation was part of the preliminary deployment of Yishuv agents to initiate a renewal of Zionist activity in the region.[31] All were astounded by the political culture they discovered among the Jews of Romania. Long-standing personal quarrels, political infighting, and crumbling leadership made it almost impossible to organize activity or to create a basic sense of solidarity.

The director of the Zionist Organization, the right-wing leader Abraham Zissu (called "Sweetie" in the Mossad documents), was one of the obstacles to any concerted action. Averbuch, like the paratroopers before him, considered Zissu a divisive figure who turned people away from Zionism. Like his predecessors, Averbuch tried to reach some sort of arrangement that would make cooperation possible, but this effort was not successful. As the head of a special committee on Jewish immigration to Palestine, established during the war by the Romanian government through the agency of the Red Cross, Abraham Zissu was given authority over Jewish emigration by sea. The committee was composed of people with ties to revisionist immigration activities "and other Jews of that kind and even worse," as Averbuch put it.[32] In fact, this committee was originated by the Greek ship contractor Yanaki Pendelis (the "fat man" in Mossad parlance), who was connected with Mossad activities before the war, to circumvent Zissu's obstacles. Pendelis was also involved in an old, unresolvable quarrel with Zissu about control over Jewish immigration. Ironically, Zissu was appointed head of the committee in January 1944, and the various conflicts Zissu was involved in, and which all the Zionist operatives tried in turn to resolve, paralyzed this body for all intents and purposes.[33]

If that were not enough, upon arriving in Bucharest Averbuch discovered that the government was allowing Jews to leave Romania, but only with a license from and under the supervision of the Romanian Red Cross. Zissu, for his part, tried to pry the management of emigration away from the Red Cross and requested several times that the Romanian government revoke the regulation, but without success. In Averbuch's first meetings with Zissu he tried to persuade him not to fight the Red Cross but cooperate with it, especially in light of the pending sailing of the first Mossad ship. Better that the Red Cross take care of the Russian sailing permit required of every ship than an institution known to be Zionist, "which could raise doubts among the local commanders about whether the matter is legitimate and [lead to] the transfer of the decision to Moscow," Averbuch argued. A meeting between Zissu and the president of the Romanian Red Cross, meant to ease the tensions and bring about cooperation, ended acrimoniously. The president accused Zissu of a "war crime." When Zissu was found to be blocking all efforts at cooperation, the members of the Yishuv delegation decided to dismiss him from the directorship of the Zionist Organization on the grounds that he was doing damage to the entire Zionist cause. Averbuch accused him personally of megalomania, of pushing the Zionist Organization into a corner and turning it into a hostile, belligerent force that was repelling both the right (Filderman) and the left (the socialists) despite their sympathy for Zionism and the Yishuv.[34]

Still, the arrival of Averbuch inaugurated a new era. One cannot exaggerate the qualities of this man. He was one of the most experienced Mossad operatives, a man whose temperate mien could not overshadow his proven bravery as a veteran of rescue and immigration missions in Austria, Romania, Greece, Turkey, and Iran, both before (in his face-to-face negotiations with Eichmann in Vienna) and during the war. Equipped with a press card and a cover name, he and his team managed to send two ships from Romania very shortly after their arrival, in November and December 1944, with 1,500 women and men aboard. Then a year and a half went by with no ships departing at all. The entire operation seemed about to collapse until, in May 1946, another Mossad ship, the *Smirni,* sailed from Romania with 1,600 refugees on board. This was the last ship to sail from a Romanian port. Because of the special political circumstances in the region, subsequent ships sailed from Yugoslavian and Bulgarian ports. Romania continued, however, to be a focus of Mossad activity in Eastern Europe; it was the country from which the illegal immigration enterprise was run and the major supplier of the tens of thousands of Jewish refugees sailing from this part of the continent. Eastern Europe was thus a unified field of action, and the Mossad's work in Romania, Yugoslavia, and Bulgaria had to be well integrated and coordinated.

Averbuch wanted to launch his first ship as soon as possible in order to prevent the political entanglements in the region and the many obstructing elements from taking their toll. By immediately sending out a ship full of war refugees, whose names he himself would determine,

Averbuch wished not only "to blaze a trail—the first ship after the Russian occupation," as he wrote,[35] but also to constitute for the Mossad and the Palestinian Zionists a secure senior position in this discordant community. To achieve this goal, Averbuch was prepared to send his first ship at almost any price. The cost of sending the *Salah a-Din* (excluding the associated expenditures involved in arranging such a sailing), which was launched at the beginning of November 1944, was especially high: more than 120 million lei (the Romanian currency), equivalent to about 75,000 Palestinian pounds, or about 150 Palestinian pounds per person. These expenses were paid by the Jewish Agency and the Mossad.[36]

Because the Russians refused to issue a formal license for the ship to sail, and to prevent "a possibility of failure in the first sending and a scandal in the event of a failure," Averbuch decided to board only members of the pioneering Zionist youth groups. In the end he added a few local Jews who belonged to no community organization, as well as a few refugees from Yugoslavia.[37] "As for its composition—it's a wonderful ship," Averbuch wrote to the Mossad station in Istanbul, its liaison branch.[38] A Russian permit was obtained through people with close ties to the authorities, in exchange for a large bribe. The *Salah a-Din*'s uneventful departure, smooth sailing, and orderly passage through Turkey, with the journey culminating in its safe entry to Palestine with the help of official immigration certificates that the passengers received in Istanbul, created high expectations among the Jews in Romania and increased Averbuch's and the Mossad's popularity. The momentum created by this auspicious state of affairs served Averbuch and his team, prompting them to immediately launch another ship. The *Taurus* was leased by Mossad agents in Istanbul in mid-November from a Turkish ship owner and reached Constanta on 25 November. Averbuch reported that since no delays were expected on the Russian side, he intended to fit it out within five or six days and launch it quickly with 750 passengers.[39]

For a moment prospects for action looked promising. Turkey seemed to be favorably disposed to allowing Jewish immigration via its ports. Ship dealers called Mossad agents there and offered them sailing vessels. The Turkish foreign ministry was apparently willing to assist the movement of Jews to Palestine and, in so doing, reap the financial benefits of the migration.[40] The Mossad agents decided to do all they could to diversify their fleet—using small boats and large ships, bought and leased vessels—and thereby adjust to the organization's financial capabilities and to whatever operational circumstances might develop at any given moment. At the end of January 1945, one of the agents in Istanbul reported to Ben-Gurion that the Mossad in Romania had three ships and that the Romanian authorities seemed to have no objections to the Mossad's operations. "Currently there are some 18,000 Hungarian and other refugees in Romania, and via Romania the wretched few survivors of Hungarian Jewry may be saved. We still don't know if we will have to fight for it or not," the agent reported.[41] These hopes, however, quickly collapsed in the first quarter of 1945. Turkey was eliminated as a transit route for Mossad ships after the British formally revoked the regulation allowing any Jew who managed to reach Turkey to enter Palestine. Under British pressure, the Turks reversed their previous stance, which saw Jewish migration via its ports as an appropriate source of income. They announced that they would confiscate any Turkish ship carrying Jewish refugees that tried to pass through Turkey, and the Turkish chargé d'affaires in Bucharest declared that any sailing vessel leaving Romania with Jewish refugees aboard would be returned to its port of origin.[42]

At the beginning of December 1944, however, before the descent of the local iron curtain that prevented Jewish migration for eighteen months, a final ship was launched with 950 refugees on board. This ship was laden with symbolism not only because it was the last sailing before the long-term blockage of the Romanian seaway, but also because it carried a microcosm of the Jewish Holocaust remnants in Europe. The passengers included more than 350 orphaned children, survivors of the Transnistria camps.[43] Along with these children were two leaders of the Jewish combat organization of Vilna, Ruzka Korczak and Avraham Lidowski. They had been sent by Abba Kovner's group to join up with the Zionist operatives in Romania and to open, with their help, a route for Jewish refugees from Poland and eastern Europe to the Mediterranean ports and Palestine. They had now been asked by the operatives not to return to Poland, but to go to Palestine in order to tell the Yishuv the story of their resistance against the Nazis and of the death of their communities.[44]

A Guiding Soviet Hand

The "Romanian story," however, is the story of the Smirni's delay and of how it finally sailed, after the frustrated efforts of Averbuch and his associates over the course of almost two years, and of the tortuous Soviet and Romanian policy toward the Jewish question in general and the movement of the Jews to Palestine in particular. This story illustrates the resourcefulness and stamina of the Mossad's man in Romania, but it also reveals his helplessness in the face of the tyranny of circumstances.

Bad luck dogged the *Smirni* from the start. Its first mention in Mossad documents appears in the summer and autumn of 1943. It was an old and decrepit tugboat flying a Greek flag, bought for a huge price from contractor Pendelis, largely for the purpose of taking children out of Transnistria. By the spring of 1944 the *Smirni* had still not sailed, even though between March and May five ships carrying 1,500 refugees had sailed from Constanta.[45] In July 1944 Pendelis received 100,000 Swiss francs to prepare the ship for sailing,[46] but two months later the Soviets, Romania's new rulers, laid their heavy hand on the *Smirni*.[47] In December the Russians promised to free the ship for the beginning of the new year (only for three months) and to hand it over to the Romanian Red Cross for the purpose of taking Jews out of the country. Preparations for sailing were made, but the Soviets reneged. At the end of February 1945 the ship was freed, but the "comrades" (the Mossad word for the Russians) demanded another ship in its place.[48]

The war in Europe was in its final stages, with country after country liberated from Nazi occupation. Thousands of refugees began to gather in Romania, which, lying on the shores of the Black Sea, was by tradition a country of transit and a point of departure for Jewish ships sailing from Eastern Europe. Among these refugees were the remnants of Hungarian and Polish Jewry, who of their own volition began a great migration southward to places where operatives from the Yishuv were active.[49] Averbuch, cut off from the community that had sent him, from his organization's headquarters, and from the world (a letter he sent to Istanbul at the beginning of March 1945 reached its destination more than three months later[50]) had to embrace, almost on his own, the great drama of liberation. He was forced to cope with the demands presented by the huge migration of refugees to Bucharest, with the lack of money that restricted his ability to operate and weakened his standing with the authorities and within the community, with a growing sense of failure about the launching of the ship, and with his isolation and loneliness. He had become the Zionist forward station in eastern Europe, and like the few other Yishuv operatives in that part of the world, he had nothing to offer the flood of refugees. "A stream of people is coming from Tzivia [Poland]," he wrote at the beginning of March in the letter whose appeal was heard only months later. "For example, today another 20 members of our youth movements reached us and every day dozens of deportees are arriving. All of them require arranging stations on the border. Everything is ready for that, men and so on, and we have no money. I am literally exploding. . . . After all, we will not send our comrades to engage in trade on the black market the way, unfortunately, the rest of the refugees do."[51] The ceaseless demands for help that reached these lonely, disconnected relay stations in Bucharest (and in Sofia), especially the requests for operatives made by the survivors of Jewish communities and members of the pioneering youth movements, were appalling in their urgency and in their tacit or sometimes explicit reproof directed at the Yishuv. There was also an echo of the feeling held by these communities that the Yishuv had failed to reach them during the days of genocide and had abandoned them when they most needed help. "Each of my letters is a single scream," a man wrote to the Mossad agent in Sofia in the name of his comrades in Budapest at the beginning of 1945. "Send representatives and more representatives. The fate of Zionism in Europe depends on you. It is not enough to send money as you did and are still always doing . . . you, too, should learn for once that there are no borders and obstacles—if you want to come you will be here in one way or another." This letter, three pages filled with harsh language ("thousands of surviving children are in terrible condition . . . the liberated Jews are hungry, torn, and tattered"), also reached Istanbul in June, more than three months after it was sent.[52]

The war had ended and the *Smirni* had not yet moved. It was trapped apparently in a bureaucratic snarl, but it was actually being held back as a political act by the Russians, who turned it into a floating hospital and later into a Sunday cruise ship for Red Army soldiers. The Mossad headquarters was in the midst of reorganization. Agents were infiltrated into Eastern Europe and the Balkans,[53] and for the first time, agents were openly sent to the western side of the continent. Three were sent to France, which was meant to serve as an operational and political center for western Europe and for the entire continent. An agent was dispatched to Switzerland to organize the Mossad's financial setup in Europe. Another one was preparing to go to the United States. Two operatives were supposed to leave for Yugoslavia, where refugees, largely from Romania, were also gathering.[54] Headquarters in Palestine urged Averbuch, via the Istanbul station, not to despair and not to stop working to free the *Smirni*. Its concern was partly related to the huge effort and resources already invested, but mostly to the importance it attached to the arrival of such a big ship in Palestine, packed with 1,600 survivor children, resistance veterans, ghetto fighters, and other refugees. Averbuch was given complete freedom of action and was promised that all financial obligations he entered into would be honored. The *Smirni* was a test case for the Mossad, an episode that would determine the nature of the organization's actions in the future, the type of ships it would operate, and the composition of the "human material" it would move.

In the middle of April 1945 Averbuch reported that the *Smirni* was a lost cause. The Russians were installing special equipment against magnetic mines, and they were certainly not doing so to help Jewish refugees reach Palestine. He also reported that an accelerating flow of people from Hungary and Poland was creating dire financial and logistical problems, with there being no way out of the country. "Many thousands are on the roads, some say not thousands but tens of thousands. It goes without saying that all this is headed towards one destination—Palestine. I feel miserable and insignificant facing this great and colossal advance."[55]

Ironically, it was just after the Allied victory, a victory that came too late for European and especially Hungarian Jewry (the last community to be liquidated by the Nazis), that the Mossad's work in this part of the continent reached its low point. Averbuch now came to realize that in Romania the chances of carrying out his plans by sea were nil. The release of the *Smirni* was put off by the Russians to "an indeterminate time," and the fate of a smaller sister ship was no different. In May, however, with the help of a miracle, as he put it, and with the help of "one of the big shots in the collaborators' camp [the "collaborators" were, in Mossad jargon, the Jewish communists]," the ship was handed over to Averbuch. Payoffs apparently also helped. Averbuch even managed to visit, with Pendelis, the ship in Constanta to conclude the arrangements for its sailing. However, while there they received news that all Greek ships had to undergo a new inspection by the Russian authorities because the release certificate given to the ship in December 1944 was not valid for 1945. The door that had opened for a moment slammed shut again.[56] In Bulgaria the situation was no better. The Mossad agent's radio broadcasts were halted by the authorities, and his visa was set to expire in mid-June. The tone of Istanbul's reports to the Yishuv was somber, referring to growing Soviet restrictions that prevented any possibility of operating from the area.[57]

If the Zionist agents, each alone in his own corner, living off sporadic and sometimes deliberately distorted local information, had no clear answer to the question of what the Soviets' true intentions were, the British apparently did. As observers on the Allied committees in the different countries, they could see the Soviet hand guiding the pseudo-activity surrounding Jewish emigration to Palestine, activity that led nowhere and in which the Mossad men served as mere pawns. A British Foreign Office memo to the cabinet from June 1945 states that Jewish emigration was dependent entirely on Russian whims; it was the Russians who permitted and who prohibited. In August a British delegate in Romania reported to Foreign Secretary Ernest Bevin that during recent months, in fact since the beginning of 1945, the Soviets had not granted any exit visas to Jews and there was, therefore, no Jewish emigration from Romania. If the Russians were to change their policy, the Romanian government would not prohibit the massive emigration of Jews, "firstly because the liability which these populations present, and secondly because the native prejudice against the Jews [sic]."[58]

Averbuch, too, came to the conclusion that Jewish emigration from Romania was dependent solely on Soviet interests. Any possibility of emigration depended, he realized, largely on the political and economic relations between the Soviet Union and Romania; until relations—especially economic relations—between the two stabilized, there was not much chance of initiating large-scale emigration from Romania.[59] With no way out by sea and with no ability to take in additional refugees because of the worsening condition of the Jews already there, the Mossad people were forced to direct the Bricha movement to new channels. From Poland the routes were switched to Hungary. From Romania Bricha agents began to send people, mostly those who had come from Poland, to the Jewish units based in northern Italy. Within two weeks several hundred refugees had been removed from Romania, and their number grew each day. At the beginning of August there were eight thousand Romanian, Hungarian, and Polish refugees in Italy, of whom five thousand were from Romania.[60]

The tiny mission in Romania began to fall apart. Its members abandoned it one by one. Even though he had asked to return to Palestine after an absence of a year and a half and despite his sense that the Yishuv and his own organization had not given him and his people proper backing, and had in fact abandoned them, Averbuch gritted his teeth and held ground for the time being to keep the lights of Palestine burning in Romania. To his colleagues in Istanbul and Palestine he signaled his intent to resign and return home no later than the end of

September, by which time he would have completed a full year in Romania. "I see my mission as over," he wrote.[61]

As he planned his return home, however, the "miracle" that he had so many times before thought was happening, actually happened. The Russians suddenly, at the end of September 1945, released the *Smirni* and its companion boat (referred to as "the sisters" in Mossad documents). The boats were simply handed over to their owners, without explanation. Just as their confiscation had been arbitrary, so was their return. Was this local act connected to a deliberate Soviet attempt to ease up on the Jewish situation in Romania? Was it timed to coincide with the first session of the Allied foreign ministers conference, held in London, to prepare the peace agreements with the former enemy countries of Romania, Bulgaria, Hungary, Italy, and Finland? What makes the latter hypothesis doubtful is the insignificance of this issue in the global context of the reorganization of spheres of influence on the European continent, although it would be wrong to downplay the importance that the Soviets attached to such symbolic details in the communization process they imposed on the eastern European countries. In any case, the refusal of the Soviets, and with them the Romanians, to respond to American and British demands to include noncommunist political parties in the Groza government as a condition of Western recognition led to the immediate dissolution of the conference. It is more likely, then, that the decision to free the two Mossad ships in Romania was a local Russian decision, although there is no hard documentation to either interpretation.

Ready and Waiting

From the date of the *Smirni*'s release in September 1945 to its sailing at the beginning of May 1946, more than eight months of unrelenting effort were spent outfitting the ship and preparing the financial, economic, and political conditions that would allow it to sail. During these months a new Zionist mission was established in Romania. Four of the paratroopers who had parachuted into this country during 1944, and who were forced by the British at the end of the war to leave, now returned as members of the Mossad. Romania's isolation had come to an end. For the first time telephone contact was established between Averbuch and his senior colleagues in the Mossad.

As 1945 turned to 1946, Yugoslavia was put on the agenda as a launching country and not just as a transit point en route to Greece or Italy. In November 1945 the first Zionist agent reached Yugoslavia and "swiftly entered into any possible hole." A senior Mossad official who joined the first agent in Yugoslavia two months later reported that "the authorities are sympathetic, Yugoslavian Jews are dedicated and in key positions" and that there was an experienced and excellent "team of workers" (refugees ready to sail, in Mossad language). At a meeting with the authorities, he submitted an official request to bring over ships and board them with Jewish refugees so that they could sail from the Yugoslavian coast. The Yugoslavian response was quick and positive. A written response would be issued within two weeks, they promised.[62] Once again, the Mossad found its crucial local link. This time it was Moshe Piade, one of the founders and leaders of the Yugoslavian Communist Party, a Jewish revolutionary intellectual who displayed sympathy for the Zionist effort and who laid, at his first meeting with the Mossad representatives, the political foundation for Mossad operations in this country.[63] It once more became evident, as it had in France and Italy, how vital the local Jews planted deep in the new regimes were to the operations of Zionist agents in European countries after the war. With the help of Piade Yugoslavia became, without advance planning, a vital support station for the Mossad's main station in Romania. During the second half of 1946, in the space of only four months, three Mossad ships sailed from its shores carrying close to 7,300 passengers.[64] By an intensive and brief effort that exploited the political and logistical opening created by a specific historical moment in Yugoslavia, thousands of refugees from the Nazi destruction were extricated from Europe.

In the meantime, the Soviet position continued to cast a shadow over the ill-fated *Smirni*. In October 1945 Averbuch reported from Bucharest that the Russians were showing understanding and goodwill with regard to the sailing, but they did not want to do any damage to relations between Romania and Britain, which were already touchy. "On the part of the comrades [the Russians] there is a great deal of understanding of the matter, but in recent days they have begun to hesitate about giving a permit (for B [an illegal sailing]) because of their unwillingness to complicate the locals even more with the guardians [the British, in Mossad documents]," he wrote.[65] It was at this juncture, on 2 October, that the foreign ministers conference broke up because of the American and British refusal to recognize Petru Groza's communist government in

Romania. Only two months later did the Soviets agree to the dispatch of a three-man delegation, composed of representatives of each of the three powers, to Romania in order to incorporate opposition representatives in the Groza government, paving the way for Western recognition.[66] Later Averbuch reported that the Russians had promised him that as soon as the Romanian-British crisis was over, they would permit the sailing. Since the outfitting of the ship was going to take another month in any case, Averbuch believed that there was still an opportunity for the ship to sail from Romania. Nevertheless, he also looked for a way to transfer it to Yugoslavia so that it could sail from there.[67]

Ben-Gurion's visit in the DP camps in Germany, at the end of October 1945, and the new Labour government's announcement that it would continue the closed-door policy in Palestine (13 November 1945) returned the Zionist movement, after a period of waiting in suspense for political developments to unfold, to the path of offensive struggle. "Now more than ever we must get things moving no matter what" was the message of the Mossad headquarters to its office in Istanbul (to be passed on to Romania) one week after Bevin's declaration in Parliament.[68] Istanbul urged Averbuch on. One ship, he was told, was "more important now than all the declarations by our top people."[69]

Negotiations with the Soviets in Romania continued, but activity stepped up considerably after the Soviet agreement to add opposition representatives to the communist government and as the West prepared to grant recognition. In December 1945 the Zionists openly proposed that they operate in the same way that the Mossad agents in Italy had—with the full knowledge, but without the formal approval, of the authorities.[70] The very fact that such a proposal could be made to the authorities evinces no small measure of confidence and trust in the relations between the two parties. This ad hoc alliance of interests between the Soviets and the Zionists may have been born out of a Soviet attempt to circumvent its exclusion from the effort by the great powers to determine the future of the Middle East, under the auspices of the Anglo-American committee of inquiry.[71]

In January 1946, the activity surrounding the *Smirni* became operational. The Mossad headquarters transferred money and the first radio operator.[72] At the beginning of February, the *Smirni* was anchored in the Constanta port, "ready and waiting."[73] In the final week of March 1946 a group of Palmach agents, sent from Italy, arrived to accompany the ship. The cost of the sailing was 80 Palestinian pounds per person;

the sailing date was set for 13 April.[74] On 4 April, the British began to take notice of the *Smirni*. The British legation in Romania reported to the Foreign Office in London that the ship was scheduled to sail within a few days with 1,500 refugees on board.[75] According to the ship's papers, it was to sail to Port Said; its passengers received collective passports without visas. The group's leaders held letters from the Romanian Red Cross certifying that there were on deposit in the Red Cross offices letters from the Mexican consulate and the Costa Rican legation in Budapest containing entry permits for 1,500 people to Mexico and for 800 people to Costa Rica. According to the Mossad plan, on the night of 11 April two trains carrying 1,700 passengers were to set out from Bucharest to Constanta, but further complications ensued. At the last minute before the trains left from Bucharest, as Averbuch reported to headquarters, the British legation, which had received instructions to operate through the agency of the Allied Control Committee to prevent the sailing, succeeded in foiling the trains' departure.[76] The day after the trains' delay, it was discovered that the shipping contractor, Pendelis, without Averbuch's knowledge, had arranged with the Romanians an exit permit for the ship, but one that specified that the ship was sailing to Palestine. This detail did not correspond with the Red Cross's letters, which had been prepared in coordination with the Soviets. With the help of an officer in the Romanian navy, a Jew who covertly aided the Mossad, the documents and permits were harmonized. At the same opportunity, with Soviet assistance, a radio transmitter was installed on the ship and its generator replaced as conditions of sailing. The entire operation was carried out openly, almost blatantly, under Soviet protection; in any case, it was no longer possible to hide the two thousand Jewish refugees who had massed in Bucharest and who "had made too much of a ruckus in the country," as Averbuch put it.[77]

From the voluminous documentation, and from what may be read between the lines, it is clear that Averbuch knew that the sailing of his ship represented a firm interest of the Soviet Union, and that the delays along the way were temporary, only paper exercises, to provide the appearance of interpower cooperation in the control of Romania. According to Mossad reports, among those involved in arranging the sailing were the director-general of the Romanian Ministry of the Interior, a Jew named Joseph Schreier, and Prime Minister Petru Groza, who personally coordinated the sailing with General Susaikov, head of the Russian delegation. A new date, 4 May, was set for the launch. The two special trains left Bucharest two days prior to this and arrived the next day, the first in the morning and the second in the afternoon, at the port of Constanta. In the afternoon the Romanians examined the passengers' documents and belongings, and the refugees began to board the ship. By midnight about a thousand people had boarded, and then an order was received to halt. The intervention came this time from the Jewish Democratic Committee, whose members suddenly claimed that the ship was not fit to carry so many passengers and that the sailing was dangerous. They somehow succeeded in involving the Communist Party's strongwoman, Anna Pauker, in their effort to stop the sailing, but the opposing interests won out. Toward morning boarding was resumed; however, the ship was delayed for two additional days, during which it was visited by a government committee including a representative of the navy, the Communist Party, and the Red Cross, set up to inspect the conditions on the ship. Disturbances broke out on the docks among those whose boarding had been delayed. On 6 May the ship received approval to sail, and in the afternoon it set out, aided by a Soviet harbor pilot, but it was forced to return because of heavy fog.

The next morning the *Smirni* finally set sail with 1,666 passengers on board. Apart from the 220 orphans, the composition of the passengers was different from what Averbuch had planned. There were refugees from Poland who engaged in "speculation," according to reports from the Mossad agent on the ship. There were many old people and several hundred Jews from Hungary. Members of the pioneer youth movements who had been designated to sail on the ship were forced by Mossad agents to stay behind in Romania because of lack of space.[78] The trip was made almost without interference. In Cyprus the sailors' and passengers' documents, which could have revealed the Mossad's operational methods in the country of origin, were collected, and on the morning of 14 May the ship, accompanied by a British airplane and destroyer, entered Haifa port. The next day the passengers were already in the detention camp at Atlit.[79] The Mossad's most complex and largest refugee ship operation to date—and its longest and most convoluted—had come to an end.[80]

The *Smirni* on its own breached the limit of 1,500 certificates that the British had approved for each month. In Romania the Soviets rebuffed the British protest against the ship having been allowed to sail, arguing that the passengers had carried entry visas to Mexico. It was only a few weeks later that the British discovered the deception the Romanians had perpetrated, in cooperation with the Mossad and under the Soviets' supervision, in the issuing of collective travel permits to Mexico and Costa Rica by the Romanian Ministry of the Interior.[81] In its size, its human makeup, and in the impression it made, the *Smirni* did top the scales. On 20 May, six days after its arrival in the country and after its passengers' detention at Atlit, the British high commissioner in Palestine, Sir Alan Cunningham, wrote to the colonial secretary in London that it was urgently necessary to find an additional detention camp and that under the current state of affairs it was impossible to keep so many detainees in acceptable security conditions. The danger of serious riots caused by the illegal immigration, he warned, was imminent.[82] The way to the cabinet decision "refouling" the refugee ships to Cyprus, which would to be made two months later, was paved.

An Opening in Yugoslavia

While the Mossad in Romania fought to send another ship from a local port, more than 2,500 Jewish refugees were quickly transferred to the Yugoslavian port of Bakar. This border-crossing operation was also accomplished with the help of a top-ranking Soviet officer. On 24 July 1946 the *Balboa* (the *Haganah*) set sail. This was a new corvette that the Mossad's agent in the United States had purchased, and it carried close to 2,700 passengers—some from the shipment just sent from Romania and some refugees who had been brought by train from Zagreb. Toward the end of June Colonel Borisov, director of administration in the Soviet delegation in Bucharest, supplied exit visas to the passengers on the *Smirni*'s smaller "sister" ship, in contradiction to his promise to the British consul. A. C. Kendall protested against what he saw as "Soviet collusion with the enemy country in illegal measures directed against her ally Great Britain" and demanded that the Russians delay the sailing until they received certification from the destination country, Costa Rica, that it had indeed issued entry visas for Romanian Jews.[83] Like the French before, the Soviets rejected this demand on the grounds that the destination visas were none of their business.

The British, after their failure with the *Smirni,* used all the political and diplomatic tools at their disposal. What they perceived to be an inexhaustible potential for Jewish immigration to Palestine via Romania was their worst nightmare. The sailing of the smaller ship, carrying only four hundred passengers, was taken by the British as a sign that their fight against this movement was futile and that "the flow of illegal immigrants might increase alarmingly."[84] They acted simultaneously in Bucharest, Moscow, and Paris. In Bucharest the British submitted a protest to the secretary-general of the Ministry of Foreign Affairs. In Moscow the British ambassador protested to the Soviet Ministry of Foreign Affairs on the operational methods of the organizers of the illegal immigration and the Soviet assistance given to them, and he demanded that Soviet representatives in Romania be instructed not to assist in these acts of deception.[85] In Paris, the site of the foreign ministers conference, the British pressured the Romanian representatives.

At the beginning of August British consul Kendall toured Constanta, where the small boat was still anchored. In his report, Kendall stressed the close cooperation between the Romanian communists and the Zionists, and he singled out Emil Bodnaras, chief of Romania's secret political police and one of the most influential figures in the communist regime, as helping the Zionists. Bodnaras, the report noted, was especially close to the Soviets, traveled constantly between Bucharest and Moscow, and enjoyed the privilege of a direct line to Stalin. The report also mentioned the head of the state security department and the head of the department in the Ministry of the Interior charged with supervision of foreigners. The connection with the Zionists, the report said, was conducted through Bodnaras, who dictated Ministry of the Interior policy while opposing the Ministry of Foreign Affairs guidelines.[86] As in the case of France, the British tried—as did the Zionists—to exploit the differences in attitude within the government represented by the two central ministries. In his conversation with the Romanian foreign minister on 8 August, British chargé d'affaires Adrian Holman said that he did not accuse the Ministry of Foreign Affairs of intentionally deceiving Britain, but he was sure that certain officials in the Ministry of the Interior were collaborating with the Jews, perhaps with Soviet consent. He warned the foreign minister that if the ship set sail, he should not be surprised if he received a "frigid reception" in Paris.[87]

The threat that Romania would suffer at the peace conference because of its policy toward Jewish illegal immigration was apparently what changed things. In October the Soviets were compelled to admit that the visas held by the ship's passengers were forged, and for this reason the sailing was prevented.[88] The truth was that the benefits derived from letting the ship go could not compare with the political damage likely to befall Romania and its guardian, the Soviet Union, at the peace talks in Paris and at the foreign ministers conference in New York. The Russian "temptation," as the British high commissioner in Palestine put it in 1945, to cause embarrassment to Great Britain could not justify the deterioration of Soviet relations with Britain at such a sensitive moment on the way to the signing of the peace treaty. In mid-October, before the Soviets acknowledged the invalidity of the visas held by the ship's passengers, the Mossad station had already begun making preparations for sending the ship to Yugoslavia in anticipation of negative developments in Romania. "The opening in Yoram [Yugoslavia] remains the only one."[89]

Yet the opening in Yoram did not last long—less than half a year. During this period, however, the Mossad sent out four ships from Yugoslavia's Adriatic ports, carrying close to 7,300 people, thus managing to confound the coordinated British campaign in eastern Europe. In all four cases high-ranking Romanian, Soviet, and Yugoslavian officials assisted in border crossings from Romania, preparation of the vessels, their boarding, and their launching.[90] Throughout this period the British exerted ever-growing pressure on the Yugoslavian government to prevent the sailings, and they succeeded in extracting a Yugoslavian acknowledgment that this movement of Jewish migrants was not in Yugoslavian interests and that everything would be done to prevent it.[91] British diplomats, however, were skeptical about these promises. One of them reported, after meeting with the deputy foreign minister who had promised Yugoslavian cooperation, "I do not however think this will amount to more than an attempt to stop entry of Jews into Yugoslavia."[92] The British were also aware that "the atmosphere in Yugoslavia is not very favorable to any representations which H.M. Ambassador might make."[93] However, on the eve of the November sailing of two of the ships, a Mossad agent was summoned to the Yugoslavian Ministry of Foreign Affairs and was informed of a delay in the sailing as a result of British pressures. An interministry commission, made up of representatives of the foreign and interior ministries, accompanied by the Mossad agent, visited the temporary camps near Zagreb where the refugees designated to sail were gathered, and ruled that it would be a mortal danger to leave the refugees in these camps during the winter; permission to sail was therefore granted.

Marshal Tito was also involved in the British attempts to block the Yugoslavian coast, especially when, despite the explicit promises of the Yugoslavian deputy minister of foreign affairs, the Greek ship *Athena* sailed during the final days of November, carrying 785 refugees from Romania. On 14 December, Tito confirmed to the British ambassador that he did not approve this emigration of Jews from and through his country, and that it was not in Yugoslavia's interest. After that meeting the British presented Tito with a report on all the measures they had taken since the summer of 1946 with the Yugoslavian authorities in the matter of Jewish emigration. The report contained evidence of Yugoslavian cooperation with this movement of Jewish refugees. In response to this report, the Yugoslavian deputy minister of foreign affairs, General Vlatko Velebit, said that he would be surprised if "another ship was to sail . . . because . . . the Marshal had given instructions that transit traffic was to cease."[94] In fact, no more ships sailed. Tito's instructions were scrupulously followed, and Mossad agents were not allowed to use dry docks in Yugoslavian ports as they had done in the past.[95]

With the Yugoslavian window closed, Mossad agents in the region were free to dedicate themselves fully to what they called the "Grand Plan": getting tens of thousands of Jews out of Romania in a single coup. A key figure in this project, and a central and particularly interesting character in the Romanian administration, who has not been given the attention he deserves in Romanian and Zionist historiography, is Emil Bodnaras. In Robert King's book on the history of the Romanian Communist Party, considered to be a very reliable text on the subject, Emil Bodnaras is mentioned only in connection with the Communist coup of 23 August 1944 and for his part as a leader of the "patriotic struggle" units. Then he disappears.[96] This lack of coverage is intriguing, since Bodnaras continued to be a central and authoritative figure in communist Romania. During these years he held senior positions in the country, such as general secretary of the Council of Ministers and chief of Romania's secret political police; later he was minister of war in the Romanian government.[97] Moreover, General Bodnaras, who had been an active communist in the 1920s, had a long history of political imprisonment in noncommunist Romania, from which he was freed by the Soviets. During his seventeen years in Moscow he became very close to Stalin. It has been said that Stalin himself chose him to direct, from behind the scenes, the communist coup of 23 August 1944.[98] The British consul in Bucharest, whose reports to his London superiors indicate an intimate acquaintance with the

Romanian political arena, reported that Bodnaras served as Moscow's man in Romania, that he made frequent trips between the Romanian and Soviet capitals, that he had a direct line to Stalin, and that in practice he imposed his policies on the different Romanian ministries, especially the Ministry of Foreign Affairs, which tried to remain more independent. The Mossad agent who maintained direct contacts with Bodnaras reported the same.[99] According to both the British consul and contemporary Mossad documents, Bodnaras personally followed the Jewish emigration from Romania and supervised its operations through his personal secretary. The same sources show that the Mossad's operations in Romania could not have been carried out, and were not carried out in practice, without Bodnaras's approval and assistance—that is, without the personal approval and inspiration of "Joseph" from Moscow (the code name the Mossad agents used to refer to Stalin).

Grand Plan

The beginnings of the *Pan* operation, the biggest and most ambitious in the Mossad's history, lay in the unofficial decision of the Twenty-second Zionist Congress, at the end of 1946, to place clandestine immigration at the forefront of the Zionist campaign for the establishment of a state, and to bring "100,000" Jews to Palestine.[100] The number 50,000 originally appeared in the transcript of a telephone conversation of 1 February 1947 between the Mossad's secretary, who was in Czechoslovakia at the time, and the Mossad center in Paris. The secretary reported that "Yosef the journalist [Mossad agent Klarman] visited 'Big B' [Bodnaras] and discussed work matters with him. B told him that he is prepared for 50,000 immediately after the signing of a peace treaty. The matter is very encouraging and serious. B is a practical man, B requests that preparations be begun."[101] The next day the Romanian station in Bucharest sent the Paris center a message containing an additional report on the meeting with Bodnaras. "The latter [Bodnaras]," the report states, "accepted the idea of taking 50,000 Jews out via Romania's ports, even without final exit sowings [country of destination visas]."[102]

Dire hunger and deprivation among the Jewish population in Romania made the Romanian question a burning issue not only for the Mossad but also for the Romanian authorities. These Jews became an agitating and destabilizing element, and many of them began to move on their own toward the borders in an effort to flee the country.[103] "Hundreds of people are streaming towards the western border. Neither we nor the police have yet succeeded in overcoming and controlling this phenomenon," the Mossad's man in Bucharest reported to Palestinian headquarters.[104] Independent sources indicate that in the spring and summer months several hundred (up to one thousand) Jews were fleeing Romania each week.[105] "The situation in Agami [Romania] is appalling . . . all the efforts to stop this panic-stricken stream have been futile because of the desperate devastation in Agami," the Mossad's center in Paris concluded in the last days of June.[106] In other words, a huge community had uprooted itself well before conditions were ripe for getting them to Palestine. Furthermore, the authorities, headed by Bodnaras, were willing and making efforts to move many thousands of Jews out of Romania immediately, before the Zionist organizations had time to make preparations.

A report from Romania sent on 25 February 1947 stated that the removal of all the "50,000" could begin within three months.[107] Another report set out the working arrangements with the authorities: Klarman would maintain direct contact with Bodnaras while Rico (Lupescu, a former paratrooper and now a Mossad agent) would maintain contact with Bodnaras's personal secretary, Popescu, who had promised to be available to the Mossad's men day and night. Rico added, in Bodnaras's name, that it would not be necessary to wait for the dismantlement of the Allied Control Commission after the conclusion of the peace treaty, and that preparations could begin immediately.[108]

In the meantime, the Mossad's representative in the United States, Ze'ev Schind (Danny), received a report on Romania's "Grand Plan," which required organization on a scale the Mossad had never attempted: ships of another league and huge quantities of equipment, food, and personnel. On 24 March, at 4 P.M., Schind was informed about the discussions with Bodnaras that were under way in Romania. He was already in the process of preparing and equipping four ships he had purchased. Three of these could carry more than two thousand passengers each. The *President Warfield,* later to become the *Exodus,* could carry more than four thousand passengers. In that same telephone conversation, which was transcribed in the operations log in Paris, Schind hinted about "two large vessels" he was bargaining for, which would together cost $440,000. These vessels, he said, would be able to carry "tens of thousands."[109] On 2 April Schind purchased the first ship and a week later the second.[110] In May the outfitting and loading of these two huge ships, the *Pan Crescent* and the *Pan York,* were completed in the port of New York. To conceal the operation from the British, who were tracking the Mossad's activity in the United States, and also to recoup some of the purchase price and bring money to the Mossad's coffers, Schind refitted both ships as cargo vessels; he was thereby able to earn the tidy sum of $196,00 in exchange for carrying goods to Europe. The first ship sailed on 21 May, and the second one left at the beginning of June. Both flew the Panamanian flag.[111]

Mid-1947 was a hectic time for the Mossad. Its ships sailed from Western European ports at the rate of two and sometimes three (in May and July) a month. Yet not a single ship sailed from eastern Europe. Bulgaria had not yet become a possible country of origin for such sailings. In Romania, the ground was being prepared for the "Grand Plan," and the Mossad were waiting. Averbuch was far from the theater of action—in Palestine, where he had arrived for home leave at the beginning of February with counterfeit documents. The sailings from Yugoslavia ceased, as the British noted with satisfaction,[112] and all Mossad attempts to renew them encountered a brick wall.

The Mossad's preparations, with Bodnaras's approval, for the resumption of sailings from Balkan ports were discovered by the British in August. The first ship to capture the attention of British intelligence was the *Paducah,* which was purchased in the United States at the beginning of the year and which flew a Panamanian flag. The alert was sounded to the British delegations in Romania and Bulgaria on 18 August 1947.[113] The British immediately launched a coordinated campaign, both in the Allied Control Commission in the Romanian capital and with the Soviet deputy foreign minister in Moscow, aimed at preventing the resumption of sailings.[114] On the morning of 19 August the *Paducah* entered the Bosphorus and stopped to anchor at the port of Burgas in Bulgaria. A second ship, the *Northlands,* was already waiting at Constanta.[115] On 23 August Bodnaras promised that the ships could sail from Constanta itself, but his subordinates were less sure. The ongoing *Exodus* affair on the western side of the continent, with its international repercussions, as well as the multipronged British offensive in Bucharest and in Moscow, cooled Romanian enthusiasm.[116]

At the end of August the Romanians decided, in coordination with the Bulgarians and almost certainly, though there is no direct documentation asserting this, at the behest of the Soviets, that the two ships would sail from Burgas in Bulgaria. The passengers would be Romanian Jews. The Bulgarians still refused to allow the emigration of Bulgarian Jews, but after a meeting with a high-ranking official in the Bulgarian establishment ("the equivalent of Rashi [a Mossad code name for Bodnaras]") two Mossad agents reported that the Bulgarians' sole motivation was financial, and that in exchange for an appropriate sum of money they would be willing to provide the Mossad with a protected and safe port of departure. "They don't have," the two agents cabled Paris, "any other explanation of why they want to work with us. Interested in large projects, with tens of thousands of people." The agents' proposal was for twelve thousand passengers sailing on three ships. The Bulgarians demanded a sum of $20 per person to sail from their port; the Mossad offered $10, hoping to compromise on $15, but the Bulgarians would not budge. Moving thousands of Jews from Romania to Bulgaria would cost another $3 per person. The payment, the Mossad agents reported to Paris, would have to be made "in unofficial Wises [U.S. dollars, in Mossad code], apparently with Danny"—in other words, in black-market dollars and in the United States. The same was true of the additional payments. The Bulgarians demanded an answer within a day's time (by 30 August), payment up front of $50,000, and the initiation of preparations immediately. They also promised to arrange for the use of an isolated port reserved specially for the purpose of Jewish emigration. The two Mossad men reported further that the Bulgarians had said fairly openly that if the answer were negative, the two of them and the ship already anchored in Burgas would have to leave Bulgaria immediately.[117] The next day, on 30 August, the Mossad in Paris conveyed its consent. In an additional round of discussions with Bulgaria, it became evident that they were not willing to reduce by even one dollar their $20-per-person offer. On the Bulgarian side the negotiations were curt and blunt, in the form of "take it or leave it."[118] Once the agreement between the Mossad and the Bulgarians was concluded, however, in the first stage for the passage of only four thousand people, the Bulgarians kept it to the letter. They were as firm with the British as they had been with the Zionists. They did not explicitly reject the British demands to thwart any Zionist attempt to launch Jewish refugee ships from their ports, but in practice they ignored all British warnings and protests.[119]

The first agreement with the Bulgarians was thus for $80,000 in exchange for the use of a Bulgarian port. The entire sum had to be transferred to the Bulgarians five days before the sailing—half of it in the

United States and the other half in cash in Austria, Czechoslovakia, or Romania, at addresses the Bulgarians were to give to the Mossad.[120] All the preparations were made in two and one-half weeks, in Bulgaria and in Romania. More than four thousand people were taken over the border by train, and from the train station closest to the port of Burgas by truck. The British chargé d'affaires in Bulgaria tried to apprise the Bulgarian Ministry of Foreign Affairs of the large, organized movement of Jews between Romania and Bulgaria, and he specifically demanded that the *Northlands,* anchored in Burgas, not be allowed to sail with Jews on board. It was of no use. On 26 September both ships sailed, with the names *Redemption* (in Hebrew, *Ge'ula*), carrying 1,388 passengers; and *The Jewish State* (in Hebrew, *Medinat Ha'Yehudim*), with 2,664 passengers.[121] All the onshore arrangements, as well as the sailing itself, were accomplished, as before, with the assistance of the local authorities, namely, the Bulgarians and the Soviets. Four days after their departure, while the ships were sailing through the Mediterranean, the Mossad chief sent an order from Paris to headquarters in Palestine to organize favorable "press and Jewish public opinion" for the two-ship operation, in order to prepare the ground for the "Grand Plan." He asked that clear indications of the assistance that the Romanian and Bulgarian governments extended to the two ships, and of Soviet approval ("the blessings of Uncle Joseph"), be planted within the news items and articles.[122] British intelligence's claim that the Soviets were behind the entire enterprise, and that it was part of their plan to frustrate British policy in the Middle East, thus had evidence to support it.[123] From the Mossad's point of view, the dress rehearsal for the "Grand Plan" was successfully concluded. The theater had been prepared for the two big ships and an operation unlike anything the Mossad had yet attempted.

At the end of September the *Pan Crescent,* which the British had tried on 30 August to sink at Venice,[124] sailed through the Dardanelles, and by the beginning of October it was anchored at Constanta. Ten days later the second ship, the *Pan York,* sailed into the port. From that moment the preparation of the ships was carried out in Romania itself, and in full daylight. This work took place along five parallel courses: reworking the ships to convert them from cargo to passenger vessels; choosing and sorting the passengers and preparing them for the trip; organizing overland transport, including the collection of 15,000 people from all over Romania and their transportation to the Bulgarian border, and from there, by another day-long train ride, to the Burgas port; administrative organization and the outfitting and supervision of the two ships; and, finally, orchestration of the political activity concerning the sailings, conducted in Bucharest, Sofia, Paris, Tel Aviv, Jerusalem, and the United States. The most complex and demanding of these preparations was the collection of this large number of people from all over Romania—distraught and frightened people from villages, towns, and cities—and turning them into a responsible, disciplined community that could be boarded on trains at the proper stations according to a precise timetable and brought together, on the target date, to the port of sailing.

This would not have been a simple operation even in more hospitable and convenient circumstances and in territory more familiar and welcoming than Romania was at the end of 1947. The operation did not proceed without tension or mishaps. Heavy pressure was put on the head of the Mossad station to accept passengers according to political criteria, but Averbuch made it clear he would have none of that. On the lists sent to him from Paris and Tel Aviv were people, he said, "whose *aliya* we cannot justify"; without explanations about the lists, he had no intention of taking any of the candidates being imposed on him,[125] and he had the upper hand. Evidence of the heterogeneity of the human makeup and of how Averbuch's choices were made primarily on humanistic rather than utilitarian political grounds can be found in a report by a British officer, Captain Linkletter, on the disembarkation of the two ships' passengers at Famagusta in Cyprus. "Once more," he wrote, "it has been possible to see that the passengers were taken out of Romania as families—including parents, the elderly, and young children. . . . In these ships the percentage of children was greater than in any of the other ships of the past year . . . the *Pan York* alone carried 700 children under the age of five. . . . The passengers were dressed well, only very few of them appeared dressed in rags and destitute. Most were of short stature, fat, and serene. Almost all of them spoke Romanian, Yiddish, French, or German. Because of the hastiness with which the action was carried out, it was impossible to conduct a precise examination of the Russian-speakers, but it was clear that these did not recall in their external appearance typical Russian types."[126] Yet there were some small, last-minute failures in this almost perfectly organized project. Some people who had not been on the lists managed to get onto the trains and the ships. A snowstorm delayed the trains somewhat and set back the schedule. In the end, however, the planning and the organization of gathering the people and moving them through Romania and Bulgaria were exemplary and represent the

Mossad's greatest logistic coup. What could have been, for so many reasons, a resounding failure ended up a splendid success.

A Jewish Tale

The preparations for the ships' great journey took about two months and involved hundreds of people in Romania. All the work was carried out under the direction of a special "operations department" run by Averbuch and composed of people from the Mossad, Haganah, and Palmach. The British kept close tabs on the work. "The intelligence service of the enemy is getting more sophisticated," the Mossad chief claimed at the beginning of November. "Its informers are penetrating ever deeper and the diplomatic pressure against us is operating in all areas: in all state, financial, and commercial negotiations."[127] Britain during these two months was conducting its rear-guard campaign against Jewish clandestine immigration, using all means at its disposal in the regional capitals, Turkey, the United States, and the Middle East.[128] Paradoxically, it found a temporary ally in the Zionists themselves, through a flanking movement made in Washington in an effort to activate the American administration against the Zionist leadership. As early as October, Secretary of State George Marshall was informed by the British about the presence at Constanta of the two *Pan* ships and of their operators' intention of launching them with thousands of Jews on board. The ships, he was told, were manned by American citizens and financed by American money. However, more seriously, "only those well-indoctrinated with Communist faith are allowed to go. Illegal immigration has thus now become part of the Russian plan to use Palestine as a springboard for their influence in the Middle East and the principal source of confusion and instability throughout the area," the secretary of state was notified, apparently in an effort to spark his interest.[129] For the first time since the British began attempts to exert their influence in Washington on the issue of illegal Jewish immigration, in June 1946, the State Department adopted a favorable tone. Marshall's response to Bevin was a display of goodwill.[130] Among the Zionists, too, before any decision on the ships had been made on the political level—it should be recalled that the Mossad's work was known to very few, even in Zionist circles, outside the organization itself—there were some who opposed provocative clandestine measures likely to interfere with the sensitive diplomatic dynamic that was then at its height, prior to the UN discussion of the partition plan. In a meeting with Dean Rusk of the State Department, a Jewish Agency official declared that his organization "would do everything within its power to prevent further incidents," but he added that the Jewish Agency "did not have complete control on the Jewish underground [sic]."[131] The Americans began applying direct pressure on the Zionists and the Jews to thwart the sailings. Marshall warned American Jewish leaders he summoned to his office that, unless immediate and effective measures were taken to stop the clandestine activity, he would "treat the matter publicly."[132]

One day after the UN decision on partition, the members of the Jewish Agency Executive met in Jerusalem to discuss the information they had just received that the two ships were set to sail in a few days, carrying 16,000 people. Four of those present, including Golda Meyerson (Meir) and Ben-Gurion, opposed the sailing, and two supported it. Ben-Gurion proposed that the decision be postponed and that the authority to make it be delegated to Moshe Shertok, head of the political department, since he was "on the front." In other words, Ben-Gurion wanted to toss the hot potato over to Shertok, who was then in Washington. This was a classic Ben-Gurion move—assigning responsibility for a decision on a secondary matter, about which he was ambivalent and on which he did not want be in the vanguard, to someone else, being relatively certain about what the answer would be.[133]

The ambiguous decision sent the Mossad's communications into a frenzy. Moshe Sneh, the Executive official in charge of clandestine immigration, who had informed the Executive about the imminent sailings, reported that same day to the Mossad chief in Paris on the discussion and on the decision to consult "your brother-in-law" (Shertok), noting that the sailing of the ships was to be delayed until a decision was made. "In the meantime it has been decided that the departure will not take place without the Executive giving indication of its agreement. You are to notify Agami [Averbuch] of this," he ordered the Mossad chief.[134] The Mossad's headquarters in Palestine also sent a message to the chief, stationed in Paris, demanding his immediate return to Palestine to participate in the discussions being held in the various Yishuv and party institutions. "The discussions have begun," the cable announced. In this telegram and the one following it, the Mossad station in Palestine informed the chief that both

Meyerson and Ben-Gurion favored the continuation of sailings from
the west and that Ben-Gurion was very anxious about what was likely
to happen in Romania.[135] As in previous instances, Ben-Gurion spoke
in several voices. He neither granted his permission nor explicitly
withheld it. The Mossad chief, in a Kutuzovian manner that was characteristic of him, was slow to react; he generally needed time to digest
information of this type and establish a position. Three days passed
between the time he received the news of the Zionist leadership's decision to delay the sailing and his passing on of this information to
Averbuch, the person in Romania whom it directly affected. The
phrasing of the Mossad chief's directive is interesting. As a sweetener,
Meirov first wrote of the great possibilities opening for the Mossad.
Only afterward did he touch on the matter itself, dealing the blow that
he knew would be painful to Averbuch and his people in Romania.
"In view of the negotiations taking place between the Jewish Agency
Executive and all the external elements involved," Meirov wrote, "it
has been decided to open the large immigration to Palestine at the
nearest possible moment." He continued: "We have received an instruction from the official institutions to delay the sailing of the two
ships from Agami [also the code name for Romania]. The delay order
applies only to the sailing of the two vessels from Agami."[136]

The cable was a shock to the Mossad's men in Romania, to dozens of
other activists from the Haganah and the Palmach, and to all the other
people connected with the "Grand Plan," who had invested all they had
during the preceding months to bring to fruition this ambitious project.
Averbuch's reply, quiet, bold, and trenchant, sent the same day he received the message from the Mossad chief, says all there is to say.

Received from S [Shaul Meirov] the Executive's decision on delaying the
departure of the two big ones. Request to pass on to the Executive and to
David [Ben-Gurion]: 14,000 people remain without any way to support
themselves, since they have liquidated their businesses and sold their belongings. They cannot remain here in the winter, because no preparations
have been made for heating materials or products. Note that the exit gate
here is entirely open. Could close as soon as this shipment. Have been
asked to remove from the list of immigrants all the technicians [!], engi-
neers, and those with industrial professions. . . . The Jewish collaborators
[the Jewish communists] will exploit the situation to destroy our standing
in the government, by painting us as responsible for the fate of 14,000 people. The delay is likely to destroy completely the Zionist movement in
Romania. The immigrants are sitting on their suitcases because departure

was already set for 14 December. You are requested to discuss the matter again and our demand to revoke it.[137]

This exchange of cables illustrates the great difference between two temperaments, two types of responsibility: that of the Mossad chief directing the headquarters work, accountable to both the political leadership that sent him and to the people of his own organization, and that of the senior field operative, sharing the fate of the thousands of human beings whose lives were in his hands. In addition, it exemplifies the classic Zionist dilemma, pitting "the work of the future" (*Zukunftsarbeit*) against "the work of the present" (*Gegenwartsarbeit*), the vision of a future realization of Zionism in the land of Israel against the immediate obligation to rehabilitate Jews in distress, wherever they are. On one side lay the destiny of the Jewish state as it was seen by the political leadership, and on the other lay the immediate fate of fifteen thousand displaced Romanian Jews as seen by a group of Mossad operatives. Were these goals really incompatible? Did the ships really endanger the state? Did the Mossad agents in Romania constitute a threat to their leadership?[138]

The backstage struggle between these two positions continued for three weeks. In the end (on 27 December 1947) the ships set sail. These were American ships carrying thousands of Romanian Jews, sailing from a Bulgarian port with the help of a Soviet pilot and under the supervision of Jewish agents from Palestine.[139] A Jewish tale. Did the ships sail because the strength of the Jewish refugee was greater than that of the great powers, to paraphrase the words of Berl Katzenelson at the Zionist Congress on the eve of the war? Did they sail because there was no power in the world that could stop these refugee ships, not even "the power of the Executive's decision," as the Mossad chief said?[140] Or were there other reasons, less poetic and much more political, that made the sailing of the ships inevitable? The final chapter of this book will return to the significance of the struggle between the Mossad and the Zionist leadership over the sailing of the ships from Romania, a struggle to which Zionist historiography has applied many false meanings. Five months after these ships sailed, the state was declared. It was not the refugee ships from Romania that put the creation of the Jewish state at risk.

PART II

Organization

CHAPTER 4

Visibility and Resistance

The seminal events discussed in the preceding chapters owe their potency to their visibility. The power of the people who orchestrated these events and made sure that the whole world witnessed them, however, lay in their invisibility. They were invisible to their avowed adversary, the British in their various guises: the Mandatory administration, the diplomatic delegations, intelligence, and the navy. Yet, more important, they were also invisible to a certain extent to those who sent them: the Zionist leadership. The operatives were thus relatively free to act as they saw fit, according to what they understood circumstances to require.

At least two of the three major staged events—La Spezia and *Exodus*—were carried out by the Mossad agents with the indispensable assistance of the Jewish refugees, in what were truly morality plays for their time. They had, or were understood to have, everything needed to turn a happenstance or an unremarkable marginal event into a historic one. There was something about these events which made members of that generation see in them the reflection of their times and of themselves. These events condensed yet amplified the social and political experiences of that generation. Forged in them were the materials of the collective memory. The emotional and historical import with which these events were charged turned these dramas into a metaphorical struggle between might and morality, between obtuse bureaucracy and basic justice and human rights. These dramas had sharp, clean, almost overly simplistic plot lines; there were good guys and bad guys, and no doubt who was who. They took place in well-defined locations rich with symbolism, usually at sea, in a kind of no-man's land between the accursed continent that had become a vast graveyard for the Jewish people and the yearned-for homeland, on jerry-built ships or boats that in many cases had not been built for human passengers. The time frame of these displays was focused, with the activity staged before a live, proximate audience. In addition, the events were assimilated in broader circles through mediators, already processed and interpreted by the period's instruments of dissemination.

The two events—La Spezia and *Exodus*—stand apart from the dozens of other clandestine immigration actions occurring between the end of World War II and the establishment of the Jewish state, which contained many of the same dramatic components. They constitute a different category because of their visibility and publicity and also because they became model showcases. (The *Pan* episode was different because, among other reasons, it took place in eastern Europe, far from the eyes of the West and its media, and was thus directed largely inward, toward the Yishuv's leadership and institutions.) The other events of the clandestine immigration campaign—in fact, each of these events and every one of the launches that the Mossad organized from Europe toward Palestine during those three years—involved clashes, either physical or symbolic, direct or indirect, and sometimes bloody, between British force and Jewish rights, between the arbitrariness of the government and the humanity of the victim. Yet not one of these events turned into what Léon Blum called, in another historical context, a "political school";[1] none became an indelible part of the generation's memory as these two events did, precisely because these other events were not exposed to the world as they were unfolding, and because their images did not become part of the world vista.

In a moment of insight, empathy, and self-abnegation, Yehuda Arazi, the mover of the La Spezia episode, assimilated himself into the reality of the refugees and became their leader. In this single act and in this one character the ultimate in visibility and invisibility were conflated. He became the Jewish refugee whose body incarnated the Jewish tragedy of World War II and the inevitable clash between that tragedy and the old British colonial order, and who carried on his shoulders the staggering burden of this morality play. Yet, at the same time, he was the essential invisible, a member of the Palestinian Jewish underground who from the spring of 1943 had been pursued by British intelligence, living under false identities with changing addresses and occupations, until he emerged as the refugee leader at the port of La Spezia. The Land of Israel and the Diaspora, so incompatible and yet with such plainly mutual interests, thus became one in Arazi's real and metaphoric assumption of the refugee identity. The one sheltered the other, and this mutual protection allowed each to play its role in the manipulated political spectacle. This cohesion between the Jewish refugee from the Exile and the Zionist activist from the Land of Israel made La Spezia unique: other clandestine immigration episodes preserved the distinction between the Jewish refugee and the organizer from Palestine, who used the refugee in his political battles. This was the source of the singular moral force of the La Spezia episode. In this sense, Arazi crafted, almost inadvertently, a lesson plan for the "political school" of Jewish clandestine immigration after the war. The tactics he used there were studied and incorporated in the Mossad's modes of action and were thus duplicated, though in different form, in the orchestrated and well-publicized episodes that came later.

Arazi was the first to use the press in a systematic way to convey his message to the world. The world, for his purposes, was not just the British and the Italians; it included the Zionist leadership and even the Mossad command itself. It was mainly through the medium of a young reporter from a local Genovese republican paper that Arazi dispatched his messages. In fact, from the moment Arazi decided to turn the fate of the La Spezia refugees into a moral and ideological-political lesson, there was not a single move he made or a single text he produced, whether for the refugees on the ship or for the relevant British and Italian authorities, that was not also directed at other, more distant recipients. The ship had been detained only a single day when Arazi issued, in his capacity as the refugee leader and through his spokesman, the Italian reporter, a public proclamation. Addressed to the Italian prime minister, the Pope, the president of the United States, and to "anyone with a humane spark in their hearts and all those whose souls have not been marred by the Nazi-Fascist disease," it declared that the 1,014 Jews, "part of the surviving remnant of the German slaughter," were willing to pay with their lives to reach their homeland and that "no power on earth" could stop them.[2] When he learned of the British intention to enjoin the Italians to force the refugees off the ship and send them back to the DP camps, he threatened publicly to sink the ship with the refugees on board. He thus demonstrated the paradigmatic Zionist formula of life in the Land of Israel, namely, Zionist redemption or death and devastation.[3] The Holocaust survivors were, according to him, "wonderful propaganda material for the entire humane world."[4] Exposing the tattooed numbers on the refugees' arms to the British soldiers and to reporters, the declaration and execution of the hunger strike, the refugees' suicide threats, and the huge banner in Hebrew lettering at the port entrance reading: "1,014 *Ma'apilim* Will Not Get off the Ship Except on the Soil of Their Homeland"—all these were elements in Arazi's political campaign. "All of Italy is on our side," he cabled to the Mossad headquarters in Palestine when he believed his propaganda war was going well. He did so in order to declare his intention—not to ask for permission—to "set sail with the vessel [the refugee ship] *at any price*" (emphasis added).[5]

Post-war Italy was open to the world and a focus of media interest, so a relatively minor episode like the confinement of a ship carrying a thousand Jews in a small port town could turn into a well-covered and photographed event. Thus, the international press coverage given to the La Spezia incident,[6] and especially the photographs that appeared in Palestine and Western newspapers as the episode progressed, enhanced its significance and charged it with the quality of an "event," made of it something worth photographing, in Susan Sontag's formulation. It should be made clear that the photographic testimony about La Spezia did not shape the event; it did not give it a name or define its character. "It is still ideology (in the broadest sense) that determines what constitutes an event," wrote Sontag. "There can be no evidence, photographic or otherwise, of an event until the event itself has been named and characterized."[7] The particular historical situation at La Spezia, however, imbued with ideology, whose characters were concrete and whose circumstances specific, created the precise context in which photographs could become the catalyst of moral impulse, "images that mobilize conscience."[8]

The lesson of La Spezia was learned by the organization, even though not all the Mossad's leaders readily accepted Arazi's methods; the tactics were his own and were never discussed in advance and vetted at the command level. After La Spezia, however, many sailings of refugee ships were accompanied by press coverage orchestrated by Mossad agents. The Jewish American journalist I. F. Stone, who learned about the Mossad's activities from his meetings with Ze'ev Schind in the United States, was put on the *Biria,* an old Turkish ship that, on the high seas, took aboard the 999 refugees who had embarked from the port of Sète on another ship, in order to prevent the second

ship from being captured by the British. Stone reported on the agonizing journey of the Jewish refugees, publishing his impressions of
that floating hell in the press and later in a book.[9] The *Arba Heruyot*
(*Four Freedoms*) (formerly the *Fede,* the same ship that was captured at
La Spezia), which sailed from Bocca di Magra in Italy not long after the
end of the La Spezia incident, was accompanied—at Arazi's initiative
and with his technical assistance—by American journalist Claire
Naikind, who mixed incognito with the refugees and covered their
journey. The ship, which reached the Palestine coast after the British
decision in August 1946 to send the captured refugees to detention
camps in Cyprus, was the first one whose passengers engaged in organized resistance to their capture at sea. The violent confrontation with
the British, although relatively restrained on both sides,[10] was widely
publicized by her press reports. The *Theodor Herzl,* which sailed from
a French port at the beginning of April 1947, was accompanied by a het-
erogeneous collection of reporters and photographers headed by
Moshe Perlman, who was recruited by the Mossad with his British
passport as cover. A few months later he would play a central role in
managing the English-language press in the *Exodus* episode.[11]

As a clandestine organization, the Mossad conducted a comprehensive investigation of the personal history, connections, and political sym-
pathies of every journalist who was taken onto one of the refugee ships.
All were cautioned in advance about what to expect and the risks they
were assuming, and all had to obey the instructions of the Mossad agents
and the ship's officers. Twenty-four-year-old François-Jean Armorin, a
former combatant in the French Resistance at Vercors and a rising star in
the French media after the liberation, was taken along with a colleague
from the French press onto the *Theodor Herzl.* In his newspaper, *Franc
tireur,* and later in his book *Des Juifs quittent l'Europe* (The Jews Leave
Europe),[12] he recounted his brief initiation ceremony and how he was recruited by a Mossad agent in Paris, at night, on a deserted side street near
the Champs-Elysées (where the Mossad European headquarters was located). "'Do you want to go?' asked the Mossad man. His face was hidden, and a car whose engine was running waited for him nearby. 'Fine.
We know you . . . when the time comes, we'll call you, but you should
know what awaits you.'" As a kind of secret password, Armorin held out
a telegram from one of the news agencies reporting a distress signal,
picked up by an amateur radio from a boat carrying 800 clandestine immigrants from Savona to Haifa, which had begun to sink near Sirina in

the Dodecanese archipelago. "We've already received a report," the Mossad agent said. "Unfortunately, we haven't yet managed to purchase the Queen Mary." Then he disappeared. A while later, Armorin received instructions to report at a given hour at a large printing establishment; in one of its halls a funeral service was being held for a leader of the French Communist Party. A man with a foreign appearance and accent approached him and said, "Tomorrow . . .," and gave him a rendezvous time at the Invalides station. From there he was taken by plane, with his colleague from *Le Parisien libéré,* to southern France.[13]

As with Rastani in La Spezia, the Mossad could not have wished for a more loyal and effective journalist-mediator than this young, non-Jewish Frenchman; in fact, his being a gentile only enhanced the importance and credibility of his testimony. He managed to infuse his articles, and later his book, with an impressive knowledge of Jewish history and a rare identification with the people he accompanied and with whom, for a time, he cast his lot. In a way, he considered the Jewish refugees' struggle to attain a homeland of their own a continuation of the war he waged to liberate his own country from Nazi occupation. Armorin wrote in his newspaper on the invisible movement of the Jews who were abandoning the continent that had incinerated millions of their kind ("this people is quick to burn"):

On this continent, which has barely returned to a state of peace, there are still those who crawl on their bellies, short of breath, along the old underground arteries that were patiently bored during the years in which Europe remained silent and licked its wounds. Their skin is still gray like the skin of one who has no identity card; they walk at night, they do not sleep in a hotel bed, they fear the police, soldiers, the bark of a dog. They have code words, an address in Lyons, a secret path in the Carpathian Mountains, a transit point in the ruins of Munich; so they progress slowly from city to city. They are unheard, no one sees them, but all along those mysterious trails, which are sometimes broken, all too-often ruined, which return to life after others have been lost or undone, these miserable creatures continue to trek in search of a country.[14]

He shared the crowded berths in the ship with the refugees; ate their thin soup, dates, and stale bread; and took notes of their stories. He heard from Georgette Zuckerman about how her hands had frozen at Auschwitz and about the tattooed number A.16 833 on her left arm. He heard the story of Norbert Klinger, who had been born in Vienna, grown up in Czechoslovakia, and moved to Hungary after the occupation. There he lost his family, fled into the forests, was captured and tortured, fled again, joined the partisans, was again captured and tortured, and then was sent to the Sachsenhausen death camp, "a horrible den of death, deportation, flight, capture, torture, betrayal, injury, heroism, flight, torture, death, liberation." Armorin was also there when the coastline appeared on the horizon and the cry "Eretz! Eretz!" ("Land! Land!"—it appears in transliterated Hebrew in the French original) went up, and soon everyone was joining in. "There were several seconds of collective fury suddenly igniting the crowd, holding on to it, making it laugh and cry. Only rarely is a man privileged to experience a moment like this more than once in his life . . . and we experienced it, it feels as if a long time has gone by since then, when the first tank entered our dead city, and the windows of the homes and the prison gates opened wide," Armorin wrote, recalling the moment of the liberation of his own town.[15] Later he was with the refugees during the battle on the ship before its capture by British vessels, a battle between unequal forces that lasted an hour and a half and cost the lives of three refugees (two immediately and a third who died later of his injuries). Among them were Aharon Malberg, twenty-three years old, number 23 340 from Mauthausen, and another refugee who was lost at sea.[16]

Horror Equals Headlines

The link that the French journalist made between World War II and the right of the remaining Jews to their own homeland, this meta-story of the two thousand–year martyrology on which Ben-Gurion based his post-Holocaust militant Zionism,[17] has never been more obvious. The bloody clash on the *Theodor Herzl*, however, was only a dress rehearsal for the *Exodus*, which was to become the quintessence of the Jewish clandestine immigration movement in terms of the use of refugees for political and propaganda purposes and the full exploitation of the press as a mediating agent in the propaganda war. The press was present at all of the *Exodus*'s major phases, and it worked on two tracks. First, it mediated between the events and the target audiences. Second, by its very presence as mediator and disseminator of the message behind the events and of the pictures and images "that mobilized conscience," the media changed the character of the events, influencing them and imbuing them with a power and meaning they would not have had otherwise. Thus it is hard to imagine that, without the consciousness of the presence of the press and its effect on the actors, the ship would, upon approaching the coast, broadcast to "the world" an appeal to listen to the voice of the illegal immigrants' (*ma'apilim*) ship of the Hebrew resistance movement.[18] It is only reasonable to suppose that the refugees' resistance and ardor in their hopeless war against the British navy would have been less fierce had they not anticipated the presence, at the Haifa docks, of representatives of the United Nations Special Committee on Palestine (UNSCOP) and of the world and local press.[19]

By the time the three British prison ships returning the 4,500 refugees to the continent approached the French coast during the next stage of the incident, the refugees were already classic media products. They became, even before the long wait along the coast began, a historical "event" with international repercussions,[20] one that condensed all the scenes from previous chapters in the *Exodus* story as well as scenes from similar previous episodes. To these were added elements of international struggle over power and prestige and images of an intolerable violation of justice and basic morality. Could the French, who had endured five years of Nazi occupation, be blamed for "the feelings of compassion that they feel in the face of the agonies of the gas chamber survivors?" asked the author of *Le Monde*'s editorial on 23 July 1947, following the French government's decision to open France's gates to the refugees but not to force them to disembark. "After all, we can easily understand what dilemma France will find itself in if it is forced to hunt down and reincarcerate people whose only crime is that they have been deprived of their documents, their legal status, and their homeland by [a country] that not long ago was the common enemy of France and Great Britain."[21]

Moshe Perlman, who was responsible for international press relations for the Mossad (and who was also a correspondent for British newspapers)[22] had little to do, at least during the first days after the prison ships docked on the French coast. The ships told their own story, attracting hundreds of French journalists and foreign correspondents who were in France to cover the foreign ministers conference then under way in Paris. The story of the *Exodus* refugees, the "gas chamber survivors," forcibly returned to Europe in despicable and humiliating conditions, needed hardly any mediation. The British protagonist in this morality play was defeated from the start. At a meeting with British reporters, the British press attaché admitted that the entire affair had been a huge mistake since the French had no intention of "playing the British game."[23] The horrors observed by the journalists who managed to get close to or board the ships evoked expressions of disgust and protest that included comparisons, both implied and explicit, of Nazi deeds during the war with British deeds after it. "Auschwitz on the Water" was the headline of a French communist newspaper on 30 July 1947.[24] Another newspaper spoke of the transfer of Jews from Nazi concentration camps into British barbed-wire enclaves.[25] In a message to Mossad headquarters in Paris, the chief agent in Marseilles reported that many journalists had wept at the sight of the refugees in the deportation ships.[26] At one point, Mossad agents tried to replicate the La Spezia affair by inviting Harold Laski, who had mediated between the La Spezia refugees and Foreign Minister Bevin, to make a documented visit to Port de Bouc and see for himself how the refugees were faring. At the same time, the agents tried to organize letters of protest to British newspapers from "good" British subjects, "the few righteous men in Sodom."[27] After a few days, when the attraction of the *Exodus* began to wear off, as it does with all stories, it was necessary to help generate new interest in it. The refugees' hunger strike—a replay of the well-orchestrated hunger strike of the La Spezia refugees—was called for mainly to recapture the media's attention and not allow the world to forget them.[28] It was scheduled, in coordination with Mossad agents on the coast, to take place at a convenient hour for newspaper publication. Perlman reported it to the international news agencies, and the strike, having achieved its purpose, was promptly brought to an end.[29]

It was a remarkable example of the "horror equals headlines" equation that would come to characterize mass communication in the second half of the twentieth century: the greater the agony and the terror, the greater the event's attractiveness to the media. When the event reached its lowest point—the deportation of the Jewish refugees back to Germany—it also attained its climax in terms of propaganda effectiveness from the Zionist point of view. The concluding chapter of the visible, public *Exodus* incident—the forced disembarkation at Hamburg—was thus truly the media apotheosis (as distinct from other parts of the episode that remained far from the public eye and did not engage public opinion, such as the refugees' long stay in German camps until the last of them had been brought to Palestine, or to Israel after its establishment). "Far from making an example' of the *Exodus* and rallying the world against the organizers of illegal immigration, Bevin succeeded [in the Hamburg chapter of the affair] only in shocking the world community into deeper sympathy for the Zionist enterprise," wrote the British Lord Bethel.[30] Bevin's fury during the summer of 1947 thus led him into a folly that coincided with the Zionist leadership's unwillingness to give up the great potential political and propaganda victory that the unexpected German stage of the affair offered.[31]

In the disembarkation at Hamburg, most of the refugees on the first ship stepped down quietly and without protest. Others—members of the young, tough nucleus of the refugee community—were dragged off the ship by British soldiers. Some of the refugees were injured, and the press reported shocking scenes. Disembarkation from the second ship—on which, it was later discovered, the head of the Palmach escorts had planted a bomb, on orders of his commanders—also proceeded quietly and without disturbance. It was so quiet that Moshe Perlman, who did not know about the bomb, accused the refugees of having lost the pride they displayed in France and of leaving the boat "like sheep."[32] The passengers on the third vessel, the *Runnymede Park*, who were the most organized and active because of their internal leadership,[33] stubbornly refused to leave the ship. Yet even for them the disembarkation was accomplished relatively peacefully, with only minor injuries to the refugees. There was no need for a "war to the death," as the leader of the *Runnymede Park* passengers ordered to expose the infamy of the British decision and arouse the reporters' emotions. The forced deportation of the Jews to Germany and their dragging on the docks caused many of the journalists (there were said to be about two hundred of them in Hamburg), some of them moved to tears, to override their professional obligation and submit an official protest to the American president and to the British authorities in Hamburg.[34] "It was for the world that we did this," one of the refugee women from the ship wrote, "for the Jewish people's honor, and that was the whole of the matter.[35]

"The world" was thus the object of all the resistance activities on the ships and the justification for the deaths of refugees in these actions. Even Moshe Averbuch, in his isolated theater of action in Romania, far from the sphere of influence of the Western media, considered the public relations effect of his plan to send the *Smirni* up the Danube to Budapest in order to save hundreds of orphans. He talked about shaking "the entire world" with this ship.[36] The Mossad chief himself, the most secretive of men, understood the propaganda effect of the historic events his subordinates were organizing. After the *Ge'ula* and the *Medinat*

Ha'Yehudim (the *Redemption* and the *Jewish State*) sailed from Burgas, Bulgaria, with many thousands of Romanian refugees on board, he issued an order to Palestine headquarters to coordinate "the press and Jewish public opinion" and to plant news items about Romanian and Bulgarian assistance and references to "the blessings of Uncle Joseph [Stalin]" for the whole operation.[37] Thus, Yehuda Arazi assuming the leadership of the La Spezia refugees, the *Exodus* affair, the refugee woman on the deportation ship writing a diary in Polish, and the graves of the dead clandestine immigrants in Haifa were all "broadcasting to the world." After the resistance battle on the *Negev* (the *Merica*), during which one refugee was killed, the newspaper *Davar* wrote that, although the list of the dead was growing, such deaths had a purpose since they gave the Zionist movement its saintly martyrs and because their graves "broadcast the call to the entire world for additional ships."[38]

"That was the whole of the matter"—the purpose behind the Mossad's orchestration of resistance aboard the refugee ships. The refugees' resistance on the ships, which had no chance whatsoever of succeeding, was meant mainly to arouse the conscience of the world. Resistance granted the clandestine immigration movement visibility; it made the struggle newsworthy on a worldwide scale. Without the spectacles of the violent clashes between Jewish refugees, with only sticks and cans of food for weapons, and uniformed British soldiers with firearms, the events surrounding the ships would have been much less attractive to the media. Such resistance was, therefore, the Zionists' most effective political weapon in the years after the Holocaust. Arazi, who "invented" the weapon of public, media-oriented resistance—even though at La Spezia it was still largely passive—acknowledged this explicitly: "I utterly opposed *Aliyah Gimmel* [the immigration campaign of young, armed fighters that Ben-Gurion attempted to put into action in the autumn of 1945]. We did not have the strength to confront them with arms. In contrast: we immigrants [*ma'apilim*], survivors of the Holocaust, want to go to Palestine—don't prevent us . . . great propaganda material for the whole humane world."[39] Mossad agents told François-Jean Armorin, who covered both the *Theodor Herzl* and the *Exodus,* that, unlike the "breakaway" (*ha'porshim*) terrorist organizations (Irgun and the Stern Group) that used knives and submachine guns in their bloody war against the British, Mossad people preferred to use a less deadly but much more effective weapon: the secret boats and their refugee passengers.[40] The resistance on the ships was thus organized to provoke serious incidents, sights difficult for the world to watch passively, and thereby challenge the legitimacy of British policy. The briefings given to the refugees on the eve of embarkation or later in preparation for confrontation with the British had the character of revival meetings and were meant to get the refugees to identify with the Zionist struggle and to be willing to get hurt or even killed fighting for it.[41]

There was resistance of some kind to British capture in almost all the Mossad ships, but it became established Mossad policy beginning with the British government's Cyprus decision in August 1946. The Mossad then issued instructions for passive resistance during the transfer of refugees to the British deportation ships. The initiators of this resistance policy and its escalation were Palmach headquarters in Palestine and members of the Mossad's operational arm there. They were responsible for bringing the refugees from ship to shore, and thus the potential sites of clashes with the British were within their "jurisdiction." Their commander was David Nameri, a kibbutz member and one of the founders and senior officers of both the Mossad and the Palmach and the liaison between the two. An activist in both his views and actions, he had no direct contact with the refugees as did his colleagues in Europe. He therefore formulated his positions without being influenced by the specific fate of the refugees, their sufferings and fatigue, or their ability to fight or resist. The first instructions on resistance were transmitted from Palestine to ships that were already at sea, before a comprehensive policy had been adopted: "If there is an attempt to take control of the ships outside the territorial waters, there should be passive resistance such as: preventing them from coming up the ladder, blocking the approaches to the helm and the engine room, interference with handcuffing and creating havoc."[42] A few days after publication of the British decision on deportation to Cyprus, Nameri demanded that the refugee ships be transformed into true vessels of war. His opinion, and that of some of his colleagues, was that "shouts and curses" were no longer sufficient and that it was time to act, to conduct a fierce and violent battle against deportation including deliberate sabotage of the deportation ships. Explosives were put on the ships and were sometimes attached to the bodies of refugee women, who thus became living bombs. Instructions were given as to how and when to carry out the sabotage. "If they are deported without any response we will never be forgiven," Nameri stated in a cable to the Mossad in Tel Aviv (he was himself in Haifa, where the refugee ships were held until deportation).[43] Nameri, who undoubtedly remembered the *Patria* tragedy six years previously—more than 260 Jewish refugees drowned as a result of a badly executed dynamiting of the ship that was supposed to deport them—and his own role in it,[44] was still not deterred from renewing his demand to sabotage ships loaded with thousands of refugees.

The decision to resist came from above, from the Mossad leadership, under pressure from the Palmach and from Nameri, rather than spontaneously from the ranks of the refugees. Before the hurried sailing of the *Four Freedoms* (previously the *Fede*) from Italy, Arazi gave the ship's captain explicit instructions for the eventuality of an encounter with a British vessel that would try to capture it: "Don't stop and do not respond to the warning shots. And should the British board the ship, resist and interfere and steer the ship to a different place."[45] The instructions to the commander of the *Palmach* (the *Ariana*) were even more explicit and unequivocal: "Proceed to the shore *at any price,* even if [the British] shoot" (emphasis added).[46] In many cases, the refugees were not at all capable of fighting. On the *Four Freedoms,* for instance, conditions were so harsh that all the refugees were weak and many ill. Since there was no doctor, they could not receive even basic medical attention. Eventually the ship's commander asked permission to speed up the journey and to bring his passengers ashore for treatment. When he did not receive such permission ("You are not permitted under any circumstances to arrive during daylight. Make an effort to hold out until evening," was the order), he decided to organize resistance anyway, under his command and that of the two escorts. After the ship was discovered by the British, there was a battle that lasted three hours and ended when, after British boats battered its hull, the ship was in danger of sinking. A few refugees were hurt; some of them were treated by the British, and others were hospitalized.[47] The *Henrietta Szold* set sail from Greece on 30 July 1946 and was at sea when the Cyprus decision went into effect. It carried a large number of pregnant women, and more than a third of its passengers were children, many of them babies—"very difficult human material," as the Yishuv escorts reported,[48] certainly not "material" fit for a physical struggle with armed soldiers. The *Bracha Fuld* (previously the *Fenice*) was a similar case. Its journey lasted longer than planned, and its food stores almost completely ran out. The eight hundred refugees on board reached the Palestinian shores in such a state that there was no one left "to conduct resistance."[49]

The orders to resist came, as noted, from the Yishuv officials and were passed on to the refugees through the ship commanders, most of them members of the Palmach. It should be stressed, however, that the refugees, especially the young members of Zionist parties or youth movements, accepted these orders willingly and even enthusiastically, at least at the beginning. After the first British deportation campaign, the Mossad station in Palestine reported to the center in Paris that "the immigrants acted according to orders during the transfer and fought with the army like lions."[50] The fight on the *Palmach* was also evidence of the refugees' commendable bravery. The battle was both shorter and fiercer than previous ones, demonstrating an escalation in weaponry. Water jets, tear gas, and in the end small arms were used by the British, and the results were what might have been expected. Thirty-one of the passengers, among them the Palmach ship commander, were wounded. This was the only time during all the campaigns of resistance on the refugee ships that a Palmach operative was injured in resistance action; in contrast, hundreds of refugees were wounded and thirteen were killed. One of the thirteen was killed on the *Palmach,* the first victim of the violent confrontations with the British on Mossad ships. Ben-Gurion immediately turned this victim into a symbol of the new Zionist martyrology and referred to this individual time and again in his rally-'round-the-flag speeches of the period.[51] This victim still did not deter the Mossad from its policy of physical confrontation, even though not everyone was favorably disposed to the idea.[52] The *Latrun* (the *San Dimitrio*), which sailed about a month after the *Palmach,* was seized and its passengers transferred by force to Cyprus; Mossad agents in France had equipped it with sticks, bottles, and several gas masks in anticipation of the battle. While at sea, some 130 young refugees were trained to use these "weapons" to defend the ship against British capture. Another group of young people were trained to jump from the ship and swim to shore. These preparations did not make much of an impression on the British. Although there was a brief attempt at resistance, the ship was quickly captured, and the refugees obeyed British orders and quietly boarded the deportation ship.[53] Apparently, the reports of wounded and dead among the refugees on previous ships had an effect, even if explicit documentation would appear in internal Mossad correspondence only later.

Hands, Sticks, and Bottles

The resistance on the ship *Knesset Yisrael* (the *Assembly of Israel*), under the command of Yossi Hamburger (later Har'el), is worthy of a more detailed discussion. It constituted a break in the resistance campaign, and its commander, one of the most prominent and responsible of the ship commanders, found himself at odds with his leaders and direct superiors. The first Hebrew name given to the ship, before it set sail from Yugoslavia, was *Tnu'at Ha'Meri Ha'Ivri* (the *Hebrew Resistance Movement*), and the commander told a presailing muster of the 3,200 passengers that they should consider themselves accountable to this name.[54] The ship carried an entire *shtetl*, with a "kindergarten" and an "old-age home," to quote the derogatory terms used by one of the Yishuv leaders to describe the composition of the passengers.[55] It was certainly not a combat unit. Indeed, when Hamburger passed on to the refugee leaders the instructions about resistance that he had received from headquarters—very moderate ones, it should be stressed ("to the extent of your abilities")[56] the leaders expressed doubts about whether the people on board would be able to fight and whether they themselves would be able to persuade them to do so. They asked Hamburger to meet the people and persuade them himself, since his words carried special, "sacred" weight and would be accepted without challenge. "We will resist with everything we have," Hamburger said to the refugees, "first with our hands, then with sticks and bottles, with hoses and with fuel." The concept of resisting "with hands, . . . sticks, and bottles" derived not only from the concern about putting firearms in untrained hands and losing control of events should such weaponry be used by both the refugees and the British. It was a deliberate choice, a calculated consideration of the powerful and highly desirable effect that fighting between unequal forces would have. The intention was to elicit the kind of moral outrage produced by any David-versus-Goliath battle.

The resistance group on the *Knesset Yisrael* included about two thousand people, most of them from youth movements. The leaders of these groups explained the idea of resistance to the passengers and prepared defiant banners to be unfurled during the British capture operation. One read: "Every Jew murdered or wounded on the ship will be paid for in English blood!"[57] This campaign to foster a fighting spirit was directed not only inward, at the refugees, but also at the Yishuv and its institutions. In an exceptional display of personal confidence, Hamburger cabled a message not only to Mossad headquarters but also, in a circumvention of the chain of command, to the headquarters of the Haganah and Palmach: "Making all preparations for disembarkation on the shore. Also preparing vigorous resistance. Our intention is to *force* the Yishuv to fight for immigration. Huge technical preparations. The third reserve alone contains 750 partisans and soldiers of the great [red] army. . . . *Prepare a strong reaction by the Yishuv.* Request confirmation from all three institutions on receipt of this memorandum" (emphasis added).[58] In the end, orders were received from the shore to cancel the resistance, apparently because the ship's case was under legal adjudication, but actually as a result of political considerations that required a cooling down of the anti-British resistance campaign, in which, from mid-1945 until mid-1946, the Haganah, Palmach, Irgun, and the Stern Group collaborated. Even the ship's name was changed unilaterally, and symbolically, from the *Hebrew Resistance Movement* to the *Assembly of Israel.* The ship's commanders tried to protest the decision, but the orders from the Yishuv were categorical. "We request that you not revise our instructions about the name. Your name will be *Knesset Yisrael.* Accept the deportation order under this name."[59]

During the transfer of the refugees to the deportation ship at Haifa port, a bitter struggle was nevertheless organized, one that soon became desperate, lasting three hours and ending with the death of one sixteen-year-old refugee and dozens of wounded, both among the refugees and among the British soldiers.[60] The Yishuv was not moved and did not display the "strong reaction" that Hamburger had asked for, unless such a label could be applied to poet Nathan Alterman's newspaper column headlined "Division of Roles": "The Yishuv may not demand [of an illegal immigrant girl]/what it does not of itself and its children demand."[61] Later, when a baby died on board one of the British deportation ships carrying the *Exodus* refugees from the coast of France to Hamburg, Alterman would write almost identical words: "The nation may enlist [the refugee babies]/only if the heart believes/that it will be worthy of looking upon them/and declaring the death a needful one."[62] The harshest and most painful protest against the resistance action on the *Knesset Yisrael* came, however, from within the organization, from the native-born ship commander. Yossi Hamburger, the Mossad's great hope and future commander of the two largest clandestine immigration operations, those of the *Exodus* and the *Pan* ships, wrote, "Someone has to give me an answer. If no one fights on the shore, why do the *ma'apilim* have to fight? They are the remnants of the six million who were destroyed, who have already been through all of hell. Why do they have to be victims again? We have to tell them not to resist because all resistance is the spilling of blood and it is untenable that the *ma'apilim* fight while here on the shore everyone sits quietly."[63]

The fight on the *Theodor Herzl*, five months after the *Knesset Yisrael* incident, was the most violent and wasteful of all the resistance operations up to that of the *Exodus*. It ended with three dead and more than twenty wounded, some of them seriously. Was the British reaction so severe because of the escalation of Jewish terrorism in Palestine and the increase in tension and violence there, as some historians claim? Was the refugees' resistance so resolute because of the diverse coterie of journalists and photographers on board? François-Jean Armorin, who depicted the battle and its outcome with compassion and admiration in his articles and later in his book, concluded by saying, "The *Theodor Herzl* did not surrender. The refugees held out to the end, until their pitiful amount of ammunition ran out, until the unnecessary bloodletting by submachine gun. One of the [British] officers told me afterwards that his men had lost control of themselves. . . . At midnight, two hours after the ship was captured, the blue-and-white flag still waved on the flagpole and the sea breeze beat at it."[64] As in previous cases, the heroism of the exhausted refugees was exemplary, even if pointless and thus heartbreaking. "We resisted," wrote a refugee woman, "and we have three dead and 16 wounded. We simply did not want to surrender to them like sheep."[65] It was the refugees' heroic contribution to a war in which, at that time, the muscular Yishuv displayed no heroism at all.

A Mapai member of the *Va'ad Le'umi* (National Council) directorate, David Bar-Rav-Hai, cried out at a directorate meeting against this senseless and unjust bloodshed. "The course that was determined in the past and which was correct for the first ship," he said, "has turned into political nonsense and organized bloodshed within this routine of the transfers to Cyprus. No one dares say it out loud. I'm saying it."[66] The general public reaction to the deaths of the three refugees, however, was not exceptional in the routine of those days; this is probably linked to the tense atmosphere prevailing in the Yishuv at the time due to the execution of four members of the Irgun terrorist organization in Acre Prison and the escalation of the British fight against Jewish terrorism.[67] In other words, a link was already created between the terrorism of the "breakaway" groups, which were condemned by the Yishuv's political leadership, and the violent struggle taking place on the clandestine ships, which got all the acclaim. Ben-Gurion himself would denounce this unjustified link with unprecedented fury during the *Exodus* episode.[68] When, however, the bitter consequences of the resistance on the *Theodor Herzl* became known, the Mossad section in Palestine immediately rallied to support the resistance policy it had led from the start. They denounced the "provocation" of the British soldiers in capturing the ship. The use of British firepower had far exceeded what was necessary, they claimed, and amounted to "premeditated murder." They spoke as if it were not foreseeable that the policy of physical resistance followed by the refugees would lead to an escalation in violence and refugee casualties, and as if it were possible to expect the British to play according to the rules set by the Mossad. As an additional step in the escalation of the resistance campaign, the Mossad demanded of Golda Meyerson, the most senior political leader present at the time in the country, "an appropriate response."[69]

The Refugees' War

There was never a universally acceptable solution to the active resistance on refugee ships, nor any consensus on its extent, cost, or results. It divided the Mossad's agents as it did the Haganah's ranks. The political leadership's stand on resistance was ambiguous, partly because most of the political leaders were out of the country at the time. Indeed, Ben-Gurion thought that when refugees jumped from the captured Mossad ships and swam to their homeland, this said "more than any Zionist book or speech" he had read in his life, and he turned the first refugee killed by a British soldier into a new Jewish martyr who sanctified the Zionist goal.[70] He was in Europe during these months, however, far from the events. He could experience only their tragic-glorious halo and their strong propaganda effect, not the harsh concreteness of their actual unfolding, which gradually roused more and more discontent among various groups within the Yishuv. The issue became public largely after the resistance actions began to result in a loss of life. Whereas *Davar*, which generally echoed the political leadership's line, claimed that a purpose was being served by the growing ranks of the dead and by the "hundreds of exhausted, stunned, abused people now entering another concentration camp," going so far as to promise in their name that "their spirit has not been broken, and the spirit of the Yishuv will not break, either,"[71] others found this "division of roles" intolerable. The poet Nathan Alterman, newspaper columnists, editorials in *Ha'aretz*, and even young Palmach soldiers who served as escorts on the ships or as instructors in the temporary camps set up by the Mossad in Europe, all raised the same question: how could the Yishuv, which was brought up on resistance to the British and was much better equipped for it, impose the entire burden of fighting on the weakest and most oppressed, those who had not yet set foot in Palestine, the survivors of the Holocaust, women and children, who were left alone on a battlefield that was largely political and that ought to belong to the Yishuv as a whole?[72] "How could you, how could the 'resistance movement' remain silent, sit idly while *ma'apilim* are being murdered on the country's shores and deported from it? Did we not shout, did we not swear, that the days of the *Patria* and the *Atlantic* would never return—and here they are returning. Do [we] really intend to leave things that way and to leave the *ma'apilim* alone in their war?" wrote a Palmach member to his comrades and commanders.[73] At the time of the violent disembarkation in Hamburg, *Ha'aretz* correspondent Robert Weltch wrote that even if "a certain measure of resistance was perhaps understandable in principle," overly stubborn resistance was "pointless in the face of such great force" and given the risk "of precious, pointless casualties."[74] There was nothing new in his words. This was the established position of his newspaper, which had opposed escalating the resistance on the ships, especially in view of the loss of life among the refugees. The refugees, the newspaper claimed, had already done their part simply by coming to Palestine. There was no reason for imposing additional burdens on them and intensifying the resistance because the illegal immigration operation was already achieving its goal, "even without the horrifying scenes of unarmed resistance against the British war machine," *Ha'aretz* wrote as early as May 1947, after three refugee ships in a row were captured by the British.[75]

Despite *Davar*'s promise that the refugees' spirit would not break, the reality proved otherwise. The price was apparently too high, and the refugees were affected by the large number of victims. On the *Hatikva* (the *Hope*) and the *Mordei Ha'Getaot* (the *Ghetto Rebels*), which both sailed from Italy after the capture and battle of the *Theodor Herzl*, no spirit of resistance was evident among the passengers. The Mossad, and even the Palmach commander who during this entire period had pressed for intensifying resistance on the ships, were forced to admit this.[76] The escorts on the *Mordei Ha'Getaot* spoke of the refugees' "fear of shooting."[77] On the *Yehuda Ha'Levy,* which sailed from Algeria, the passengers actually fled for their lives and threw away the sticks they had been given when a British destroyer began bashing the ship's hull.[78] There were reports from the crews about passengers who asked, in the middle of the journey, to turn back and "go home."[79] Even before this, after the battle on the *Theodor Herzl,* the Mossad was forced to begin a retreat from its resistance-at-any-cost line and send orders to cool down the physical struggle despite "the serious implications of the order for us [the Mossad]."[80] It was only when the Israeli commander of the ship *She'ar Yishuv* received orders to engage in passive resistance that this change in tactics became official. When the commander demanded clarification, saying that if he received none he would interpret the order to mean "handing over the ship without resistance," the Mossad made the order explicit: "We wish to avoid casualties."[81]

This minor episode of unclear or contradictory orders was characteristic of the policy concerning the resistance issue. The people in the heart of the storm were the ship commanders, escorts, and radio operators, most of them from the Yishuv and members of the Palmach who were torn between conflicting loyalties to the Palmach command on the one hand and to the Mossad leadership on the other.[82] The Mossad and the Palmach issued resistance orders differing in character and force.[83] The debate over the issue of resistance on the refugee ships was the major theater in which a conflict of command, organization, generation, and image between the Mossad and the Palmach was played out. Palmach commander Yigal Allon was the most fervent advocate of resistance by the refugees. All through the period during which resistance was an issue, from August 1946 to the summer of 1947, he constantly fought for the continuation and intensification of the resistance. He also demanded that the Palmach—and its commander—have the authority to direct the resistance on the ships and to be the source of the orders to the Palmach escorts on board.[84] Allon used every possible method of persuasion and injunction to impose his view—letters, articles, personal meetings with his soldiers, and direct orders. He demanded compliance, if not obedience, to his orders "which are not in any way ambiguous."[85]

After the first casualties, at the end of 1946, when the question surfaced within the Palmach itself, the *Palmach Newsletter* published Allon's apologia on the issue. The author of the unsigned article conceded that the fight was a lost cause and that there seemed to be no immediate benefit because it did not prevent the refugees from being deported. The true purpose of resistance, the article admitted, was the transformation of the refugee's character. After all, the article said, when one retreats—that is, when one does not fight deportation even if the fighting is without practical consequence and involves casualties—one "turns into human sheep." Resistance, according to the article, is meant to turn the *ma'apilim* from a passive to an active force, into people who determine their own fates, and so to counter the British claim that the *ma'apilim* were no more than pawns in the hands of an extremist group of "unscrupulous men" who were exploiting their plight for their own political purposes. The refugees' willingness to take risks and lay down their lives for the right to immigrate was testimony to the fact that they had not been "transported" but had become active *ma'apilim* of their own volition, out of devotion to their homeland and its redemption and from their willingness to face war and sacrifice.[86] Indeed, this was a glaring example of meaning reversal: the refugees were exploited in order to prove that they were not exploited, that they were not pawns, weapons in the Zionist political struggle. It was also testimony to the Yishuv's condescending attitude toward the refugees, who had to be thrown into a bloody conflict in order to be transformed, forged into "new" men and women.[87]

Visible and Anonymous

The number of casualties—dead and wounded—among the refugees and the refugees' fears of violent clashes with British soldiers did not deter Allon. A day after the capture of one of the ships without any resistance from the refugees,[88] who displayed, according to the report of the Mossad agents, "fear of shooting," Allon sent the following cable to his subordinates in France: "My order with regard to unarmed resistance to the capture of our ships and to transfer to deportation ships still stands. Organize properly, instruct the *ma'apilim*, give encouragement to the escorts before each sailing."[89] It is hard to know what the main motivation for this message was—Allon's determination to remain the supreme and sole commander of the Palmach agents in this clandestine operation or his resolve to uphold the principle of resistance. It may also have been that he was already trying, perhaps not even fully consciously, at the end of 1946, to sabotage the negotiations with the British planned for the first quarter of 1947. Not long after this cable he wrote that there could be no doubt that armed conflict would break out "after it becomes clear that negotiations alone still cannot obtain political gains under the circumstances we find ourselves in."[90] Allon's letter of 21 June 1947, which is a broader and clearer exposition of his previous statements on this subject, indicates that all three of these factors determined his position. He may have believed everything he wrote in his letter, or he may have written it largely to persuade his subordinates; in any case, Allon weighted down the refugees' resistance with way too many things for them to shoulder, and more than it was fair or ethical to expect from them. First, Allon stated that even if the Yishuv remained on the sidelines, the refugees' resistance served a purpose because it was one of the last manifestations of the fight against the foreign regime. Ending resistance on the ships would mean the end of the fight. Continuing resistance on the ships was "the best guarantee that the Yishuv will find a way to identify with the refugees, even though that way has not been found so far." Second, the resistance operation, which from time to time aroused the conscience of the public and its leadership, served, according to Allon, as a link between the resolute struggle of the past and the intensified struggle that would break out eventually, "if we do not want to surrender." Resistance, Allon added, "in and of itself is the end and the goal." With regard to the humiliation of being dragged away by British soldiers, Allon wrote, "We cannot allow an imaginary concern for our honor to lead to the absence of resistance being interpreted to mean that the *ma'apilim* are going to Cyprus of their own volition. . . . We would be devaluating our national and human honor . . . if we do not oppose deportation." Allon also believed that resistance was delaying and would continue to delay British plans to return the refugee ships to their port of origin, "a real danger that awaits us at any time." Reality, as it turned out, contradicted him. Less than a month after Allon's letter, the refugees on the *Exodus* were sent on three deportation ships back to their port of origin in France, despite their fight against the British close to the Palestinian coast.

Finally, when it came down to it, the role of the resistance, according to Allon, was "to reawaken, from time to time, the Diaspora's support for us and its willingness to extend assistance, and the consciences of those of the world's nations that have not yet lost theirs."[91] Allon thus placed much too heavy a burden of expectations and aspirations on the

Holocaust survivors: to carry the sputtering torch of the Yishuv's fight against the British, to awaken the Yishuv and get it back to fighting, and at the same time to atone for the decline in fighting. Did the lives or the well-being of the refugees, survivors of the Nazi death industry, enter into Allon's considerations? "Correct, comrades," Allon wrote to his soldiers, "we must not take human life, and especially the lives of the *ma'apilim,* lightly. There is nothing more disturbing than the death of these remnants from the sword, who have managed to live through the seven circles of hell and here they fall at the gates of the country. . . . We should not delude ourselves—as in the past, in the future *ma'apilim* are likely to fall to enemy bullets. . . . I am convinced in the depths of my heart that these sacrifices will not be in vain. Their spilt blood is the blood of fighters sacrificing themselves in their nation's war of independence. Our pain at their death, and at their absence from our camp, is great, but in the end we are saving ourselves additional sacrifices and directly helping to save many who could expect destruction. Yes, my comrades, with a full sense of the responsibility I take on myself, I say: we must maintain resistance despite the sacrifices."[92]

There were sacrifices, and refugees did indeed die "at the gates of the country." Thirteen people died in the hopeless and futile resistance battles against deportation,[93] all of them refugees. The deaths did not prevent deportation, and the Yishuv suffered no great "pain at their death, and at their absence from our camp," to use Allon's pompous phrasing. In fact, the Yishuv suffered no pain at all. Most of the dead refugees remained anonymous, and the locations of their graves were not always known. A ship that sailed from Italy in October 1946 was named after Bracha Fuld, a young woman of the Palmach who was killed in Tel Aviv during the disembarkation from a refugee ship on 26 March of that year.[94] Her burial, which the British tried to carry out quickly and secretly in order to avoid the anticipated crowds and demonstrations, became in the end a huge display of solidarity, both spontaneous and organized.[95] In contrast, not many showed up at the funeral of Herbert Lazar, a refugee killed in battle on another ship. The residents of Haifa were invited by the community council to pay their respects ("The Yishuv will honor the martyr by its participation in the funeral"), but he was a stranger, a man without a name. When the death notices were posted on the city's notice boards he was still nameless, referred to as "the unknown *ma'apil,*" the anonymous immigrant. That is how he went down in history. The name of the *San Miguel,* which sailed from the French port of Sète on 3 February 1947, was changed to *Ha'Ma'apil Ha'Almoni* (the *Unknown Ma'apil*)—"named" after Lazar[96] and all the other anonymous dead. This is indeed a paradox: the refugees' deliberate visibility as arranged by the secret agents of the Yishuv and as the result of events that drew their power from their conspicuousness, not only failed to save the refugees from anonymity but actually seemed to contribute to it. As a rule, they remained a mass of "anonymous *ma'apilim*," unknown immigrants.

There should be no doubt about it: If the refugees' resistance fulfilled the Palmach commander's wishes and orders, it was with regard to the part about "to reawaken from time to time . . . the consciences of those of the world's nations that have not yet lost theirs." The refugee ships were captured in spite of the brave fight put up by their passengers, whose bodies bore the tragic imprint of Jewish history, and they were deported to camps in Cyprus. In the case of the *Exodus,* they were driven back even to Germany. Some of them died. Yet there was no power on earth that could withstand the "conscience-mobilizing" force of the events in which the refugees played a major role. In this sense they were Zionism's great asset of that time, its winning story. In contrast, the Yishuv's organization, the Mossad, which produced these winning political and media productions and which operated the most effective political weapon that Zionism had in these post-war years, succeeded in preserving, during the entire period of its operation, its invisibility. However, although it was a covert, invisible organization, its operatives were never anonymous. Each of them had a name, a role, a background, and status within the organization—a status as a member of the organization and a status as a result of being wanted by the British as a member of the organization. These non-anonymous people left many traces that make it possible to reconstruct, almost completely, their movements, actions, ways of organizing, personal and group profiles, priorities, rivalries, relations with other organizations, aspirations, and spoken and written words. These people are the subject of the next chapter.

CHAPTER 5

Ordinary People

Organizations and institutions take on the contours of their history, the people who compose their membership, the character of the groups that coalesce within them, and the relationships woven between these groups. Organizations beget characteristic patterns, values, and vested interests. The network of agreements they create and carry out with other bodies, how they adapt to changing circumstances, and the continuity of their activity provide the source of their power and prestige. The Mossad, which was responsible for one of the major enterprises of the Zionist community in Palestine in the years preceding the founding of Israel, and which was one of the key factors in building consciousness and forging self-identity,[1] had a clear and distinctive history. It was driven by a constitutive set of images and ideas manifested in strategies representing specific interests, under the leadership of a group of individuals with similar characteristics who developed lifestyles and work patterns, norms of cooperation, and constellations of interests, and who set the tone for the organization from its inception until it was absorbed into the network of state institutions.

This embryonic group was conceived in late 1937 (and formally became the Mossad about a year and a half later) by those in the inner circle of Yitzhak Tabenkin, leader of Ha'Kibbutz Ha'Meuhad (hereinafter referred to as the Kibbutz), a radical, activist faction advocating settlement and a militant approach within the labor movement. This group was assigned two functions: to undermine the restrictive British quotas on Jewish immigration to Palestine and to force radicalization

153

of the political leadership of the Zionist movement itself, which, according to Tabenkin, was unduly self-restrained and cooperative with the British government.[2] There is no documentation of any decision by the Kibbutz to establish an organization for clandestine immigration. Silence surrounds its inception. The absence of documentation tells us something about the decision-making process of the Kibbutz secretariat and Tabenkin's inner circle, which were characterized by informality of practice and style. Key decisions were often made after random consultation—in spontaneous encounters on the kibbutz paths or in the communal dining room—and were not documented.[3] The absence of records also reinforces the claim that this clandestine operation, at least at its inception, had a double profile—with its goals directed toward the British and also toward the central Zionist leadership—and that decisions and initial activities were done in the oral tradition of the deliberative fraternity that was the leadership of the Kibbutz. This democratic dimension of the Kibbutz leadership was passed down to the first operatives and was a key feature of the group that led the Mossad during the post-war years discussed in this book.

The anguish of the thousands of members of the HeHalutz Zionist youth movement in Poland who had been uprooted from their homes in a series of edicts and pogroms in their country,[4] their demand to circumvent British immigration quotas and force an independent immigration to Palestine,[5] the special historical bond between the two movements, and the desire of those close to the leader of the Kibbutz—the founders and leaders of HeHalutz in Poland before their immigration to Palestine—to respond to the plight of their former followers, all contributed to the founding of this unique immigration enterprise. In my view, however, the catalyst for moving the process along was the political interest of the Kibbutz, which was based on political and security circumstances in Palestine and on the power struggle in the Zionist movement, as perceived by Tabenkin and his followers. This merits an explanation.

The Arab Revolt of 1936 not only exacted a price in bloodshed and Jewish immigration;[6] it also provoked controversy within the Jewish community about Zionist strategy in reacting to this uprising between what was called "restraint" and "response." The activist wing within the Zionist leadership was represented by those who wanted to end the reliance on the British government. In what came to be known as "going beyond the fence," the activist wing advocated not only the active defense of Jewish settlements but a policy of military initiatives against the local Arabs. In addition to matters of defense and security, the activist tendency also marked an internal political struggle about the direction of development of the Jewish community and the positions of power and influence within it.[7] Following the defeat of the Tabenkin camp, which had opposed the principle of partitioning Palestine at the Twentieth Zionist Congress, the Kibbutz's decision in late August 1937 to establish an integrated political and operational front against the "co-operationist" policies of the central Zionist leadership could thus be seen as one more step "beyond the fence." "Some usurpers took over the Zionist Movement in order to change Zionism's direction and I'll fight it to the end," said Tabenkin in a closed Kibbutz seminar right after the congress.[8] This was also the moment when Yehuda Braginsky, one of the founders of HeHalutz and a confidant of Tabenkin, was sent to his "brothers" in Poland to organize their clandestine immigration to Palestine, although these "brothers" had cried out for help for more than two years.[9] There is no unambiguous, documented link between the congress decisions about the partition of Palestine and the Kibbutz decision to launch this double-headed clandestine campaign, but one should not be blind to the circumstantial connection between these two developments. Thus, this solidarity operation, launched in late 1937, should be seen also as a political move taken by a group with an elitist self-image and aspirations in its struggle over Zionist policies, as well as with positions of power, influence, and hegemony within the Yishuv.[10]

This observation, together with the documentation highlighting the gap between the ideological-ethical discourse that was the leitmotif of this clandestine campaign and the local factional political interests that actually drove the enterprise, are important in understanding the inception of the Mossad and its evolution. From the outset, various Yishuv groups and institutions promoted the ideology of rescue, that it was the role of Eretz Israel to take responsibility for Diaspora Jews in need, in effect using this ideology to advance political interests and improve positions internally. It was this ideology that conferred legitimacy and prestige to the Yishuv groups, which conducted their political and power struggles in its name.[11]

The first agents sent to Poland after Yehuda Braginsky to organize the clandestine immigration campaign—Ze'ev Schind, Zvi Yehieli, Moshe Averbuch, Pino Ginsburg, and, later, Shmarya Zameret—were handpicked by Tabenkin. All were members of the Kibbutz, and all were in their thirties, family men, deeply involved in their kibbutz communities.

Except for Zameret, who was born in the United States, they came from eastern or central Europe, where the clandestine immigration was to originate. They had experience in public activity and knowledge of the languages of the target countries, and they were cut in the mold of Tabenkin and were his personal ambassadors in the mission. Before their departure for Europe, each met for a long conversation with the leader and was given a personal send-off.[12] This style of personally selecting people and bringing them into the secret inner circle plays a key, if invisible, role in enhancing the power of a given society. The selection was thus based on personal ties to the leader or those close to him, and it remained the distinguishing feature of the Mossad even in its later years, when it was no longer under the direct authority of Tabenkin and was composed of dozens, even hundreds, of people. The recruiting of agents for the Mossad from the closed circles of the Kibbutz, and later from other kibbutz organizations and the Labor movement of Palestine, on the basis of personal, political, and even family connections, preserved the group identity of the Mossad, the ethical and personal codes of the operatives, and the organization's ideological and political homogeneity. Thus, despite the expansion of its size and scope of activities after World War II, the Mossad maintained intense loyalty and closeness within its ranks and preserved the communal deliberative character of its decision making. This enabled its operatives, sovereign in their respective domains scattered throughout Europe, to direct operations through ongoing consultations with their colleagues, who were peers in responsibility and status.

Five ships carrying a total of 715 people from Europe reached the shores of Palestine in 1938, and their passengers secretly disembarked without harm.[13] This small number could not effect any fundamental change in the statistics of immigration to Palestine or the proportion of Jews in that land, although these first sailings did reverberate throughout the Jewish communities in Poland. These beginnings, however, forged a sense of power and avant-garde mission among the small group of the Kibbutz members who executed the campaign. During the course of that year, the hard core of the organization, its members already spread throughout Europe, began to coalesce and proved capable of orchestrating the complex logistics for moving hundreds of people in a multitude of vehicles and routes across the face of Europe—a silent, massive flow of which the sailings from the southern ports of the continent were only its visible tip.[14] The organized Nazi pogrom in Germany and Austria of November 1938 (known as *Kristallnacht*) and Britain's al-most concurrent retreat from the plan to partition Palestine following the Woodhead Commission report, along with the vigorous activity of the Jewish right-wing organizations in bringing Jews into Palestine clan-destinely,[15] led to the "nationalization" of the Kibbutz immigration campaign and the emergence of an all-Labor organization to carry it out—the Mossad—from the initial group created by Tabenkin.[16] Although *Kristallnacht* sent shock waves through the Yishuv,[17] it was the political events in Palestine itself, the internal tension within the Zionist community there, and relations between the Jewish community in Palestine and the British government that placed the clandestine im-migration on the central political agenda and turned it into the main channel of Zionist activity. In December 1938, when Ben-Gurion re-turned to Palestine from an extended visit to Britain, he began to preach his "immigration revolt" idea in various forums and to recruit support-ers. He spoke of a new technique for political war with the British, call-ing it "the immigration war"—"not a war for immigration, but a war through immigration . . . not a secret immigration in order to maximize the number of Jews in Palestine, but immigration as a means of politi-cal warfare, that will keep the English government under pressure."[18]

A Political War

The failure of the London Conference in early 1939 gave the signal for the nationalization of the immigration campaign and its use by the central Zionist leadership. In April 1939, during confidential delib-erations in the Jewish Agency Executive under the designation "Clarification of the Situation," a decision was made to have the Executive itself organize the clandestine immigration through "parallel institutions." After three meetings held on 16, 18, and 30 April, Ben-Gurion was authorized to entirely reorganize the effort, in the frame-work of his reorganization of the security apparatus, and "to reach agree-ment with minimum opposition."[19] These meetings were so cloaked in secrecy that their minutes were kept separate from the regular protocols of the Jewish Agency Executive and the names of those in attendance and of the speakers were not recorded, but indicated by code numbers: Ben-Gurion was noted in the minutes as number 4, Weizmann 8, Shertok

30, and Eliezer Kaplan (the treasurer) 100.[20] In his party's Central Committee, Ben-Gurion announced more overtly, "It was decided that the Agency would organize the immigration. . . . There will be only one Jewish aliya [*bet*, that is, clandestine], and the Executive will direct this immigration through its Immigration Department." He made immigration the top priority of the leadership and asserted that most of the financial resources would be applied to this.[21] Previously, Ben-Gurion's intention had been that, on the day the 1939 White Paper was published, a ship of Jewish immigrants would publicly and defiantly set sail for Tel Aviv, carrying young pioneers willing, with Haganah support from shore, to defend by force their right to immigrate to Palestine[22] and even to die in battle, as "Jewish immigration to the land is worthy of victims."[23] The concept of resistance, with its toll of victims inflicted on the refugees and its generation of international press coverage, was thus not the product of the post-war years, but had crystallized with the process of nationalization of the underground immigration on the eve of the war.

Shaul Meirov, a Haganah commander, was appointed to run the Mossad, and the organization was placed under the command of the Haganah, that is, under the overall authority of the Jewish Agency Executive. Meirov was well placed within the various historical, political, and familial networks of the Jewish elites, and this made him an ideal choice to head an organization encompassing a great many political and operational sensitivities, both local and international. He was a member of a kibbutz, and thus belonged to the elite's elite; he benefited from the aura of having participated in the historic Tel Hai battle in 1920, which had become a legend; both political strongman Ben-Gurion and spiritual leader Berl Katzenelson were considered his patrons; and, by virtue of his background in security and activism, he was acceptable to the first Kibbutz operatives of the organization. The act with which the Mossad arrogated the Haganah, making it answerable to the national institutions and placing it high among Yishuv organizations, was the order issued in early July 1939 to the Haganah district commanders to place themselves and their units at the service of the Mossad.[24]

The Twenty-first Zionist Congress, held in Zurich in August 1939, renewed and broadened the Mossad's mandate of operations,[25] but the practical work was put on hold several days later with the outbreak of World War II. The ship *Tiger Hill*, which sailed from Constanta in August 1939, still managed to deposit hundreds of refugees from Poland on the shores of Tel Aviv the day the war broke out. Although additional groups of refugees waited in Germany, Austria, and Bratislava, the Mossad operatives left the continent and froze their operations. "A cessation of all our activity," wrote Shmarya Zameret in his diary in Paris. "Air travel halted several days ago. International trains yesterday. Telephone and telegraph connections are unreliable and practically inaccessible. Several borders are closed . . . and we are a small group of people stuck here in Paris."[26] Braginsky, who had directed the Mossad from Paris, instructed his colleagues throughout Europe—Ze'ev Schind, Zvi Yehieli, Moshe Averbuch, and Pino Ginsburg—to leave their posts and return to Palestine. "One has left today. Tomorrow another two are leaving. . . . There is no escape—my job now is to safeguard what there is and to wait for the coming days," Zameret wrote in his diary.[27]

This spur-of-the-moment decision at the outbreak of the war, followed by the departure from Europe of most of the operatives from Palestine just when the subjects of their activity and the Jewish communities in general needed them most, sparked harsh criticism within the Mossad itself and among the leadership in Palestine. It violated the ethos of the mission of the Zionist community vis-à-vis the Diaspora while revealing the limits of this ethos. Berl Katzenelson, the spiritual mentor of the Labor movement and a man who cherished and cultivated symbols, spoke about "a terrible sense of shame" regarding this exodus of the Zionist operatives from Europe. "I would have liked," he said, "to see ten of them fall martyred in the occupied territories."[28] Yet only in retrospect, given the dimensions of the Jewish catastrophe in the war, was the great burden of guilt placed on this decision, with some injustice.

In any case, the Mossad soon reconsidered the repercussions of its decision and began to return the operatives to their work in Europe toward the end of 1939. Geneva, Bucharest, and Athens were the permanent strongholds of the Mossad in Europe. Geneva served as a center of communications and relay station for Mossad agents and community leaders in contact with them, and also between the headquarters in Palestine and Europe. Schind and Zameret traveled where this was still possible in an effort to locate ships owned by the Mossad or negotiated with ship agents and middlemen to purchase other ships in order to resume the immigration to Palestine. Schind maintained communication with the American Jewish Joint Distribution Committee (JDC) in Europe, and Pino Ginsburg was the contact person for various Nazi agents who aided Jewish immigration before the war began. Other Mossad people also occasionally met with German officials in the first months of the war in an effort to rescue Jews from Germany and Austria and to ferry them out of Europe.[29]

With great effort, the Mossad managed to dispatch two ships from Europe at the start of the war. The *Hilda*, launched in January 1940 from Belchik on the border of Romania and Bulgaria, with 728 refugees on board, was the product of pre-war planning and work. The *Darian* sailed from Constanta in February 1941 with 800 refugees on board and docked in Haifa on 19 March.[30] Following this, during the first four years of the war, no Mossad ship left a European port with the exception of a few small boats from Romania in spring 1944. It was not the blocking of sea routes that halted the enterprise (ships continued to ply some Black Sea and Mediterranean routes) or the inability to move Jewish refugees along the roads to the Mediterranean ports still open to traffic. Rather, it was the changed attitude toward the rescue mission within leadership circles in Palestine. The retreat of the political leadership from its policies of immigration as soon as World War II broke out was what stopped, at least during the war years, the Mossad's attempts to launch refugee ships from the continent. Ben-Gurion replaced "militant immigration" with what he called "militant Zionism," a movement intended to fortify and consolidate the Zionist movement and settlement in Palestine.[31] Just as the original clandestine immigration campaign was launched as a product of internal political interests of the Yishuv in late 1937 and early 1938, it was halted when the Jewish Diaspora needed it most because of attitudes within the Yishuv. In a conversation with Moshe Shertok on whether demands should be made on the British to allow the entry of Jewish refugees who held immigration certificates issued before the war, Ben-Gurion said, "Our political future is more important than saving 2,900 Jews." "He [Ben-Gurion] was willing to give them up," wrote Shertok in his diary on 13 November 1939.[32] In these and other words, Ben-Gurion articulated the fateful equation that posed the grand political vision of a Jewish state against rescue efforts that, even in the best of circumstances, could be but marginal. From then on, the political future of the Jews in Palestine topped Ben-Gurion's list of priorities, and, because of his dominance and power in the Yishuv, determined the limits of the rescue efforts throughout the war. Thus, the Mossad agents in late 1939 and 1940, whether in Istanbul or Geneva, with their meager resources and in isolation from their home in Palestine, for which the catastrophe in Europe was distant and incomprehensible, were virtually powerless with their pathetically small rescue efforts in the face of the enormous tragedy. What Moshe Averbuch, one of the Mossad leaders, wrote to Eliahu Golomb, head of the Haganah, in December 1939 became true of the Mossad activities in general throughout the war: "The truth is that we have been failing miserably ever since the war erupted."[33]

For lack of action, the war years were an incubation period for preparing the organizational infrastructure for the post-war days, although no one knew for sure whether the Mossad would resume operations when the war was over. Most Mossad activists spent 1941–44 in Palestine at their homes, mostly in kibbutzim, except for various missions to Istanbul or Egypt by some of them.[34] Only a thin organizational skeleton remained active. An administrative officer operating under the cover of a Tnuvah Dairies Cooperative employee kept open the office in the Executive House of the Histadrut (room 17) and performed administrative tasks. Ruth Klieger, then the only woman active in the Mossad leadership, was assigned to negotiate with institutions in Palestine and abroad; Yosef Barpal was designated as her advisor, and Zvi Yehieli wandered between Palestine and Istanbul and then went to Egypt to manage the operation of parachuting into occupied Europe.[35] The Mossad diaries from the years 1943–44 document extensive activity around this mission of a tiny group of volunteers under the joint command of the Mossad and the British. In January 1943 the Palmach inaugurated its first course to prepare a naval force for future Mossad activity. In late 1943 the naval force of the Palmach, no longer under the exclusive control of the Kibbutz, was formally declared a permanent division. In April 1945 the Palmach naval company "Palyam" was established.[36] The logistics, training, and budget for the course were borne jointly by the Palmach and the Mossad, with the Palmach, in effect, placed at the service of the Mossad.

The issue of the relationship between the two organizations, the Mossad and the Palmach, was raised at that point during the war and was an offshoot—like the relationship between the Mossad and the Kibbutz—of the larger struggle for control of the Zionist community's resources in the context of the political and ideological contention within the Labor movement. During the war years, with Mossad activity at a standstill, the struggle over the Palmach—born in 1941 out of criticism of Haganah methods as too docile—became the key issue in the political and party dissension. The Palmach was then completely identified with the Kibbutz. All senior staff officers of the Palmach, except for the treasurer, were members of the Kibbutz. In 1942 members of the majority in Mapai claimed that the Kibbutz was exploiting both its control over the security apparatus and the paralysis within the Mapai party to operate independently on security issues.[37] Saving the party, said Ben-Gurion in an informal discussion in early October 1942, "calls for power"—that is, control over the tools of power—and therefore, "one should be wary of the Kibbutz which wants to hold the reins of power."[38]

The scope of the Jewish catastrophe in Europe was becoming clear in Palestine. Ben-Gurion himself, who had recently returned from a lengthy stay in the United States, had heard the news and knew the dimensions of the destruction even earlier. Just as he had been able in the party's Central Committee in December 1938, with *Kristallnacht* fresh in their minds, to talk about the situation in the party branch in Tel Aviv while asking forgiveness for his preoccupation with "petty" party matters during such a difficult time for the Jewish people, Ben-Gurion and other Labor leaders found the time and energy in the fall of 1942 for their intraparty squabbles and viewed "saving the party" and local political gains as the most urgent issues.[39] The Labor movement conference at Kefar Vitkin, which supposedly had done away with party factions, was perceived in the Kibbutz circles as a declaration of war. "We must cease to feel embarrassed, for the war has just started," it was said in a Kibbutz activists meeting. In reaction, the decision was made "not to yield the party any position we hold."[40] As it happened, with that conference and the decision to disband the various factions within Mapai, began the process of strengthening the central leadership of the party; the Kibbutz, which had boycotted the party institutions, gradually diminished in power, its political influence dissipating,[41] and its initiatives regarding the combat forces of the Palmach and youth in general declining.[42] In practice, the departure of the Kibbutz from center stage, which begun in late 1942, eased the way for Ben-Gurion to establish his status as the leader and his Mapai associates as the ruling elite of the state-in-the-making.

Cooptation and Patronage

Following a series of meetings of senior Mossad people in late 1944 and January 1945, and at the request of the Mossad commander, an outline of the group's organizational structure was drawn up, with suggestions for improvements and a plan for the deployment of Mossad agents abroad at the close of the war. To the organizational chart were added the following comments: "It is urgent to send a key person to the United States; to place someone in charge of all matters concerning North Africa, Egypt, and the Orient; to send another five operatives to Italy [two Mossad people were already operating there] in order to expedite penetration into France, Belgium, Holland, and Yugoslavia [there was already a senior Mossad agent in Romania, and three were operating from Istanbul]." Another suggestion stressed the need to deploy fifty agents in Europe, citing the number for each country, and twenty-one in Asia—twelve from Palestine and nine locals.[43] At the end of 1944 the Mossad began to search for candidates for its missions abroad and recruit additional people for its ranks of operatives. The principle derived from the prosopographic concept, in which an organization expands by reproducing its profile again and again in order to perpetuate itself and tighten internal bonds, was enacted classically in the Mossad's recruitment of new members. The political, social, economic, and even personal-familial web of connections that bonded the agents within the organization also drove the pattern of recruitment. The Mossad, which had always drawn its members from those close to the dominant political circles in the Zionist community, and which relied on a human network that was politically and operationally trustworthy, cast its net over people who were formed in the same school of life. Of the twelve agents recruited by the Mossad in late 1944, eleven were current kibbutz members and the other a former kibbutznik. Those recruited were known to Mossad leaders or personally recommended by others known to Mossad members. All were born in Europe and were graduates of the Zionist pioneer youth movements there, knew European languages, and, in their thirties, had already acquired some public service experience either in the Labor movement's educational forums, economic activity, or operations. Head of the Mossad Shaul Meirov talked with most of them before their recruitment and before each signed on as "ready for the mission."[44] What Yonatan Shapira wrote about Mapai's mechanism for dominating the foci of power in Palestine—the recruitment of those belonging to the same generational cohort and social circles for key organizational positions, so that the party could strengthen and reinforce itself—applied to the screening and recruitment of new Mossad agents. Through these methods of "cooptation and patronage," the ruling elite ensured control over expansion and turnover in its ranks.[45]

The recruitment of Ada Sereni to the Mossad was not exceptional in this sense, but it added new dimensions and was emotionally charged, as the relations between her and Mossad leaders would be in future joint work. Her recruitment cannot be treated separately from the remarkable and tragic mission of Enzo Sereni, a legendary figure and member of the Mossad. In October 1944, half a year before Meirov met with Ada Sereni to ask her to join "our institution,"[46] Meirov and Zvi Yehieli had tried, like all the Labor movement leaders in Palestine, to dissuade Ada's husband, Enzo, from parachuting into occupied Europe. He was too old, they argued, too important, and too dear to the movement and to the country. In response, Sereni announced that if he were forced for administrative reasons to rescind his decision to parachute and compelled to return to Palestine, "that will be the end of all ties between us." The opposition retreated. About a week prior to his blind night jump somewhere over northern Italy, Enzo Sereni wrote a generous and wonderful letter to his friends in the Mossad, as only he knew how: "I want you to know that the months I worked with you were among the happiest in my life. I knew that I was among my people, working for my people, and engaged in holy work. I ask your forgiveness for my rashness, my temperament, all my mistakes. I go—I am certain—in your name also, and I shall try not to sully our name and to accomplish our work under all conditions. If I do not return, shalom to you all."[47]

When Meirov first proposed to Ada Sereni that she join the Mossad, Enzo's fate was not yet known, and perhaps this was before his murder at Dachau, which was disclosed only months later. Ada herself needed no recommendation. In a community as small as the Yishuv, everybody knew everybody else. Certainly among closed circles of the elites of this community, being the wife of Enzo was recommendation enough. Ada Sereni, however, was more than that. A kibbutz member for eighteen years, she had just joined the kibbutz secretariat and was put in charge of the kibbutz industry. Furthermore, she had never been just Sereni's wife; she had always held her own opinions, was impressively articulate, and, like her husband, had belonged to the aristocracy of the Italian community in Palestine. Now, in late 1944, approaching the age of forty and her three children grown, she could get away and become an agent herself. Perhaps the guilt-stricken Meirov had thought of allowing her to go to Europe to be nearer to the area where her husband had disappeared, to help in the search for him. Above all, however, the Mossad was in need of people like her. Italy would become a key link in the Mossad's operations, and Meirov wanted the best people there. Only seven months later, at the end of the war, when word did not arrive from Enzo, did Ada Sereni decide to join the Mossad in Italy. Less than two years later Sereni's two daughters, Hannah and Hagar, members of the Palmach, were also recruited by the Mossad.

The spring and summer of 1945 saw a massive dispatch of agents to Europe. Several senior Mossad personnel were already positioned in key locations. Averbuch had been in Bucharest since October 1944; Ruth Klieger and David Shaltiel were in France; Ehud Avriel was in Turkey; Shmarya Zameret was making his way, together with Ada Sereni, to Italy, where Yehuda Arazi was already in place; Yani Avidov was in Egypt; and Levi Schwartz in Greece.[48] Three of the former parachutists to Romania were sent back there to help Averbuch in his work.[49] Because the sea routes from Romania were still blockaded, however, and thousands of refugees had begun to gather in Italy, the latter became the main country of embarkation. Until 29 July more than ten thousand refugees had reached that country, with "thousands more on the way," as reported by Meirov to Ben-Gurion in late July 1945 at the historic Zionist conference in London,[50] the first after the war. In mid-September 1945, Pino Ginsburg left Haifa on his way to Italy, Portugal, and France, from where he would head to Switzerland to coordinate all the Mossad's financial activity in Europe.[51] On the *Pietro*, the second ship to sail from Italy after the war and which was now returning to Europe, another nine Mossad operatives were dispatched—one to Austria, one to Hungary, three to Poland, and four Palmach people—three naval officers and a communications expert.[52] In the fall of 1945 Ze'ev Schind left for the United States to do fundraising, especially from the JDC, with which he had had close contact all through the war years, and to procure ships; by early 1946 he had already settled into the work and was about to close his first deal for the two largest ships yet to be sailed by the Mossad. By October 1945 dozens of Mossad agents were stationed in Europe,[53] moving thousands of uprooted, downtrodden, homeless Jews across the continent and beginning the task of transferring them, bit by bit, to the shores of Palestine. It was therefore the Mossad that was on Ben-Gurion's mind when he decided, after his visits to the DP camps in Germany in October–November 1945, not to return to Palestine but to stay for a while in western Europe to coordinate a joint effort for moving tens of thousands of Jewish Holocaust survivors to Palestine. In those camps he discovered, by his own account, the unique political potential with which he could found a state—Jewish refugees. The agreement he reached with the senior JDC representative in Europe about covering half the cost of the Mossad activities raised this operation to an unprecedented level (see Chapter 6).

Thus, in the early months of 1946 the Mossad infrastructure was in place in Europe and began to step up its activity, as reflected in the number of sailings and passengers on the ships. In April 1946 the Mossad head arrived in Paris to be closer to his people and to the action.[54] Geneva, home base for Pino Ginsburg, treasurer of the Mossad's European branches, Aryan-looking and a diplomat by nature, became the communications center of all European operations. The expansion of the Mossad, its organizational consolidation during those months, and the unified front presented by its members against outside attempts to divide them and take control all mark the Mossad as a full-fledged organization. It provided its members with incentives to win and maintain their loyalty for the long haul, it had an efficient system of internal communications, it had the means to ensure that its efforts were directed toward achieving its aims, and it adapted itself to changing circumstances to protect its autonomy and freedom of action. These conditions—incentive, communications, supervision, and self-protection—commonly regarded as ensuring the effectiveness of an organization, were fostered by the special character of the Mossad as an organization, the unique brand of its activities, and its leaders. The incentive was enhanced by the high level of socialization within the group and by the prestige and privileges bestowed upon its members—not necessarily in monetary terms, but by virtue of belonging to an exclusive and secret organization considered to be the vanguard of the Zionist national struggle.

Difficult Wedding

The high level of cohesiveness within the Mossad leadership, except for the occasional refusal of the leaders of the Italian delegation to toe the line set by the commander, and the flexibility in administration and command eased the difficult wedding of the Mossad with the Palmach, resulting in the relatively uncomplicated and rapid absorption, especially during 1946, of dozens of Palmach personnel at all levels of operation. These young people, some under age twenty,

were recruited to the Mossad and served as deck hands, ship commanders, security personnel for the convoys, communications experts, drivers, instructors at the transit camps near the harbors, and other trades
needed for the preparation of the ships and odd jobs assigned by the
Mossad. In Italy alone there were forty-five Palmach men and women
by the end of 1947.[55] In France and, temporarily, in Romania—other
key bases of embarkation for the Mossad—large groups of Palmach
members were also stationed. The clandestine immigration and the operations entailed by it became the most important enterprise of the
Palmach in the post-war years[56]—in fact, since its founding in 1941.

For that very reason, however, and since no other outlets existed for
the Palmach's thirst for action, the match between the two organizations was not natural. Formally, the Palmach was under the command
of the Mossad, but in reality it was hard for the Palmach people to accept the authority of the Mossad, especially that of the middle-level operations personnel recruited after the war who were their direct supervisors. The senior Palmach command not only worked to undermine
the authority of the Mossad, but even encouraged the young Palmach
recruits to remain separate, to preserve their organizational framework,
and to accept direct orders from the Palmach command only while demanding more and more autonomy. Palmach commander Yigal Allon
called the Palmach-Mossad relationship "joint ownership" and spoke
explicitly of the "lack of clarity of authority" and "duality of framework
and administration."[57] During the three years of joint activity, especially the most intense period of 1946–47, Allon tried to create a command within a command inside the Mossad and to assign to Palmach
personnel involved in immigration work their own commanding officer, to whom they would answer directly. Taking their cue from the
upper echelon, Palmach rank and file engaged in many clashes with the
Mossad. The wedding of the Mossad and the Palmach not only led to
inter-generational clashes—the Palmach people, in some cases, were
the children of the Mossad leaders—but conflicts related to the political and cultural distance between these bodies erupted as well.
Whereas the Mossad activists were mature family people, somewhat
rooted in Diaspora manners and culture, old-fashioned in work methods, and overly cautious, the Palmach were perceived as "the paragon
of Jewish youth in the Land of Israel and the crowning glory of the
Haganah."[58] The youth and birthplace of the Palmach members were
perceived to have intrinsic value. As written in the *Palmach Newsletter*,

"Those born in Eretz-Israel are different: Perhaps they could be viewed as impertinent, superficial, empty-headed. But ingrained in them are the freedom of the mountains in the land and the heat of its sun. And behold them here, bearing themselves proudly and walking tall, untouched by fear of the ruling foreigner. They long for the true expression of the power within them . . . two feet planted in this earth and head erect."[59] From its founding, the Palmach reality of life was dull and its operations sparse while the aspirations and fantasies of the group were grand; this gap nurtured a compensating spirit and a supercilious, separatist culture of an elite unit. "The Palmach pride [as opposed to arrogance] stems from its 'family ties,'" said Allon, explaining the Palmach spirit.[60] Against the horse trading and administrative work done by the Mossad leaders—political machinations, fundraising, ship purchasing, bookkeeping—lacking glory and generally done in isolation and behind the scenes, the Palmach juxtaposed its "esprit de corps," the ethos of "the group," the "camaraderie" that evolved beside the campfire in the new land, its communal values, the new Israeli-born audacity, and the myth of "bearing arms," even though these arms were often no more than sticks.[61]

The question of bearing arms in the context of the clandestine immigration—that is, resistance on the ships—was destined to create friction between the Mossad and the Palmach. The Palmach commander questioned the Mossad's stance concerning resistance on the refugee ships. Of the passive resistance organized by Yehuda Arazi in La Spezia, Allon said, "It was [at first] viewed bitterly by the Palmach ranks as a *Diaspora* phenomenon, for the heart wanted to strike back at those who treated us cruelly" [emphasis added].[62] Allon wanted to give the Mossad ships a "fighting character" and spoke of "the military aspect of the clandestine immigration." In his diary Ben-Gurion wrote, "The 'navyists' hate the Mossad" and reported a conversation he had with the Palmach company commanders, who demanded that the immigration campaign be taken from the Mossad and given to the Palmach. "Why is there no open resistance to the deportation of refugees? Why is the scale of the campaign so small? Why?"[63]

The decision to sabotage the deportation ship *Empire Rival*, which carried the *Exodus* refugees from French shores to Hamburg, as a token of resistance was made jointly by Palmach people on the ship and in France. The Mossad agents on shore opposed the plan, and the Mossad commander gave explicit orders not to sabotage the ship. He was not so concerned with the risk to innocent victims—the bomb was to be activated after the disembarkation of the passengers—but that such an act of sabotage could ruin the Mossad's relations with the French and thus endanger the entire Mossad enterprise.[64] Just as there was no consensus about the issue of active resistance on the ships within the Mossad and other concerned institutions, Palmach people also did not always agree among themselves and with their commanders. Decisions were made on a case-by-case basis and were contingent primarily upon the temperament and inclination of those involved. While some organized resistance at almost any price, others calculated the cost and benefit, especially with regard to victims. With the deportation of both the *Catriel Yafeh* and the *Twenty Three,* orders came from shore to those accompanying the refugees to conceal and transfer explosives on the bodies of women refugee passengers. This appalling order was carried out, and a bomb was detonated on one deportation ship. On another the Palmach agent was deterred by the fear of sabotaging a vessel with passengers on board.[65] Eliezer Klein, the much-praised commander of the *Catriel Yafeh,* was determined to carry out the sabotage, notwithstanding the victims. "A situation might arise in which a significant number of victims cannot be avoided," he noted, asking his shore contact to define a reasonable number of victims and "the limits of the operation."[66] Those who sailed with the ship *La Negev* decided to end the refugees' fight on board after thirty minutes of dodging British water jets and "submachine guns and revolvers (and live bullets)" because they wanted to prevent "more victims . . . the people were feeble and exhausted." By the time they disembarked in Cyprus, despite the orders for sabotage there, too, they balked at "arousing the people to resistance, because we did not see any value to it."[67]

Fighting on the ships had value as propaganda, as Zionist indoctrination, and to relieve frustration, "for the heart wanted to strike back at those who treated us cruelly," in the words of the Palmach commander. It also, primarily, had domestic political value. The more significance resistance was given in the constellation of factors that composed the clandestine immigration campaign, the greater the importance of the Palmach among the organizations running this key Zionist endeavor. This was the area in which the Palmach fighters could display their excellence, and certainly their superiority over the Mossad. The conflict over resistance was thus a battle for power and control, for positioning in the Zionist struggle and the future retelling of this undertaking. No attempt was made to conceal the arrogation of as many aspects as possible of the immigration campaign, or to inflate and embellish those aspects already handled by the Palmach. "Officially, the Palmach General Staff had no authority over the Mossad. Its one and only realm of authority was the military aspect of the clandestine immigration, that is, directing evasive action and resistance to the deportations, disembarkation, and accompaniment of the passengers, and sabotage of hostile sea vessels. But because the Palmach played a major role in the work itself, in practice it reached a level of influence and authority in the clandestine immigration operation as a whole," acknowledged the Palmach commander.[68] The Palmach therefore made a vigorous effort not just to expand its authority but to continuously instill in its people a sense of the importance and breadth of their activity, and to immortalize it. The "nights of disembarkation" on the shores of Palestine, clearly the turf of the Palmach, and the carrying of Diaspora Jews on the shoulders of Palmach young people, though a rare occurrence, thus became the symbols most strongly associated with the clandestine immigration, its grand story. This was so even though the attempts to circumvent the British naval blockade off the coast of Palestine not only failed, but were not even the main goal of the organized immigration. Out of sixty-four ships sent by the Mossad to Palestine in 1945–48, only thirteen, all of them small, managed to reach shore and discharge their passengers—a total of 2,500 people, constituting only 3.5 percent of the seventy thousand dispatched by the Mossad in its ships.[69] Nevertheless, these nights were immortalized in prose and poetry, pamphlets and speeches, and were presented as the most immediate, direct, and symbolic encounter between the Diaspora and Eretz Israel, well beyond their actual importance. Poets and writers such as Nathan Alterman, Yitzhak Sadeh, Hayim Guri, Hayim Hefer, and Zerubavel Gilead did their share to create the mythology of the nights of disembarkation, to glorify "bearing their nation on their shoulders," thereby deflecting attention from the true heroes of the immigration campaign—the refugees themselves and the ordinary people of the Mossad.[70]

Horizontal Hierarchy

In the pyramidal structure of the Mossad in its heyday, Palmach personnel represented the lowest, widest base of workers. At the middle, narrower level was the operational bureaucracy of the Mossad, drawn primarily from the new Mossad recruits, who mediated between the leadership and the rank and file. A survey of the Mossad leadership is now in order, since even after the organization became large and complex, encompassing hundreds of workers managing enormous resources and moving masses of people, it preserved the egalitarian, democratic spirit of its leadership under the principle "obey your peers, command your peers, and only peers are leaders."[71] The command hierarchy of the Mossad, especially within its leadership, was horizontal rather than vertical in its decision making and dissemination, and also multidirectional—not just from the center to the periphery, but also from the periphery (the various stations) inward. In an internal discussion of Mossad and Kibbutz leaders, the Mossad head admitted that "the functions of the center are limited. The work is done by the people in the field, on shore, and under their authority. The center approves the general plan, provides money, arranges for technicians and for the initiative. The center shifts and should be on site."[72] Mossad stations and agents were widely dispersed; in 1946–47 the Mossad had people in almost every European country as well as North America, South America, northern Africa, and some countries in Asia, sometimes one or two people at each site. The nature of the work and the distinctive circumstances at each location demanded maximum independence and discretionary decision making by the station heads. The station heads had a common character, background, and social and political culture and, except for Arazi and Sereni in Italy, were veterans of the Mossad and comrades-in-arms before the war. All these factors, plus the unique leadership style imparted by Shaul Meirov, shaped a flat hierarchy in the Mossad, a kind of collective leadership whose commander was the first among equals. The term "group of peers" can thus be applied to the Mossad leadership, referring to a community whose members have a common background in terms of age, origin, and cultural and social experience, enabling them to forge long-lasting social ties.

The Mossad leadership after the war was homogeneous in many respects, above all age. At the close of the war, when the Mossad again began to fan out, its senior people were all around forty or fifty. Three were born in the previous century: Shaul Meirov in 1899, Yosef Barpal in 1896, and Yehuda Braginsky in 1897. Seven were born in the first decade of the twentieth century: Zvi Yehieli and Ada Sereni in 1905, Moshe Averbuch and Yehuda Arazi in 1907, David Nameri in 1908,

Ze'ev Schind in 1909, and Shmarya Zameret in 1910. Two were born in the early part of the second decade: Pino Ginsburg in 1911 and Ruth Klieger in 1914.[73] Eleven of the dozen were born in Europe (three in Russia, four in Poland, two in Romania, Ada Sereni in Italy, and Pino Ginsburg in Germany), and one was born in the United States. Nine of the twelve immigrated to Palestine during the 1920s and two in the early 1930s. All except for Shaul Meirov, who had come with his family in 1912, were thus members of the Fourth Aliya, which supplied the majority of the secondary serving elites of the Yishuv. At the time the Mossad resumed recruitment at the end of the war, these people were relative veterans in Palestine—with fifteen to twenty years of service, deep roots in Jewish Zionist society, committment to the ethos of the ideological-political movements dominant in the Yishuv, and a record of public service in managing people. Thus, not only were most of the senior Mossad officers (ten of the twelve) imprinted with the stamp of the kibbutz—the most prestigious of the pioneering Zionist groups in Palestine, which functioned as an exclusive social elite in the Yishuv—each was also hewn of the material of which the operatives were made and which shaped its *aristocratie de service*.[74]

Although they had the same age and origin, social and political background, operational experience, personal status, and other attributes, these twelve people differed from each other in various traits. Some were very colorful and others more drab, but all were individualists as well as team players. Courageous in their own ways, all were underground agents who knew how to be loners, sometimes using borrowed identities. They operated by themselves or in pairs in the twilight zone between the safe and the dangerous, the legal and the illegal, their work often bringing them into contact with merchants and dealers at the margins of the underworld. "I can't take it anymore. Oh how I have sunk. The work has forced me into contact with the scum of the earth. Contacts that drive me crazy, obscure my humanity. If you only knew to what depths I have sunk, a nightmare to the point of madness," wrote Shmarya Zameret from Europe to his wife in Palestine.[75] Nobody could resemble the refined Zameret, usually smiling and pleasant, the only American amidst the always-tense group of eastern European Mossad leaders, who quoted English and American poetry in moving letters to his wife, visited museums when he had a spare moment, and through all his years of Mossad work kept a diary in which he drew sensitive profiles of his comrades-in-arms.[76]

A brief look at the biographies of some of these operatives provides insight into the functioning of the Mossad leadership during these years and a deeper understanding of the ethos of the society that sent them on their mission. According to Lewis Namier, it is through the biographies of individuals who are not necessarily "great men" but secondary figures of history—ordinary people, those not in the spotlight, and about whom there is usually little documentary evidence—that the historian gains insight into the past.[77] Does the top echelon of the Mossad fit the definition of ordinary people? How does one define ordinary people? One way is to take Burckhardt's definition of "great men"—those "who are all that we are not"[78]—and turn it upside down: ordinary people are like us. According to this definition, the Mossad activists may indeed be seen as ordinary people who acted in extraordinary circumstances, which made them extraordinary.

Zvi Yehieli, for example, a senior operative in the Mossad when it was still an embryonic group of Kibbutz members, is one of those ordinary people seen by Namier as makers of history. With all that was special about him, he was a prototype of the Mossad operative. He was born in Romania (Bukovina) in 1905 to a family of merchants. He graduated high school, immigrated to Palestine in 1925, and joined a kibbutz, where he worked with the cows. By the time he was first drafted into the clandestine immigration in early 1938 he was a father and family man.[79] Yehieli was a member of the Haganah and spoke Hebrew, Romanian, Yiddish, German, and English—prerequisites for working in the Mossad. His first mission was to Vienna to coordinate the Zionist youth movement. A short time later he joined the agents in Athens who were trying to expand immigration from there.[80] On the eve of World War II Yehieli worked with Braginsky and Schind, moving between Austria, Yugoslavia, Greece, France, and England, involved primarily in matters regarding ships and money.[81] From then on he served almost exclusively with the Mossad. On 20 November 1939 he went to Geneva after the main operatives left Europe at the outbreak of the war, and never ceased in his efforts to save Jews—not just through immigration to Palestine, but by transferring money to Jewish communities, maintaining contact with them, and negotiating with Nazi agents to extricate Jews from the occupied countries.[82] After his return to Palestine in late 1940, Yehieli alternated between Istanbul and Mossad headquarters in Palestine. In the years 1943–44 he coordinated in Cairo and Palestine the Mossad's parachute missions into occupied Europe.

He was a soft-spoken, tight-lipped, and refined man, whose immediate family were not even aware of his doings other than that they were on behalf of the Haganah.[83] A negotiator by nature, Yehieli was a moderate and was meticulous in his reports. His comprehensive accounts of his activities and those of his comrades in Europe from September 1939 to the end of 1940 are trustworthy, scrupulous, and free of hyperbole. They indicate the precise boundaries of rescue operations and the aid capability of those from Palestine. He was a kind of Jewish-Palestinian version of Smiley, John Le Carré's fatigued hero—of average height, round-faced, soft-spoken, warm, with tired eyes behind spectacles. "The Jews are being led to slaughter in numbers that approach catastrophic proportion . . . every day is too late . . . and I look at Zvi Yehieli—this is our local barometer [in Cairo, the launching site of the parachutists], and behind his glasses I discern worry and sadness in his weary eyes. Although to the outside he seems quiet and relaxed, cautious and reassuring, you feel the storm churning inside," wrote one of the younger parachutists who worked with Yehieli.[84]

Although he was no clone, the biography of Moshe Averbuch is almost a carbon copy of Yehieli's. Both were quiet pillars of Mossad leadership, modest almost to the point of anonymity, people of a kind without which no organization can exist. Averbuch was two years younger than Yehieli, had immigrated to Palestine two years later, and was recruited to the Mossad several months after Yehieli's enlistment (in late 1938). The two worked together a great deal, especially prior to and early in the war.[85] Like Yehieli, Averbuch was recruited for the clandestine immigration campaign from his kibbutz (Kefar Giladi), and for ten years, except for short visits, his family and friends almost never saw him. He served in Austria, faced Eichmann alone in Vienna as war loomed (after the *Anschluss*) in an effort to get Jews out of Europe, moved throughout the continent alone or with his partner Yehieli, dealt with ship owners, raised funds, maintained ties with the Jewish communities, fought with headquarters in Palestine, served in Istanbul, operated in Iran under a false name for about a year, and in the fall of 1944 was sent to Romania, from where—and from eastern Europe in general—he directed the Mossad's largest operations. The style of operation and cooperation of the two, with their comrades and with each other, was similar: moderate, judicious, and to the point, generally free of political or partisan interests that were irrelevant to rescue or immigration.[86]

David (Davidka) Nameri was, in a sense, the opposite of these two. The story of his life is like a colorful Zionist poster that encompasses all the mythologies pertaining to Palestine in his day. He was the most rooted in Palestine of all the Mossad leadership—colorful, charismatic, unforgettable by those who met him; tall, lean, swarthy, with a deep, hoarse voice. He was a natural leader of large organizational operations. Nameri was born in 1908 in the town of Skidel in Belorussia, which was annexed after World War I to independent Poland. His Zionist father was a member of the independent Haganah there, and Nameri graduated from a Hebrew high school. In 1926 at the age of eighteen Nameri immigrated to Palestine and worked as a construction laborer in Haifa. He then joined the Kibbutz brigade near Acre and worked at drying out the swamps. A year later he moved with his group to kibbutz Gesher, worked at the electric power plant in Naharayim on the Jordan River, and finally settled in kibbutz Ashdot Ya'akov in 1934. That year he participated in a Haganah course for commanders of settlements. In early 1938 Nameri organized the first disembarkation of the passengers of the first clandestine boat, *Poseidon,* and also participated in a course for division commanders of the Haganah. Between 1936 and 1939 he was in charge of the Stockade and Watchtower campaign, directing the establishment of dozens of new, instant settlements. In short, he was always being called to missions at hand, and he always came. "How did I get to 'Stockade and Watchtower'? I was in Naharayim. I was a member of the Gesher group. I knew the [Jezreel] Valley. I knew many of those from the settlements. I was also a member of the Haganah. In short, they knew they could call on me and that I'd come."[87]

For the clandestine immigration campaign, they also called on him and he did the job. Nameri's task until 1947, when he went to the United States to represent the Mossad in place of Ze'ev Schind,[88] was to organize the reception of the clandestine ships from the moment they landed. Before the end of World War II and later, he was responsible for smuggling many people out of Haifa using forged passports or by other means. He thus smuggled out many Mossad agents, several Yishuv leaders, and the Mossad chief himself to Paris.[89] Unlike his Mossad colleagues, Nameri spent most of his years of activism in Palestine: "He would disappear for a day or two and then reappear just as suddenly. Even when he returned at midday, he always wore work clothes as if nothing had happened. Even if he was up the previous night for some action, he would show up for work the next day full of energy, as was his way, and the kibbutz would know: Davidka's back."[90] Thus, he "moved from job to job, from scene to scene, to wherever the main battle was then being waged," said Yigal Allon.[91] After the founding of the Palmach, Nameri was made a member of its general staff of three. In organizational terms, it was he who built the Palmach and "bore it on his shoulders."[92] He was in charge of training for special jobs and a liaison with the British division for special actions, with which the Palmach cooperated in the face of the threat of Nazi invasion of Palestine. In January 1943, in cooperation with the Mossad, he set up the first training course for the Palmach naval force, wrote the "Ten Commandments" of the Palmach sailor, and generally sought to shape Palmach young people in his image. Until 1948 he served as a bridge—a problematic yet vital bridge—between the Palmach and the Mossad and pushed for greater radicalism of Mossad operations, especially encouraging active resistance by the refugees on the deportation ships to Cyprus from August 1946—apparently because, working mainly in Palestine, he had not witnessed the devastation of the Holocaust in Europe and had not been in direct contact with its weary survivors.

The Fox and the Hedgehog

The inclusion boundaries of this exclusive and relatively closed organization and the limits of tolerance and control of the Mossad head were put to the test almost daily by Yehuda Arazi. For these reasons, and because it sheds light on the personality and leadership of Shaul Meirov, the Mossad commander, I return briefly to Arazi. In his age, place of birth, background, and total devotion to the Zionist community in Palestine, which sent him on his mission, Arazi conformed to the collective profile of the main Mossad group, but he was also their diametrical opposite, especially in relation to Shaul Meirov. Arazi was born to a bourgeois family in Lodz in 1907, and, unlike his colleagues, he remained an avowed bourgeois. His true loyalty was to Eliahu Golomb, who headed the Haganah, and to what Golomb represented. From the moment of his recruitment in 1926 to the Mandatory police force as a representative of the Haganah, Arazi was dedicated to the Zionist community's security issues. From 1936 to 1939 he worked on weapons acquisition for the Haganah in Europe, especially in Poland, as Golomb's personal envoy where he set up a munitions factory.[93] The matériel and machines for the manufacture of guns and bullets, as well as four small planes, which he purchased and sent to Palestine in the late 1930s, changed the face of the Haganah, according to its leadership.[94] Just before the outbreak of World War II he attended the Zionist Congress in Geneva at Golomb's request, where he received a budget of £40,000 to buy weapons. He did not wait for the final fall of the gavel. "The smell of war was in the air," and he returned to Poland, reaching Warsaw the day before the war broke out. There he sat "between bombs" with the young leaders of the Zionist pioneer movements—he himself had never been a party member—and discussed their fate and future work. He left Poland the day the government fled from Warsaw, and after a wild car drive through Romania, Yugoslavia, and Italy he reached Paris, where he was received by the Mossad people still there.

Arazi often walked on the edge, risking his life and sometimes the lives of others. He was an adventurer, a lover of life, and a hedonist. Into the weapons shipments to Palestine from Poland he would slip some high-quality chocolate and sausages and expensive bottles of liquor.[95] He was never a member of the Histadrut or of the well-placed political party, and he paid a price for that. When his friends were awarded senior posts in the new state apparatus after 1948, becoming members of the constitutive and ruling elite of the state, Arazi turned to private business and was almost forgotten. His rivalry with Meirov dated back to the 1930s and the investigation into the Arlosorov assassination, when Arazi, an officer in the Mandate police, refused to play the role assigned to him by Mapai and forge documents.[96] In the spring of 1945, Arazi was forced on Meirov by Golomb, who sent him personally to Italy. The changes wrought by Arazi immediately upon his arrival in Italy, however, and the dramatic results of his work, made him vital to the Mossad. Rather than fight him or try to prevent him from directing the station, Meirov brought him into his camp by cooptation, and this was the beginning of a reluctant and problematic friendship. "I had serious reservations about whether or not Yehuda Arazi was the right person for the clandestine immigration work . . . and behold he turned out to be an indisputable leader," Meirov later wrote.[97] In Arazi, Meirov probably found all the qualities that he felt lacking in himself: "boldness, an extraordinary sense of orientation, wild imagination, magnificent and varied talents, a man of powerful appetites . . . a dictator, who embodied in his entire being, actions, and 'tricks' the doctrine of the advantage of the dauntless individual, or the advantage of a small group of dauntless people entirely dedicated to a mission, struggling against a large and mighty, but convoluted, rusty, witless, and inflexible machine."[98]

How, then, could one who so lacked uniqueness and charisma, who was wanting in all the characteristics he saw in Arazi and, to some extent, in other Mossad people—boldness, imagination, impressive talents and powerful appetites, a sense of orientation, and decision-making ability—lead throughout the 1940s an organization that was at the forefront of the Zionist endeavor and be accepted by those who appointed him and those under his command? How did Meirov, who had never directed any operation, who did not inspire followers, who was hidden from view of those he commanded, and who often delayed decisions until "tomorrow,"[99] become an undisputed authority figure? Michel de Certeau speaks of the power and presence of the absent personality, who delimits a site of power and attraction by not being there.[100] One of his peers in the Mossad leadership spoke of the mystique in which Meirov shrouded himself and of the information he kept to himself as a means of maintaining power and control. Up to the end of his life, Meirov never broke his silence concerning several matters in the history of the country in which he was involved.[101] On the eve of World War II and just after, when Meirov headed Mossad affairs from Europe, and especially during the flare-up of his chronic glandular disease, he would seclude himself in the hotel room where he lived and hold meetings with a select few. He conveyed his instructions by telephone or through the communication stations of the Mossad, and many Mossad people came to know him only as a bodiless voice.[102] Thus, without extraordinary leadership skills or an array of personal qualities that make for charisma, Meirov's uncontested leadership was the product of a pedigreed personal history of Zionist activism and a reputation from previous work. It was also the result of a network of contacts within the political leadership (especially with Ben-Gurion), family and marriage ties with the "Mayflower families"—Shertok, Golomb, and Hoz—and an unqualified loyalty and devotion to the greater Zionist cause that superseded differences of opinion, "that thing by virtue of which one believes in him . . . because his voice shook when he said 'What have they brought us to?'"[103] By avoiding high-handed, rigid command, and by not forcing his will on subordinates, he both tightened his hold on the Mossad and increased its ability to adapt to changing circumstances. "He will not bring any plan of his own. He will not devise or undertake anything, but he will hear everything, remember everything, and put everything in its place. He will not hinder anything useful nor allow anything harmful. He understands that there is something stronger and more important than his own will—the inevitable course of events, and he can see them and grasp their significance, and seeing that significance can refrain from meddling and renounce his personal wish directed to something else."[104] This is what Prince Andrew thought about General Kutuzov. The same may be said of Meirov. Meirov had his own explanation for his style of leadership in the Mossad: "In full awareness, I chose not to intervene in the details of activity of our people on site . . . I was careful to give them all the feeling of space for their initiatives, imagination, and ability to implement. In total clarity, I understood that for this grand enterprise spread across almost the entire face of Europe and the seas, it would be a practical impossibility to manage from one center, one headquarters, and that the 'modest' job of headquarters was to assist, encourage, stimulate, and come up with appropriate resources and people in the field. I would coordinate and intervene in operating details only when there was an absolute need to do so. It was also the job of the center to represent this work to the other Zionist institutions and Jewish bodies, and also to represent those institutions to the enterprise for clandestine immigration."[105]

Meirov belonged to every primary sociological grouping in the Palestinian Zionist community. He was a student in the renowned Herzliya Gymnasium and belonged to the inner circle of its illustrious alumnae. He still lived on a kibbutz and was an officer of the Haganah from its inception. He was well connected through family ties with key people in the areas of settlement, security, and politics. These qualifications made him a natural choice to head the clandestine immigration when this responsibility was removed from the Kibbutz and nationalized in the summer of 1939. He wrapped his past in mythological trappings, transforming every event in his childhood and youth to a portent of future meaning, and this past followed him and gave meaning—in his eyes and the eyes of others—to everything he did. The Mogilev pogrom in 1905, when he was a boy of six, was "etched deep" within his heart. When proto-military drills began in his school in 1910, and wooden rifles were distributed to the pupils, he was excluded from the drills. "I knew in absolute clarity that I was kept out because I was a Jew, and for that reason only."[106] The solution: immigration to Palestine and studies at the prestigious Gymnasium. At the age of sixteen, he sought work near Zikhron Ya'akov. After running for his life, riddled with "shame," from a confrontation with two men, "tall and dark, daggers tucked into their belts and long clubs in their hands," he swore "never to be on the road unarmed, if only with a good-sized stick."[107] Later he held his first revolver in his hands, "a major experience in those days."[108] He saw the ill-fated yet much mythicized battle in Tel Hai in 1920, in which his role is veiled, as the event "which shaped the direction of my life," leading him to view "reality in the country in a different light" and placing him in the midst of security issues.[109] As a writer of history—he was one of the editors of the official multivolume history of the Haganah, which shaped generations of young Israelis—he helped transform the story of Tel Hai into a national pedagogy of heroism, advocating the sacrifice of life for the fatherland and the expansion of its borders.[110]

Unlike most of his colleagues in public service and Mossad work, Meirov had immigrated to Palestine as a youth with his entire family. His studies in the Gymnasium in Tel Aviv introduced him to the contacts that he kept all his life and the friends who shaped his world view, most of whom eventually held key positions in the political elite of Palestine and later Israel. These primary connections, which predated his family ties, were able to withstand tests of ideological and political differences and eventually provided a base of political influence.[111] Meirov's political path did not follow the pattern of a young man cut off from his immediate environment and parents' home, struggling against his social surroundings, which characterized most leaders of the Zionist movement and community in Palestine. On the contrary, his parents' home, his schools, and the leadership of this community in the first decades of the century encouraged him to choose the path of national service. He thus missed the sometimes painful experience of independence during adolescence and young manhood and in the early stages of his political work, and he lacked the toughness that marked socialist Zionist leaders who grew up and were educated under more trying conditions.[112] This duality—a dense network of connections that accords political support together with personal "softness" and a certain weakness of character—can, perhaps, explain the type of leadership and political strength of Shaul Meirov, drawn from external rather than internal sources, and which ultimately marked the management style of the Mossad.

However, the man should not be misunderstood. In the course of his long career, he showed that he could bare his fangs. For his involvement in some of the more controversial affairs in the pre-state Israeli history, he neither took responsibility nor expressed regret. Of his role in forging documents during the investigation of the murder of Arlosorov, he later said, "I was one finger in the hand of the incident."[113] After the tragic sinking of the *Patria,* as a result of sabotage by the Haganah, in which more than 260 Jewish refugees drowned, Meirov, who was among those responsible, did not participate in the mea culpa of his colleagues but continued to blame "the enemy," the British: "People like us had no other way to operate," he wrote to one of his subordinates who demanded an explanation. "Despite all the terrible, fierce pain over the victims . . . our political, moral right was drawn from our absolute recognition that we had no other way of fighting the war of immigration and freedom . . . not that we were happy about these methods; we sought to avoid them without surrendering the goal. And when the hostile regime blocked off all other approaches, we were forced into these ways. The responsibility falls on the enemy regime, despicable and cruel, and on its representatives. Clearly the conscience of anyone with a heart cannot be stilled to his dying day, even after all these considerations . . . but we could not deviate from our path without betraying ourselves and our cause."[114] He also knew how to eliminate from the Mossad those in whom he had no interest, those who he believed could upset the harmony of the system or undermine the policies of the organization and his control of it. He was able to do this with iron fists wrapped in velvet gloves. Zvi Yehieli, the least political of the Mossad leaders, left the organization in August 1947 because his actions were being restrained for political reasons. "I want you to know that I am not leaving of my own good will, but circumstances arose that meant, in effect, my being removed from the work," he wrote to the Mapai Executive. The situation in the Mossad, especially at the top, calls for a serious and comprehensive review, he wrote, and the party has no right "to ignore what is happening in the Mossad, coordinator of the most important activity in the Zionist struggle."[115] Arazi and Braginsky also left the Mossad because Meirov did not want them around anymore.

The Mossad apparatus thus "purged" itself of undesirable elements and adjusted itself to the needs of the state-in-the-making. Those who had carried out the clandestine immigration in the field began to depart one by one. Meirov remained. If Isaiah Berlin's categories of hedgehogs and foxes are applicable to people of action, Shaul Meirov was a hedgehog, "a man who knows one big thing," a man of one principle, one faith, and one cause, all of whose deeds, in every circumstance, were focused on realization of that big thing.[116] He also viewed himself in that way: "a man of one task. I engaged in several tasks that were actually one task," he said.[117] Indeed, of all the attributes that lent to his stature, the "hedgehog" quality was one of his greatest sources of strength. Amid that colorful group of foxes who led the Mossad along with him, and whose preoccupation with this campaign was ephemeral because they were called upon to carry out a temporary mission that suited that revolutionary period, this gray security bureaucrat, corporate man, man of one big thing and one faith, was fixed and stable like the system itself in the constituting state.

CHAPTER 6

Vision and Provision

At the end of the war the Mossad agents in Europe found themselves once again using the good offices of the American Jewish Joint Distribution Committee (JDC), particularly its financial resources, to achieve their goals. In return, the more the Mossad expanded the scope of its work, the more the philanthropic Jewish-American organization became involved in operations diametrically opposed to its traditional ventures. This was an alliance of no choice, wonderfully fertile, conceived and developed under extraordinary circumstances between partners with opposing views who were historically wary of each other. Despite the shattering upheaval of the war, the JDC remained true to its basic, generation-old views and adhered to the rules of conduct it had imposed upon itself. The founders and leaders of the JDC continued to perceive their organization as a charitable institution established to help Jews in need throughout the world, its main goal being the "reconstruction of Jewish life" wherever Jews lived—"restoring Jews to their economic position" and retraining "those who cannot return to their former homes."[1] "The JDC makes the basic assumption," wrote its secretary, Moses Leavitt, at the height of the Nazi destruction of European Jews, "that Jews have a right to live in countries of their birth or in countries of their adoption; they have a right, as human beings, to reside there with full rights."[2] As the war drew to a close, the foreboding of the JDC officials in the field grew—they knew that the situation of the Jews in Europe would never return to what it had been and believed that their organization must transform itself profoundly, because that which had been will never be the same.[3] In March 1946, almost a year after the war had ended, with the roads of Europe clogged with hundreds of thousands of Jewish displaced persons who had survived but would never return to their former homes, Moses Leavitt wrote to Dr. Joseph Schwartz that, based on information he had, those returning to their Polish homeland will probably dig in and remain, while the survivors who have lost their families will most likely continue on to Palestine and other destinations.[4]

Even Dr. Schwartz, though well aware of the situation on the European continent, believed (at least until fall 1945) that many of those displaced persons would seek out their former homes. In addition, the mass migration and enormous confusion in the wake of the war constituted a challenge, perhaps too formidable, to the directorate of an organization whose raison d'être and strategies were focused on restoring things and people to their former place.[5] What is more, the JDC defined itself as fundamentally an American institution. The organization and its representatives saw themselves as part and parcel of the American ethos, loyal above all to the American government, especially to the traditional views of the U.S. State Department.[6] Consequently, the JDC openly avoided, to the best of its ability, activity having political implications or involving any political organizations. When the Rescue Commission of the American Jewish Conference of major Jewish organizations convened in 1943 to prepare the post-war Jewish demands, the JDC declined the invitation on the grounds that it would not associate with political organizations.[7] It responded similarly when Dr. Nahum Goldmann, administrative chairman of the World Jewish Congress, offered in early 1945 to set up another forum of Jewish organizations that would coordinate the rescue and rehabilitation efforts after the war.[8] Even when the war ended and the JDC was up to its neck in the illegal operations of the Zionist agents in Europe, Moses Leavitt continued to view himself as the representative of a law-abiding American agency that shunned involvement in Jewish clandestine activity.[9]

Any struggle on behalf of the political rights of Jews was thus, by necessity and definition, beyond the limits of the JDC. This was not just a passive stance toward any Jewish political aspirations—particularly Zionism, the essence of these aspirations—but indicated moral reservations about Jewish nationalism and the concept of a Jewish state. The fundamental difference between this Jewish-American organization and the Zionist movement concerning how to resolve the Jewish question created a continuing turf rivalry between the JDC and the Zionists. This rivalry, which periodically snowballed into open conflict, created a climate of mistrust between the two sides. "There is no way of knowing who will get here first," commented a Jewish soldier from Palestine in refugee-burdened Italy in late 1944, about the fight between the JDC and the Zionists over the bodies and souls of Jewish refugees there, "but whoever arrives first in these countries will take the path that we began."[10] The mistrust reached such proportions that the *Daily Forward,* the Jewish newspaper of New York, published an article during the Holocaust years noting that God should be praised for creating the "*Yahudim*" ("uptown German Jews") of New York, a reference to the founders and leaders of the JDC, for "if the Zionists would have been the leaders of the JDC, the Jews of Europe would not have received a single cent; all the money would have gone for Zionist purposes."[11] Like other non-Zionists on the American scene, the people of the JDC were indeed worried about the rising power of the Zionists in the Jewish world and the crass, no-holds-barred methods they used in their struggle for primacy.

The Zionist camp felt similarly toward the JDC and its policies. JDC work was perceived to be more of a "work of the present" *(Gegenwartsarbeit),* meaning aid and relief here and now, wherever there were Jews in need. As such, the present orientation of the JDC clashed with the future, grand vision of the Zionist movement, for which "the suffering of the Jews" was soil for growth and a source of strength, and which considered future redemption in the Land of Israel and a thorough transformation of the mold of the Jew to be the only solution. "Besides the approximately 600,000 pounds that the Yishuv raised for rescue operations, it conveyed a more important 'supplement' to the Diaspora, of much greater value than the money it raised, and that is the *vision of redemption*" (emphasis added), said Ze'ev Schind, a veteran Mossad activist, at the Ha'Kibbutz Ha'Meuhad Council in September 1944.[12] Reporting on the rescue efforts and immigration operations of the Mossad during the war years, Schind also contrasted the rescue activities of Zionism, suffused with the vision of redemption, with the assistance rendered by the Jews of America during World War I, which was permeated by the spirit of philanthropy and "controlled by petty clerks, lacked any sense of movement, and never knew a vision."[13]

Upon returning from a four-month journey to the liberated countries of Europe in the fall of 1944, the director of the Immigration Department of the Jewish Agency reported to the Agency Executive and to the Mapai Central Committee; this was one of the first comprehensive reports compiled by a Jew from Palestine about the survivors and activities on their behalf in Europe. He had only harsh words for the dangers inherent in the aid rendered by the JDC. "It's hard to describe the demoralization brought on by the relief work of the Joint," he said to the Jewish Agency Executive, "how it affects people . . . getting them used to the dole." To illustrate, Eliahu Dobkin told the story of a German Jew who had been a member of a Zionist pioneering movement and was now a refugee in Lisbon surviving on the JDC allocation. "I'm willing to end my life this way," said the man. "I'll come every two weeks and get the dole."[14] Ben-Gurion sharpened the issue in his own way. In deliberations of the Jewish Agency Executive in early 1945, which revolved around the JDC's work and which also praised the American organization, Ben-Gurion asserted that "all assistance to the Jews of Europe must be given from a Zionist perspective."[15] In meetings of the Rescue Council in September and October 1944, as well as May and October 1945, Ben-Gurion repeatedly insisted that it was not the task of the Jewish Agency to be a relief organization; its only task was to bring Jews to Palestine.[16]

The Jewish tragedy, which was revealed fully only after the war, and the unprecedented suffering of those who survived the destruction not only failed to budge Ben-Gurion from his views, but even entrenched them. After visiting the DP camps in late 1945, Ben-Gurion remarked to a soldier from the Jewish Brigade, who demanded more extensive Zionist work in the camps, that "the Zionist mission is not to save the remnant of Jews in Europe, but to save Palestine for the Jewish people."[17] The efforts of various Jewish philanthropies to provide immediate succor to the Jewish refugees, especially children—to extricate them from the camps and transfer them to foster families or institutions in Britain, France, and Switzerland—were halted at once by Ben-Gurion. When he reached Heidelberg at the end of his tour of the camps in Bavaria, he transmitted telephone instructions to the Jewish Agency representative in London "against removing people from the American zone [of occupation]—not to France, England, or Switzerland. . . . I demanded that the removal of children and adults be stopped . . . unless for purposes of 'aliya,' under instruction of the Jewish Agency."[18] To Zerah Wahrhaftig, a member of the Rescue

Commission of rabbis in the United States, who had also visited the DP camps, Ben-Gurion explained "the extent to which the removal of children from these camps and their temporary lodging in France could weaken the struggle for immigration of all the refugees to Palestine."[19]

Division of Labor

Thus, though entrenched in their opposing views, the two sides knew that in the final analysis they had an identical goal: rescue of the Holocaust survivors. Already in 1944 the Jewish Agency had negotiated to cooperate with the JDC in providing aid to the Jews of Europe, and a kind of division of labor and influence emerged between them.[20] In a meeting of the Executive on 25 February 1945, the Jewish Agency treasurer Eliezer Kaplan reported on the conclusion of negotiations and the seven points on which the sides had agreed.[21] These points related to the open, legal activities of the Jewish Agency. Nothing even hinted at its massive future participation in the clandestine activities of the Mossad. In the spring of 1945 Dr. Joseph Schwartz and Charles Passman, the JDC official in Cairo, told the Mossad agent there that the JDC had no intention of "changing its politics concerning the allocation of travel expenses for *aliya* to Palestine and aid to *hakhsharot* ["trainings," one of the code words used by the Mossad for the illegal sailings] anywhere that these could be arranged."[22] Dr. Schwartz added that in the future there might be "a change concerning *bet* [*aliya bet,* that is, clandestine immigration]. Not at present."[23]

A month later, in a meeting in Paris between Ben-Gurion and Dr. Schwartz, not a word was spoken of the clandestine immigration.[24] At the time, some cooperation, albeit loose and not without problems, already existed between the operatives from Palestine—soldiers of the Jewish Brigade, the first Mossad agents—and representatives of the JDC stationed in Europe. In Italy, the first country in western Europe where the Mossad renewed its activity and where soldiers of the Jewish army units were actively assisting Jewish refugees, the initial meeting with the JDC was filled with recriminations. A soldier from Palestine wrote in June 1944,

As you know, we carried out all the work among the refugees in southern Italy with no help at all from the Joint. We established schools, training courses, shops, and work cooperatives. We set up organizational, economic, and social institutions. And we accomplished all this with our own resources and instruction. When the Joint arrived a month and a half ago, they walked into a ready-made situation. . . . We didn't criticize or settle old scores with them—why the Joint was so late in coming. We accepted them with open arms, despite their lateness. And now that Rome was liberated, there are thousands of Jews in terrible distress. Six weeks have passed since Rome was conquered and the Joint has still not arrived. . . . This isn't new. For years we saw how "nimble" the JDC machine is—we remember this from the previous war—but there's a limit to everything under certain circumstances. . . . It's imperative to demand that Dr. Schwartz and America wire the required moneys, and promise from now on to send people with decision-making authority so that the refugees can be met at once and their needs attended, and not drag at the heels of developments presented to us by these days of liberation.[25]

In October of that year, this attentive soldier had no better words for the JDC. "More than once," he wrote, "we witnessed the heavy Joint machine with a budget of millions not moving properly or being responsive to the misery of the refugees and their appeals. Something is missing at every stage and, in the final analysis, the suffering of the refugee increases."[26] The contacts of the first Mossad agents with that organization in Italy were also difficult, and nothing came of their efforts to elicit its support. Anything related to immigration, Dr. Schwartz had told the Mossad people, was not of primary importance to the JDC. "We barely managed to elicit from them a commitment to work across the German border," said a senior Mossad official later. Their attitude was cynical and "very Jointy," he added.[27] An official of the Diaspora Center, established in Italy in October 1944 to coordinate rescue operations there, following a trip to Austria, attacked the JDC and its representative there with unprecedented harshness, demanding that he be replaced. "There are 8,000 Jews in Vienna. Starvation, and many are dying. In a women's camp there are 600 young women, most infected with sexual diseases. . . . The exodus from Vienna has begun. They were given instructions to go to the DP camps in Germany. . . . The Joint is oblivious and there is actual famine in the Modena and Graz camps. The Joint is totally indifferent."[28] Going beyond charges of personal incompetence and rivalries, these harsh comments reflected fundamental differences in approach and organizational style. Those from Palestine were unfettered by higher organizational and political considerations and were able to act quickly based primarily on local circumstances, improvising and responding according to their own understanding of things. In contrast, the JDC was nourished on a work tradition that was many years old. Its staff functioned according to plans and budgets that were drawn up in advance—clear and rigid rules about what is permissible and what is not. Because the JDC was such a large institution, the pace of adjusting to each location and the start-up of work there was slower than seemed reasonable in the eyes of the soldiers and agents from Palestine.

In August 1945 Charles Passman was appointed by the JDC to head its Mediterranean operations. Passman was closer in spirit to the agents from Palestine, and some of the Zionist impatience and zealousness seems to have clung to him from his years of living there. This appointment presaged a major change concerning the common activities and assistance rendered by the JDC to the Mossad's rescue work and clandestine immigration operations.[29] In February 1946 the Diaspora Center and the JDC reached an agreement on full cooperation in Italy. According to the agreement, the JDC undertook to provide 600 Italian lira to each refugee in the camps, in addition to the allocation from the United Nations Relief and Rehabilitation Administration (UNRRA), and to give financial support to refugees who lived outside the camps. It was also agreed that the training courses and their supervision would be organized by the Diaspora Center, while the JDC would assume financial responsibility for them.[30] Agreement with the center meant, in effect, complete and open cooperation with the Zionist movement and the clandestine immigration, for which Italy at that time was the primary country of embarkation. This transformation in the JDC perception was profound and philosophical, evolving over a period of months. One might pinpoint the beginning of the change in the JDC's view in the role played by Dr. Schwartz in the August 1945 delegation led by American law professor Earl Harrison to investigate the conditions of the displaced persons. Schwartz's involvement in preparing the Harrison memorandum, and the memorandum itself—to which the JDC was committed, as one of its senior people had helped formulate it—were crucial to this shift in the JDC attitude. Funding of the Diaspora Center in Italy was important not just to meet the perceived need but also because it signified that the JDC would stand shoulder to shoulder with Zionist activity, including financing of the Bricha (the underground escape enterprise) throughout Europe. Until the fall of 1945, and even later, though the matter was not fully elucidated, the Bricha also received funding from the Diaspora Center and from the Mossad. Funding for Bricha activities came from Palestine by way of the Mossad and the Jewish Agency, especially the Rescue Commission.[31]

From fall 1945 the JDC began direct funding of the Bricha operations in most places, and bore the brunt of the financial burden almost single-handedly—supplying food, clothing, and shoes for the refugees; transporting them along Bricha routes on JDC vehicles or allowing Bricha vehicles to bear the JDC insignia to facilitate border crossings; preparing the papers required for border control; and providing money for the bribes needed by Bricha agents at difficult border crossings.[32] Not only did the JDC allow the use of its name and organizational resources, but it did not hesitate to put at the disposal of the operatives from Palestine its contacts with officers of the American army and officials in charge of the departments dealing with refugees. These connections opened many doors. One telling incident was reported by Walter (Erich Frank) from Vienna to the Mossad headquarters in Palestine in January 1946: "In mid-November we came to an agreement with the American army (that is, with Stevens who was in charge of the DP division in Vienna, known for his good work in Lisbon, and Dr. Schwartz's friend from the Joint). According to this agreement, we could submit a list of 100 names every day and receive under some terms a collective travel document to Linz. Linz was already beyond the demarcation line in the American zone. There a second transit camp was set up (kleine München) also under the authority of the American army. The camp was less good, but heating, food, and caring were also provided by the Joint. . . . The agreement was reached through intermediaries from the Joint, considered by the army to be a kind of liaison to all the local Jewish bodies."[33] Other reports of Bricha agents at transit points in central Europe, who shouldered the main burden of the migration movement during these months, had only praise for the cooperative efforts of the JDC people, from Dr. Schwartz[34] through the hierarchy of personnel in the organization—American representatives and local workers. About the JDC delegation in Vienna, headed by Dr. Sachs, Efrayim (Erich) Frank wrote, "They are devoted Zionists and diligent workers" who "help us out with anything we ask of them and also do much at their own initiative."[35] In the letter, Frank remarks that the JDC is a "one hundred percent" partner in the Bricha activities and that its powerful influence on the military authorities is a blessing to the clandestine work.[36]

Yitzhak Steiner (Parenta), a Mossad agent and commander of the Bricha central European zone, also reported "excellent" relations with the JDC and good contacts with its people in Prague and Vienna. "Only Hagar [a code name for Hungary]," he wrote to the Mossad headquar-

ters in Palestine, "does not yet understand our work. All the Joint's
American representatives are close to our work and to Zionism in general,
and hence we get very important help from them. In most places the Joint
sees to the food, lodging, and supplies for the journey. . . . They [in
Vienna] are very well connected with the American army who is responsible for the upkeep of the refugees. They are also about to sign an agreement with the army to move our people legally into Bavaria. The Joint
and the Jewish soldiers have been helpful in all this."[37] As noted, in
September 1945 the JDC had already begun to cover most of the Bricha
costs. At first this was an immediate, local response to the pressing needs
of the Zionist agents, and later—following meetings of Dr. Schwartz with
the heads of the Bricha—it became an unwritten agreement to cover all
expenses.[38] Schwartz met with Bricha agents at the sites of action and
helped them on the spot as best he could, but he also tried to introduce
an orderly system and wanted to transfer JDC money through Pino
Ginsburg, the Mossad treasurer in Europe, who was based in Geneva. The
urgent needs, however, and the apparent desire to be independent of the
Mossad's central financial administration, induced the Bricha leaders to
insist that Dr. Schwartz transfer the money directly to them.[39] From headquarters in Palestine, they demanded that a special organizational and financial body be set up "so that not every agent and site would be conspicuously fighting about money matters."[40] Thus, in late 1945 Bricha
agents met in Paris to establish an autonomous organization.[41]

The fall and early winter of 1945 was a period of Zionist organizational
expansion in Europe. It was also a significant time in terms of the deep-
ening involvement of the JDC in the underground activity of the Zionist
agents on the continent. In September 1945 the JDC took a crucial step
toward institutionalizing its problematic, ambiguous relationship with
the organization for clandestine immigration. Departure of the first boat
from Italy and the successful disembarkation of its passengers on the
shores of Palestine seemed to present a solution to the problem of the
displaced persons crowding the temporary camps. This and pressures
from the Mossad led to a JDC decision to provide aid on an ad hoc basis
to transport two thousand people from Europe to Palestine at a cost of
£30–40 per person, without taking any responsibility upon itself. The rationale used by Dr. Schwartz to convince the JDC Executive Committee
to share the cost of "transferring" Jewish refugees to Palestine—that ex-
tricating refugees from Europe would cost the JDC less than maintaining them there and would be a one-time expense—was expressed by

Ben-Gurion shortly after in their late October meeting, following Ben-Gurion's tour of the DP camps. Indeed, this meeting—a series of meetings in Germany and France, to be precise—is another milestone, perhaps the most important one, in the JDC involvement in the Zionist clandestine activities in Europe. After this tour, Ben-Gurion felt that the hour and circumstances were ripe to revive his 1939 idea of "a militant immigration," which had never been implemented because of the outbreak of the war, and use the Holocaust survivors as the main weapon in the struggle. ("I saw that this could be crucial in our political war," he said to his colleagues in the Mapai Political Secretariat.[42])

Donors and Recipients

Once the anvil (the displaced persons) had been found on which his plans could be forged, Ben-Gurion began to gather the resources required. In talks between the two men, the JDC's share of support for the immigration was agreed upon. "Schwartz agrees that the Joint will bear the burden of the immigration," wrote Ben-Gurion in his diary on 28 October. "I offered him a partnership based on his providing the means and our providing the people."[43] The next day Ben-Gurion was more generous with details of his talks with Schwartz. The two had also discussed the situation in Poland and other eastern European countries in which the JDC representatives were already operating. The entire monthly budget for Poland was half a million dollars. "I told him," wrote Ben-Gurion, "that we'll bring the children and the 'kibbutzim' to Germany." Schwartz responded that many would not go to Germany and that the Polish government pledged not to interfere with the departure of the children to Palestine "when certificates arrive." Twenty-five percent of the entire JDC budget should be allocated to immigration, noted Schwartz, without specifying which immigration he meant. Knowing well the point of view of the organization that Schwartz represented, Ben-Gurion stressed the economic feasibility of transporting Holocaust survivors to Palestine, noting that every person who reached Palestine would be "sheer profit for them [the JDC] because they spend there [in Europe] over $200 for each Jew in need of help."[44] Finally, Ben-Gurion and Schwartz agreed that the JDC would cover 50 percent of the cost of immigration. Once more, it is not apparent which immigration specifically was under discussion, but Ben-Gurion's writings clarify that it referred also, or primarily, to the clandestine immigration, because the two agreed that the JDC would cover half the costs of the first seven hundred clandestine immigrants who had already reached Palestine in Mossad ships after the war (PP130 [Palestine pounds] per person).[45] The language used by Ben-Gurion and Schwartz is interesting: everything was said, but nothing explicitly. The clandestine immigration and the Zionist organization running it—the Mossad—are not cited at all, although everything revolved around them. Discourse in which the word "Mossad" never appears characterizes all the JDC deliberations about the operation.

Meanwhile, the head of the political department of the Jewish Agency, Moshe Shertok, armed with instructions from Ze'ev Schind (Danny), the official Mossad liaison with the JDC, also met with Schwartz in late October 1945, at the time that Schwartz was holding talks with Ben-Gurion. In a letter to Palestine, Shertok reports that Schwartz "cannot commit himself to involvement at all and certainly not to the amounts." It was clear to him, however, that "they will be involved, though not to the extent that I had called for." Shertok added that Schwartz stressed that his organization had to prepare for "the financial burden that *Aliya Aleph* [legal immigration] would place on them, based on the new quota." He promised, however, to convey the Mossad's request to New York, "where it will be decided."[46] Again, the word "Mossad" was not mentioned. The day that Shertok wrote his letter in late October, he received confirmation that New York had decided to support the principle of clandestine immigration.[47]

It was not only Ben-Gurion and Shertok who met with Dr. Schwartz in an effort to enlist JDC support for the underground Zionist enterprise. The Mossad itself launched a lobbying campaign among JDC representatives across Europe, but directed primarily at Schwartz, who was the most powerful JDC man on the continent. The effort reflects the importance ascribed by senior Mossad operatives to the participation of the JDC in their campaign. It also reveals the methods used by the Mossad, its highly diffused structure, and its flat hierarchy. The Zionist conference in London in August 1945, the first after the war, provided the Mossad with an opportunity to lay virtual siege to Schwartz, who attended the event.[48] Schwartz's itinerary through Europe was also known to the Mossad agents; station heads in each country monitored his movements and met with him frequently during his visits to their areas, trying to pry some money from him. Pino

Ginsburg, treasurer of the Mossad in Europe and based in Geneva, also met often with Saly Mayer, the JDC representative in Switzerland, and with Schwartz himself.[49] It was Ben-Gurion's talks with Schwartz, however, and the agreements they reached that are considered the foundation of cooperation between the Mossad and the JDC, the reference point and basis for their claims from then on.

By early November 1945, apparently based on the conclusions reached in his talks with Schwartz, Ben-Gurion placed $100,000 at the disposal of the Mossad.[50] One month later, Mossad headquarters in Palestine began pressing the treasurer in Geneva to provide more and more money. "Tell us if you received the loans and how much. Did money arrive from America, did you get money from the Joint, etc. How many *parashim* [cavaliers, a code word for Swiss francs] do you have now?"[51] The JDC office in New York, however, was more difficult and less flexible than its counterpart in Europe. It is possible that the New York people felt less committed to the agreement reached with Ben-Gurion in Europe. The different pace of work and the gap in perspective between the two sides provided fertile soil for the continuing misunderstandings and tension between the two organizations, beyond the natural tension between donors and recipients. Indeed, from the beginning, the JDC did not meet the expectations and demands made by Mossad agents for funding their activities, and thus Mossad representatives practiced aggressive lobbying through the entire period in the corridors of the JDC. By the first half of December 1945 the treasurer of the Mossad in Europe had declared that he was "a profound pessimist" about everything having to do with support from the JDC, and that despite enormous efforts he had not yet managed to "get a penny" out of them.[52] A month later, however, the agreement began to bear fruit: $175,000 was deposited for 1,100 refugees transported by the Mossad by the end of December 1945, and an additional $150,000 was transferred to cover the passage of 960 people on Mossad ships during January 1946.[53]

More than anyone else, the person who bridged the gap between the two fundamentally different ideologies and the conflict of interest between them, and who eased the cooperation between the agencies whose people, methods, and goals were often diametrically opposed, was Dr. Joseph Schwartz, director of the JDC-Europe during most of the war and the immediate post-war years. Yehuda Bauer has commented at length about this unusual personality: a rabbi and Orientalist by training; a social worker by occupation and calling; a courageous, independent, and knowledgeable individual who, during the war years, made the name of the JDC synonymous with rescue and hope, limited as the prospects were for the Jews of Europe.[54] So great were his authority and stature following his activities during the war, so dominant his presence, so primary the activities he instituted, and so immense the resources at his command—at least in comparison with those at the disposal of the operatives from Palestine—that he was regarded as the cornerstone of all the rescue and rehabilitation activities of the Jews of Europe. He thus enjoyed special status among both the agents from Palestine[55] and the representatives of the American government in Europe. He could come and go at will in the European offices of senior American military officers, presenting his case directly to them.[56] His participation in the Harrison Commission (Harrison was appointed by President Truman to investigate the situation of the Jews in the DP camps) and the great influence he had on the writing of the conclusions and recommendations of the Harrison memorandum, including the demand to allow one hundred thousand Jewish displaced persons to enter Palestine—Bauer presumes that it was Schwartz who introduced this number into the text[57]—further enhanced Schwartz's prestige, establishing him as a recognized authority on the issue of displaced persons to both his own organization and the Zionist agents.[58] Some suggest that the Harrison report sparked a chain of events that ultimately led to the founding of the State of Israel. Without a doubt, this memorandum, with the 100,000 figure, became a basic tenet—supported by an American president—of the post-war Jewish demand.[59] While still in the field directing the JDC's activities in Europe, Schwartz became one of the key decision makers of his organization, because of the fact that Europe was the main arena of the JDC's dramatic activity after the war and also because of the personal authority he had accumulated during the war years.

Perhaps something more occurred to change the deep-seated, traditional views of the JDC, something historiography has overlooked. Although this is not documented, the possibility cannot be ignored that Schwartz's encounter with Harrison and his staff and his profound imprint on the memorandum adopted by the American president, albeit for his own reasons, created a new sense of loyalty and commitment for the Jewish organization. Until then, the JDC's fealty to the State Department had been evident. However, the State Department not only disagreed with the principles and recommendations of the Harrison memorandum, but had objected from the outset to the premises and terms of reference accorded to Harrison before he left on his mission, recommending that Truman not interfere on the issue of Palestine and not pressure Britain to change its policy.[60] With this memorandum there may have been a parting of ways, if only temporary, with Schwartz and the JDC finding themselves not only in support of the president's policies but a partner to its implementation. The JDC's change of heart also reflected a more general change of attitude among the American Jewish public and its organized leadership—a more confident self-image, a sense of empowerment, and greater identification with Jewish Palestine and with the aspiration of the survivors to get there.[61]

A discussion of the decision-making apparatus in the JDC Executive Committee is beyond the scope of this book. It can be said unequivocally, however, that Schwartz's intimate acquaintance with the dire circumstances of the Jewish survivors in Europe and the longing of many of them for Palestine, his stance toward Zionism and the Zionist enterprise, his frequent contacts with the operatives from Palestine—including Mossad agents—during and certainly after the war all contributed to the JDC's decision to take a major role in funding Mossad efforts despite its basic ideology opposing involvement in illegal activity. Eliezer Kaplan, treasurer of the Jewish Agency, who said with irony that he was considered "a Joint man" in both Palestine and America, spoke in the Jewish Agency Executive about the impact of certain individuals on the positions and policies of their organizations. He was referring primarily to the influence of Schwartz on the JDC.[62] Schwartz made a memorable appearance on behalf of the JDC at a special United Jewish Appeal conference on 15–17 December 1945 in Atlantic City, a conference that turned into a mass demonstration of solidarity by American Jews with the Holocaust survivors. This event was a turning point in the attitude held by wide segments of American Jewry, including traditional non-Zionists, toward Palestine and the Jewish survivors.[63] Schwartz's appearance and his moving testimony to the Anglo-American Committee at the start of its deliberations in early 1946, continued the line he took in the Harrison delegation and placed the JDC openly on the side of the Zionist campaign. In his testimony Schwartz stated that thousands of Jews were indeed flowing from eastern to western Europe, disregarding borders and armies, being pursued and in danger for their lives. He admitted publicly that the JDC was helping them, providing transportation, food, and shelter. He offered a shocking account of those penned up in DP camps and warned of fur-

ther demoralization and deterioration of the survivors of the great massacre. The Holocaust, said Schwartz, strengthened the bond of Jews to
the homeland in Palestine, extinguished hopes that legal arrangements
would guarantee security for Jews in their former homes, and under-
mined faith in the value of good laws and human rights treaties. True
to the long-standing JDC tradition, Schwartz refrained from using political language. When asked by the British committee chairman if his
words referred to a Jewish state, Schwartz replied that he did not think
at all in political terms, but in terms of settlement and the aspiration of
human beings to live in hospitable and friendly conditions.[64]

Early 1946 was thus a kind of honeymoon period between the JDC
and Zionism. "In terms of the Joint, there is a great and whole-hearted
desire, at least this year, of making common cause with the Jewish Agency
and Eretz-Israel," Kaplan reported to the Jewish Agency Executive in
February.[65] He added that, although Dr. Schwartz claimed he was not a
Zionist, "Jewish pride still emerges from his words . . . and he has accordingly replied to Bevin . . . but this is not to say that [the Joint] have
become Zionists or changed their spots. This comes from no-choice, not
from love, but that's the situation."[66] This change is at the heart of the
transformation in early 1946 of the work of the Mossad, its self-perception,
and its position at the vanguard of the Zionist struggle. Ben-Gurion's plan
to revive the pre-war notion of "a militant immigration," waged mainly
through the Mossad, could be realized only in a climate of cooperation
between the JDC and the Zionist organizations, and with the financial
leverage of American Jews. Thus, here was an alliance of the human resources that Palestine offered—a strong, action-oriented leadership in its
prime, motivated, resourceful, and intimately acquainted with the
European continent—and the financial resources of American Jewry.

With the Ben-Gurion–Schwartz agreement, the Mossad entered a
new phase. A new organizational structure was formed. Senior Mossad
personnel fanned out across Europe and began to direct the stations
there; Ze'ev Schind was already settled in the United States to serve as liaison with the JDC Executive and also to arrange for the acquisition of
large ships to step up the immigration campaign.[67] The effects of this reorganization were soon felt. Whereas the Mossad had managed to extract
1,032 refugees in eight small boats in the five months from August to
December 1945, within the first five months of 1946 it quadrupled this
number.[68] In March and April 1946, simultaneous sailings were planned
from Italy, France, Greece, and Romania, with the transportation of

some seven thousand people.[69] Based on the Mossad documents, which reveal ceaseless lobbying of the JDC to finance the increased pace of the clandestine sailings, the JDC was apparently surprised by the scope of Mossad activity—as indicated by the number of immigrants in Mossad ships for which payments were due—and was unprepared financially to meet its obligations based on the agreement with Ben-Gurion.[70] More significantly, when it signed the agreement with Ben-Gurion, the JDC almost certainly did not take into account the dramatic political reaction provoked by the Mossad operations. Although the Mossad cables—and there were many from the period in which the communications channels were up and running—convey the financial pinch, they also radiate a sense of confidence that the rich uncle from America was on their side ("the wealthy man," "the central bank," or "the great treasurer," as Dr. Schwartz was sometimes called in Mossad correspondence[71]) and that he would eventually fund their most imaginative visions under almost any conditions. "We hope that within a few days," noted a cable from Palestine to the treasurer in Geneva, "we will inform you of new opportunities for obtaining *parashim* [Swiss francs] through the treasurer [Kaplan]. Meanwhile continue your efforts to get *parashim* by any means to meet the needs of the comrades and not delay the operation."[72]

Political Spectacle

In early March 1946 the Mossad finalized its Grand Plan, scheduled for March and April of that year. The plan was to sail from every country in which the Mossad was operating—Italy, France, Greece, and Romania—and land an unprecedented wave of refugees on the shores of Palestine within a very short period, overrunning the British blockade. This was the Mossad's contribution to the two-tiered struggle waged by the Zionist community against the Mandatory rule, then at its height. To obtain the funding required for this plan, the Mossad enlisted the treasurer of the Jewish Agency; the director of the Jewish Agency's Immigration Department; Dr. Judah Magnes, rector of the Hebrew University and representative of the JDC in Palestine; and anyone else with useful contacts. The following cable, sent from the Mossad headquarters in Palestine to Eliahu Dobkin, director of the Immigration Department, then in Paris, reflects the Mossad's tactics, style of operation, and critical dependence on the JDC:

Information arrived from Rudolph [Romania] that final preparations are underway for the departure of thousands. Binyamin [Italy] has five vessels for 2,700. Kassuta [France] and Tenor [Greece] are preparing over a thousand. Our plan is for the vast majority to arrive in March and the remainder in April. We are in urgent need of three million *parashim* [Swiss francs] to fund these transports until we receive payment from the Joint. This calculation is based on 55 pounds per person, on condition that we can immediately come up with official *parashim*. You are required to help us find the immediate means to fund this and, in this sense at least, prevent failure. We are pressed to give the go-ahead to another thousand [people] from various locations, in addition to two vessels for two thousand that Danny [Schind, U.S.] purchased. Here we have appealed to the rector [Dr. Magnes]. He does not seem willing to approach his superiors without first hearing the opinion of P-n [Charles Passman, resident representative of the JDC in Palestine and a confidant of Dr. Schwartz] who is returning soon. . . . It's imperative that you get immediate approval from Shachor [Blacky, i.e., Dr. Schwartz] for an additional allocation as above, and please look high and low for some immediate operating capital.[73]

More than the details, which reveal the wide-ranging and very confident activity of the Mossad operatives in Europe and the United States, the tone of the cable and its appeal to a member of the Jewish Agency Executive reflects exceptional self-assurance, personally and institutionally. The appeal to Dobkin is not a request but an instruction, which indicates the high rank of the Mossad in the hierarchy of Yishuv organizations and the self-image of its members.

Several days later Dobkin conveyed the news through the Mossad network and the treasurer in Geneva that the JDC was willing to support the Grand Plan and double the quota to 6,600 people by the end of April.[74] Because the JDC had so far paid for 2,100 people, added Dobkin, the Mossad would have at its disposal sufficient funds for another 4,500. "After April, we can present new demands, and I will attend to finding operating capital together with Itai [Ehud Avriel] and Berg [Pino Ginsburg]."[75] In the first three months of 1946 the JDC transferred advances against its commitments in the amount of PP40 ($160) per person.[76] The sum of PP40 for the conveying of each refugee was calculated based on the costs of immigration from the first months of operation until February 1946 as follows: According to the Mossad calculations, seven of the first ships that arrived from Italy, with 1,685 people on board, cost PP143,500, for an average of PP85 per person; and two ships from Greece with 251 people on board cost PP19,235, for an average of PP76 per person. Thus, combined immigration expenses from the two countries were PP162,735, or the equivalent of about $650,000 based on the exchange rate at the time.[77] Based on the calculation of PP40 per person—half the cost of bringing each refugee into Palestine—for 6,600 refugees, the JDC was to give the Mossad $1,056,000 by the end of April.

Before this amount was paid, however, word suddenly arrived from the JDC offices in New York that support for the Mossad activities had ended.[78] It is not clear if the reason was the unexpected and unbudgeted financial burden or the political rumpus raised during those months by the Mossad ships, all of which were intercepted by the British, peaking with the La Spezia affair in Italy.[79] At any rate, in the second week of April, when the arrest of the refugees on board the ships in La Spezia was drawing international attention—and while Zionist leaders in Palestine were fasting to protest the arrest, the JDC decided to halt its financial support of the clandestine immigration. The explanation given by the JDC, as conveyed via the communications network of the Mossad, was that these operations were not actually adding immigrants to the official, approved quota, and that those who arrived by ship were virtually legal but were brought into Palestine at a cost much higher than the cost of a regular immigrant.[80]

Only later, when the Mossad people applied pressure and demanded explanations, was the political cat released from the bag. "The Joint announced that it is not prepared to continue to pay 40 pounds per person because from now on, it does not want to support political activity," read a cable from Mossad head Shaul Meirov and Pino Ginsburg to Palestine on 13 May, following their meeting with Dr. Schwartz.[81] They also reported that Schwartz himself was not happy with the decision and had twice recommended the renewal of JDC support. They were told that the decision had been made in a special session of the JDC Executive in New York, where it was also decided that the JDC would pay the Mossad only PP15 ($60) per person, the same amount that it allocated for immigrants with certificates.[82] It became clear that Kaplan had been right when he warned his colleagues in the Jewish Agency Executive not to believe that the JDC had changed its spots and adopted goals and tactics matching those of the Zionists from Palestine.[83] The JDC announcement, which added to the financial disaster of the La Spezia affair,[84] sent the Mossad network into a tailspin. It is hard to assess exactly how many sailings were delayed or canceled, because even during relatively stable times the situation on the ground

did not necessarily match the plans on paper, so profuse were the political and operational obstacles.[85] The JDC decision and the Mossad
reaction to it testify, however, to the Mossad's utter dependence on
American-Jewish money, leaving the clear impression that without this
money the organization and its activities were in effect paralyzed.

Nevertheless, while the Mossad brought out its biggest cannons
(the head of the Mossad himself, who generally avoided contact with
people outside the organization; the Jewish Agency treasurer; and even
Ben-Gurion) to lobby the JDC to revoke its decree,[86] and while contact with the JDC was fully coordinated in Paris and New York to increase the effectiveness and control of the Mossad chief,[87] the Mossad
did not halt its activities for even one day, and its stations continued to
function. On 7 May Moshe Averbuch launched the *Max Nordau*
(*Smirni*) from Constanta, the first "illegal" ship from Romania and the
largest since the end of the war, with 1,666 refugees on board.[88] A day
later the *Fede* and *Fenice* set sail with 1,014 refugees, who were allowed
to dock on the shores of Palestine.[89] In May Ze'ev Schind received orders to appeal to Jewish donors and Jewish institutions in the United
States (such as the World Jewish Congress or Keren Hayesod) in an effort to secure funds for the Mossad operations, even in the form of
loans. "Work hard to get *weisim* [dollars, after Stephen Wise] in
America from individuals," Meirov cabled to Palestine on 13 May. "We
can now get one pound for nine or ten-and-a-half [Swiss] francs."[90]
The funds were intended primarily for what the Mossad called "creating money."[91]

"Creating money" meant taking advantage of the differences in the
currency exchange rates and clever trading in the stock markets of
Europe, which increased the amount of money held by the Mossad
manifold. Dollars were received in America, either from institutions or
individuals who wished to launder their money, and these were officially transferred to Switzerland. The cover for transferring the funds
was a license received by Jewish institutions to send relief money to the
DP camps in Germany. The dollars were transferred to the bank accounts of wealthy Swiss Jews who lent their assistance to the Mossad financial people. The dollars were exchanged for Swiss francs at the official exchange rate of 4.28 francs to the dollar. In the black market,
however, the value of the dollar and the value of the pound sterling
were much lower (the dollar, for example, was worth only 1.5 francs, a
third of its value on the official exchange). With the francs in hand, the

Mossad treasurer could then buy back dollars at a low rate and return the loans he had received from America, with a decent profit remaining for the Mossad. When there was time to play with the money, every dollar received from other countries went through three or four such conversions. During that period of political and economic turmoil in Europe, a nice profit could also be made by transferring money to countries where the Mossad operated; the difference between a legal and illegal transfer was approximately 30 percent but could reach 100 percent. In these deals, the Mossad was assisted by financial experts who were friends of Zionism, especially in Switzerland, Italy, and England.[92] In early June Pino Ginsburg reported to Mossad headquarters in Palestine that he had begun "money transactions to Danny [America] and back. Details to be announced."[93] The Mossad, it should be noted, was not the only agency to engage in such "creative" activity, bridging the area between the legal and illegal; it was joined by representatives of the Jewish Agency and other perfectly legal Zionist institutions.[94]

At the same time, efforts continued to prod the JDC to revoke its decision. In June the Mossad appealed to renew the PP40 agreement with the JDC to pay for immigration activities from eastern Europe. The Mossad argued that there was no hope of immigration by certificate from these countries, and therefore the JDC's claim that the Mossad was bringing in only regular immigrants, at an exorbitant cost, had no basis.[95] In the summer of that year, another surprising turnabout occurred in the position of the JDC. A series of meetings between Ze'ev Schind and Eliezer Kaplan, treasurer of the Jewish Agency, and the JDC people yielded an agreement according to which the JDC would place $100 at the disposal of the Mossad for each of its immigrants. Kaplan, who was close to the JDC Executive Committee, was not satisfied and demanded that the amount be raised to $120, but to no avail.[96] For the 6,370 Jewish refugees transported by the Mossad in June and July 1946, the JDC paid $637,000. It also pledged $100 for each of the 1,590 refugees who had already sailed or were scheduled to sail by the end of August. Interestingly, these sailings took place after the media storm over La Spezia, which is what prompted the JDC Executive Committee to halt its support of the Mossad operations. In other words, after the initial, almost instinctive misgivings of the American organization about the political spectacle that had occurred in La Spezia, its directors reconsidered. This reversal was apparently influenced by the growing boldness of the Mossad exploits and the use of larger ships that exceeded the official immigration quotas. The new agreement made JDC funds conditional on an ongoing review. Every three months the agreement would come up for consideration prior to renewal.[97]

Close and Distant

In mid-October 1946 the Mossad treasurer submitted to the Jewish Agency treasurer a plan for bringing 19,500 immigrants to Palestine based on $2,000,000 from the JDC, $500,000 from the Jewish Agency, and $300,000 from revenues "created" by the Mossad treasurer. Simultaneously, agreement was reached with Schwartz to cover the costs of an additional two thousand refugees who had arrived in Palestine in August and September, and the JDC Executive Committee in New York confirmed this agreement and its financial implications.[98] Parallel to the plenary meetings of the Twenty-second Zionist Congress, the Mossad held discussions about a massive plan to bring 100,000 Jewish refugees to Palestine through the course of 1947,[99] taking full advantage of the political power of the clandestine immigration enterprise. Dr. Schwartz was in Basel for the congress and also took part in the Mossad discussions,[100] which is evidence of the intimacy and trust that prevailed between the Mossad and Schwartz, if not the organization he represented. Following the congress, the Mossad submitted an official request to Schwartz for "an advance for ten thousand in the sum of a million *weisim*," which meant initial payment of $1 million to fund the transport of ten thousand refugees as the first stage in the massive "hundred thousand plan." There was also a demand to increase the JDC subsidy for each person brought in by the Mossad. Schwartz "promised to endorse" this, and so he did to the Executive Committee ("the Council of Stephens," the Mossad code for the JDC Executive). He also recommended regular advance payments to ensure that the activities could take place without interruption.[101] Schwartz flew twice to New York to convince the Executive Committee to increase its support or at least to promise regular payments over the long term. He was helped in this by Shertok and Kaplan. Ben-Gurion also pledged his assistance. JDC approval, however, was not forthcoming until mid-March, and meanwhile the Mossad was forced to call off negotiations for purchasing ships due to lack of funds.[102] Again, the JDC limited its support to $100 per person until June 1947 and would not commit to a larger amount or an extended time period.[103]

In April and May a series of meetings was again held between those from Palestine and New York. Dr. Schwartz and Moses Leavitt, secretary of the JDC, met in Paris with Kaplan and Meirov.[104] On 23 May 1947, a lengthy meeting was held in New York with Pino Ginsburg and Ze'ev Schind representing the Mossad, and Louis Sobel (the new JDC secretary) Boris Yoffe, and Dorothy Speiser representing the JDC. This is one of the few meetings between the two organizations in which detailed minutes were kept that revealed the complexity of relations between the Mossad and the JDC, the history of the relationship, and the model of cooperation between them. The two main speakers at the meeting were Ginsburg, who had come from Geneva for the meeting,[105] and Sobel. Ginsburg was familiar with Mossad methods from the pre-war period and aware of the details of the deals that had been struck. He was based at the scene of action, Europe, for a year and a half and was one of the key figures around which Mossad activity revolved. By virtue of his responsibility for finances and his long experience in Mossad activities, he often served as mediator between Mossad stations or arbitrator of conflicts between key leaders. The treasurer of the Mossad in Europe opened the meeting by saying that of the "running quota" of 10,000 refugees that the JDC had promised to fund in the amount of $1 million, 8,200 had already reached Cyprus. In other words, the JDC owed $820,000. Of the $500,000 due for 5,000 people, they had received FF600,000 and $60,000 from Saly Mayer (the JDC representative in Switzerland), with an agreement that the balance of $250,000 would be paid in New York. Thus, for the 8,200 people who had already arrived, there was an outstanding debt of $320,000. Louis Sobel said in response that no additional payments would be made by Saly Mayer and that the money due to the Jewish Agency would be transferred in New York and not Switzerland.

The two Mossad representatives stressed the difficult financial straits of the Mossad and the urgent need for money. They explained that there were ships and signed agreements for ships that would allow the passage of 40,000 additional refugees. All the money contributed by the JDC and the Jewish Agency was already spent, and the organization was running out of money. Louis Sobel explained that because of a shortage in cash, the JDC was forced to delay some other payments as well, and thus he could not promise when the resources would become available against the JDC debt of $1 million. Sobel asked the two about the Mossad's short-term immigration plans. Pino Ginsburg reported on the plan to get Jews out of Germany by two routes. The first was from Germany to and through Italy. In recent months, said Ginsburg, they managed to bring 2,500 people from Germany to Italy, despite obstacles posed by the American forces. The other route for transporting refugees was through France. According to a report published by the Jewish Telegraph Agency (JTA), six hundred people were being held at the German-French border, and Ginsburg said he did not know how this would affect their plans. He reported that the British authorities demanded that the French prevent the entry of Jewish refugees from the German camps into France. The French response was that they would not make distinctions between Jews and non-Jews, and that they must be true to the tradition of the French Revolution. So far the Jewish Agency had entry visas into France for fifteen hundred people. This was part of a larger plan to bring ten thousand people from Germany to France, but in light of recent developments the agency was not optimistic about realizing these hopes. Pino Ginsburg added that they were testing a third route, from Germany to Romania, explaining that the situation in Romania was dire and that Mossad representatives there were authorized to move out fifty thousand people.

The two Mossad representatives also reported that their organization was in contact with the Yugoslav government, which had promised safe passage for five thousand refugees en route from Germany to Palestine. Sobel asserted that from the JDC point of view, priority should be given to the camps in Germany, which was the reason for JDC support of the Mossad activities. The JDC demanded that most of the candidates for migration to Palestine be taken from camps in Germany to ease the plight there. The Mossad representatives asked that the JDC increase its support for the immigration of another ten thousand refugees and provide the Mossad with an additional $1 million. In response, Sobel said he would convey this request to the JDC Executive and Administrative committees, and he added that the chances of a positive response would increase if the ten thousand came exclusively from Germany. He noted, nevertheless, that he could not commit himself and that this should not be taken as a pledge of JDC support.[106]

The discussion, which was very detailed and conducted in good spirit, reveals both the distance and the closeness between the two organizations. This pattern of relations between the Mossad and the JDC recurred throughout the post-war period, characterized by the desire of the American organization to know how its money would be spent but not wanting to know too much about the details in order to avoid being implicated, and thereby maintain its law-abiding appearance. Hence Sobel asked about the Mossad plans but did not delve into the details concerning the transport of people, illegal border crossings, contacts with various police units, and the payments needed at sensitive locations. In this conversation, the Mossad seems eager to reportmore—if only to bolster its claim for increased funding—than the JDC wants to know. In the JDC files are reports and correspondence about the clandestine immigration, but the discussion about them was usually limited to the number of refugees transported by the Mossad in its ships, and nothing more.[107]

Also revealed at this meeting was an attempt by the JDC to consolidate all money transfers to the Mossad in New York, apparently to control the flow of cash, which, in the first months of cooperation, had passed through a great variety of channels. An additional topic raised in this talk was the JDC's paramount commitment to dismantling the time bombs—the DP camps in Germany—and its efforts to influence the Mossad in this regard. These camps were burdensome to the American government and army, and the JDC wanted to be the key factor in lifting this burden. Also, the camps consumed most of the JDC budget in those years; their elimination was worth almost any price. To get the Mossad to focus its efforts on helping to empty these camps, the JDC was willing to fund Mossad operations in other parts of Europe. Indeed, in July the JDC renewed its commitment for an additional $1 million to offset the transport costs of the next ten thousand immigrants,[108] but it refused to support the illegal immigration from north Africa or the Zionist training centers there.[109] The discussion with the JDC over north Africa was particularly strained, and disdainful tones slipped into the conversation. "What was particularly hard for me in my talk with 'Blacky' [Schwartz] was the matter of 'Atlas' [north Africa]," reported the Mossad head. "I was told explicitly and bluntly that they will not bear either past or future costs. Discussion on this point was extraordinarily harsh. I won't go into the reasons—they are typical of the distinctive perspective of Schwartz's society and its superfluous considerations when it appeals to donors for fundraising. However that's the situation about this matter."[110]

Diverging Paths

The year 1947 marked the peak of JDC's international activities up to that point and since. In that year, the JDC spent $69 mil-
lion (the amount dropped to $63 million the next year.)[111] The year 1947
also marked the peak of Mossad activity. In that year alone, twenty-two
Mossad ships set sail from Europe and two from north Africa, with
more than forty thousand Jews on board.[112] In the second half of 1947,
however, the paths of these two organizations began to diverge. The
JDC continued to turn over its share, $100 per person, based on short-
term, periodically renewed agreements, but it did so with great effort,
showing its weary and cumbersome side to the Mossad, even more than
in the past.[113] The JDC's commitments throughout the world, and in
Europe in particular, were draining its budget, and, as Louis Sobel
noted to the two Mossad representatives with whom he met in May
1947, the organization even found it hard to meet previous commitments. What's more, the unequivocal political character of the Mossad
activity that year, including operations initially meant for political show,
such as the *Exodus* in all its incarnations, forced the New York JDC officers to face the question of dual loyalty. On one hand, the *Exodus* incident, especially at the height of media interest, aroused American public opinion, both Jewish and non-Jewish, and sympathy with the fate of
the Jewish refugees and their yearning to reach Palestine. On the other
hand, the *Exodus* affair increased the involvement of the State
Department, a body that had not been sympathetic to the Zionist cause.
Having clung faithfully to its quiet work ethic—within the law and the
spirit of the law—and sensitive to the winds blowing from the State
Department, the JDC was torn between its heart and cold calculations.
Paradoxically, but in a manner typical of the agency for which emergency humanitarian work was the raison d'être, the JDC in France
buckled down to help the 4,500 refugees from the *Exodus* who were
moored off Port de Bouc on three British deportation ships—this while
on the diplomatic level the old-new gaps between the JDC and the
Zionist movement were again becoming visible. During the month that
the refugees languished opposite the French shore, the JDC rounded
up and delivered more than a ton and a half of food, clothing, medicine,
and other supplies.[114] Directed by Laura Margolis, the JDC workers did
what they did best: run a humanitarian aid organization providing

emergency relief to Jews in need. On the political level, however, with the Americans and the State Department now compelled to intervene unwillingly in an affair in which they had earlier refused to become involved,[115] the JDC returned after this incident to the path of loyalty and obedience to Washington. The decision taking shape in the wake of UNSCOP's recommendations to partition Palestine also contributed to the partial freeze of JDC support for the Mossad. Why support illegal activity that might within months, by international decision, become legitimate and cheaper? Professing financial constraints and cash flow problems, the JDC started to slow payments for commitments it had already made.[116]

At the end of October 1947 the Mossad station in France calculated the amount still owed by the JDC, beginning with the sailings from Italy in March (with 1,563 refugees on board, who were sent to Cyprus) and ending with the ship from Burgas, Bulgaria on 26 September (with 2,664 refugees on board). According to this reckoning, 18,405 people had sailed. The JDC had paid its share for the first 10,000; for the second 10,000, the JDC had deposited 225,000 "stephens" (dollars) by the end of October.[117] There is no hard evidence that the remainder of this debt was ever paid, and none to the contrary, but in October, November, and December 1947, the months of preparation and energy gathering for the *Pan York* and *Pan Crescent* sailings from Romania—the most demanding Mossad operation of all times, which the U.S. secretary of state had openly denounced—the JDC Executive Committee froze on payments to the Mossad.[118] The conflicting interests and ethos of the two organizations could no longer coexist in that alliance of no-choice that joined a unique historical situation, a resolute and calculated Zionist ideology, impassioned and resourceful people, and large sums of money—an encounter that produced an unparalleled national endeavor. By the time the JDC decided to end its support, the political effect of the Mossad operations, which had become their main objective that year, was already a fait accompli, and the founding of a Jewish state was only a matter of time. As in the past, however, the JDC, a pragmatic humanitarian institution, seemed to observe a policy of "never say never." What had appeared in November and December 1947 as a final, binding policy of nonsupport for Mossad activity seems to have retreated before the forces of circumstances and necessity. The huge operation of launching the *Pan York* and *Pan Crescent* with more than fifteen thousand Romanian Jews on board, the UN decision of 29 November, and, above all perhaps, the improved financial situation of the JDC were factors in the unexpected Executive Committee decision to share in the funding of transporting ten thousand additional Jewish refugees to Palestine and to discharge the JDC's prior debts to the Mossad.[119]

Ideology and Practice

JDC activity in the detention camps of Cyprus could constitute a chapter in itself. The Cyprus episode deserves more extensive exploration than is possible here.[120] For present purposes, it should be noted that the opposing ideologies of the JDC and the Zionists were fully expressed here, too, and that the Cyprus episode serves to illustrate the two basic approaches in the Jewish world between the JDC and the Mossad; the philanthropic approach of the JDC, based on instant remedies, versus the future-oriented, revolutionary, all-encompassing solution of the Zionists. Charles Passman, representing the JDC, showed up in Cyprus the day after the British cabinet decided to deport the refugees to the island,[121] and on 6 September the first JDC-sponsored contingent reached Cyprus. The team—including teachers, social workers, and a medical staff—stayed a month and a half and submitted a detailed report on the situation in the camps and the needs of the refugees,[122] a report that was the basis for all future relief work sponsored by the JDC in the camps. For over two years, beginning 12 December 1946, JDC representatives in Cyprus were managed by Morris Laub, a veteran and specialist in relief work. Having no formal status and constantly fighting for autonomy, Laub and the organization he represented were the key, if not the only, agency doing relief work in the Cyprus camps. Throughout this time, the Jewish Agency Executive refused to aid the refugees deported to Cyprus on the grounds that taking responsibility for their lives could be construed as Zionist recognition of the legality of the camps.[123]

Not all members of the Zionist establishment accepted this approach. The issue of Cyprus was raised in the Jewish Agency Executive several times and was swept away. On 10 September 1946, after the first fact-finding mission to the detention camps had departed, one Executive member reported that although the JDC was willing to bear the expenses of the delegation, "we must consider whether this is desirable."[124] The chairman of the Committee for Cyprus Deportees declared it "unacceptable that we should always have to turn to the JDC to arrange our affairs." He suggested upon his return from a tour of the camps that the Jewish Agency open an official consular office in Cyprus that would represent it politically and attend to the matter of immigration. It is inconceivable, he noted, that Jewish Agency operatives would appear before the British government as officials of the JDC. He was defeated. The large majority opposed any step that could have been construed as recognition of the camps.[125] The Zionist logic was indeed unique. During the years the camps existed, the JDC had spent $1,800,000 on direct relief and aid work there, while the Zionist community in Palestine, through the Committee for Cyprus Deportees, spent less than PP15,000 ($60,000).[126] The Zionist leadership chose this policy knowing that the JDC would fill the vacuum and perform its traditional role. Each side thus served its function according to the traditional division of labor: Zion provided the supposedly eternal component of the equation—the vision—while the American Jews supplied the transitory—the provisions. The Zionists set in motion their "clever manipulations" and harnessed to their grand vision the American-Jewish organization's commitment to Jews in trouble, while American Jews contributed the philanthropy in keeping with their organizational ethos and also, perhaps, to partake in their share of the eternal.

What was the total JDC contribution to the Mossad venture in absolute numbers? What was JDC's share of the expenses for the organized clandestine immigration? And a question that might enrich the discussion: what would have happened if the JDC had not shared the costs of the clandestine immigration? Could the Mossad have pulled it off with the help of another agency or with no outside help? Would the organized clandestine immigration have been as politically effective had it not reached the massive numbers it did? There is no definitive answer to these questions. The financial record of the Mossad's activities between 1945 and 1948 has not been found, though we know from oral testimony and documentary evidence that a detailed balance sheet was prepared for the Mossad and signed by certified public accountants.[127] In addition, the JDC has no single document that summarizes its outlays for the sailings to Palestine, as payments were made under various covers, often with no advance notice or oversight. Based on documents, it has been ascertained that the direct outlay by the JDC for Mossad operations during these years totaled about $7.5 million.[128] To this should be added JDC support for the Bricha, which brought the Holocaust survivors to the DP camps and ports and made possible the Mossad's immigration activity. Statistics

about the Bricha are also not complete or accurate. The cost of transporting one person ranged from one to five dollars.[129] Bauer speaks of
230,000–250,000 refugees transported by Bricha people throughout
Europe.[130] How much, then, did the Bricha cost? What part of this cost
came from the JDC? A Bricha agent mentioned the figure of $4 million
as the JDC's direct share of funding the Bricha and claims that another
million dollars should be added to this, to cover the cost to the JDC for
upkeep of the camps, equipment, work shops, and transports.[131] This still
doesn't include everything. Was the Mossad's purchase of large ships,
most of them acquired in the United States with JDC money, included in
the accounting between the Mossad and the JDC? Was not the $1,800,000
spent by the JDC on the deportation camps in Cyprus an integral part of
its support for the clandestine immigration? There is no accurate information about these issues. The network and routes of money flow were
so diverse and intricate that there is no way to follow it with precision.

The basic agreement between Ben-Gurion and Dr. Schwartz in late
October 1945 laid the foundation for the JDC to shoulder half the cost
of the illegal immigration. The agreement, as noted, underwent many
transformations. The amount paid by the JDC for the transport of each
refugee changed over time, as did the cost to the Mossad. In calculat-
ing costs, numbers can be manipulated and papers can be changed.
Indeed, in its reports to the JDC, the Mossad, as a matter of course,
rounded up the figures concerning those who sailed on its ships.[132]
The JDC was no stickler for accuracy either. Based also on the Jewish
Agency's share of funding the clandestine immigration, there is more
than ample evidence to suggest that the JDC covered much more than
half the cost of the Mossad operations.[133]

Finally, more important than pondering what would have happened
had the JDC not contributed to funding the transport of some seventy
thousand Jewish refugees to Palestine in the post-war years, we can
state with confidence that the Mossad could never have functioned as
it had without the enormous assistance of the JDC; that the imagination and daring demonstrated by the Mossad in those years could never
have taken flight without the material infrastructure provided by the
JDC; and that the sense of confidence reflected in the words and tone
of the Mossad operatives, who were almost always sure that the JDC,
though the product of another world and driven by another ethos,
would always—albeit with reservations and hesitations, and always a bit
late—stand by their side and enable them to realize their design.

Jewish clandestine immigrants intercepted and deported by British soldiers. Haifa, Palestine, 1947. (History of Haganah Archive)

Imprisoned Jewish immigrants breaking the fences between two British detention camps. Cyprus, no date. (Labor Archive)

Newborn in a British detention camp. Cyprus, 1947. (Ha'Kibbutz Ha'Meuhad Archive)

Jewish immigrants with their belongings after deportation to British detention camps. Cyprus, 1947. (History of Haganah Archive)

Jewish holocaust survivors on the ship *Fede* arrested by the Italians and the British. La Spezia, Italy, April 1946. (History of Haganah Archive)

Hunger strike of Jewish immigrant Holocaust survivors. La Spezia, Italy, April 1946. (History of Haganah Archive)

On a deportation ship on the way to the British detention camp in Cyprus. 1946. (History of Haganah Archive)

Romanian Jews boarding the *Pan York*. Burgas, Bulgaria, December 1947. (History of Haganah Archive)

Holocaust survivors from a displaced persons camp in Germany boarding the ship *President Warfield* (later to become the *Exodus*). Sète, France, June 1947. (History of Haganah Archive)

The damaged ship *Exodus* after the battle with British warships. Haifa,
Palestine, July 1947. (Labor Archive)

Clandestine Jewish immigrants disembark on the shores of Na'haryia,
Palestine. Winter 1945. (Ha'Kibbutz Ha'Meuhad Archive)

David Nameri, Mossad's liaison to the Palmach and head of operations in the Palestine station of the Mossad. (History of Haganah Archive)

Shmarya Zameret, head of the Marseilles station of the Mossad.
(Ha'Kibbutz Ha'Meuhad Archive)

Pino Ginsburg, a senior Mossad member from 1939 and treasurer for
Europe in the years 1945–48, Geneva. (Private archive)

Moshe Averbuch, Senior Mossad man and head of the Romania station, 1944–48. (History of Haganah Archive)

Zvi Yehieli, Senior Mossad man from 1938, active during the war years and responsible for special missions. (History of Haganah Archive)

Yehuda Arazi, head of the Italy station of the Mossad. (History of Haganah Archive)

Ada Sereni, head of the Italy station of the Mossad, 1947–48.
(Private archive)

Shaul Meirov, Head of the Mossad, 1939–48. (History of Haganah Archive)

PART III

Consciousness

CHAPTER 7

The Bearers and the Burdens

In the shifting power struggles within the Jewish community in Palestine and among the leadership of the world Zionist movement, Ben-Gurion's preeminence at the end of the war was indisputable. The death of Haganah commander Eliahu Golomb—Ben-Gurion's close colleague and one of the few friends who did not hesitate to disagree with him—combined with the death earlier of Berl Katzenelson and the withdrawal of Tabenkin from political activity on the national level, to leave Ben-Gurion with no rival to his stature. Even though his coronation as the foremost political figure in the Zionist movement and the Jewish nation would come only in late 1946, at the Twenty-second Zionist Congress, it was Ben-Gurion who already, by the fall of 1945, directed the entire Zionist campaign and set its tone and rules.[1]

To understand Ben-Gurion's position, the cognitive discourse created by him and his colleagues toward the clandestine immigration after the war, and the role of this immigration in the overall Zionist campaign, it is instructive to look at Ben-Gurion's attitude toward the Holocaust survivors and the role he assigned them in his plans for this political campaign. The encounter between the most senior Jewish leader of Palestine and the survivors of the massacre of European Jewry was fateful in many ways. In immediate and concrete terms, it provided Ben-Gurion with the object he needed for the complete realization of his concept of "exploiting the Jewish tragedy"[2] in the establishment of a Zionist Jewish state. The creation of this state on the ruins of the

Jewish nation and from the devastation of the Holocaust—the ultimate Jewish catastrophe—was perceived as the ultimate Jewish secular redemption. This encounter was fateful also because of its significance in forging the ethos of the Zionist community and the official discourse in Palestine toward the victims of the Holocaust within the physical and cognitive space whose two poles were the ruined Diaspora and the Zionist community of Palestine, a sovereign state in the making.

The encounter was imbued with deep fear and a sense of guilt, incorporated by the Zionist discourse that placed a wall between "us" and "them," transforming the other side, the "diasporic," into an object, a faceless mass of people waiting to be redeemed while performing the historic Zionist role assigned to them. "It will be hell if all the [DP] camps come [to Palestine]," Ben-Gurion was told by rescue operatives in Europe in early 1946, in response to his question about what would happen if the Jewish Agency got the one hundred thousand entry permits it demanded. "All this filth, just as it is, you [the Jewish Agency/Ben-Gurion] plan to move to Palestine?" protested the Zionist agents sent to Europe to deal with the needs of the refugees and bring them to Palestine. Ben-Gurion responded that it would be better for them ("the filth") to be in Palestine than elsewhere, implying that only in Palestine could the survivors be of any benefit and fulfill their historical function. "When these Jews come to Palestine, we'll have trouble," said Ben-Gurion, "but it will be Jewish trouble." Reporting the conversation to the Jewish Agency Executive, he never commented on the use of the term "filth" by rescue agents, and he repeated it without elaboration.[3] To the Central Committee of his party, more than four years after the war was over, he said that "some were people that, had they not been what they were—bad, harsh, and egoistic—they would never have survived. . . . What they experienced, extinguished every good part from their soul."[4]

David Shaltiel, a Mossad operative and Jewish Agency representative who served as Ben-Gurion's personal envoy to western Europe, returned from his own visit to the DP camps in Germany in the fall of 1945, having witnessed what was left of the devastation. He also expressed belief in the unique political power of the Holocaust survivors, if only Zionism would hurry to make correct use of them.[5] Vowing that he would never again set foot in Europe, Shaltiel expressed to his colleagues in the Mapai Central Committee his revulsion with the human profile of those who survived the Holocaust and the danger they carried for the Yishuv. "The fact that an individual was in a camp cannot be sufficient reason to send him to Palestine," said Shaltiel. "Those who survived did so because they were egotistical and cared primarily about themselves." One should understand but not pity them, he added. "They [the survivors] would have to work, otherwise they'll die from hunger, they'll steal, go to jail; otherwise there will be terrible things here."[6]

There were other expressions, more sensitive and less arrogant. "We were not burnt out together with the millions. Shall we now desert our last strength . . . and despair of its future seed?" wrote a soldier from the Jewish Brigade who protested the desire of most of his friends to leave Europe as soon as the war was over, abandoning the Jewish refugees and returning to Palestine.[7] Another young soldier from Palestine, who had learned while serving in Europe of the harsh reactions in Palestine toward the survivors and the crude treatment of them, wrote, "Must the nuns in Italy be more driven by their mission than the people of Palestine for their brothers who survived?"[8] The common reaction, however, was condescension and rejection, and the constant reference to those who survived the massacre as a "factor" or as "human material" reveals the psychological and discursive process of objectification and instrumentalization to which they were subjected. "The refugee element is very bad," commented a Zionist soldier serving in Italy. "In the convoy that was sent, they tried not to approve this material . . . sunk into prostitution, theft, and trade in military goods. They're making a fortune, and thus the question arises whether we should be extending them any help."[9] The head of the Jewish Agency Absorption Department, who went to the camps in Cyprus to select the first immigrants to be brought to Palestine as part of the approved immigration quotas, did not like what he saw. Facing the agitated and desperate mass of people who had survived the Holocaust and, for the last two years, had been dragged through backroads, detention camps, quarantines, and political displays, he asked how these wretched people could be of any use to the Zionist community in Palestine. Meeting with the refugees who had just arrived on board the ship *Knesset Yisrael* and had fought valiantly in Haifa against their transfer to British deportation ships, which took them to Cyprus, he wondered openly before the board of the *Va'ad Le'umi* (National Council) about the quality of the people flooding the country through immigration: "They [the immigration organizers] took a whole *shtetl* with a kindergarten and an old age home and moved it to the ship."[10]

Ben-Gurion made five trips to the Holocaust survivors in Europe—in late 1944, fall 1945, early 1946, and late 1946. The first trip, before the war had ended, was to the Jewish communities in Bulgaria and Romania (though he was eventually not allowed to enter Romania) and provided him the first window onto the object with which he would wage the Zionist war, a war that would also be the object's redemption. "Either we save them quickly," he said after his visit to Bulgaria, "or they're lost. . . . Either we bring them into Palestine or all the remainder of European Jewry is lost . . . to the Jewish nation and Zionism."[11] His second journey brought him into what he saw as the heart of the new Jewish center of power: the former death camps and the DP camps in Germany, in which Jews from all over Europe gathered. Ben-Gurion's first visit to the camps, the first meeting of the survivors with a senior Zionist leader, took place in October 1945, immediately after he had formulated for himself and his colleagues the Zionist guidelines for action against the British Labour government's policies of closing the gates of Palestine.[12] Ben-Gurion made two more visits to Germany in late January 1946 in an effort to enlist support among the displaced persons for the Zionist viewpoint, prior to the survey by the Anglo-American Committee of the camps' inhabitants. ("European Jewry's response to the committee was not pre-arranged," reported Ben-Gurion to the Jewish Agency Executive, "although there had also been some organizing."[13]) He made another visit in October 1946, prior to the Twenty-second Zionist Congress. During his first two visits he toured the DP camps in Bavaria, and he met with representatives of the camps, with soldiers from Palestine who were active there, and also with Haganah, the Mossad, and Bricha operatives there.[14] These visits helped him review the forces and resources at his command.

Vow of Silence

Rarely did Ben-Gurion make public his personal feelings during these visits, intimating little about them in his diary and keeping most of his thoughts to himself. During his first visit to Germany after returning from Bergen-Belsen, he copied into his diary, filling entire pages, the words engraved on the common grave in Belsen, Hirsh Glick's "Song of the Partisans" in Yiddish, and the poem "Es Brent"

"[It Burns]" by Mordechai Gevirtig. He copied the verses without comment.[15] This was not the first time he had expressed himself through sublimation in his diary—emotions that his own words could not express. Ten months earlier, during his visit to the Jews of Bulgaria, at the end of a particularly tumultuous day, Ben-Gurion copied into his diary the poem by Hannah Szenesh "Blessed Is the Match That Burns and Ignites Hearts." Again, he did not add a word or explain.[16] Just as he forced silence upon the survivors he met, not allowing them room for their pain and anguish or letting them sink into mourning, he took a vow of silence with regard to his own innermost feelings. Only once, during a visit to Bulgaria, did he allow a cry of rage to leap from his heart and enter his diary. "Horror, disgrace, abyss . . . terror," he wrote,[17] adding nothing. "I shall not try to express the feelings within me," he said after his visit to the German camps, "which would be impossible."[18] Ever since, from these first encounters with the devastation of the Final Solution, he almost never allowed himself to reveal personal feelings, grieve in public, or express empathy with the tortured remnants. Most of his remarks about Holocaust survivors were from a perspective of realizing the Zionist vision in the context of the survivors' recruitment for creating the state and forging a new Jewish individual.

On only a few occasions, out of the innumerable public appearances during these years, did Ben-Gurion express genuine compassion for the survivors. At a meeting of the Jewish Agency Executive upon his return from a second visit to the camps in Germany, he praised the "sanctity and devotion" of "the boys of the Brigade" and the indescribable "emotional strength in their work," adding, "Among those in the camps there are *also* truly holy people" (emphasis added).[19] In a letter from Paris to the Mapai conference in August 1946, he wrote extensively of the Holocaust survivors and the role they should play in the Zionist campaign. Beyond his usual words about their potential political power, Ben-Gurion devoted attention to the suffering they endured, the "terrible and cruel" experiences of "this crowd of people," who could not return to the path of life by charity or guardians or inundation with gifts, nor by politeness or sermons. "Only friends who come to live among them, be with them, are like them, who will share of themselves in every way, in loyal love, in natural and simple friendship; which in their deeds and lives will set an example and role model—only these can be accepted by them and will anoint their spirit and selves." Yet even to these rare words Ben-Gurion added a political-instrumental ending,

aimed at gathering all activities on behalf of the survivors under his political umbrella. Their enlistment will be possible under one condition,
he said: "unity of action . . . not futilely divided, but united around the
basic values of our pioneer movement."[20] Some ten months later Ben-
Gurion lectured to the youth of the farming movement that "if they
[the survivors] arrive and perceive us as the prosecuted and they the
prosecutors, we will have to bear it, to get used to it, to understand their
soul, to treat them with love, even if it arouses anger and revulsion
within us. If we do not gird ourselves with love, we shall not be able to
work with them."[21] This remarkable passage, never repeated, reveals not
only Ben-Gurion's deep emotions, but also belated (if unconscious and
unacknowledged) guilt feelings and recognition of his failure, and that
of the Zionist community in Palestine, to mobilize to the utmost for the
rescue of and aid to the dying Diaspora during the war years.

Ben-Gurion's description to young people in the fall of 1947 of the
personal and collective devastation of the Holocaust survivors, who
had spent more than two years in the DP camps in Europe, was intended to awaken their feelings toward the newcomers, to criticize
their insularity, the factionalism of some, and their lack of a sense of citizenship and nonpartisanship, and also to recruit them for his statist
ethos. "What a life they had the last few years," said Ben-Gurion to the
youth, "I didn't see all the camps, but I saw some. There are very few
young people because the Jewish children were killed. . . . Those who
remain from the great massacre are all adults, aged twenty to forty or
fifty. They have no children, their character is already formed, their
habits are set, they will not be able to get used to a new language, new
work, life in society. People who barely escaped from the crematoria,
who tried to live without working, a life of the black market—[their ab-
sorption] will require new strength that I don't know if we have within
us. . . . [We should teach them] the language, organize them in the
Histadrut, absorb them in public life, in the Jewish community, in the
Yishuv, turn them into citizens of the Jewish state. For 1800 years, these
Jews were not citizens. There is no sense of it [citizenship] among
European Jews. I'm afraid there is none in this room. . . . In Europe
the Jews only make demands, and justifiably so. Who can demand
something of a man whose wife was killed, whose children and parents
were annihilated."[22]

It was not in sackcloth and ashes that Ben-Gurion approached the
remnants of his people in Europe, nor did he ask forgiveness for his

blindness or for the Yishuv's priorities during the years of systematic murder of European Jewry. Instead, he demanded, in tough voluntaristic and
exclusivist language, that they enlist in the Zionist cause. Language was
one of the main tools in this exclusivist effort at imposing one culture
upon another, expediting the creation of a new political and cognitive reality while repressing the other. In his first speech to Jews in Bulgaria,
Ben-Gurion chose to speak Hebrew. This deliberate ideological choice
was intended to distinguish between those "with us" and those "against
us." When the Bulgarian Jews gathered there asked that he speak
Russian, a language they all spoke and understood, Ben-Gurion replied,
"No. Although I am fluent in Russian, speak English, French, and other
languages, here I will speak only Hebrew—the official language of the
future Jewish state, the language of the Bible. Who ever doesn't want to
listen can leave."[23] In another meeting with partisans and ghetto fighters who survived and reached Palestine, he defined the Yiddish they
spoke as a "jarring language" and abstained from speaking it with
them.[24] These political acts were typical of someone belonging to the
dominant elite engaged in reorganizing the political and cultural hegemony—acts meant to establish the social-political hierarchy and the intimate, secure relations between the dominant stratum and the lower
one.[25] Thus, even though it was the Jewish refugees who made the clandestine immigration campaign possible, and bore it "on their shoulders"
much more than they were borne by the sons and daughters of the Land
of Israel, it was these Zionist natives who were immortalized in poem
and mythic tale. Although it was the refugees who were casualties in the
war for immigration, nearly all the Mossad ships that carried them had
symbolic names chosen by the political elite in Palestine for their political significance to the Palestine-Zionist society. Neither the refugees nor
their local leaders were given any say in this; they were denied the right
to name ships in ways that would express their lives, their war, their victims, their language, or their memories.[26]

   To his demands that those from the Diaspora undergo a swift, fundamental change, Ben-Gurion added accusatory rhetoric placing responsibility for what happened, at least partially, on the survivors themselves,
making a moral judgment by way of comparison with the Yishuv. "Hitler
was not far from Palestine," said Ben-Gurion to Hitler's victims during a
visit to a hospital in one of the DP camps of Europe. "A terrible tragedy
might have transpired, but what happened in Poland could never happen
in Palestine. No one could have slaughtered us in the synagogues; every

boy and girl would have shot every German soldier."[27] Only later, when these survivor-refugees reached Zionist territory on board the Mossad ships, only after they had become *ma'apilim* ("summit climbers," the Zionist loaded term for the clandestine immigrants) and had found within themselves the power to resist and to display physical courage, did Ben-Gurion begin to extol them, turning them into a symbol of embedded power in the Zionist revolution.

The Immigration Martyr

This opportunity arose when the Mossad ship *Catriel Yafeh* reached Haifa port following the British cabinet decision in August 1946 to transfer the illegal immigrants to Cyprus. When the ship passengers, 604 refugees from Italy, learned that they were about to be deported to Cyprus, several of them jumped into the water and tried to swim away. British destroyers closed in on the ship, and boats captured the fugitives. Ben-Gurion immediately transformed them into a symbol of Zionist heroism that no empire can defeat. "In the last six months, the British government has shown that it can enforce its policies in Palestine by force of arms," he said in an interview in Paris on 9 September 1946, "and we have never doubted this. The power of Britain is much greater than ours. But we have something that I believe the British people, especially the Labour Party, despite its Foreign Office, know and acknowledge to be stronger—the strength of the spirit. Jews who jump into the sea and swim to the shores of Palestine are stronger than warships."[28] Several weeks later, he wrote in a programmatic article for the Twenty-second Zionist Congress that "a nation that contains this vital power and these *ma'apilim* will never be defeated or vanquished."[29] In his speech to the congress plenary, he made clandestine immigration and the illegal immigrants not just "the central campaign, the campaign of fate and honor," equal in value to the conquering of the land forty years earlier, but he raised them to a metaphysical level of an entity that emerges "by itself from the depths of the survival instinct of the nation."[30]

After one of the refugees in the ship *Palmach (Ariana)*, Yehiel Schwartz, was shot and killed in the fight with the British, and fifty refugees (including three women) jumped into the sea in an effort to reach shore when the British overpowered the ship,[31] the clandestine immigration had found its first victim to fall in an actual battle, the first dead hero, the martyr who sanctified the homeland. Ben-Gurion could now raise the cause to the heights of mythic courage in the history of the Jewish settlement in Palestine from ancient times to the beginning of the new Zionist era, from Masada to Tel Hai. "Meanwhile the deportation of clandestine immigrants continues," wrote Ben-Gurion to Abba Hillel Silver in the United States, "and the first Jewish refugee has already been shot and killed by the British fleet because of the heinous crime of wanting to reach his homeland. I'm sure you have read that several immigrants jumped into the sea, even though the ship was several kilometers from shore, in a desperate attempt to swim ashore, and the sailors of the British fleet forced them into the deportation ships and brought them to Cyprus, to the detention camp. I have no idea what this event meant to the world, but to me it said a lot—more than any Zionist book or speech that I have read in my life. To me, this was a great, albeit tragic, message, one of courage and encouragement. A nation who has such sons is not easily defeated, if this leap will serve as a symbol to the people."[32] The name of Schwartz, who jumped into the water in his desire to reach the shore of Palestine but did not make it, like Moses who saw the promised land but would never enter, was woven into Ben-Gurion's words innumerable times in those days.[33] He wrested Schwartz from the anonymity of the mass of immigrants and, with a master stroke, gave him a name and a face, continually engraving both into the new Zionist consciousness, transforming them into a symbol and establishing them in the revolutionary Jewish pantheon on a par with Trumpeldor. "Two or three weeks ago something happened," Ben-Gurion told the Zionist Conference in America. "It did not cause a sensation in the world press. . . . A small ship was intercepted by the British Navy three miles from the shore . . . and these unfortunate Jews, who went through all the hell of Hitler in Europe, they jumped into the sea, to swim to the shore of their homeland. Behind that jump there is a greater historic power than behind the mighty navy of this empire which tried to prevent these people from their home." He then linked the story to the tale of Tel Hai: "The few small and scattered Jewish villages in Galilee, sixty years ago, forty years ago, had to resist not a mighty empire, but forces that were ten, a hundred times as many as they were. They were not afraid. Some twenty Jewish young men and women resisted in Tel Hai for months against thousands of armed Bedouins [sic], and they did not retreat. They fell. Joseph Trumpeldor fell, Sarah Chisick fell, but Tel Hai is alive. And the Yishuv will resist. It cannot surrender. It is against its essence, its very soul."[34] To the French or British, Ben-Gurion spoke in a language they understood, using examples familiar to them from the recent past. "We have no fear of conflict with England, not because we are stronger than England, but because we have no choice," he said at a public gathering in Paris.

Several years ago was a decisive hour in the history of the British army, when it was caught in the Nazi pincers in Belgium. At that moment, the British army was extricated with sailing vessels, every kind that came to hand, even ramshackle, filthy, little boats. There was no choice, and Dunkirk became a name of honor in England. All the British people were proud of Dunkirk, and rightly so. It was a great military disaster turned into a greater moral triumph. Palestine is our Dunkirk. Our immigrants are sailing there in small, broken down boats. England mobilized its fleet, seized our small ship, the *Palmach*, and headed toward Cyprus. At a distance of three miles from the shores of Palestine, some of those aboard jumped into the sea to swim to the shores of our forefathers, to their home. But they never reached the shore. The British sailors, armed with automatic guns, caught them in the water and forced them to Cyprus. There is something stronger than the British army and the British navy, and that is the Jewish awareness that there is no choice. Someone who has no choice will jump into the sea, swim, and reach his destination, and he will build homes in the sands of the desert.[35]

These tirelessly repeated descriptions of the heroic act of the refugees were meant not just to establish a solid and unifying ideological connection that overrides conflicts and antagonisms, but also to create a discourse utilizing a mythic terminology (also evidenced by the use of Masada, Tel Hai, Dunkirk, and the crematoria of the death camps in the same context) about both the clandestine immigrants and the sons of Palestine who helped them. These words of Ben-Gurion were intended to entrench the story of immigration to Palestine as a fundamental component in the body of Zionist mythology, along with other elements such as "Jewish labor" and martyrdom for the Zionist cause, and, at the same time, to pay tribute to it. More than he viewed these refugees as sovereign beings, free to choose their path and preferences, Ben-Gurion assigned them their life challenge: to serve as raw material in the hands of the Zionist maker—that is, he himself or the Yishuv and revolutionary Zionism under his leadership. In this sense, one sees here a return to the previous Ben-Gurion attitude about the relations between the Diaspora and the Yishuv, which the Holocaust—about which Zionism was utterly helpless—did not change and even strengthened. According to this view, the Yishuv and its leader, Ben-Gurion, were the "new rendition" of the Jewish people, "the interpreters of what is deep within the souls" of those from the Diaspora—the bearers, in other words, of the one and only key to their "redemption."[36]

Present Tense Imperative

Most of Ben-Gurion's references to the survivors in statements addressed to the Yishuv operatives in Europe or to his colleagues in the Jewish Agency Executive and his political party, took the form of "thou shalt" commandments, transforming the survivors into passive objects. These instructions are heavy with active verbs: gather together (the Jews), send (movement leaders), strengthen (the morale), teach, safeguard (the youth movement),[37] or, elsewhere, recruit (forces), step up (immigration, settlement, security), resist, activate (the Jewish survivors in Europe), transport, inculcate (the pioneer spirit), deepen (Zionist awareness), impart language, organize in the Histadrut, transform into citizens of the Jewish state, and so forth.[38] The words are permeated with a sense of urgency and almost always use the present tense imperative, leaving no room for weighing the past, for reflection, or for a full encounter, painful and shocking as it may be, with the Holocaust and its victims.

To the victims of the Holocaust, Ben-Gurion assigned a role. Before he met the survivors, prior to leaving for Bulgaria in late 1944, Ben-Gurion had already formulated with remarkable clarity, the role they would assume in the Zionist struggle, and he characteristically rushed to share his thoughts with the world. In September 1944, in his parting words to the soldiers from Palestine about to leave for Europe, Ben-Gurion said, "More than anything, the fate of our cause hinges on the will and fortitude of the [surviving] million and a half Jews of Europe. Whether they, the moment they can raise their voices, are downtrodden, stricken, and disheartened, making do with the crumbs of rights . . . and the good graces and help they get from their rich brothers in America and international charitable organizations; or they—as proud and self-respecting Jews—join our demand for a homeland and independence for the Jewish nation, and are willing to storm the gates of Palestine."[39] After his first visit in the camps of Germany, Ben-Gurion frankly informed his colleagues in the Jewish Agency Executive of the motivations for his visit: "I was concerned about European Jewry. I knew that we stand before a prolonged and difficult struggle. . . . They [European Jewry] could be a major hindrance or a big help."[40] To the Mapai Central Committee he reported upon his return that he had never, in the entire world, found "such a Zionist public as I found in Munich and its surroundings, and I saw that this could be a hugely powerful factor in our political fight."[41]

More than a year later, when the British began to deport the Mossad ships to Cyprus and the refugees on those ships were placed at the forefront of the Zionist war, Ben-Gurion again extolled the historic power of those who came out alive, but he also noted the dangers and threat they pose. "When there's a need to mobilize and activate air-borne divisions and large fleets to stop the Jewish clandestine immigration," he wrote from Paris to the Mapai conference, "it is a sign that behind the clandestine immigration and the Jewish attraction to Palestine lies an historic, mighty, and powerful force that cannot easily be vanquished. And it shall not be vanquished! Therefore, do not be afraid and do not despair! . . . Here [among the survivors] are hidden huge forces of fulfillment. There are major dangers as well! Everyone who meets with the Jews in the German camps or the refugees of Poland, Hungary, or other countries will not dispute these words. No other segment of Judaism except ourselves will have such a great impact on the fate of Zionism in formation as the Jewish remnant in Europe, for better and for worse."[42] Indeed, Ben-Gurion's plan was to base his Zionist war on the triad of the refugee camps, the active Zionist forces in Palestine, and the Jewish community in America.[43] To the scenes of horror in the death camps and the fortitude—or lack of choice—he found in the DP camps, to the guilt feelings of the Western world, and to the power of the Jews in America and Palestine he assigned key roles in the transformation of the Jewish catastrophe into a liberating and redeeming force. The Holocaust not only devastated the Diaspora; according to Ben-Gurion, the great massacre also eliminated the option of a renewed cultural-national Jewish life outside Palestine. "I met with thousands of Polish Jewish refugees who escaped to Russia at the start of the war and then returned to Poland in order to immigrate to Palestine, and in their wandering from the distant reaches of the Urals and Turkestan through Poland and Czechoslovakia to occupied Germany [by the Allies], they regard themselves as on the threshold of their homeland," he reported to his colleagues.[44] Thus, before it was created, the Jewish state in Palestine claimed custody over continued Jewish existence and preservation of Jewish history and memory, "nationalizing" the Holocaust and its survivors.

From his visit to Bulgaria in December 1944 until the end of the war, Ben-Gurion was immersed in planning the Zionist campaign for the post-war period. Using primary and secondary sources, and with the help of the statistics department of the Jewish Agency, he gathered data about the Jews in Europe and the world. He was particularly interested in the Zionist pioneer youth movements and their spin-offs and in the demographic composition of the Jewish communities that remained.[45] By March 1945 Ben-Gurion had formulated a plan for the immigration of a million Jews in the eighteen months following the war. The thousands of pieces of statistics that he gathered, all recorded in his diary,[46] were the basis for the "Zionist Accounting after the War," which he presented before the Zionist Conference in early August 1945 in London[47]—the first international Jewish gathering since the Twenty-first Zionist Congress, which had dispersed on the eve of World War II and many of whose delegates did not survive the war. The immigration into Palestine of a million Jews within a year and a half from the war's end was viewed as part of the realization of the third phase of Zionist history: the statist (étatist) era.[48] Ben-Gurion wanted to carry out the immigration plan along two channels: a Zionist underground and the training of Jews—primarily young people—for the fight through an educational system exported to the Diaspora. The Holocaust, he wrote in his "Zionist Accounting," the étatist trends in the world, and the White Paper in Palestine cast doubt on the continued survival of the Jewish people. Only the immediate establishment of Jewish sovereignty to release the Jewish communities from the thumb of communism, and the bringing in of a million Jews "using the power of the Jewish state and the help of American Jewry," could avert this risk.[49]

It was not only because Ben-Gurion had a plan, but also because, before his colleagues did, he held a pessimistic view of British post-war policy, that the general disillusionment with a Labour Party solution to the problem of Palestine did not surprise him. By June 1945, following Churchill's letter to Weizmann noting that a discussion about Palestine would not take place until after the Allies meet at the peace table,[50] Ben-Gurion had concluded that the White Paper policy would continue indefinitely. In his words several days later to the Zionist

Emergency Committee in the United States, followed by a press conference, he suggested the possibility of resistance in Palestine if London
cannot be convinced through the United States to change existing policy.[51] It was a kind of encore to what he had done in December 1938,
when he made a quick visit to America prior to the Saint James
Conference to enlist the resources and support of American Jewry for
his "militant Zionism" program and to bring American leverage to
bear on the conference.[52] Now, as then, he sought to influence British
policy through American Jewry and the American government.[53] As in
his pre-war visit, he demanded that American Jewry supply money,
weapons, machines, science, technology, and professionals "in preparation for the battle about to be waged in Palestine."[54] This time, however, American Jews, fraught with guilt after the Holocaust, when they
had done so little to help European Jewry,[55] were generous in their
support of what he called the "battle" for the future state.[56]

While on the *Queen Elisabeth* en route to the Zionist Conference in
London, Ben-Gurion and the American Zionist leaders traveling with
him were informed about Churchill's electoral defeat and the Labour
Party's rise to power in Britain. This was ostensibly good news for the
Zionist camp, because Labour had traditionally been sympathetic to
Zionism and the party's recent platform, from December 1944, was
even more Zionist than the Zionist program itself.[57] Ben-Gurion, however, was not carried away by the rejoicing of his colleagues in London
and Palestine (where the Labour victory was greeted by displays of joy
in the streets, flag waving, and slogans). In contrast with the words of
Chaim Weizmann, who spoke in the London conference about the
great development and massive immigration in a gradual five-year
process under the auspices of the British government,[58] Ben-Gurion's
speech cautioned against illusions and complacency and conveyed an
open threat of war against Britain. "Do not rely on this great change
[the rise of Labour]," were his words, intended both for the conference
delegates and the new British government, "and do not assume that
this will solve the problem of the White Paper." He concluded, "If for
any reason the White Paper regime will be continued for an unspeci-
fied period . . . we in Palestine shall not fear nor be deterred by the
great power of England—and we shall fight her. . . . I feel an obligation to say this to the Zionist movement, to our friends in England,
and to the Labour movement: Either we are on the threshold of a
Jewish state, because without a state the Jewish people cannot survive

in the world as it exists today, or we are on the verge of a grave struggle, bitter and harsh, which the best of the Jewish nation will shoulder—whatever the price shall be."[59]

Jewish Post-War Triad

The heart of the conference fell in line with Ben-Gurion's impatience and aggressiveness, and not with Weizmann's moderation or appeal for continued cooperation with Britain. The conference delegates adopted the Biltmore plan and spoke of "increasing the tension in Palestine" if Britain failed to redress the problem.[60] In August 1945 matters became clearer. While Earl Harrison, the envoy of President Harry Truman, was composing the report of his tour of DP camps in Germany and his recommendations for the immediate immigration of 100,000 Jewish refugees to Palestine, the Colonial Office announced to the Jewish Agency the approval of 1,500 immigration certificates in keeping with the White Paper, confirming Zionist fears that nothing had changed in British policy. In a special meeting of the Jewish Agency Executive the very next day,[61] Ben-Gurion was extreme in his reactions. He demanded an end to talks with the British government, an intense press campaign in England and the United States, and activity to step up immigration to and security measures in Palestine. In a statement he wanted the Executive to publish, he called for the incorporation of a paragraph stating that "the gates of Palestine cannot and will not remain closed. They will be opened by Jews who are resolute, just as it is their natural right to return to their homeland." He also noted his intention to return to Palestine at once to initiate the necessary measures.[62]

Instead of going back, however, Ben-Gurion remained in Europe to organize the Zionist underground there. He wrote an eight-point summary of the strategy and tactics of the struggle, which is a key document for understanding Ben-Gurion's mood at the time and the priority he assigned to the different elements in the Zionist campaign. It was also the first step in establishing the large, post-war Zionist underground center in Paris, in which the Mossad played a key role. The second paragraph of Ben-Gurion's document stressed the need for a militant armed immigration, capable of defending itself from attack at sea or on shore, and for squads equipped with machine guns, hand grenades, and pistols to accompany the ships. The third point in the document asserted that comprehensive activity in Europe for arms acquisitions, military training, funding, communication, and recruitment for militant immigration would require a "central command in France." The fourth point dealt with mobilizing moral resources among the Zionist community in Palestine. "We should not wait to 'react' to the [British government] announcement. It is possible that no announcement of policy will be issued. What is decisive is the continuation of the White Paper policy in practice. The existence of the White Paper is a declaration of war on the Jewish people, and it is up to our nation—non-sovereign and oppressed—to fight with all the means at its disposal." In the seventh point, Ben-Gurion called for a prolonged and persistent campaign, "daring and calculated for longer than a brief period. No expectation of a final battle or a quick and easy victory." The eighth point dealt with informing the world about the Zionist campaign, stating that "its importance [world opinion] is almost equal to the strategy itself."[63]

This was a duplicate, though on a much grander scale, of his "militant immigration" plan from before the war. This immigration would, according to Ben-Gurion, have two purposes—a declaration of war on England and the movement of thousands of Jewish refugees to Palestine—and would attract the attention of the entire world. The operation was anticipated to be complex and long term, requiring the mobilization of all available resources: the Yishuv in Palestine, the Holocaust survivors in Europe, and world Jewry, especially American Jews. To the broad mobilization of the Jewish post-war triad—the Yishuv, refugees, and America—Ben-Gurion accorded special value beyond the immediate, practical gains. He saw the harnessing of the three post-war Jewish centers of power in terms of the symbolic struggle of overcoming the present Jewish condition, readying hearts and minds for a war of survival, the coming of which he had already envisioned.[64] As before the war, public opinion was considered an essential part of the plan, and Zionist propaganda was integral to the overall struggle.[65] Ben-Gurion threw himself into the task of drumming up public support, making many public appearances during the post-war years. He spoke in various forums in Palestine, before his party, and before British officials (the high commissioner in Palestine and government people in London). He appeared before Jewish organizations in Europe and America, he met the press, and he preached to whomever would listen. Again and again, he tirelessly outlined the basic points of his program, seeking to strike while the iron was hot and trying to instill in listeners the tenets of his belief. In his rhetoric, the refugees act of jumping into the sea embodied the drive of Jews to return to their land that no power on earth could stop.[66] It also represented grounds for the moral demand on the world to provide the survivors of the Holocaust—an event the likes of which the international community had never before seen and perhaps could have prevented—with a state. The importance of the Holocaust survivors in his formula derived from his belief in the crucial role of international public opinion. With the international media fed and orchestrated by a well-run Zionist propaganda machine, no power in the enlightened Western world would have the strength to prevent the Holocaust survivors from reaching their only refuge—the "home of their lives"—in Palestine. When the British dared to block the refugee ships and later deported the refugees, especially after some were killed in clashes with British soldiers, Ben-Gurion did not hesitate to compare the British deeds with those of the Nazis.[67]

October and November 1945 were a period of setting up the Zionist network in Europe and planting the operatives within the community of Holocaust survivors. The combination of operatives from Palestine with the Holocaust survivors represented, according to Ben-Gurion and others from Palestine, the crux of post-war Zionism and the thrust of the struggle against the British. It was, however, Ben-Gurion's political standing, personal authority, and persuasive skills that transformed this mixture into a movement on which the Jews could build their campaign for abandoning the continent of their death and around which favorable world opinion could be mobilized—including, if not the support then the latent and cautious sympathy, of other governments.[68] In Paris, his temporary headquarters, Ben-Gurion established the center from which the underground Zionist activity throughout Europe would be managed, where intelligence would be compiled, decoded, and analyzed and from which political contacts would fan out. He wanted Ehud Avriel, a kibbutz member born in Prague and a Mossad agent, to run the Paris center.[69] To finance the underground activities in Europe and the other Zionist enterprises, Ben-Gurion called for establishing four centers—London, Switzerland, America, and Palestine—for key people who would engage in the financial activity. He suggested that the procurement of ships be transferred at once to America because of the difficulties encountered by Mossad people in many European countries, and decided that the Mossad vessels sail under the flags of Latin American countries.

In his meetings during his visits to the DP camps with Edward Warburg and Dr. Joseph Schwartz, who were visiting the camps on behalf of the JDC, he spoke of transporting thousands of Jews across the continent, feeding and lodging them in transit countries, maintaining them in Germany and Austria, smuggling them to Mediterranean ports, and then moving them by sea to Palestine. He then reached a key agreement that changed the face and scope of Zionist activity.[70] In late 1945 the Zionist movement placed the clandestine immigration at the center of its priorities in formal, not just practical, terms. "In addition to the regular political activity, constructive and defensive," asserted the Jewish Agency Executive upon Ben-Gurion's return from Europe, "the struggle for the realization of Zionism now requires a special effort in the following directions: (a) increased clandestine immigration from all countries; (b) active defense of the clandestine immigration at sea and the entry points to Palestine; (c) establishment of a movement to protect and promote clandestine immigration across the entire Jewish Diaspora; and (d) removal of obstacles in Palestine that prevent clandestine immigration."[71]

Between Two Cities

While organizing the Zionist underground in Europe from Paris, Ben-Gurion made a trip to London, where, together with Moshe Shertok, he met with Colonial Secretary George Hall and his deputy Creech-Jones on the morning of 13 November 1945. He heard from them the announcement about Palestine that Foreign Secretary Bevin was to make in the House of Commons that day.[72] It is impossible not to see the far-reaching, if ambivalent, significance of this conjunction of events. Because in October and November 1945, when the plan for the Zionist clandestine campaign was conceived, Ben-Gurion was moving incessantly back and forth between the two capitals on either side of the channel. This was not just an oft-repeated journey but a border crossing in the deepest sense—from the legal realm in London, where he functioned as chair of the Jewish Agency Executive, bearing an official position, and coming and going in the chambers of the British government, to the illegal realm in Paris, where he ran the underground campaign against the British, spearhead of the resistance movement of

Palestine.[73] The repeated crossing of this line between the open political realm and the covert underground was a metaphor of Ben-Gurion's ambivalence toward the clandestine immigration and his frequent passage from the political-diplomatic domain to the radical sphere of illegal activity when political channels were blocked, and back again.

Ben-Gurion had faith in this dual strategy of diplomatic navigation combined with militant struggle, the legal and the illegal, which was referred to as "controlled struggle" or "restrained activism."[74] The intention was to maximize the sophisticated and subtle use of all the tools at the disposal of the Zionist movement: the Jewish population in Palestine, for demonstrations, protest, sabotage, and resistance; the clandestine immigration operations in Europe and at sea; and diplomatic and political activity in the various capitals of the world. These tools were to be used simultaneously or sequentially, according to the demands of changing circumstances. Clandestine immigration was meant to be an instrument used by the Zionist leadership in the struggle to attain a state and was bound by the decisions of the leadership. It developed, however, an inertia of its own. This effort to activate various instruments of the Zionist struggle had for Ben-Gurion another dimension, that is, the "last battle" he waged (ending in December 1946) in his personal struggle with Chaim Weizmann. This battle was not just about the strategies of Zionism but about the leadership of the movement. Here, too, clandestine immigration served Ben-Gurion in his war against Britain and also in the fight—political, personal, and partisan—for the command of the movement. When he demanded that the clandestine immigration not be halted for even one day, not even to restore strained relations with Britain—which he still believed should not be irrevocably severed, even when at their lowest ebb—he was concerned not just with the immigration itself, but with how to strengthen his own leadership and undermine Weizmann's power base, which rested on Weizmann's special relationship with Britain. This was evident from the summer of 1946 through early 1947, that is, the period from the British Broadside operation to dismantle the Zionist power and leadership (Black Saturday, 29 June 1946) to the conclusion of the Twenty-second Zionist Congress, with Ben-Gurion's victory and Weizmann's removal from the center of the Zionist movement. Indeed, one of the goals of the British Broadside operation was to eliminate the radical elements from leadership in Palestine, which were responsible for directing the resistance movement and the clandestine immigration campaign, then at its height. From January until the end of

June 1946, the Mossad brought eight ships from Italy, Romania, Greece, and France, carrying 7,500 refugees. Many other ships were ready to go; in July alone, five more Mossad ships set sail.[75] The British Broadside operation also sought to restore and strengthen the influence of Chaim Weizmann's moderate leadership.[76]

All of Ben-Gurion's efforts from the moment in Paris when he heard the details of the British operation were focused on thwarting the political dimension of the operation and foiling the British plan to return the mantle of Zionist leadership to Weizmann.[77] Losing no time and setting all else aside, Ben-Gurion first worked to strengthen the control of the Jewish Agency Executive by tightening and streamlining the coordination among its various centers: Jerusalem, Paris, London, and New York.[78] For that purpose he went to the United States and obtained a joint decision with leaders of American Jewry about the need to hold a special meeting of world Zionist leaders to formulate Zionist policy.[79] He ascribed special importance to setting the rules of the game, and he succeeded. His choice of Paris as the nerve center of operations was not coincidental. Although there was a legal matter preventing Ben-Gurion from conducting his affairs out of London—after Black Saturday, the British issued an arrest warrant against him—the British capital was Weizmann's town, the territory in which he operated for years based on his political concepts and in which he excelled. Transferring operations from London to Paris represented not just a profound change in Zionist policies at the time, but also the transfer of leadership from Weizmann to Ben-Gurion. Paris was intended to be the actual and symbolic site of realizing the Zionist revolution, of shifting from Weizmann's traditional policies to the alternative, militant Zionist strategy. The choice of Paris was a declaration to the Yishuv and the world that Zionist affairs were no longer determined by lobbying in the corridors of power in London, but in Palestine and the European continent centered in Paris, where Ben-Gurion reigned.

Weizmann understood this well. He used various means to prevent the conference of Zionist leaders from convening in Paris or to postpone it to a later date, and to avoid looking like he was being manipulated by Ben-Gurion. Ultimately, he avoided the conference, citing "health reasons."[80] This was a low point in relations between the two, following a long series of resignation threats by each side. More important, it widened the rift between the strategies of the two leaders, a rift that would never be closed. While Weizmann persisted, even after Labour's change of heart about Palestine came to light, to adhere to political moderation and diplomatic lobbying—which had always been his strategy—Ben-Gurion urged more extreme action and radicalization of the Jewish reaction. When Weizmann renewed his meetings with the British government ministers in October 1945, after Labour's position about Palestine had become known although not officially published, Ben-Gurion demanded an explicit decision from the Executive to sever ties with the British government. "This phony friendship, which ostensibly prevails in talks, only conceals the terrible truth from the public and members of the government: the murder of our refugees in Germany and the attempt to choke us in Palestine. Today I renewed my proposal to 'sever' ties with the government here—for as long as they implement the White Paper—and I demand that all members of the Executive participate in this vote. I announced that until an official decision is taken, I do not see myself represented in these talks."[81] Two days later, on 10 October, Ben-Gurion again warned Weizmann not to attend a second meeting with Bevin (the first had ended fruitlessly), and he announced that he was unwilling and unable "to take fictitious responsibility."[82] In a meeting between the two at Weizmann's request, apparently in an effort to heal the rift, Ben-Gurion threatened to resign if the Executive and the General Council, including its English and American members, were not convened in Jerusalem. "I am prepared to submit my resignation to these institutions to enable them to arrange the necessary reorganization of the Executive should there be a need. If for any reason this meeting cannot be held, I cannot continue to serve in the Executive."[83] Weizmann, on the other hand, was appalled by the renewal of the Jewish resistance actions following the first lull in the campaign, upon the visit to Palestine of the Anglo-American Committee of Inquiry. When on 25 April 1946, the day after the submission of the committee's report, members of the Stern group murdered British soldiers, Weizmann informed the high commissioner that he opposed these Jewish actions and would try to halt them.

Controlled Struggle

Paradoxically, the Paris conference of the expanded Executive was a great victory both for Ben-Gurion, who convened it and was the dominant speaker, and for the moderates of the Zionist leadership—Ben-Gurion's opponents, led by Weizmann, who did not show up. The very convening of the Executive at a time and place chosen by Ben-Gurion over Weizmann's opposition was itself a significant achievement. Beyond that, the deliberations and decisions of the conference reflected the "controlled struggle"—alternating militancy and restraint, depending on the circumstances—that Ben-Gurion had advocated. Ben-Gurion played a sophisticated game at the conference. He participated intensively in the deliberations but then abstained from voting. He seemed reluctantly to go along with the moderate initiatives of Dr. Nahum Goldmann—a Weizmann man—and accepted the principle of partition that Goldmann proposed. In fact, Ben-Gurion, who not only welcomed but quietly encouraged this moderate direction, created the impression of being dragged to accept Goldmann's initiative only for the sake of not appearing too moderate and risking the support of activist parties back home. He needed that support for the last battle with the moderates and their leader, Weizmann, planned for the Zionist Congress. To his supporters who were perplexed by his positions, Ben-Gurion explained that "the unity of the leadership and the camp must be preserved until decisions at the Congress."[84] He further said, "At this crucial hour, one must not jolt the movement and exacerbate differences."[85]

Ben-Gurion viewed the decisions of the Paris conference to be "historic,"[86] and they constituted the program of the Zionist movement from then on. The question of illegal immigration, even if not central to the conference, ran like a scarlet thread through the lengthy deliberations of the expanded Executive. On the day the conference opened, Weizmann met in London with Colonial Secretary George Hall to discuss the Morrison-Grady plan. This meeting, on the margin of events, was one of those minor yet revealing occurrences signifying some far-reaching change. Just when the Zionist leadership, headed by Ben-Gurion, had convened in the French capital for the elaboration of a new political breakthrough and to galvanize the Zionist camp around it, Weizmann was still clinging to the old system in his own, anachronistic, territory. Following this meeting, on 2 August, the colonial secretary handed two letters to Weizmann. In the first letter Hall wrote that the members of the Jewish Agency Executive jailed in Latrun (as part of the British Broadside operation), or those who would be arrested upon their return to Palestine, could not participate in the Jewish Agency delegation to the conference set for London in September, and he asked Weizmann for a list of who should be invited among the Jews. It was clear from Hall's letter that the final decision of who would be invited would be made by the British government.[87] The second letter to Weizmann referred to the illegal immigration. It stressed that the government had resolutely decided to put an end to the illegal immigration so that it would not destroy chances for an agreement, and that the announcement about the measures to be used to halt it would be published in the newspapers.[88] In Paris Ben-Gurion demanded, of course, that Hall's proposal be "firmly and clearly rejected."[89]

Ten days later, on 12 August, the British government carried out Hall's threat and published its new measures to prevent illegal immigration into Palestine—above all the transfer of the illegal immigrants to camps in Cyprus and elsewhere until "a decision can be taken as to their future in the context of a permanent and just solution is reached." The announcement stated that the "illegal traffic [was] not, as has been maintained, a movement arising spontaneously among the European Jews who see in Palestine their only hope for the future. Nor are those who encourage and direct it inspired solely by the sympathy which is so widely felt for suffering." It was further stressed that the traffic was "a widely ramified and highly organized movement supported by very large financial contributions from Zionist sources, which has been built up and put into operation by unscrupulous persons in an attempt to force the hand of His Majesty's government and anticipate their decision on future policy in Palestine." The British described the organizers of the immigration campaign as a "minority of Zionist extremists" who maintain "a closely knit network of agents in the countries of eastern and southern Europe," which are—rather than the camps in Germany—the main source for a large number of the immigrants. The announcement also claimed that the illegal immigrants reinforced the terrorist element among the Jews and that, therefore, "their promiscuous introduction cannot be tolerated any longer."[90]

The first deportation was carried out by the British the day after the publication of the "Cyprus decision," on 13 August. A total of 1,280 refugees on two Mossad ships (*Yagur* and *Henrietta Szold*), captured and brought to Haifa port, were deported that same day. Although a curfew was placed on Jewish Haifa on the day of deportation and the day before, thousands of Haifa residents violated the regulations and walked through the streets toward the port. Work was halted from 6 A.M. to midnight. A large crowd gathered in the Jewish neighborhoods and clashed with British soldiers. In one incident, soldiers fired into a crowd of demonstrators and killed three people. Demonstrators also gathered in Tel Aviv, and Jerusalem protesters closed their stores and recreational facilities.[91] The feeling, however, among the Mossad people who accompanied the ships, the Palmach soldiers, and the refugees on board was that the Jewish population did not rise to the occasion.[92] It should be noted that the country lacked its central leadership at the time; some were in Latrun jail while others were attending the expanded conference of the Zionist Executive in Paris.

From Paris, Ben-Gurion tried to use the refugee deportation as proof that Britain ruled Palestine by brute force alone. "The Mandate was destroyed in 1939. They broke down Jewish representation, they expel Jews from Palestine. Only after we make this completely clear to the world, can we talk about [a strategy of] non-cooperation. The question is not purely ethical. It may very well reach the UN. France and America for their own reasons will hesitate to oppose Britain. And we must wage the struggle against Britain as a power that uses brute force to oppress Palestine and the Jewish people. That is our basic starting point."[93] The next day Ben-Gurion was even more blunt. He attacked the British actions, even comparing their deeds with Hitler's. He also condemned the weak reaction of the Jews in Palestine and did not hold back a swipe at Weizmann. "We must not forget," he said, "that while Hall is talking politely with Weizmann, Jews are being killed in Palestine. . . . Things are happening in Palestine such as have never been seen before in the history of the Zionist movement and the Jewish nation—with the exception of Hitler's deeds—and we did not react. Each one of us who speaks to the government must feel that he represents the six hundred thousand Jews of Palestine who suffer the insults and attacks of the government. If our political efforts fail, we must have a defined plan for continuing the struggle. . . . Let us not forget that Jews will not always be willing to be shot and removed from Palestine without finding a way to respond."[94]

At the end of August, after deliberations had ended at the expanded conference in Paris and in keeping with the two-pronged course of action he had espoused, Ben-Gurion again demanded at the Political Committee of the Jewish Agency Executive—in defiance of the position of the London (Weizmann) group—that clandestine immigration be given top priority in contacts with the British. It should be declared, he said, that the British policy of restricting immigration to 1,500 certificates a month had no basis in law, "not in accordance with the Mandate and not in keeping with any UN decision." He also called for more intense diplomatic efforts in various European countries—Poland, Yugoslavia, and France—to counter Britain's demands of these governments to prevent Zionist operatives from working in their territories and sailing from their ports.[95] The tumultuous congress which convened in December 1946, ultimately making Ben-Gurion head of the Zionist Executive and leader of the Zionist campaign in its final stages before realization of the goal of a state, gave him an even broader base of support than was expected.[96] From then on, Ben-Gurion dedicated himself mainly to building up military power, based on his belief that an armed confrontation was looming ahead. He did not, however, withdraw entirely from the issue of clandestine immigration. In addition to making public statements about the critical importance of this specific instrument,[97] he increased the Mossad's resources for preparing for the fateful year.[98] His ambivalence toward clandestine immigration, however, which was especially notable on the eve of the war,[99] never disappeared and returned in full force with the two large Mossad operations of 1947, the record year for the clandestine immigration campaign—the *Exodus* and the two *Pan* ships.

Changing Agendas

Ben-Gurion's direct involvement in the *Exodus* affair was recorded only at its conclusion, upon the British deportation of the refugees from Port de Bouc in France back to Germany. He monitored the incident, however, from the time it made headlines and turned into "the affair"—when British destroyers attacked the ship, with 4,500 refugees on board, several miles off Palestinian shores. Ben-Gurion carefully entered into his diary the details of the clash with the British, the course of events, and the victims, without comment.[100] The enormous propaganda value he attached to the ship and its 4,500 refugees after their deportation, to France from Palestine, and then to the international publicity the passengers drew while anchored opposite the French port in three British deportation ships,[101] is evident from his remarks to the Histadrut General Council following the hanging of two British sergeants by the Irgun on 30 July 1947, one week after the ships had reached France. Ben-Gurion was furious with the Irgun action and the harm it brought to the Zionist cause. He believed that the drama of the *Exodus* could yield unprecedented political dividends for the Zionist campaign at a critical historical moment—just when UNSCOP was about to complete its deliberations—and that the murder of the sergeants could wipe out these gains. He compared the Irgun's deeds to the Nazi horrors and referred to collaboration between Jewish "hooligans" and the "hooligan" British government, both of which were subversive of Zionist goals. In demanding that the agenda of the meeting be changed to allow discussion of this matter, Ben-Gurion asserted that "there has never been [a situation so shameful and embarrassing] as this in the history of the Yishuv." First, Ben-Gurion cited the murder in Haifa of a Jewish bank clerk during an attempted robbery by members of Irgun,[102] extolling him as the anonymous martyr: "The first and only Jew who dared stand up to a band of murderers . . . was killed in the heart of a Jewish city, no help proffered to him," and the press remained silent. "He [the murder victim] was dropped from the agenda," said Ben-Gurion. These words about the martyred clerk only prefaced his oration about the truly great martyrs of the hour—those on the *Exodus*. Most of his speech was devoted to the refugees being "dropped from the agenda" because of the Irgun's irrational act—the hanging of two British sergeants—at the height of the heroic *Exodus* affair: "Four thousand and five hundred Jews, the like of which has never been seen before, who sanctified the name of Israel, were dropped from the agenda because of a gang of hooligans in Palestine who wanted to perform a Nazi-type deed here. . . . I view this situation of the government and Ezzel [Irgun] as that of a nation under siege, the siege of a mighty and cruel enemy, cheating and hypocritical. And within the besieged city is an outbreak of the plague. Some say: Perhaps the plague will also enter the enemy camp. I think that the plague and the enemy are both our foes, and we must fight each with all our might and at the right moment. . . . I will not stop battling the plague because there is an outside oppressor, and I will not stop battling the oppressor because the plague rages within."[103] Through the *Exodus*, added Ben-Gurion, the world has been shown the baseness of the White Paper regime. "In our generation, there has never been an epic of the Jewish war like this one, which is greater, in my opinion, than the war in the ghetto, because in the ghetto there was no choice, while these Jews had a choice. They could have gone to France, and the French state wanted to accept them. Among them are those who languished in camps for years. Pregnant women, small children. They had a choice of going to France and they refused. This was one of the greatest expressions of the Jewish struggle, of Jewish pride, and of the connection with Palestine." In closing, he spoke of the Irgun's cooperation with the British ("allies to Bevin"), about the "mutual help" between them ("maybe they don't speak to each other, but they don't have to speak at all, and still there is mutual help"). "It [Irgun] presented a Nazi spectacle among us, caught two Englishmen and hanged them. After such a deed, who in the world will pay attention to the war of these five thousand Jews [the *Exodus* passengers]? Even we don't notice it."[104]

Two days later, in Mapai Council, Ben-Gurion was even harsher. In a "trial" for the breakaway organizations (Irgun and the Stern group) he played the role of both prosecutor and judge, condemning them to total elimination. "A week ago," he said to his party, "we reached the apex of this great tragic battle—the *Exodus 47*—and seemed somehow to shake the conscience of the world. Until these Jewish patriot-crooks came along, made the world forget this great campaign, and presented them with a different spectacle—the hanging of two hostages in a Jewish city in Palestine. They gave Bevin a gift that his entire fleet and anti-Semitic system would not have been able to deliver. . . . For this treachery alone, erasing the great tragic struggle of the *Exodus 47* from the memory of the world, they should be obliterated from the face of the earth."[105] In this address, Ben-Gurion again placed the clandestine immigration at the heart of the struggle, "the focal point of the campaign of the Jewish people." This time, however, he bound it together with the UN—again integrating the legal with the illegal, the political move with the violent action—and also hinted at his preference for the UN arena that would soon take precedence, already relegating the Jewish refugees and clandestine immigration to a lower priority in the overall Zionist campaign. Even on this occasion Ben-Gurion did not pull his punches regarding Weizmann, saying that he represented "the Zionism of yesterday, Zionism from before the deluge" and criticizing Weizmann's "pathetic" appearance before the UN committee, "when an old Jew stands up and talks about the catastrophe of his life's work" without mentioning a word about the clandestine immigration. "Zionism like [Weizmann's] no longer exists," said Ben-Gurion. "Zionism without clandestine immigration, the tragedy of clandestine immigration, the courage of clandestine immigration, and the agonies of clandestine immigration—is not Zionism of our times."[106]

Yet while attacking the "old Jew" Weizmann for his Zionism of yore—devoid of the tragedy, bravery, and suffering of the clandestine

immigration—and while himself characterizing the story of the clandestine immigration in every possible public forum as "the most tragic
and sublime spectacle in the contemporary Zionist war," Ben-Gurion
had already decided on a new order of priorities and was drawing the
new battle lines of the future Zionist front. The role of the clandestine
immigration was diminished considerably in this new battle plan. The
sentiment he expressed in public about the Jewish refugees gave way to
a more pragmatic and instrumental approach, manifested in behind-
the-scenes deliberations and decisions. What Ben-Gurion defined as
the "security of the country and establishment of an armed Jewish
force" now became of paramount importance to him. He argued that
"our entire immediate and distant future is at stake, and these must
guide the Zionist strategy, both externally and internally."[107] These
were Ben-Gurion's words at a special meeting of a select group of
members of the Zionist General Council held in Zurich in late August
1947, in which, according to Ben-Gurion, "frank things can be said." In
the confusion, sense of failure, and lack of direction that permeated the
conference[108]—which was poorly timed in Zionist terms, especially in
the context of the work of UNSCOP[109]—Ben-Gurion confronted his
associates with his forecasts of imminent war in Palestine and his recommendations and claims derived from these forecasts. "It will not be
political opponents [i.e., the British] who will be up against us," he
told his colleagues, "but the disciples and even teachers of Hitler, who
know only one way of solving the Jewish problem—*total destruction*."
"The goal of the Arab onslaught now," he added, "is not theft, terrorism, or halting the growth of the Zionist enterprise, but rather the
eradication of the entire Zionist enterprise."[110]

Facing the apprehensiveness of most of his colleagues ("the Zionist
movement was not then prepared, it seems, to hear these things," he said
several months later[111]), Ben-Gurion demanded that the movement free
itself from the beliefs and perceptions that belonged to the past, and face
the imminent events open-eyed: "The movement dealt with other matters entirely such as the UN Committee, viewing these as the center of
gravity. We refer to these as political issues, and they are endlessly discussed. I'm sorry I have to differ with the prevailing view and focus on
an entirely different issue—the security of the Yishuv, which now means
whether or not Zionism will be realized or extinguished."[112] He directed
an inner, closed committee to devise a detailed plan for establishing an
armed force, but his demand for funds to build up the force—which,
jointly with the national command and general staff, reached an initial

sum of three million Palestine pounds[113] according to a conservative estimate—met with reservations and mistrust.[114] In fact, there was nothing new in Ben-Gurion's proposal. Nine months before the Zionist
General Council met in Zurich, at a meeting of the Political Committee
of the Twenty-second Zionist Congress Ben-Gurion had asserted that
the question of security is the key issue that the Yishuv must contend
with, and at stake was the very existence of the Yishuv.[115] At the conclusion of the congress, he demanded that his colleagues in the Jewish
Agency Executive entrust him with the security portfolio, and he got it.
The dramatic transformation of Ben-Gurion upon the conclusion of the
congress—in his Zionist priorities, status in the movement, and self-perception—was already evident in his meeting with the high commissioner
in Jerusalem immediately upon his return to Palestine after the congress
and after eight months of absence from Palestine. At this meeting (cited
in the Introduction), after giving the usual emotional speech, as the high
commissioner phrased it, about the right of immigration, he acknowledged almost in passing that no ships were expected in the near future.[116]

It was not the absence of Mossad ships that was on Ben-Gurion's mind
at the time. In the last days of January and through February 1947 loomed
a series of talks in London with the foreign and colonial secretaries of the
British government. Ben-Gurion intended to attend these talks with his
sword sheathed and to discuss the possible partition of Palestine if the
subject were raised by his British partners to the talks.[117] His top priority
now was the security of the Yishuv in Palestine. The action was no longer
on the naval front, where ships were plying the seas toward the shores of
Palestine before the eyes of the world, enthralling public opinion. He no
longer had to use this tool in his political battles within the Zionist movement, as the primacy of his status had been formally acknowledged at the
congress. Thus, upon his return to Palestine from the failed talks in
London, where British foreign secretary Bevin had announced to the
House of Commons that the question of Palestine was being transferred
to the UN,[118] Ben-Gurion devoted himself almost entirely to the security
issue and to training the army-in-formation for war.[119]

Refugees or Security

The synchronization of the Zionist General Council
conference in Zurich and the *Exodus* affair—yet another historical

coincidence that provides a subtle key to decode a deeper process—allow us to locate with greater precision the point at which the Jewish refugees and the clandestine immigration enterprise lose, almost simultaneously, their relative importance in the Zionist campaign. This timing also helps reveal the dissonance between what was made public and what was concealed, between the declarative, rhetorical, and the concrete dimension. These two events also brought together the top political leadership (Ben-Gurion), representing the change that had already taken place in the movement's priorities, and the secondary, operational leadership (Mossad head Shaul Meirov), representing the illegal immigration enterprise and still embodying the old set of priorities. The watershed with regard to the refugees and clandestine immigration, their importance all at once diminished in Zionist considerations, was the battle over the *Exodus* waged by British destroyers on the morning of 18 July 1947 and the dragging of the passengers of the disabled ship that evening to the three British deportation ships in Haifa harbor in full view of several members of UNSCOP.[120] In these events the refugees fulfilled their part in the Zionist political campaign to persuade the world of the link between the fate of the Holocaust survivors and the creation of a Jewish state in Palestine; in fact, they did so beyond all expectations and planning, winning them lavish praise in the Zionist rhetoric.[121] In the coming days, however, there was less need for the courage shown by the *Exodus* refugees. Indeed, at a time when the Zionist leadership warily awaited publication of UNSCOP's recommendations about the partition of Palestine, the bravery of the refugees, anchored off France and then in Hamburg, was almost superfluous from the Zionist point of view. After the publication of the recommendations, as the focus of political activity shifted to the UN, the steadfastness of the refugees, though bringing additional gains to the Zionist publicity campaign, became redundant. The shocking fate of the *Exodus* refugees, about to be returned to Germany after a harsh month on prison ships off France, did not offset the political considerations of the Zionist policymakers at the time, as is evident from the mildly worded press release issued by the Jewish Agency Executive on 24 August 1947 following the deportation announcement of the British government.[122]

Officially, the Zionist General Council, meeting in Zurich between 25 August and 2 September 1947, just as the *Exodus* deportees were making their way to Hamburg, was staunch in its support for the clandestine immigration and the refugees. The conference decisions asserted that "The *Ha'apala* [clandestine immigration] to Palestine" is "the main front of the *political struggle* [emphasis added] waged by Zionism against the conspiracy of the White Paper" and has a "vital role in the campaign to rescue the Jewish masses."[123] There were some who still held this opinion. Moshe Shertok, for example, argued at the conference that "the clandestine immigration cannot lose its first place on the agenda of Zionist policies." In his opinion, there was no certainty about how things would develop following publication of the UNSCOP decision, when and if a UN decision would be taken, and how favorable the conclusions would be from the Zionist perspective. "We are kneading material that is not entirely in our hands," said Shertok. However, he continued, "Some matters are in our hands. The clandestine immigration is still in our hands to a large extent, though not entirely." He thus called for the focus of "all efforts and all energies upon the clandestine immigration."[124] Behind the scenes, however, the new perception of "the Zionist political agenda" was already at work, shaping decisions on the ground. Ben-Gurion's words in the closed meeting of 26 August, in which he placed security and the very existence of the Yishuv at the core of Zionist energies and actions, have already been cited.[125] His stand concerning the deportation of the *Exodus* passengers to Hamburg, however, expressed far from the public eye, is much more telling. Even among the chief operatives in Europe, who were in direct contact with the survivors and the ship passengers themselves, opinion was divided about what action to take or to assign to the refugees when their ships reached Hamburg. Shaul Meirov, the Mossad head, and Hayim Hoffman (later Yahil), head of the Jewish Agency delegation to Europe, claimed that force should be used to prevent disembarkation of the refugees "on German soil" and that an "extreme action, to exacerbate events and cause serious clashes with the British" should be taken.[126] Others, such as Kurt Levine, the Jewish Agency envoy to the British occupied zone in Germany, opposed extreme action on the grounds that the *Exodus* passengers had gone through enough, and the battle must not be waged "on their backs." Levine suggested acting quietly and cunningly to smuggle the *Exodus* refugees out of the camps the British had prepared for them near Lübeck, transfer them to Belsen, and then bring them to Palestine with immigration certificates that he had in stock.[127] The three presented their views to Ben-Gurion in his hotel room in Zurich at the time of the Zionist General Council meetings and asked for his reaction. Ben-Gurion sided unreservedly with Levine. For humanitarian reasons, he explained, he opposed the kind of extreme activity desired by Meirov and Hoffman; he noted that the *Exodus* passengers had already done their bit and should not be mixed up in activity that might "end in bloodshed."[128]

Humanitarian considerations and the desire to avoid bloodshed, then, ostensibly guided Ben-Gurion in his decision not to involve the *Exodus* refugees in any violent reaction to their deportation to Germany. Things were not as unequivocal as they appear, however. How can such humanitarian considerations be reconciled with Ben-Gurion's harsh reaction to Weizmann's efforts to prevent the disembarkation in Hamburg of the *Exodus* refugees in the first place and to have them returned to France? Does not Ben-Gurion's reaction to Weizmann's efforts contradict the claim of humanitarian motives? From the Twenty-second Zionist Congress, it should be recalled, Weizmann did not have an official role in the Zionist movement. Old, infirm, and politically vanquished, he tried to work out a solution from his residence in London, at the initiative of colleagues in the London office who were pushing him to intervene. The fate of relations with Britain in the context of implementing the UNSCOP report and the possibility that an "open scandal in Hamburg" would exacerbate relations that were already stretched to the limit gave him no rest. "Insistence in the matter of the ships," he believed, "can only exacerbate relations and give the Foreign Office an opportunity of saying that they are throwing in their hand, and will have nothing further to do with the whole business. . . . For the sake of getting a firm and satisfactory basis for the execution of the UNSCOP report," he believed, "it is very necessary that we should find some way back to approximately normal relations with Britain."[129]

The immediate fate of the refugees, who had been at sea for two months in abysmal conditions and who were about to be forcibly removed from the ships onto German soil, disturbed him too.[130] For a combination of reasons, Weizmann wanted, at almost any price, to "avoid any open scandal at Hamburg, even at the risk of having the ships turned back to France." His request to meet with Bevin on this issue was denied; the British foreign secretary "was anxious to avoid any risk of discussing the UNSCOP decision" because that might constitute "intervention" in the matter on his part. If Weizmann's issue was "the ships," he was told, "it would be best . . . to discuss the matter first with the Undersecretary of State at the Colonial Office, who would report to Bevin."[131] Indeed, in the first week of September Weizmann was invited to the Colonial Office, where he met with the undersecretary, Ivor Thomas, and warned him of the dire results that would ensue from the British decision to forcibly disembark the refugees in Hamburg.[132] In response, the undersecretary suggested that the ships be returned to France on condition that the Jewish Agency undertake in writing to recommend that the ship's passengers disembark there voluntarily. At his own discretion (all members of the Jewish Agency Executive were then at the Zionist General Council in Zurich and thus unreachable), Weizmann appealed to Léon Blum in Paris and asked him to intervene personally—to influence Bevin and to persuade the *Exodus* refugees to disembark without riots in France.[133]

Brinkmanship

Information about Weizmann's activity reached Ben-Gurion in Geneva from two sources. From Paris a Mossad agent reported Weizmann's appeal to Blum, and a telephone call from the Jewish Agency offices in London reported the meeting between Weizmann and Thomas and the undersecretary's proposal.[134] The information about Weizmann's involvement and the way this information reached Ben-Gurion immediately set into motion Ben-Gurion's characteristic double emotional reaction, especially where Weizmann was concerned: the need to have his views prevail and the need to retaliate against anyone posing an obstacle to his forward motion, which he expressed by threats of resignation and by disrupting the Executive. "Any separate activity in London that is not approved by the entire Executive," wrote Ben-Gurion to the Executive members in London, "is liable to blow up the Executive and also possibly the Zionist Organization."[135] He then sent instructions to the Mossad agent in Paris to immediately halt any activity by Léon Blum that was related to the affair, while warning the people in London that acceptance of the colonial undersecretary's proposal—the quiet return of the ships to France—contradicted the decision of the Executive, and that he himself vigorously opposed it. Ben-Gurion's letter to the members of the Agency Executive in London is almost unprecedented in its harshness of tone, actually calling Weizmann a collaborator with the British government against the Zionist cause. "The

English are using Weizmann to apply pressure on us to their advantage," said Ben-Gurion, supposedly in the name of Shertok.[136] He wrote that he "opposes the assignment of any political job whatsoever to CW [Chaim Weizmann]—whether in England or America," and he added that "there is no need to explain this." Ben-Gurion also demanded that Weizmann not interfere in the activities of the Executive or serve as an envoy or mediator between the British government and the Jewish Agency. "If there is a need—and there is—to approach the government, Executive members should be the ones to do so—accountable to the Executive and in adherence to Executive decisions. The intervention of CW will be damaging both externally and internally." Despite his understanding of the delicate situation of the Jewish Agency in London vis-à-vis Weizmann, Ben-Gurion cracked down, demanding that they not take action "about the clandestine immigrants" that would oppose "our joint decisions," that they not violate the "instructions decided upon" or lend a hand to "a new devils' dance in London, of all places." What was done, added Ben-Gurion, has already brought great damage. "Today I read an item in Reuters—and it's clear to me that this is a lie—that the immigrants agreed to disembark of their own free will, the only condition being that it not be publicized, and therefore the government forbade journalists and photographers from being there. This is slander and an incitement campaign by the propaganda machine of the Foreign Office against the clandestine immigration and the Zionist movement, and I already read a version in the *Times* yesterday of the type we used to hear in the good old days of Hitler: Zionists = Marxists. Let us be cautious that none of us is coopted in any way for this campaign."[137]

The measures taken by Ben-Gurion—the instructions he sent to the Mossad agent in Paris and the Jewish Agency representatives in London, and the harsh letter to the members of the Executive there—call for an examination. First, although his attack on Weizmann conformed to the pattern of relations between the two, it was certainly unjustified this time. Although Weizmann had stressed to Léon Blum that he was approaching him as a "private individual only,"[138] it was the members of the Jewish Agency Executive in London who had initially pressed Weizmann to use his office and contacts with Blum to resolve the problem.[139] Second, at the time Ben-Gurion sent the instructions to London and Paris, no Executive decision had been made regarding the proposal presented to Weizmann by Ivor Thomas to return the ships to France on condition that the Jewish Agency recommend that the passengers disembark there quietly.[140] Third, and most important, if humanitarian motives were behind Ben-Gurion's desire for a moderate Zionist reaction to the deportation to Germany, and if he was so concerned about sparing the *Exodus* passengers anything that might "end in bloodshed," why did he not immediately accept the British offer to quietly return the deportation ships to France and remove the refugees there?[141]

In truth, the two conflicting positions in the *Exodus* affair, the Zionist and the British, had become so complex and suffused with internal contradictions and irrational motivations that the task of unraveling them has become nearly impossible, although it is essential for understanding one of the key events of the period. From the outset, both sides sought to exploit the *Exodus* to make a point. The Zionist leadership and Mossad command hoped to transform the launching and journey of the ship, the largest Mossad operation to date—all of whose details were known to the British, who monitored every stage of the operation—into a worldwide media event in the struggle to crash the gates of Palestine.[142] The British foreign secretary, on his side, wanted to transform the *Exodus* into a publicity tool of the first order, seeking to frame the Zionist operation as a cynical exploitation of Holocaust refugees, who were already victims of fate and were now being incited to break the laws of civilized nations. The *Exodus* was the first Mossad ship that the British decided to send not to Cyprus but to its port of origin, thereby forcing the countries that allowed such sailings to pay for their deeds by having the refugees returned to their shores. Bevin's original plan was to demonstrate to journalists that the strategy of sea war was hopeless and that the Jewish refugees would be returned to their point of departure on the same ship in which they sailed, as is the policy for anyone entering a country illegally, and that all this was the product of the irresponsible and inhumane behavior of the Zionist leadership.[143]

Neither side planned, nor could it envision, the progression of events. From the Zionist perspective, the political climax came during the transfer of the refugees in Haifa port to the three British deportation ships, witnessed by members of the UN committee who were winding up their visit to Palestine and formulating their recommendations.[144] The next high point came outside Port de Bouc in France; the journey to Hamburg was an unexpected dividend, though not without dilemmas in terms of the fragile balance between Zionist political interests and concern for the physical and emotional ability of the refugees to endure the challenge. Bevin's plans, on the other hand, had already been upset with the transfer of the refugees from Haifa to France;[145] matters grew worse off the French shores as a result of the refugees' refusal to disembark and the French refusal to force their disembarkation, in spite of British demands.[146]

Bevin's attitude toward the illegal immigration had already become imbued with personal anger and frustration. "You are making a fool of us. . . . You are making us look ridiculous. No government can tolerate this," said Bevin to Dr. Goldmann a year earlier; and to Ben-Gurion he said, in early 1947, that the situation of Britain in Palestine was humiliating, and in another meeting at the time he defined the illegal immigration as a gun at his temple.[147] By the summer of 1947 the anger and frustration had reached such levels that they clouded Bevin's judgment, as even Allan Bullock, the author of Bevin's semiofficial biography, has written.[148] Bevin's extraordinary touchiness about the issue was well known and became a consideration in the formulation of the American attitude toward the issue.[149] The decision to deport the refugees to Germany can be defined as politically foolish and desperate and could be counted, in the words of Arthur Koestler, among cases "that could not be explained in terms of logical reasoning and expediency."[150] Indeed, the British made this decision without enthusiasm and against the opinion of several of Bevin's colleagues in the British government who were handling the Palestine problem.[151] Bevin himself anticipated that the deportation to Germany would arouse disgust and protest, especially in the United States, but his fight against the illegal immigration had already transcended the bounds of reason and taken on a bitter personal hue. He had driven himself into a dead end from which he could extricate himself only by identifying the British interest with his own feelings, seeing brinkmanship as the only way out.[152]

The Missing Element

As for Ben-Gurion, he and his colleagues regarded the first violent deportation in Haifa, in full view of the UNSCOP observers, and the staunch stand of the refugees off the French shore, in full view of French and world media, to be an enormous moral and publicity victory for Zionism. "We have been able to show the world the baseness of the White Paper regime," said Ben-Gurion in early August 1947, and "seemed somehow to shake the conscience of the world."[153] He then elevated the courage of the refugees off France to a level higher than that of the Warsaw ghetto fighters.[154] The Zionist achievement, then, went well beyond expectations. It undoubtedly contributed to the final draft of the UNSCOP conclusions, which was met with satisfaction in the Zionist camp and was perceived as a political victory.[155] Yet when UNSCOP's majority decision to partition Palestine and establish a Jewish state—the goal for which Ben-Gurion had struggled for years, sometimes nearly alone—was tabled at the UN and the Zionist campaign shifted to the corridors of the international body, even then Ben-Gurion vehemently refused to accept the British compromise to quietly return the refugees to France, which would have spared them the horror of returning to Germany. Even more astonishing is that Ben-Gurion, no less than Weizmann, believed that the truly important matter, after 1 September, was implementation of the UNSCOP report—that every obstacle to the implementation of the recommendations must be removed, and thus every effort must be made not to gratuitously aggravate the already strained relations with Britain. Hayim Hoffman (Yahil), who had in late August 1947 proposed along with Meirov that a major demonstration with the *Exodus* refugees be held on the docks of Hamburg, even at the price of bloodshed, a proposal that met with Ben-Gurion's unequivocal opposition, later wrote that even then he felt Ben-Gurion did not reveal his true reasons for opposing militant activity, and that his considerations were primarily political: "Perhaps he already knew the contents of the recommendations of UNSCOP, which had just finished its work in Geneva; he certainly hoped the committee would recommend partition and creation of a Jewish state in part of Palestine, and perhaps he was concerned that violent confrontation with the British on German soil might jeopardize the committee report."[156] Even this late testimony, however, which presumably drew upon hindsight and which reveals Ben-Gurion's disingenuous stance, cannot reflect all the twisting complexity in Ben-Gurion's position, about all aspects of which there is no direct evidence. We know of Ben-Gurion's decision concerning the disembarkation of the refugees in Hamburg—a demonstration, but controlled and without violent resistance—which he made in the presence of Meirov and Hoffman in late August; we know about his attempts to thwart the compromise proposed by Weizmann, which would have brought the ships to France and allowed the refugees to disembark quietly there; and we have his words at the closing session of the Zionist General Council in Zurich on 2 September. Nevertheless, circumstantial evidence of the complexity of Ben-Gurion's stance does exist.

Upon the arrival of the information about the vehement public reaction in England to the British decision to deport the refugees to Germany and of the British cabinet's plan to reconsider this decision, Shertok cabled Golda Meyerson in Jerusalem, instructing her to make sure that "no event in Palestine ruins our chances."[157] Shertok does not explain what he was referring to as "chances," but based on the energetic Zionist effort in the days that followed to avoid all compromise, it can be concluded that Shertok was instructing Meyerson to ensure that nothing happened in Palestine (anti-British terrorist activity?) that might change the British decision to send the *Exodus* refugees to Germany or that could influence the negative public response to the deportation (which was positive from the Zionist perspective).[158] What is more, information reached the Zionist General Council in Zurich several days later to the effect that Britain, in an effort to remove Germany from the odyssey of the *Exodus* passengers, requested of the Danish government that the refugees be allowed to disembark at a port in Denmark. In response, the Jewish Agency Executive shot off a cable to the Danish prime minister demanding that his country assume the French approach—accepting only refugees who enter of their own free will and not forcing the others to disembark anywhere other than where they chose to be (i.e., Palestine).[159] Even a possible Danish solution was thus rejected out of hand by the Zionist leadership. All this evidence indicates that no real effort was made by the Zionist leadership to have the deportation order to Hamburg rescinded or to circumvent it by a compromise, but that the Zionist interest was to bring the affair to a full-blown, if controlled, conclusion on German soil. Moreover, upon publication of the UNSCOP report, no effort was made by the Zionists to link the report with the fate of the individual refugees. Zionist reaction to the disembarkation at Hamburg received perfunctory ceremonial attention and rhetoric—nothing more. An example is found in Ben-Gurion's closing words at the Zionist General Council. "Two climaxes epitomized the [incomparably serious] situation," said Ben-Gurion, "on the one hand the tragic courage of the *Exodus* immigrants; and on the other hand, the cruel folly of the White Paper government, which deported the Nazi victims from the shores of their homeland and forced them to return to the land of the Nazis."[160] This statement was uttered by Ben-Gurion at the very moment that Zionist leaders were working behind the scenes to remove any hindrance to the deportation of the refugees to Germany.

The action of the Yishuv with regard to the German chapter in the *Exodus* affair is illuminating in that it reflects the gap between words and deeds, declaration and action. After publication of the UNSCOP report on 1 September, Golda Meyerson in Jerusalem asked Ben-Gurion in Zurich for direction about leading the public reaction to the disembarkation of the refugees in Hamburg.[161] Ben-Gurion's response, if there was one, is not on record. By decision of the National Council (*Va'ad Le'umi*), presumably after consultation with the Zionist leadership in Zurich, "Hamburg Day" was routinely marked by a two-hour work stoppage in the late afternoon, public gatherings, and flying the national flags wreathed in black at half-mast.[162] Thus, the organized reaction of the Jewish community in Palestine to the decision to deport the refugees to Germany, and the actual deportation and removal from the ships, was unexceptional; it was restrained and ceremonial, resembling the reactions to previous diversions of ships to Cyprus.[163] For the Hamburg chapter of the *Exodus* affair, Ben-Gurion wanted the best of all worlds: to avoid obstructing the decisive political moves begun with publication of the UNSCOP report; to take advantage of the unexpected moral dimension in the media offered by the nightmarish aspect of the deportation of Holocaust survivors back to Germany; to drive another nail into the coffin of the White Paper policy; to bring the Americans, who had until then avoided significant involvement, into the fray;[164] to put Weizmann in his place, that is, to allow him no place in the Zionist leadership circles;[165] and also to display, for domestic and external consumption, an organized, responsible, and controlled Zionist camp whose decisions were made and implemented in an orderly manner under the leadership of one and only one person.[166]

The only element missing from Ben-Gurion's "best of all possible worlds" scenario was the human aspect—the fate of 4,500 Jewish refugees, the "saints" of the previous chapter of the affair, according to Zionist laudatory speech. Many of the refugees, especially the leaders, accepted with understanding and some degree of love the additional agony imposed on them by the affair, regarding it as a necessary extension of their survival struggle during the war years. There are more than a few contemporary testimonies to this effect,[167] although most expressions of this kind are the product of nostalgia. When Ben-Gurion made his decision, refusing any compromise solution, he did not consult the refugees. Their opinion was not included in the web of considerations and plans. One month earlier, while the *Exodus* refugees suffered bravely in service to the Zionist cause, Ben-Gurion had expressed his fury over the terrorism in Palestine, "the irrational acts by Etzel" that would diminish the moral outrage over the *Exodus* incident and "remove from the agenda" the refugees, "four thousand and five hundred Jews, the like of which has never been seen before, who sanctified the name of Israel."[168] At the climax in Germany of the *Exodus* affair, however—the high point or the nadir, depending on the vantage point of the observer—it was Ben-Gurion himself who removed the Jewish refugees from the agenda. The personal fate and wishes of all of the *Exodus* refugees were not on the Zionist agenda, or on his.

Question of Authority

An addendum to the *Exodus* affair, which relates it to the sailing of the *Pan York* and the *Pan Crescent* from Romania in December 1947 (against the better judgment of the Zionist political leadership, including Ben-Gurion's), was the bomb that the Palmach people detonated on the British deportation ship *Empire Rival* near the Hamburg dock on 9 September 1947. The bombing defied Ben-Gurion's explicit instructions to the Mossad head some ten days earlier to abstain from any act that might end in bloodshed.[169] Ben-Gurion did not allow the action to pass unnoted, even though the bomb did not take lives and only damaged British offices in the port,[170] and he demanded an accounting from the Mossad head. It is not known when or in what form this demand was transmitted, as there are no written documents to that effect.[171] The only time Ben-Gurion referred to this incident in his diary was on 17 December 1947, when the struggle between the Mossad people and the political leadership over the sailing of the two ships from Romania with fifteen thousand refugees reached a climax.[172] On that day Ben-Gurion met with Shaul Meirov and conveyed a request from Shertok in the United States that Meirov not come there to discuss the *Pan* sailings because Shertok would be going to Palestine to consult with his colleagues before the final decision was made.[173] According to Ben-Gurion's writings, Meirov brought him a letter written by the senior Palmach officer in the south of France to the Palmach person accompanying the ship, with instructions to sabotage it "without approval from the Mossad, because sabotage is parallel to self-defense. In these matters, we take orders only from the [Palmach] division and there is a standing order—to sabotage the deportation ships everywhere. . . . The explosion must take place after disembarkation of the passengers."[174] Meirov added, according to Ben-Gurion's diary, that he himself gave explicit orders *not* to sabotage (emphasis in the original). "His [Meirov's] reasons: France's attitude if they're caught and the damage to the clandestine immigration enterprise." Meirov said further that the order of the Palmach commander on site was given after orders from the Mossad commander not to sabotage the ship, and with knowledge of those orders—that is, in explicit defiance of the Mossad commander.[175] Ben-Gurion seems to have accepted Meirov's explanations without reservation. He did not add interpretations or ask for explanations about the letter Meirov showed him (part of which he copied to his diary), even though some of Meirov's statements were not entirely reasonable; until he had received orders on the matter from Ben-Gurion (in late August), Meirov himself had been in favor of demonstrations and violent actions by the *Exodus* refugees in Hamburg, and he had no way to convey any orders to the ships during the journey, as communication with it was cut off.[176] At any rate, there was certainly no rift between Ben-Gurion and Meirov because of the *Pan* ships, as some historians have stated.[177] In fact, the written record indicates continued cooperation between them, reflecting Ben-Gurion's absolute trust in the Mossad commander. One day after the 9 December 1947 stormy session about the *Pan* ships' fate in the Mapai Central Committee, in which the full scope of the differences between the two men was revealed, Ben-Gurion sat with the Mossad head to plan future activity, and the two decided that it would be the Mossad that carried out the immigration operation—"[and that] we need our own ships"—and not the immigration department of the Jewish Agency.[178] Furthermore, Ben-Gurion's actions in the *Pan* episode, unlike his rhetoric, once again indicate either ambivalence toward the affair or a relatively low standing assigned to it in his priorities, or both.

The question of authority, both his own and that of the entire political leadership, over operational bodies of the Jewish organized community such as the Palmach and the Mossad during this dramatic and fateful period for Zionism seems to have concerned Ben-Gurion more than anything—with respect to the bomb on the ship, the deportation to Hamburg, and the *Pan* sailings; this concern is also what bound these events together in his consciousness, even though more than three months elapsed between the first and second incidents.[179] Concerning the two *Pans*, whose sailings were the largest and most complex operation in the history of the Mossad (see Chapter 3), a full-blown conflict erupted between the central political leadership and the secondary operational elite—between the political rationale perceived, at least by Ben-Gurion, as the decisive factor governing Zionist affairs and the dynamics of the Mossad, which developed momentum and esprit de corps during its years of operation and sought autonomy in its actions and involvement in the decision making. The needs of the refugees, their aspirations and ambitions, should also be included as a factor in the dispute. The face-off, as formulated by the Jewish Agency Executive and the historians in their wake, concerned the two giant ships acquired by the Mossad in the spring of 1947 and outfitted with significant effort and at great cost to the mission,[180] with fifteen thousand Jews from Romania on board awaiting rescue, versus the risk of thwarting the historical political achievement represented by the UN decision on 29 November. On one hand, thousands of refugees had sold their belongings and uprooted themselves from their homes and previous lives, orphans were taken from orphanages, "and there's no going back,"[181] with "the 'iron curtain' about to descend in the very near future."[182] On the other hand, a unique window of opportunity had opened for the creation of a Jewish state following the UN decision in late November and was at risk of closing if the ships were to sail with the refugees on board.[183]

Was this indeed a clash of mutually exclusive rationales? Or was it a manipulated dilemma based on the self-interests of two legitimate power bases struggling for turf within the evolving political and organizational system of the state-in-the-making? Ben-Gurion, who was busy at the time with security matters and with the creation of an armed force in preparation for the forthcoming war—which indeed broke out the day after the Lake Success decision—stumbled into the dispute between the two sides. More precisely, the Political Department, especially Moshe Shertok, and the Mossad, especially Shaul Meirov, pushed Ben-Gurion into the fray as each side demanded his support for its point of view, forcing him to choose.[184] At first, Ben-Gurion tried to wriggle out of the decision and a direct confrontation with the Mossad. He passed a motion in the Zionist Executive assigning the decision about the sailings to the head of the Political Department, Moshe Shertok, who was in Washington and was the one who had to conduct the political battle with the U.S. government.[185] Later, when the Mossad rejected the Executive's decision and raised the subject in internal party forums, Ben-Gurion described the dilemma of the Zionist movement and the need to take a stand between the political and the organizational-operational imperatives, including human needs (those of the refugees). He did this in surprising detail at the Mapai Central Committee:

Moshe [Shertok] wanted to be able to tell them [the U.S. State Department and Secretary of State George Marshall] in a suitable manner that until the matter [the vote in the UN] was over, we would not make problems for the American administration about this, and we agreed to that. We thought that ended the matter. Two weeks ago we were told that two ships with 15,000 Jews were about to leave Romania. We said that although a decision had been taken in the UN, the state was not yet established and there were other matters on which our people in America were still working. Let's ask their opinion. We asked Moshe, who said that in a meeting of the Executive there, they had unanimously and resolutely opposed the operation at this time; even if I held the same opinion as Shaul [Meirov] or Yeshayahu [Trachtenberg, a Mossad agent], I would accept the American view because they are now bearing the burden, and even if they are wrong, nothing must be done to suggest that we are hindering their efforts. And I would have accepted their opinion if it were like yours. But I don't want to hide behind our people in America, and I do agree with their view.[186]

Ben-Gurion, however, was not satisfied with forming a clear opinion on the matter, although tortuously put. He took advantage of the opportunity to settle historical accounts with the clandestine immigration enterprise and the Mossad. For a year and a half, said Ben-Gurion to the Mapai Central Committee, he had been debating with the Mossad about the goals of the clandestine immigration (the immigration of Jews and the political struggle—"there is no greater annoyance to the English than this"), the character of the Mossad's work, and the size of the ships. He argued that he was against the Mossad's switch to large ships[187] because he believed that small boats carrying two hundred people each would be much more effective in achieving the goals of the clandestine immigration. "It's a much greater nuisance because for a ship with 1500 people, one [destroyer] is enough, but if we send twenty small boats, they would have to keep their whole fleet in the Mediterranean. . . . Out of twenty small boats, three or four might get through to Palestine," said Ben-Gurion. He then delved into the complex of considerations that guided him. One should see the entire picture, not just one section of it, he said. The plight of the Romanian Jews was not the only difficult situation. There was also the situation of the Jews in Aden, the Jews of Egypt and Baghdad, and the Jews of other countries. In the political struggle, added Ben-Gurion, a change has taken place. With the end of the Mandate, the principle of the White Paper had been removed, even if change on the ground would not take place for several months yet. Real Jewish immigration to Palestine could not take place without a Jewish state, "and the state is not in our pockets" as "the UN is still not an implementing power." A clandestine immigration campaign of the magnitude of fifteen thousand people would not be interpreted as an operation against England, but one against the UN. "Are you prepared to take upon yourself this responsibility," Ben-Gurion concluded in a direct address to the Mossad head, "that there will be a conflagration here, that the entire matter [the UN implementing committee for the partition decision] will be a fiction? . . . At this delicate moment, when our entire existence in Palestine is in jeopardy, when the keeping of [UN] promises is at risk, at this very moment, should we come up with such a provocation?"[188]

This rebuke by Ben-Gurion of the Mossad and its commander, with whom he had met one day earlier to coordinate continued organizational activity, exhibited the flaw and ambivalence in his position, which prevented him from acting with the same resoluteness that marked his rhetoric. "Every time I was in Paris," said Ben-Gurion to the Mapai Central Committee, "I spoke with Shaul [Meirov] about it [changing the Mossad's tactics], but they went their own way." Further, "The tragedy was that they did not oppose me, but they did the opposite." Also, "I did not want to give orders about this, and things continued as before."[189] On the face of it, these expressions are atypical of the man who made authority a distinguishing feature of his leadership or the one who, less than one year later, would issue orders to open fire on the Irgun's weapons ship *Altalena* and call for the dismantling of the Palmach despite strong opposition in his political home. On closer inspection, however, these expressions do conform to a pattern in Ben-Gurion's attitude toward the clandestine immigration. This is almost an exact replication of his ambivalent behavior toward the founders of the Mossad (before it was so named)—the members of the Kibbutz at the beginning of their venture—when they told him exactly ten years earlier, in late 1937, that they were about to launch the first clandestine immigration boat from Poland. In this sense, it was the closing of a circle. Then, too, authority was his prime concern, and he strenuously opposed any activity not approved through the proper channels. At the time he even threatened to bring charges in the movement's judicial institutions against the Kibbutz people. Nonetheless, as his interlocutors were walking down the stairs of his home on their way out of the meeting, he pursued them and asked that when the first clandestine immigration ship did arrive—something to which he had so vigorously objected as a decision made outside the proper institutions—he be awakened and be the first on the beach to help with the disembarkation of the passengers.[190] One of those who participated in the meeting with Ben-Gurion (15 November 1937) wrote to his colleagues in Poland a brief sentence that is key to understanding the complex attitude of Ben-Gurion toward the clandestine immigration throughout its ten years: "The old man opposes it and is sorry . . . [but] there's no ban."[191]

Thus, Ben-Gurion opposed the sailing of the *Pan* ships, but a ban—which he knew how to impose when something provoked his passion—was not issued. Others in the political leadership furiously opposed the sailings from Romania and viewed them as a "catastrophe";[192] still, the ships sailed without consent and without authority.[193] The Mossad operatives were accused of visiting tragedy upon the Zionist movement and jeopardizing the imminent Jewish state; however, this did not stop Ben-Gurion from continuing to regard the Mossad as one of the crucial operational-organizational instruments of Zionism, and considering the head of the Mossad as one of his closest confidantes and appointing him to key, sensitive positions in the security-political system established under his personal command.[194] Why, then, did Ben-Gurion not impose the full weight of his authority on the Mossad people? Why did he not prevent the sailing if it truly jeopardized the political process at the critical moment on the eve of the state? Did the fate of fifteen thousand Jewish refugees from Romania, whose world had crumbled, touch him so deeply that he changed the tenets of his faith and priorities as a statesman? Did he really fear that imposing the heavy hand of authority on the Mossad heads, most of whom were still identified with the Kibbutz, would lead them to break away from the national institutions and openly rebel? Or does the answer lie elsewhere?

Obedient Rebels

On the whole, Romanian Jewry was not considered by the Zionist elite as one of the favored constituencies of the diaspora, and communications about them are replete with blunt words about the low quality of the "human material" from that country.[195] This did not ease the task of Ben-Gurion and other leaders who were considering the destiny of these fifteen thousand displaced persons against the special background bequeathed by their historical fate. To every argument about the specific situation of the Romanian Jews, Ben-Gurion responded with a claim about the general fate of Jews throughout the world. When he was reminded that these people had been uprooted from their homes in Romania and were unable to return, and that "this is a tragedy that has not been expressed," Ben-Gurion responded that this was also true of the Jews in Aden ("There was a pogrom there!") and that the situation in Egypt, Iraq, and "many countries" was similar. "We must take care of everybody," he declared.[196]

It was not the special fate of these fifteen thousand Jews that prevented Ben-Gurion from exerting his authority. Nor was it the fear that he, with too aggressive an approach, would push this organization rooted in the Kibbutz—an organization that had accumulated impressive power over the years—into a stance of resisting to the point of secession. The Mossad of late 1947 was not the same Mossad of earlier years. The radical elements, those with the potential to revolt and bolt out, had been driven out of the leadership.[197] Those left in positions of authority were close associates of Ben-Gurion and held similar views, and not by accident. He knew well and met frequently with all the key players of the Mossad, even those not of his own party.[198] Indeed, the Mossad developed a syndrome typical of such organizations, tending to view itself as the be-all and end-all,[199] sometimes resisting the views and decisions made by the central leadership and even disobeying its orders, as was the case with the *Pan* ships. These people, however, were not cut from the cloth of mutineers or breakaway faction leaders. On the contrary, they were more of an "aristocracy of service"—unflinchingly loyal, disciplined, and obedient to the ideological leadership. Even when it agitated to have its particular views carry the day, as happened with the *Pan*s, the Mossad did so in a dialectical way, within a consensual framework or as a reasonable deviation from the commands from above. This, then, was an obedient and controlled revolt.[200] Furthermore, even if key Mossad activists had harbored thoughts of an uprising around the *Pan* affair—and there is no evidence for this—the group's structure, the geographical dispersion of its personnel, and its style of action would not have enabled them to translate such an idea into action. This was a thoroughly decentralized organization whose key people were stationed, individually or in clusters of two or three, on four continents. Not only was there no clear power center within the organization, but because of its structure and semi-underground character, it engendered no defined culture or way of life as a political, social, or generational group, and hence no counterculture either. The views held by the Mossad people about the *Pan* affair were drawn from their direct and immediate contact with the post-Holocaust Diaspora and its needs. "I saw the Jews of Romania—starving, worn and tattered," said one of them in the debate about the *Pans*. "You have not seen them in the thousands, pushing and shoving at the borders . . . not caring if they are shot or imprisoned!"[201] This incident, then, was not an act of revolt or refusal on principle to accept commands from their superiors; rather, it was an attempt, in their own way—even if this was perceived as subversive by the leadership—to solve a human and operational dilemma that was unprecedented in their experience, and also an expression of the need, natural to every such organization, to follow through on their greatest achievement.[202]

The Mossad would never plot against the throne. "*These two* ships [emphasis added] are jeopardizing the fate of the Jewish people as decided [by the UN]?" was the angry question of one of the Mossad agents to the Mapai Central Committee dealing with the fate of the *Pan* ships.[203] Had they really believed that "their" fifteen thousand Romanian refugees were jeopardizing the creation of the state, the Mossad people themselves would have postponed the sailing, and perhaps given it up altogether and looked for alternative solutions to the problem of the refugees in Romania. Their belief, however, was that this operation not only would save thousands of Jews from devastation or communist confinement, but would also strengthen the rationale for a state and the Zionist publicity campaign even after the partition decision of late November, because "Nothing better [than the clandestine immigration] has yet been found to prove the need for a solution to our problem."[204]

More important, Ben-Gurion himself, like the Mossad operatives, though for different reasons, did not believe that two ships carrying fifteen thousand refugees could threaten the creation of the Jewish state. The proof of this is the consent he gave to the sailing by his silence. Had he believed that something there might threaten or thwart the process of establishing the state, the ships would never have set out, or those who sailed would have been severely punished.[205] Ben-Gurion's mind, however, was focused elsewhere, on the arena where he believed the fate of the state would soon be forged—the Jewish community in Palestine and the war over it in situ. He devoted most of his time and thoughts to this.[206] The colleagues and allies who continued to dwell on the previous issues—the diplomatic campaign or clandestine immigration—and still viewed them as crucial, lost him.[207] For the key question on the agenda after the UN decision—whether or not there will be a Jewish state—the clandestine immigration was no longer relevant. It could neither help nor hinder it. What was relevant was the existence and security of the Yishuv; "The security issue . . . takes precedence even over immigration, even over the state, because without the Yishuv there can be no immigration, no state, no anything."[208] Or, as he said to one Mossad agent who came to consult him and left with the impression that Ben-Gurion was already detached from the immigration issue, "A Jewish state will be created and then all the Jews will come."[209] The force of events, or the course of the historical process, which Ben-Gurion believed could be halted only by the collapse of the Jewish community in Palestine, overwhelmed the principle of obedience to authority. The winding and problematic route taken by the *Pan* ships, which ultimately led, with the consent and will of the Mossad officers, not to the shores of Palestine but directly to Cyprus and the hands of the British, was at that moment in Zionist history a detour only, a detour far removed from the main road that would lead to the establishment of a state.

Epilogue

The *Pan York* and *Pan Crescent*, with fifteen thousand Jewish refugees on board, never made it to the shores of Palestine. They deposited their passengers in Cyprus, as had most of the Mossad ships after the war. The landing on the beach, or *horada* (disembarkation) in Zionist parlance, was experienced by very few refugees—only about three thousand out of more than seventy thousand transported by Mossad ships. Yet the *horada* became a formative experience of the native Zionists in Palestine, a key element in the collective memory organized and forged around the establishment of the Jewish state. Construed into this experience and memory were the characteristic discursive elements of Zionist Palestine toward the Jews who came—who were brought—from the Diaspora. This discourse is suffused with the rhetoric of pity and Zionist patronizing, but also one stigmatizing—the other face of the deep terror aroused in the Zionist subject by this familiar stranger, this close yet distant diasporic arriving in the homeland.

The two texts I analyze in closing, those of Yitzhak Sadeh and Nathan Alterman, deal with the direct, physical encounter between the people of Eretz Israel and the survivors-refugees coming from exile, an encounter taking place at the very moment of the refugees' arrival at the shores of Palestine. These texts belong to the basic scrolls of Zionist revival narrative and were constitutive in the shaping of Israel's collective identity in the country's first decades of independence. Both were written by prominent members of the Zionist-Israeli power elite who were close to the central political leadership and were among the authors of the hegemonic

Zionist narrative. Yitzhak Sadeh was a general, founder, and first commander of the legendary Palmach (combat forces), the forerunner of the elite units of Israel's army. Nathan Alterman was the most respected national poet of the first statist period. I treat these texts as historical documents. I read them not as literary illustrations of the historical but as textual representations of the historical itself—textual representations of past reality through which this reality is mediated and becomes accessible.

My reading of these texts is "suspicious," as is my reading of any other historical document, assuming that every text contains traces of something of which its writer is unconscious—traces of the repressed, the silenced, the erased; traces of what does not want to be uttered or is not at all utterable. Both texts describe the refugees' concrete and symbolic descent—or ascent (*aliya*)—onto the shore with the help of the land's natives, who carried them on their shoulders. Those "nights of disembarkation," engraved in poetry and prose in a volume that far exceeds the historical reality, were meant, according to these texts and the Zionist myth of Jewish redemption and reception, to be encounters of love and compassion, of unconditional acceptance, of homecoming at the end of a long and agonizing journey. Within these two texts, however, intended to glorify and extol the encounter, another truth emerges—about its terror and horror and about the immanent threat it embodies for the sons of the land. While on its surface the text is a homily about the destroyed "exile" coming ashore, on a deeper, hidden level the opposite transpires—reaffirming the stigma of the "Diaspora-ness" of this mass of people and branding an even harsher mark of blame on the nature, character, and actions of those who survived the Holocaust and that accounted for their survival.

Here is Yitzhak Sadeh's love sermon to the coming Jewish refugees, "My Sister on the Beach":

Darkness. On wet sand, my sister stands before me: filthy, tattered, wild-haired, her feet are bare and her head bowed. She stands and weeps.
I know. Her flesh is branded: 'For Officers Only'.
My sister weeps and says:
Friend, why am I here? Why did they bring me here? Am I worthy that young healthy boys risk their lives for me? No, there is no place for me in the world. I should not live.

I embrace my sister, embrace her shoulders and tell her:
You have a place in the world, my sister, a very special place. Here, in our land you should live, my sister. Here you have our love to you. Dark

and comely art thou, my sister. Dark, because seared by suffering, but comely, more beautiful to me than all other beauty, holier than all holiness.

Darkness. On wet sand my sister stands before me, filthy, tattered, wild-haired, her feet bare and her head bowed.

I know: evil people have tortured her and made her barren. And she weeps and says: Friend, what am I doing here? Why have you brought me here? Am I worthy that young healthy boys risk their lives for me? There is no place for me in the world. I should not live. . . .

I embrace my sister, embrace her shoulders and tell her:

You have a place in the world, my sister, a very special place. Here, in our land. And you should live, my sister. Your feet have trodden the road of suffering, and tonight you have come home, and here with us is your place. We love you, my sister. All the glory of motherhood you carry within you, all the beauty of womanhood is in you. Our love is for you, you will be a sister to us, you will be our bride, our mother.

Before these sisters I kneel, I prostrate myself in the dust at their feet. And when I rise to my feet, straighten my body, raise my head upwards, I sense and I know:

For these sisters—I am strong.

For these sisters—I am brave.

For these sisters—I will also be cruel.

For you everything—everything.[1]

These are the words of the founder of the Palmach, whose young re-cruits supposedly carried on their shoulders the Jewish refugees as they disembarked after their clandestine voyage from Europe; they are spoken to a young refugee girl just arriving on the shores of the homeland. The importance of this text lies not in its literary merit, which is clearly dubi-ous, with the tone of the text very much in tune with the spirit of the time, but in its long-lasting influence on members of the generation and the youth of the formative decades of the state. This homily appeared in the late 1940s, when the post-war clandestine immigration into Palestine was at its height. It was originally published in the Palmach periodical, a key publication in shaping the spirit of the combat units. Its first issue, in December 1942, carried these words: "Sometimes the right word at the right time spoken with fervor can serve as a weapon."[2] What, then, do Sadeh's words really say "at the right time"? What kind of weapon do these words become? To whom are they addressed? Who is speaking of whom? Who stands that night on the beach facing whom?

Let us first look at the contraposition emerging from Sadeh's text, so symbolic and charged, as to what faces what on the shores of the Land of Israel. On one side stands a group of young Palmach boy-soldiers with their commander, and on the other a lone refugee girl. It is a squad of men facing one woman; native-born Israelis in the presence of a foreign, uprooted girl; men, "young healthy" and strong, against a beaten, filthy, and weeping woman; male power in the plural opposite female weakness in the singular—in short, strong, rooted, and brave Israeli Zionism facing a defeated, despairing Diaspora longing to die. It is Zionism as an organized discourse of manliness and power built on and emerging from Jewish catastrophe. "For these sisters I am strong . . . I am brave . . . [and] I will also be cruel." What do these words mean? Who is speaking to whom that night on the beach? Ostensibly, Sadeh's words are addressed to the foreign refugee girl, to tell her how loved, admired, and wanted she is on the threshold of Eretz Israel—their and her home ("tonight you have come to your home"). Identifying the object of Sadeh's text, however, is not as simple or obvious as it seems. The text contains a kind of rhetorical flaw. The words of love and compassion spoken by Sadeh are not and cannot be directed at the refugee girl, if only because she does not understand the speaker's language. This is not, then, what first appears and is implied by the title of the text and its form of address—a speech that crosses the boundary between the "I" and the "other," between the Yishuv and the Diaspora, between the young Israeli soldiers or their commander and the refugee "sister" who has arrived on the shores of Israel. It is, rather, an internal, intra-Israeli rallying and mobilizing speech. It is the fighting men, the young natives, who are supposed to welcome their refugee "sister" and carry her on their shoulders who are the commander's target audience—not the refugee girl.[3] This type of device—an imaginary appeal to an imaginary addressee that conceals an appeal to the real addressee—is within the bounds of the poet's tactics and part of his poetic license. The question is, then, what message is conveyed by Sadeh's heuristic, sermonizing words? What is he telling his young soldiers about the lone girl standing on the beach? What, according to Sadeh, are they supposed to learn about the girl, to know about her, so that they will love her, prostrate themselves before her, and wallow in the dust at her feet? If she is so wanted and loved, why is she crying?

By virtue of his authority and stature as commander and educator, Yitzhak Sadeh knows ("I know") the answers, and he puts them in the mouth of the refugee girl herself: "Friend, why am I here? Why have you brought me here? Am I worthy that young healthy boys risk their lives for me?" This is the equation seemingly voiced by the girl: the "young healthy" boys of Israel are risking their lives for a person who deems herself unworthy of the sacrifice, for a girl who has no place in the world, who does not deserve to live. In terms of historical accuracy, the statement about jeopardizing the men from Palestine on behalf of the refugees from the Diaspora is problematic, if not unfounded. Unlike the battles of the 1948 war, which broke out a short time after Sadeh's homily was written and which took the lives of about a thousand Palmach fighters, not a single Palmach man was killed in the clandestine immigration operations and the violent clashes at sea that were a part of these operations. As for the refugees, unarmed and unschooled in battle, thirteen were killed and hundreds injured in acts of violent resistance on the ships. It was the remnants of the Holocaust, no strangers to suffering, and not the strong healthy sons of the land, who risked their lives in the immigration campaign.

More troubling, however, is the meaning of the words that Sadeh assigns to the refugee girl—"Why have you brought me here? Am I worthy that young healthy boys risk their lives for me?"—and what these words say about the speaker and what he represents. Yitzhak Sadeh claims to "know" what the refugee girl is thinking, and he puts his thoughts in her mouth. The girl, who represents all the refugees who lived through the Holocaust and survived, believes that she has no right to live. She believes, furthermore, that she has no right to put the lives of the young healthy boys of Israel at risk for the sake of a wretched and worthless life like hers. In his role as an omniscient and omnipotent narrator, Sadeh attributes these claims to the girl and thus serves as mediator; he mediates the girl's speech for his pupils and gives her a voice—she who still has no language, who is still voiceless, mute. He ostensibly grants her the right of direct speech by quoting her, by having her speak in the first person. In fact, however, it is clear that Sadeh's knowledge is not of the girl's thoughts, but of his own. Sadeh is not mediating between the girl and his men but rather is exploiting the girl and using her to mediate between his men and himself. This is what is happening. The act of mediation here confounds the expected. The girl is not the speaker, not through her own words or through his; Yitzhak Sadeh is the speaker, and the girl on the beach is mediating between him and his men. The two voices speaking in the text are thus Sadeh's. He asks and he answers.

Further deconstruction of the text shows that the rhetorical questions supposedly asked by the girl through Sadeh's mediation contain a counterstatement, even if an unconscious one, to the bravura of the text, to its illuminated side—the Israeli love song that draws from the ancient book of Israel ("Dark and comely art thou, my sister") addressed to the Diaspora—which itself raises suspicion because of its rhetorical exaggeration and its inflated terms of adulation for the refugee girl. Yet Sadeh does not stop here. He provides his men with additional, gratuitous information that is completely unnecessary to his lesson of love and compassion—even if it is based on what the refugees said about themselves or about other refugees or is drawn from the journalistic chronicles of the time or from some specific event that transpired. This brief bit of information, which is inserted almost casually into the text, suddenly sets into stark relief what Sadeh is actually "saying" to his soldiers. First, Sadeh places a mark on the girl's body, brands her, displays her imperfection, exposes her tarnished femininity, and thereby distinguishes her from the healthy, perfect sons of the land. He does not, however, leave it at agonies having seared her or "evil people" having "tortured her and made her barren." From the outset he is explicit, revealing to his young disciples the incomparable horror, the ultimate outrage: "her flesh is branded: 'For Officers Only.'"

The deed is done. The Jewish girl, who survived the horrors of the Holocaust and has come to her homeland, is violated here once again for all the agonies she has already known. The additional blow is the gaze directed at the girl—interrogative, selective, all-knowingly hegemonic, stigmatizing, and invasive—a look that marks her and transforms her into an appropriated object whose innermost privacy is desecrated. It is a judgmental gaze that reads the body, the body's inscription, and even the body's inner sanctum. The act of seeing is not merely physiological; it is a gaze imbued with ideology and culture. The injury—the extra injury—comes from Israel itself. The body of the young girl is ravaged, her dignity defiled in her own "home," on the shores of Eretz Israel.

Sadeh's hidden, probably subconscious text thus states, in line with the popular local parlance of the time, that the girl survived the Holocaust (and reached Palestine) because she did not defend the integrity and purity of her body, because her (Jewish) body served (Nazi) officers. Her impurity, her defilement, was her ticket to life. Thus, the Jewish refugee girl has no chance of winning. She is defeated in every way, damned by the law of the Land of Israel and tainted by the masculine law of Yitzhak Sadeh, the emblematic creator of the new Israeli manliness. Her very survival, her being alive after the Holocaust, is shameful testimony to her double betrayal—her betrayal of herself, her body, her femininity, and her betrayal of her people—by surrendering her body to (Nazi) officers. We know, however, from this same structured inner logic, that had the girl defended her feminine, Jewish body, she would have brought about its—her body's—utter destruction.

This, then, is the implicit meaning of Sadeh's homily. The survivors, those now reaching Israel, who say they are not worthy of life or of putting the lives of young Israelis at risk, speak the unspoken truth. They survived because they, in some way, defiled and surrendered their bodies and souls to the perpetrators. In contrast, the righteous and decent Jews, those who did not surrender their bodies and who preserved their physical and spiritual integrity, were obliterated from the face of the earth and are not among those now returning from the abyss. What emerges from the deep layers of the text, then, is the moral judgment passed by the Zionist-Israeli community, which would later become the basis of Israeli society's hegemonic discourse, at least until the 1960s, about the Holocaust survivors who arrived at Israel's gates. This judgment, testifying to the constitutional inability of someone who was not "there" to comprehend the horror of the Holocaust and the total helplessness of its victims, is double-edged. Those who survived committed some kind of moral sin through which they were saved. Those who did not survive, however, are not absolved either, because they, according to similar Zionist criteria, went "like sheep to the slaughter." Thus the survivors, upon arriving home at their moment of redemption, are defeated again. They are victims once again. This is Yitzhak Sadeh's text; this is the text's subtext.

The Mysterious Known

Nathan Alterman's poem "Michael's Page" also describes a "night of disembarkation." Like Sadeh's homily, this text also subverts itself, but in a rather different way, making possible other readings, different from the accepted, canonical ones. Here are two of the verses from Alterman's poem:

At the night of unloading, with the star watching us
  As we shoulder those who arrive in the dark, as we carry their lives on our backs

We sense the fear in their breathing and the moaning of their tortured
and outcast bodies
But also their hands closing on our throats.

The people will multiply in this land. Not as a sect of converts
Will they wander among its masses. But a war of two
Unseen and unbridled, will crawl through like a thread,
    from outside and from within
To resolve whether its millstones will grind the grain
Or the grain grind the millstones.[4]

Ben-Gurion's poetic alter ego who, "in [his] special Alterman-ness,
educated the nation to Ben Gurionism," as stated later by another
Ben-Gurionist,[5] or the "poetic voice of the national consensus,"[6] just
two verses of whose long poem are given here, expresses forcefully the
contraposition and the condescending distinction between the bearers
and the burdens, between the strong healthy Zionist collective and
the ravaged and defeated Diaspora. The encounter on that "night of
disembarkation" is necessarily one of concrete, physical contact, of
body-to-body touch. Yet throughout the poem there is not an instant
of eye contact between the bearer and the burden, between Israel and
the Diaspora. If in Sadeh's text the gaze is imbued with ideology and
culture, here there is no gaze at all, no recognition. The fatal distance,
the chasm between the Zionist bearer and the diasporic burden cannot be bridged unless Zionist hegemony is imposed. Not both parties
to the encounter, but only the Diaspora must fundamentally and unilaterally change and cease to be what it is, and in this way fulfill its
function in the Zionist scenario. "We did not consider the remnants
and Eretz Israel to be one entity, but rather stressed the huge psychological and physical effort that the survivors should make in order to
be united with us," said the head of the Israeli Commission to the DP
camps.[7] In Alterman's words, for one to reach the other, for skin to
touch skin—"the skin of the whip-tormented [the exile] and the skin
of his brother who remained pure [Israel]"—"seven bolts must be
torn from the gate." All are children of the same nation and the same
history, says Alterman in his poem, and the Diaspora has been "our
source, the rock of our formation." The fracture between the land and
the Diaspora, however, cannot be mended—"a shadow passed between the tribes," "the links were broken," and "what has happened
cannot be undone." In contrast with "the terrible old age of the nation" (the Diaspora), behold the children of Eretz Israel and the

Zionist revolution, the new, young, healthy men, molded and created in the image of the new land and under its skies: "We were altered to the very core . . . altered in language, logic, image, pace, course of action, content of talk, flavor of the song, reactions of fear and laughter." "The change has happened and it was a marvel."[8]

Yet in this fateful encounter a totally unexpected thing happens. Another saying is insinuated into the verse, one that undermines the accepted power equation—obvious yet unbalanced from the outset—between the Zionist community and the Jewish Diaspora, between the bearers and the burdens. In this encounter of unequals, it is not the weak but the strong—the sons of Israel—who are threatened. The ostensibly omnipotent Israeli might be broken and destroyed by the presence of the previously negated and repressed Diaspora, which is now coming forth, even if only as an object to be carried. Notice how the "tortured and outcast body" of the survivors, the fear in their breathing, are threatening and then actually endangering the very breath—the fundamental, primal act of life—of the strong Zionist body ("their hands closing on our throats"), thus awakening a deep, mysterious fear. In the next verse the threat becomes even more explicit. It is a life-and-death war between the bearer and the burden, the grain and the millstone, two mutually exclusive entities that cannot dwell together: "a war of two / unseen and unbridled, will crawl through like a thread, from outside and from within / to resolve whether its millstone will grind the grain / or the grain grind the millstone." The bearing of the refugees on young Zionist-Israeli shoulders—which is more metaphoric than historic, since less than three percent of the survivors shipped by the Mossad in the years 1945–48 actually arrived unmolested on shore—is indeed a great political enterprise, a vital but terrifying act in the great project of establishing a state out of destruction. Yet this is not a welcome of unconditional love, an act of inclusion stemming from real compassion, but rather an "unseen and unbridled" war, an encounter of life charged with potential death.

To probe in depth this unexpected, mysterious, ostensibly paradoxical anxiety awakened in the strong and patronizing Zionist-Israeli subject coming into contact with the miserable, defeated object "he bears on his shoulders," I would suggest turning to an article by Sigmund Freud, "Das Unheimliche" ("The Uncanny"), published in 1919, to which I referred in the introduction.[9] In the article Freud deals with the permeable boundary between the "heimlich" (the intimate, the close, the well and long known) and the "unheimlich" (the uncanny, the foreign, the threatening, the mysterious). He studies the presence of one within the other and the possibility of breaking down the boundaries between them. "What interests us most," writes Freud, "is to find that among its different shades of meaning the word heimlich exhibits one which is identical with its opposite, unheimlich. What is heimlich thus comes to be unhemlich. . . . In general we are reminded that the word heimlich is not unambiguous, but belongs to two sets of ideas . . . on the one hand, that which is familiar and congenial, and on the other, that which is concealed and kept out of sight. The word un-heimlich is only used . . . as the contrary of the first signification and not of the second." A little further on Freud writes, "Thus, heimlich is a word the meaning of which develops towards an ambivalence, until it finally coincides with its opposite, unheimlich." According to Freud's definition of the "uncanny," anxiety of this kind is evoked through an encounter with something that, paradoxically, is experienced as at once foreign and familiar, distant and close, totally estranged and unknown and at the same time strangely recognizable and known. This imma-nence of the alien within the familiar, the distant within the near, is taken as etymological proof of the psychoanalytical assumption that the threatening otherness is a distinct version of the unheimliche which, paradoxically, emanates from something that has long been familiar, something very close, intimate, and integral to the psyche. Therefore, what is evoking profound, inexplicable anxiety is not something new and completely foreign that appeared all of a sudden, but, on the con-trary, something that in the past belonged and was close and then, under certain circumstances, became repressed, distant, and concealed and is now resurfacing. "The Unheimliche is what was once heimlich or heimisch, homelike, familiar; the prefix 'un' is the token of repres-sion," writes Freud. The sense of uncanny, the deep terror experienced in the close physical encounter in those "nights of disembarkation," is thus evoked by what was supposed to remain hidden and unseen and has now suddenly emerged from its concealment.[10]

My argument is that the encounter between the Zionist-Israeli com-munity and the post-Holocaust Diaspora represented by the sur-vivors—an encounter examined in its various facets throughout this book, an encounter the deep structure of which is revealed by the two texts analyzed here—indeed produced the uncanny effect that Freud claims is created by the return of the repressed, the coming to light of what should remain concealed, the unearthing of the unconscious. It is the return of the Diaspora in its role of Zionism's unconscious. The effect of the uncanny was, after the war, magnified sevenfold, as the returning repressed, which had survived what could not be comprehended or described and which had undergone additional estrangement, unrelated to the action of the psyche or to the Zionist concept of "negating the Diaspora," has now come to light. The terror produced by the horrors of the Holocaust and by those living dead emerging from its abyss also delineated, from the very beginning of the continuing historical encounter between Israel and the Holocaust, a kind of forbidden territory, a sacred, fetishistic space surrounding the event of the annihilation of European Jewry. The unimaginable horror of the Final Solution has thus undergone an ideological and political process of tabooing and has been ritualized and consecrated. Total horror has been converted into some kind of untouchable sanctity. The "otherness" of the horror, severed from the very logic of life and defying any attempt of being directly looked at, of being understood, represented, and memorized—is thus transformed into the awe-inspiring sacred with its terrible numinous force, menacing and attractive at the same time, revered yet potentially dangerous.[11]

The uncanny effect of anxiety produced by this meeting with the Holocaust also explains the fact that in both Sadeh's text and Alterman's poem, the encounter takes place in the dark ("as we shoulder those who arrive in the dark," says Alterman; Sadeh's homily opens with the word "darkness"). It is not only the darkness that descended on the Jewish people during the war years or the darkness of the "nights of disembarkation." In both texts the darkness signifies also the occluded vision, the obstructed view, the blindness, the nonrecognition that characterizes this encounter. It represents the screening and defense mechanisms that the Zionist-Israeli collectivity employed when confronted with the Holocaust survivors, as if the horrors of the Holocaust could only be watched or observed in the dark, that is, in a state of non-seeing, of blindness. This is the shield of Athena through which Perseus, in order to survive, had to look at the Medusa's horrific visage; to face the Medusa directly would have petrified him.[12] This was apparently the only way—in the dark, through the darkness—that the community in Palestine was able to "mobilize" in order to "see" the remnants of the Holocaust and overcome the petrifying terror that they aroused.

Before closing, it should be emphasized that the rest of the world did not want these people at all. In the years following World War II the gates of most countries were closed to Jewish refugees. The only place that wanted them, the only community that fought to have them, was the Zionist-Israeli collectivity. Young Israeli people did, indeed, carry refugees to the shore—if not on their shoulders, as the poem says, then by other means. Throughout this ongoing fateful yet blind encounter, so effective and powerful on the political level, so psychologically painful and terrifying on the human level, there was a "gaze"— the Zionist gaze, which saw what was supposed to be seen, what served the Zionist project. The act of sanctifying, ritualizing, and at the same time tarnishing the Diaspora "other," as Sadeh does in his homily, was meant, in fact, to obliterate that "other" by not seeing it, by not acknowledging it. According to Alterman, the "remained pure" son of the land does not comfort "with the dawning of light" the "whip-tormented" brother from the Diaspora, because there is no light to illuminate the encounter between the two, because the darkness of the night covers them.

It may well be that this was the only viable form of encounter with the survivors of the great catastrophe that could be sustained by the Zionist-Israeli community—which, while the Final Solution was unfolding, would not "see" it and would not harness all its resources for a great, uncalculated, even if largely hopeless rescue campaign—so that it would not break down under the overwhelming weight of horror and mourning, so that the vision of the Jewish state would not be shattered. It had to be an unseeing, blind encounter in the "dark" on such a "night of disembarkation." In order to realize the ultimate, complete Zionist redemption—a Jewish state—out of the ultimate catastrophe—the Holocaust— and in order to forge from the catastrophe of millions a redemption and power for millions, in Ben-Gurion's words, the Zionist collective had to sanctify the victims of the catastrophe and tarnish them at the same time, turning them into objects to be carried. The victims themselves, in turn, had to regard themselves as part of this collective on the collective's own terms, had to want to be a part of it in any way possible. This was the unstated deal; this was the encounter offered to the victims. Thus, the Holocaust, its victims, and its survivors all played their crucial historical and political roles according to the Zionist script.

Zionism's work of mourning (Freud's *trauerarbeit*) for the Jewish catastrophe still remains to be done.

Notes

INTRODUCTION

1. High Commissioner's Report, 17 January 1947, Ben-Gurion Archives, (BGA).

2. I borrow this definition of rhetoric from an article by the literary scholar Barbara Johnson, "Apostrophe, Animation, and Abortion," *Diacritics,* 16 (Spring 1986): 29–39.

3. Berl Katzenelson, minutes of the Twenty-first Congress, Central Zionist Archives (CZA). Also quoted in *Writings,* vol. 9 (in Hebrew) (Tel Aviv, 1948), pp. 61–82.

4. Ronald Syme, *The Roman Revolution* (Oxford, 1939), p. 7.

5. Isaiah Berlin, *The Hedgehog and the Fox: An Essay on Tolstoy's View of History* (New York, n.d.), p. 11.

6. Louis Namier, "History," in Fritz Stern, ed., *The Varieties of History* (New York, 1973), p. 372. Namier writes that "the subject of history is human affairs, people in action, things that happened and how they happened: concrete events fixed in time and space, and their basis in the thoughts and feelings of human beings—not universal and generalized things, but complex and varied events, just like the people who effected them."

7. Nathan Alterman, "The Gold of the Jews," *The City of the Dove* (in Hebrew) (Tel Aviv, 1975), pp. 272–74.

8. Nathan Alterman, "Michael's Page," *The City of the Dove,* pp. 25–27; Yitzhak Sadeh, "My Sister on the Beach," *The Palmach Book,* vol. 1 (in Hebrew) (Tel Aviv, 1953), p. 725.

9. Sigmund Freud, "The Uncanny," in James Strachey, ed. and trans., *Sigmund Freud on Creativity and the Unconscious* (New York, 1958).

10. Berl Katzenelson, "From Travels in the Diaspora Exile" (undated), *Writings,* vol. 7, pp. 369–83.

11. Gerschom Scholem defines the Diaspora as the "mother," as opposed to the "child," which is the Jewish state. See "We and the Diaspora Have a Common Utopia: From a Speech to the Central Ideological Forum of Mapai on the Subject of Israel and the Diaspora," 4 February 1956, *Another Thing* (in Hebrew) (Tel Aviv, 1989), pp. 129–30.

12. For a recent and comprehensive discussion of the concept of "negation of the Diaspora" as a central element in Zionist thought and existence from the dawn of the Zionist movement to the present day, see Amnon Raz Krakotzkin, "Exile within Sovereignty: Criticism of 'Negation of the Exile' in Israeli Culture" (in Hebrew), *Theory and Criticism,* 4 (Winter 1994): 23–55; and *Theory and Criticism,* 5 (Autumn 1994): 113–32.

13. Yosef Gorni, "The Po'alei Tsion in Palestine's Attitudes towards the Exile (in the Period of the Second Aliya)" (in Hebrew), in *Zionism,* collection 2 (Tel Aviv, 1971), pp. 74–89.

14. Haim Hazaz, "Homily," *Seething Stones* (in Hebrew) (Tel Aviv, 1968), p. 223.

15. Yosef Hayim Yerushalmi, *Zakhor: Jewish History and Jewish Memory* (Seattle and London, 1982), p. 97.

16. David Ben-Gurion, "The Redemption" (in Yiddish), *Der Yiddisher Kempfer,* no. 39 (24 Heshvan/16 November 1917): 1.

17. David Ben-Gurion, "Was un Wi Azoy" (in Yiddish), *Der Yiddisher Kempfer,* no. 41 (1917): 1–2; also quoted in Gorni, "Po'alei Tsion," p. 85.

18. Berl Katzenelson, "From Travels in the Diaspora Exile" (undated), *Writings,* vol. 7, pp. 369–83.

19. David Ben-Gurion at a Jewish Agency Executive meeting, 24 April 1946, minutes of the Jewish Agency Executive, CZA.

20. Jacques Le Goff, "Les mentalités," in Jacques Le Goff and Pierre Nora, eds., *Faire de l'histoire—Nouveaux objets* (Paris, 1974), pp. 106–28.

CHAPTER 1

1. Memo [unidentified signature], Public Record Office (P.R.O.), CAB 204/279, 9 January 1948.

2. *Ha'apala Reports,* History of Haganah Archives (HHA), 2751 (hereinafter *Reports*). From February 1948 until the date of the declaration of the State of Israel, four more ships sailed from Italy.

3. Most of the Mossad documents concerning La Spezia are in HHA, file 14/86; in the Yehuda Arazi files; and in the files of the Mossad operations record, numbered from 14/500 onward. An additional source is the testimony of those who took part in the events, to be found in HHA, in the Oral Documentation Department (ODD), Hebrew University, Jerusalem.

4. Giuseppe Mammarella, *Italy after Fascism* (Montreal, 1966), pp. 120–25, and elsewhere.

5. Ada Sereni, *Ships without a Flag* (in Hebrew) (Tel Aviv, 1975), p. 60.

6. Report by Dr. Umberto Nahon, 20 June 1946, CZA S6/3745. Nahon estimated that there were 16,000 refugees in Italy. The Bricha's statistics were more modest: from January 8 to August 1946, 6,032 people entered Italy. See Yehuda Bauer, *Flight and Rescue: Bricha* (New York, 1970), pp. 174–75, 253. A report by a committee of cabinet officials, appointed to check the findings of the Anglo-American Committee, noted in June 1946 that restrictive measures indeed brought about a reduction in this movement. See Report of a subcommittee on the problem of displaced persons in Germany, Austria, and Italy, 21 June 1946, P.R.O. CAB 133/83.

7. In addition to the United Nations Relief and Rehabilitation Administration (UNRRA) rations, the Jewish refugees received rations from the Joint Distribution Committee. See Chapter 6.

8. CID report no. 3 on underground migration to the chief secretary, 15 October 1945, HHA 18/17a. See also Yoav Gelber, *The Flag Bearers*, vol. 3 (in Hebrew) (Jerusalem, 1983), p. 590.

9. Brod to Foreign Office, no. 2149, 30 December 1945, P.R.O. FO945/655.

10. Foreign secretary's memo to Overseas Reconstruction Committee, (ORC). (46)9, 20 January 1946, P.R.O. WR212, FO371/57685.

11. The Mossad's communications system worked through Italy. Agents smuggled from Palestine to Europe were generally sent through Italy, from which they were sent on to other countries on the continent. On the transfer of Mossad operatives to France, see: To Hanum [Klieger] and to Kassuta [Shaltiel] in Paris from the Mossad in Palestine, 25 May 1945, HHA 14/176. On 22 August 1945 the Mossad reported to Arazi in Italy on the transfer of operatives through him to all of Europe: "In addition to the eight operatives who have reached you there are 12 on their way. Among them one to Hungary, two to Austria Germany, two to Poland, one to Italy, four seamen, two Gideons [radio operators]. Our plan is to bring back on the *Dalin* eight to ten operatives." See: To Alon from Artzi, 22 August 1945, HHA 14/81a. Also, the *Albertina* brought, upon its return from Palestine, twenty-six operatives to Europe, including radio operators, ship commanders, and counselor-operatives for the DP camps. See Sereni, *Ships*, pp. 43–44.

12. Dr. Nahon to the Jewish Agency's political department, Italy, 5 April 1945, HHA 14/81b.

13. The Mossad agents worked primarily with gold coins, which were given the code name *tse'hubim* ("yellows"), and with foreign currency, which was in great demand in Italy. With regard to the La Spezia affair, there is explicit mention of giving bribes to various people. Ada Sereni, who was in Palestine at the time of the affair, sent instructions to the president of the Jewish Communities in Italy, Rafael Kantoni, to offer "a large bribe." "Make money available to him," she instructed the Mossad station in Italy. See the series of cables from Artzi to Meir-Alon, 5–7 April 1946, HHA 14/86. In May 1947, when the *President Warfield* was being fitted out in Porto Venere, under a British and Italian blockade, Sereni reported that large sums of money in the right places could give her guarantees that other Mossad vessels would not be touched, "but only in exchange for large grants, and it is doubtful whether it is worthwhile." See Daniela [Sereni] to the Mossad operations center, 14 May 1947, Mossad operations log.

14. John Willar-Bennet, *The Semblance of Peace: The Political Settlement after the Second World War* (London, 1972), pp. 434–35.

15. U.S. Secretary of State Byrnes after the first foreign ministers' session in Paris, 20 May 1946, quoted in *United States and Italy 1936–1946, Documentary Record* (Washington, D.C., 1946), p. 212.

16. Brod to Rome, no. 659, WR2991, 6 October 1945, P.R.O. FO371/45348.

17. Report on illegal immigration, August 1946, E2155, P.R.O. FO371/57693.

18. Report of the ambassador in Rome and the political adviser to the Allied Mediterranean Command to the Foreign Office, 5 April 1946, P.R.O. FO371/57693.

19. Arazi testimony, HHA 18 August 1949, 4 September 1949, 27 September 1949.

20. Arazi testimony, undated, HHA, division 80, Arazi files, 21.

21. "The Socialist Congress heard that 1,114 Jewish survivors of Hitler were arrested as they tried to return to Palestine and demands the freeing of the *Fede* and permission for swift sailing to that country to which the people aspire [to go to] so that they may finally create for themselves a free existence and to carry with them the memories of solidarity and friendship of the Italian Socialists." The wording of the decision may be found in different places, in slightly different versions. See, among others, Arazi testimony, undated, HHA, division 80, Arazi files.

22. Nahon's report on his activities in the affair, 14 April 1946, CZA.

23. Acting Italian ambassador in London to the director of the West European department of the British Foreign Office, 6 May 1946, E4242, P.R.O. FO371/52527.

24. See note 6.

25. The first boat sent by the Mossad after the war, the *Dalin,* sailed on 11 August 1945. See HHA 14/81; *Reports,* 2751.

26. Brod to Rome, no. 659, 6 October 1945, P.R.O. WR2991, FO371/51124.

27. British ambassador, 10 January 1946; minutes of interministerial meeting in the Colonial Office, 12 October 1945, P.R.O. CAB 119/148. The minutes were given to the chiefs of staff for examination; Colonial Office to Palestine, 10 November 1945, no. 1767, FO371/45384. See also Arieh Yosef Kochavi, *Displaced Persons and International Politics* (in Hebrew) (Tel Aviv, 1992), the chapter on Italy.

28. See note 18.

29. Brod to the Foreign Office, 8 April 1946; and Foreign Office to Brod, 9 April 1946, P.R.O. FO945/655. The political adviser to the Commander of the Mediterranean forces recommended that the Allied military authorities themselves take steps to dispatch the refugees back to the countries from which they had come, if the Italians refused to do so: Brod to the Foreign Office, 8 April 1946, no. 345, P.R.O. FO945/655. The Foreign Office opposed this and suggested that the Allied command reach some sort of a local agreement: Foreign Office to the office of the Political Adviser (Brod), no. 479, 9 April 1946, P.R.O. FO945/655.

30. Report by Meir Davidson on the affair, 2 May 1946, HHA 14/86; Nahon report, 15 May 1946, CZA S25/2640. Worried about the suicide threat, the

British asked for instructions from London: Brod to Foreign Office, 17 April 1946; Charles to Foreign Office, 18 April 1946; and the Foreign Office's reply that same day, P.R.O. FO945/655.

31. Brod to Foreign Office, 11 April 1946, P.R.O. FO945/655.

32. Wording of the agreement reached between Laski and Arazi, 10 April 1946, CZA S25/2640. See also the large British correspondence on this matter, 11 April 1946, P.R.O. ADM 116/5561 and FO800/485.

33. Dov [Yermenovitz] to Amram [M. Sneh], 16 April 1946, HHA 14/86.

34. Trafford Smith to the Jewish Agency, 13 April 1946, E3428, P.R.O. FO371/52515.

35. Hall to Attlee, 15 April 1946, P.R.O. PREM 8/298. Attlee and Morrison supported Hall's position; an intelligence report from Palestine argued that the hunger strike was aimed at stirring up the Yishuv. Report 12 of the British Command in Palestine and Transjordan, 31 March 1946–14 April 1946, P.R.O. WO 275/63.

36. Cunningham to the Colonial Office, no. 617, 15 April 1946, E3594, FO371/52516; chief commander in the Middle East to the War Office, 17 April 1946, P.R.O. AIR20/4963.

37. Brod to the Foreign Office, no. 371, 17 April 1946, P.R.O. ADM 116/5561.

38. Charles to Foreign Office, no. 643, 1 May 1946, P.R.O. ADM 116/5561.

39. Alon to Avi-Amos [Ben-Gurion], to Ben-Kedem [Shertok] and to Artzi [Mossad], 21 April 1946, HHA 14/86; Arazi files, HHA.

40. Ibid.

41. Cunningham to the Colonial Office, 28 April 1946, P.R.O. ADM 116/5561. Charles to the Foreign Office, 1 May 1946, P.R.O. ADM 116/5561.

42. From Artzi to Alon, 17 May 1946, HHA 14/86. At a meeting of the Jewish Agency Executive on 21 May 1946, which for the most part addresssed what position should be taken in the wake of the recommendations of the Anglo-American Committee, a member of the executive, Dr. Dov Yosef, reported on his meetings with the high commissioner. Yosef told the commissioner, among other things, about the visit he had made on the *Fede,* which had arrived in Palestine a few days before. "If Jews are willing to come under these conditions then the need must be very great," Dr. Yosef said. "I told him [the high commissioner] about the conversation I had on the ship. I told one young man, 'I've seen better ships,' and he answered: 'There are tens of thousands of Jewish ready to come in ships worse than this one." Jewish Agency Executive, 21 May 1946, CZA, minutes of JAE.

43. Arazi testimony, Arazi files, HHA, testimony 89.

44. Arazi testimony, see notes 18 and 20; Yehuda Slutzki, ed., *History of Haganah,* C-1 (in Hebrew) (Tel Aviv, 1973), pp. 259–69.

45. Arazi testimony, see note 43.

46. On the secret cooperation between the British and the Haganah, see, among others, Yehuda Bauer, *Diplomacy and Underground* (in Hebrew) (Tel Aviv, 1966), pp. 96–164; Gelber, *Flag Bearers,* pp. 133–36, 138–42; Arazi testimony, 21 August 1955, no. 2506, HHA, division 106, file 6.

47. Arazi testimony, 21 August 1955.

48. Ibid.

49. At Arazi's first meeting with Aharon Hoter-Yishai, the Haganah's attorney, in Tarvisio, Arazi told him about his mission and said that he hoped Hoter-Yishai would find in Europe "say 5,000 Jews" who would be prepared to engage in illegal immigration. Hoter-Yishai relates that he questioned whether so many Jews who wanted to go Palestine in this way could be found. Hoter-Yishai interview, quoted in Bauer, *Flight and Rescue,* p. 66.

50. Arazi always considered himself primarily a Haganah man and sharply opposed factionalism and partisanship. At the time of the inquiry into Chaim Alorsorov's murder, when Arazi was an officer in the Mandatory police force (and, in fact, a Haganah secret agent in the police force) in charge of the investigation, he locked horns with Meirov, who was a member of the Mapai committee that tried to influence the progress of the investigation. See Shabtai Teveth, *The Assassination of Arlosorov* (in Hebrew) (Jerusalem and Tel Aviv, 1982), pp. 123–25, 153–54, 159.

51. To Artzi from Arazi, Italy, 1 July 1945, HHA 14/81.

52. Alon to Brother [Meirov], Benyamin [Italy] 30 June 1945, HHA 14/81a.

53. Bauer, *Flight and Rescue.* pp. 41–42, 64.

54. The state of mind of the soldiers immediately after the war may be learned from the following letter: "From the day on which the war ended I am in a horrible mood, . . . when we were on the front we knew for what reason and why, but now we have no purpose, we are waiting without knowing why." Yonatan [Nana] to Yitzhak Gruenbaum, 14 May 1945, CZA A127/382/1. This changed afterward. See the report of the Jewish Brigade delegation headed by Hoter-Yishai, 30 June 1945, HHA 33/12, CZA S25/5215; see also Bauer, *Flight and Rescue.* There were encounters, as well as mutual assistance, between the soldiers from the Yishuv and the refugees and survivors even prior to this in Italy, from 1943 onward, as the Allied armies advanced northward; see Gelber, *Flag Bearers,* pp. 207–87. But these were not similar, in terms of the force of the discovery, to the first intensive encounter that took place after the end of the war in northern Italy. On the significance of this discovery, Shertok said, "The recent tidings of the great wonder reached me only in recent days. . . . I confess that only during the past day have I really begun to grasp the revolutionary change that has taken place, and only here . . . I plumbed the depth of its significance." Shertok to members of the Jewish Brigade, 10 July 1945, CZA S25/6064.

55. Agami to Meir [Turkey], 24 June 1945, 19 July 1945, HHA 14/397; letter from Alon [Arazi], 30 May 1945, HHA 14/81a; letter of Yehiel (Duvdevani) from Italy, 8 July 1945, HHA 14/81a; to Moshe [Shertok] and Dobkin from Duvdevani, 20 July 1945, CZA S25/5243; Ben-Zion Israeli at the Histadrut Executive Committee, 25 July 1945, Labor Archives (LA); from Duvdevani to Artzi, 28 July 1945, 3 August 1945, HHA 14/81a; to Avi-Amos [Ben-Gurion] and Danny from Ben-Yehuda, 21 July 1945, HHA 14/81a; Duvdevani to Dobkin, 23 August 1945, HHA 14/81a; Duvdevani from Italy, 5 September 1945, HHA 14/158.

56. On 1 July 1945 Yehuda Arazi reported to the Mossad in Palestine on a meeting with people from the Diaspora Center to coordinate the transfer of the refugees within Italy. The transfer was to be carried out by the center, while

the Mossad's men were to take care of everything connected to the transporting of the refugees to Palestine. To Artzi from Alon, 1 July 1945, HHA 14/81.

57. Bauer, *Flight and Rescue,* pp. 97–99.

58. Testimony of Yeshayahu Weinberg, ODD; memo by Shlomo Rabinowitz (Shamir), HHA 4183/33/7.

59. To Artzi from Alon, Italy, 1 July 1945, HHA 14/81.

60. To Artzi from Alon, Italy, 9 July 1945, HHA 14/81a.

61. Daniela [Sereni] report, 8 September 1945, HHA 14/81a; Sereni, *Ships,* pp. 22–23.

62. After Company 462 returned to the Middle East, the immigration activists from the company were attached to companies 179 and 650 in Odena and Bologna, respectively; in practice, however, they operated out of the *ha'apala* center in Milan, with the knowledge of the commanders of the units. See Gelber, *Flag Bearers,* p. 579; see also HHA 14/84–14/86.

63. HHA 14/84, 14/85, 14/86, and others.

64. Minutes of the initiating committee for the *ha'apala* book from Italy, 5 December 1955, with Yisrael Livertovski, Shalhevet Freier, Matti Megged, Yehuda Arazi. HHA, testimonies, division 106, file 6.

65. Biger testimony, ODD, project 60, no. 8; quoted in Gelber, *Flag Bearers,* p. 629.

66. There were 79 people on board the *Nattuno A,* which sailed from Bari on 27 August. There were 168 on the ship that sailed after it. On the *Rondina* (*Enzo Sereni*), which sailed on 7 January 1946 from Vado Ligure and was captured by the British, there were 900 immigrants. See HHA, files 14/81b, 14/82, 14/83, as well as *Reports,* 2751.

67. S.I.M.E. report, 1 February 1946, P.R.O. WO 204/49, brought in full in Gelber, *Flag Bearers,* pp. 633–36.

68. Report on immigration, March 1946, P.R.O. FO945/655.

69. To Artzi from Alon, 1 April 1946, HHA 14/86.

70. To Artzi from Kassuta, 2 April 1946, HHA 14/86.

71. To Artzi from Alon, 8 March 1946, HHA 14/85. Ada Sereni was supposed to participate in the laying of a cornerstone for the Enzo House at Kibbutz Givat Brenner. To Artzi from Alon, 27 March 1946, HHA 14/85; to Alon from Artzi, 1 April 1946, HHA 14/86. For the full documentation of Sereni during the La Spezia period, see HHA 14/85 and 14/86.

72. Arazi testimony, 27 September 1949, HHA, division 106, file 6. In this testimony, Arazi explained why he chose this name: "First because it has a Sephardic sound to it and it is easy for the Italians to pronounce, and second because it provided an opening for questions about my background, and served as a springboard for the "story"—my family's origins were in Spain and after many wanderings they reached Danzig—in this manner I could easily integrate the matter of the Inquisition, the Spanish persecution, wanderings, and to hint at the fate that united the Jews in the Middle Ages and in the twentieth century."

73. Gelber, *Flag Bearers,* p. 653.

74. Albert Camus, *The Plague,* trans. Stuart Gilbert (New York, 1972), p. 120.

75. Ibid., pp. 125–26.

76. Arazi testimony, Arazi files, HHA 2090 (37).

77. Camus, *The Plague,* p. 126.

78. Antek Zuckerman spoke, as early as August 1945, at the conference in London, on "an abyss, a great abyss" yawning between the Yishuv and the Diaspora. Yitzhak (Antek) Zuckerman, *Those Seven Years* (in Hebrew) (Beit Lohamei ha-Geta'ot, undated), pp. 503–4.

79. On the very first evening Arazi conducted an inspection of the refugees on the ship, divided them into groups, chose group heads, and instituted a new regime of order.

80. Hayyim Nahman Bialik, "The City of Slaughter," in Israel Efros, ed., *Selected Poems of Hayyim Nahman Bialik* (New York, rev. ed. 1965).

81. Arazi testimony, 18 August 1949, 4 September 1949, HHA, division 106, file 6.

82. Arazi testimony, HHA, division 106, file 6.

83. Ben-Gurion's biographer, Shabtai Teveth, writes that "a view of the plight of the Jews as a source of strength was always at the foundation of [Ben-Gurion's] thinking" (Teveth, *The Burning Ground* [in Hebrew] [Jerusalem and Tel Aviv, 1987], p. 438). Ben-Gurion's words during the 1920s, 1930s, and 1940s prove this. After Hitler's rise to power he advocated turning the "catastrophe" "into procreative power" and the "plight" into a "political impetus." "Zionism's strength derives from the magnitude of Jewish suffering," he said to the Jewish Agency Executive in 1941, and "a redeeming idea . . . turns sorrow into a positive source of power." "The power of suffering has increased the power of Zionism" (ibid., pp. 438–39).

84. Arazi testimony, HHA, division 106, file 6. It was Ehud Avriel, then assistant to the Mossad chief, who ascribed to the British the description of Yehuda Arazi in the La Spezia affair as an "adventurer and demagogue." His writings on the affair imply indirectly, however, that this was also the opinion of many of the Mossad people. See Avriel, *Open the Gates* (in Hebrew) (Tel Aviv, 1976), p. 216. Some of the leaders of the soldiers who worked alongside Arazi in Italy were also less than pleased with his actions. Shalhevet Freier accused Arazi of bad judgment during the affair, and in Livertovsky's opinion, Arazi took too many risks in this incident and in other sailings. See Livertovsky testimony, ODD, testimony 2; Freier testimony, ibid., testimony 3c. See also Gelber, *Flag Bearers,* pp. 661–62.

85. Cables from Palestine to Italy, 5 and 6 April 1946, HHA 14/86.

86. Kantoni, who was sent by the Germans to a concentration camp in Germany, managed to jump out of the train, return, and join the Italian underground. See Kantoni testimony, ODD; Sereni, *Ships,* pp. 87–88.

87. To Meir [Davidson] Alon [Italy] from Artzi, 7 April 1946, HHA 14/86, and also HHA, Mossad Diary, 14/505.

88. See minutes of the meeting in London in which the report was discussed, and in which participated Ben-Gurion, Shertok, Berl Loker, David Horowitz, and the leaders of British Jewry, 29 April 1946, CZA Z4/10.380.

89. All of Arazi's testimonies about what happened on the ship suggest that the mood among the refugees changed from the moment it seemed that there was a point in their remaining on the ship. The refugees' psychological endurance during the affair attests to this.

90. Report of Intelligence in the Middle East, 1 February 1946; see note 67.

91. Alon to Artzi, 13 April 1946, HHA 14/86.

92. Artzi to Benyamin, 12 April 1946, HHA, 14/86; Arazi files.

93. Hall to Attlee, 15 April 1946, P.R.O. PREM 8/298.

94. Artzi to Alon, Kassuta [France], 17 April 1946, HHA, 14/186.

95. Alon to Avi-Amos, to Ben-Kedem, and to Artzi, 21 April 1946, HHA 14/86, Arazi files.

96. Dov [Yermenowitz] to Amram [Sneh], 18 April 1946, HHA 14/86.

97. Artzi to Alon, 19 and 24 April 1946; Amram and Artzi to Alon and Dov, 24 April 1946, HHA 14/86.

98. Nahon's report on his activities in the La Spezia affair, 14 April 1946, CZA; Arazi testimony, Arazi files.

99. Dov [Yermenowitz] to Ram [Sneh] and Ben-Yehuda, 21 April 1946; Alon to Artzi, 26 April 1946; Berg to Artzi, 26 April 1946, HHA 14/86; Arazi files.

100. Avriel, *Open the Gates*, p. 216.

101. Alon and Ben-Yehuda to Artzi, 2 May 1946; Alon and Ben-Yehuda to Artzi and Ben-Porat [Joseph], 4 May 1946; Ben-Yehuda to Artzi, 6 May 1946, 8 May 1946; and Artzi to Ben-Yehuda, 6 May 1946, HHA 14/86; Arazi files. Most of the copies of these documents may also be found in other files of the Mossad, such as classified files under the name "Mossad Diary" with the numbers 14/500 onward. Arazi intended to turn the arrival of the boats in Palestine into a "national holiday" and into a "demonstration," and gave instructions to the sailors to approach the shore and to sail its length as far as possible "and to deck yourselves out beforehand with flags." However, when the ships approached Tel Aviv a British destroyer commanded them to sail to Haifa. See Yehuda Arazi testimony, 5 December 1955, HHA, division 106, file 6.

102. See the war log of the Port Security Unit, May 1946, WO170/8929.

103. See Ada Sereni testimony, ODD, project 4, testimony 48a; Sereni, *Ships*, pp. 74–82; D. Solomon testimony, HHA, testimony 4322.

104. The commander-in-chief of the Mediterranean fleet to the admiralty in London, 23 July 1946, copy at P.R.O. FO371/52628, quoted in Gelber, *Flag Bearers*, p. 660.

105. Amitsur Ilan, *America, Britain, and Palestine* (in Hebrew) (Jerusalem, 1979), p. 205.

106. *Davar*, 12 May 1946.

107. *Reports*, HHA 2751.

108. Ibid.

109. See Davidson's report from the beginning of May 1946, HHA 14/86; testimonies of Sereni, Livertovsky, and Freier, ODD; and Gelber, *Flag Bearers*, pp. 661–62.

110. Gelber, *Flag Bearers*, pp. 661, 664–66.

111. Sereni testimony, ODD; Sereni, *Ships*; Gelber, *Flag Bearers*, pp. 662–63.

112. *Reports*, HHA, 2751.

113. Alon to Artzi, 13 September 1946, HHA 14/87.

114. Alon to Artzi, 17 September 1946, HHA 14/87.

115. To Ben-Yehuda from Alon, 12 October 1946, HHA 14/88.

116. Sereni testimony, ODD, op. cit.; Sereni, *Ships,* pp. 84ff; see also Charles to Foreign Office, no. 180, 4 February 1946, E1056, P.R.O. FO371/52508.

117. Sereni, *Ships;* Sereni testimony, op. cit.

118. Sereni testimony, op. cit., pp. 25–26; Sereni, *Ships,* 93–94.

119. Italian Ministry of the Interior to the Allied delegation, 10 August 1946, P.R.O. WO204/11135.

120. Neter [France] to Palestine, 23 June 1947, HHA 14/89.

121. *Reports,* HHA 2751.

122. To Artzi from Alon, 16 November 1946, HHA 14/88.

123. See report of Itai [Avriel] from Offri [Czechoslovakia], 17 April 1947, OL. Also, "Alon and Daniela request that Itai [Avriel] come to them immediately. Alon is prepared to delay his trip for one or two days with regard to Itai's visit" (Leonard [Italy] to the operations center in Paris, 13 April 1947, OL).

124. The report itself states that the numbers are rounded and not precise, and that "the material [the people] is very difficult in general and with regard to our direct purpose" (Neter to Palestine, 23 June 1947, HHA 14/89).

125. Intelligence report of the Sixth Airborne Division, August 1947, P.R.O. WO/275/87.

126. Charles to the Foreign Office, no. 713, 27 March 1947, E 2716, P.R.O. FO371/61804.

127. Charles to Sforza, 3 June 1947, E 5175, P.R.O. FO371/61811.

128. Charles to the Foreign Office, no. 1117, 16 May 1947, P.R.O. FO371/61842. See also Sforza to Bevin, 29 July 1947, P.R.O. FO371/61821.

129. Neter to Artzi, 18 May 1947; 23 June 1947, HHA 14/106.

130. OL, 12 July 1947, 16.00, 15 July 1947; 17 July 1947; 22 July 1947, 21.00; 31 July 1947; Charles to Bevin, 4 August 1947, no. 337, P.R.O. FO371/61821; report from 23 June 1947 on the entry of 1,870 people that month, HHA 14/106.

131. Interim report of the liaison officer on infiltration over the Austrian-Italian border, August 1947, P.R.O. FO371/61854.

132. OL, 19 July 1947, 14.00; 24 July 1947, 22.00; 12 May 1947, 22.00; Neter to Artzi, 14 May 1947, HHA 14/106; from Neter, 18 May 1947, HHA 14/533; from Neter, 23 June 1947, HHA 14/89. See also Ehud Avriel at the Mapai Central Committee, 23 June 1947, Labor Party Archives (LPA) 23/47; from Shimshon [Shemariya Guttman], HHA 14/106; 20 July 1947; from Yissar [France], 20 July 1947, HHA 14/107; Sereni, *Ships,* pp. 132–40.

133. To Yiftah and Arnon from Claire [Sereni], 20 July 1947, HHA 14/89, 14/533.

134. Report from Leonard [Italy], 11.30, 13 April 1947, OL; see also 15–21 April 1947, OL.

135. To Yiftah and Arnon from Claire [Sereni], Leonard, 20 July 1947, HHA 14/89, 14/533.

136. From Neter to Palestine, 18 May 1947, HHA 14/106, 14/530.

137. Foreign Office to the embassy in Rome, 30 April 1947, P.R.O. FO371/61841.

138. Ward to Foreign Office, no. 1941, 8 October 1947, P.R.O. FO371/61850.

139. Charles to Foreign Office, no. 1082, 12 May 1947, E5225, P.R.O. FO371/61845.

140. Sereni to the Center in Paris, 10 May 1947, OL.

141. Sereni to the Center in Paris, 14 May 1947, OL.

142. Sereni to the Center in Paris, 16 May 1947, OL.

143. Sereni to the Center in Paris, 14 May 1947, OL.

144. Notification from Neter by Rudi [Zameret, Marseilles], 2 June 1947, OL; notification from Ben-Yehuda [Meirov] from Milan, 3 June 1947, OL; Ben-Yehuda to Operations Center, OL.

145. André's [Avi Schwartz] report from Sidney [Marseilles], 13 June 1947, OL; Embassy in Rome to Foreign Office in London, 13 June 1947, P.R.O. FO371/61811.

146. 30 August 1947, 12.15, OL.

147. Yissar to Arnon, 3 November 1947, HHA 14/109.

148. Ward to Foreign Office, no. 1941, 8 October 1947, E9432, P.R.O. FO371/61850.

CHAPTER 2

1. André [Sidney] [Avi Schwartz of the Marseilles station] to the Operations Center in Paris, 13 June 1947, 17.00, OL; British embassy in Rome to Foreign Office in London, 13 June 1947, P.R.O. FO371/61841.

2. From Neter to Palestine, 18 May 1947, HHA, "Mossad Diary," 14/530; from Danny [Ze'ev Schind, U.S.] to Sidney [Marseilles], 2 April 1947, HHA, America files, 14/331; files of the British Foreign Office (FO/371) 61839 and 61840 and correspondence from 30 April 1947 and 10 May 1947 between the Foreign Office in London and the embassy in Rome, files 61840 and 61841. These documents are kept in P.R.O.

3. Georges Bidault, *D'une resistance à l'autre* (Paris, 1965), pp. 151–54; Roger Priouret, *La république des partis* (Paris, 1947), pp. 453–55.

4. André [Sidney] to Paris, 13 June 1947, OL.

5. 13 June 1947, 14 June 1947, OL; the British consul in Marseilles reported on suspicious Mossad ships, 18 June 1947, P.R.O. FO371/61812; interministerial committee on illegal immigration, 2 July 1947, P.R.O. FO371/61814.

6. Memorandum to the interministerial committee on illegal immigration, toward its meeting of 7 July 1947, P.R.O. FO371/61845.

7. Memorandum to the foreign secretary for the meeting of the cabinet committee on illegal immigration, 9 June 1947, E 5001, P.R.O. FO371/61811.

8. Foreign Office in London to embassy in Paris, 14 June 1947, no. 1067, P.R.O. FO371/61811; from London to Paris, 13 June 1947, P.R.O. FO371/61842.

9. From Rudi [Zameret, Marseilles] to Paris, 14 June 1947, OL; from Rudi to Paris, 15 June 1947, OL; from embassy in Paris to Foreign Office in London, 16 June 1947, P.R.O. FO371/61812.

10. From the British embassy in Paris to Foreign Office in London, 23 June 1947 and 3 July 1947, P.R.O. FO371/61813.

11. Cooper to Bidault, 21 March 1947, Archives du Quai d'Orsay (French Ministry of Foreign Affairs Archive, FMFA), Paris, 17 [unclear]/109/47, no. 283. A copy of this document is in the Blumel Archive, Paris.

12. *Reports,* HHA 2751.

13. See note 7.

14. To Yissar Or [France] from Arnon [Palestine], 18 June 1947, HHA 14/106.

15. Yitzhak Rav-Hanasi [Ike Aharonowitz, the *President Warfield* captain] from Marseilles to Paris, 20 June 1947, OL.

16. Ernst [Germany] to Paris, 20 June 1947, OL: "The French Consul will probably complicate things. Demands Army's IDs for individual visas. Afraid that the Consul has received orders from high up. . . . Demands Abbé's interference."

17. Daniela [Sereni] to Paris, 22 June 1947, OL.

18. See note 11.

19. Letter from "Yiftah" [Yigal Feikowitz-Alon], 21 June 1947, quoted in *The Palmach Book,* vol. 1 (in Hebrew) (Tel Aviv, 1953), p. 841.

20. Instructions from Paris to Marseilles, 10 July 1947, at the hours 19.00, 21.15, 24.00, OL.

21. To vessel [ship] from Arnon [the Mossad station in Palestine], 17 July 1947, HHA 14/234b.

22. *Ha'Olam,* 24 July 1947.

23. From Neter [France] to Palestine, 23 June 1947, HHA 14/106.

24. Daniela to Paris, 23 June 1947, OL.

25. Jacques Derogy, *Exodus, La Loi du Retour* (Paris, 1970), p. 70; see also notes 15 and 16.

26. From Ernst to Paris, 20 June 1947, OL. See also Ze'ev Venya Hadari, introduction and decoding, *Ha'Mossad Le'Aliyah Bet, Operations Log—Paris 1947* (in Hebrew) (Be'er Sheva and Jerusalem, 1991), p. 91.

27. It suffices to list some of the well-known books on this period, such as *La république des partis* by Roger Priouret, *La 4ème république* by Jacques Fauvet, and *La 4ème république et sa politique exterieure* by Alfred Grosser, which do not mention the topic of Jewish migration to and from France in the years after World War II in the framework of France's foreign policy.

28. From Sidney [Marseilles] to Artzi, 18 March 1946, HHA 14/100a, 14/299; from Kassuta [France] to Artzi, 8 March 1946; and from Sidney to Artzi, 16 March 1946, HHA 14/100a, 14/299.

29. To Nesin [North Africa] from Neter [France], 22 June 1946, HHA 14/180; to Ogen from Artzi, 23 June 1946, HHA 14/180; Tzidkiahu Report, 3 July 1946, HHA 14/101.

30. From Cunningham to Colonial Office, 11 April 1946, P.R.O. FO371/55215.

31. Foreign Office in London to the ambassador in Paris, 3 May 1946, P.R.O. ADM 116/5561; memorandum to the French Ministry of Foreign Affairs, 10 May 1946, P.R.O. FO371/52523; Cunningham to Colonial Office, no. 729, 21 May 1946, P.R.O. FO371/52529.

32. Bates memorandum on the appeals to European governments on the question of Jewish illegal immigration, 16 August 1946, E 7817, P.R.O. FO371/52627.

33. "Lulu" report, 6 November 1946, HHA 14/103; Cooper to Foreign Office, 24 August 1946, P.R.O. FO371/52630.

34. See 1 April 1948, J. P. Nathan, *La terre retrouvée*.

35. "Lulu" report, op. cit. Mossad and Bricha operatives used to forge entry permits to target countries, under which they transferred Jews to the ports of departure.

36. See Ze'ev Venya Hadari, *Refugees Beat an Empire* (in Hebrew) (Tel Aviv, 1985), p. 309; Abba Gefen, *The Breakers of the Barriers* (in Hebrew) (Tel Aviv, 1961), pp. 160–61.

37. Paris to Foreign Office, 26 July 1946, P.R.O. FO371/52545.

38. Ashley Clarke to Bates, 18 January 1947, P.R.O. FO371/61750; Clarke to Foreign Office, 15 January 1947, no. 25, P.R.O. FO371/61750.

39. Millard to Bates, 24 October 1946, FO371/52636; Millard to Bates, 8 November 1946, P.R.O. FO371/52637.

40. A copy of "Perier's" letter, which is numbered 6.501 and has no archival marking, may be found in the Blumel Archive in Paris. This archive preserves copies of the correspondence between the French ministries of Foreign Affairs and of the Interior, in particular from the year 1947, about Jewish migration to and from France.

41. Idith Zertal, "Le cinquième côté du triangle, la France et la question de la Palestine 1945–1948," in Irad Malkin, ed. *La France et la Méditerranée* (Leiden, 1990) pp. 412–423; "The Socialist Connection, French Socialists and the French Socialist Party—Their Attitudes toward Zionism on the Eve of the Establishment of the State [of Israel]," in B. Pinkus and D. Bensimon, eds., *French Jewry, Zionism and the State of Israel* (in Hebrew) (Paris: Sdeh Boker, 1992), pp. 178–97. In Mossad documents Blumel was referred to by the code name "Farhi." From France to Palestine, 20 March 1947, HHA 14/105.

42. From Léon Blum to Minister of the Interior Edouard Depreux, 22 January 1947, unmarked, Blumel Archive.

43. See David Weinberg, "The French-Jewish Community after World War 2: The Struggle for Survival and Self-Definition," *Forum* (Summer 1982): 45–54; Renée Poznansky, "The Heritage of the Second World War: Zionism in France in the Years 1944–1947," in Pinkus and Bensimon, eds., *French Jewry*, pp. 144–66.

44. Depreux wrote that the bonds between himself and Blumel were "relations that no power could break." Edouard Depreux, *Souvenirs d'un militant* (Paris, 1972), p. 245; see also note 41.

45. André Blumel to Paul Ramadier, 13 March 1947, Blumel Archive.

46. Cooper to Foreign Office, 4 January 1947, P.R.O. FO371/61799; Cooper to Foreign Office, 31 January 1947, P.R.O. FO371/61830.

47. The consulate in Marseilles to Foreign Office in London, 6 November 1946, P.R.O. FO371/52636; document from 9 November 1946, P.R.O. FO371/52638.

48. Cooper to Foreign Office, 4 January 1947, P.R.O. FO371/61799.

49. Hiyam to Bates, 8 November 1946, P.R.O. FO371/52636.

50. Clarke to Foreign Office, 15 January 1947, P.R.O. FO371/61750.

51. Attlee at a meeting of the Cabinet Committee on Defense, 12 March 1947, P.R.O. WO 32/1026.

52. Clarke to Bates, 18 January 1947, P.R.O. FO371/61750; Cooper to Foreign Office, 3 April 1947, P.R.O. FO371/61804.

53. Jean Pierre Rioux, *La France de la quatrième république* (Paris, 1980), p. 159.

54. From the Mossad in France to Palestine, 20 March 1947, HHA 14/105.

55. Memorandum to the French Minister of the Interior from the Directorate of the Arrangement with Aliens, Secretariat, SN/RI/SEC no. 213, National Archives in Paris (copy in the Blumel Archive).

56. Cooper to Bidault, 21 March 1947. The marking on the French version is 17[unclear]/109/47, no. 283, FMFA, Les Archives du Quai d'Orsay, Paris; the English version is marked Cooper to Bidault, 21 March 1947, E2667, P.R.O. FO371/61803. On the Foreign Office's instructions to the embassy in Paris about the wording of the application to the French, see Foreign Office to Paris, 15 March 1947, E2894, P.R.O. FO371/61804.

57. Paris to Foreign Office, no. 267, 4 April 1947, P.R.O. FO371/61804; Foreign Office to Moscow, no. 599, 5 April 1947, P.R.O. FO371/61804; Bevin to Bidault, 7 April 1947, P.R.O. FO371/61804; Bidault to Bevin, 8 April 1947, P.R.O. FO371/61804.

58. Paris to Foreign Office, no. 267, 4 April 1947, P.R.O. FO371/61804; meeting no. 11 of the Cabinet Committee on Defense, 16 April 1947, P.R.O. WO32/10260; Creech-Jones to McNeil, 21 April 1947, P.R.O. FO371/61805; meeting of the cabinet committee on illegal immigration, 2 May 1947, P.R.O. ADM 116/5648.

59. Interministerial meeting of the French government on covert immigration to Palestine, 21 April 1947; see memorandum to Minister of the Interior from the Directorate of the Arrangement with Aliens in the Ministry of the Interior in advance of the interministerial meeting with the prime minister, April 1947, no. 213, National Archives in Paris, SN/RI/SEC (copy in Blumel Archive); letter from Teitgen to Cooper, 24 April 1947, P.R.O. FO371/61805; Cooper to Foreign Office, no. 321, 25 April 1947, E3480, P.R.O. FO371/61805; Bates memorandum, 28 May 1947, P.R.O. FO371/61808.

60. Re'uven [Ritter, Bricha agent] to Operations Center, 24 June 1947, 11.00, OL; Re'uven to Operations Center, 27 June 1947, 06.00, OL; Re'uven to Operations Center, 1 July 1947, 18.00; 2 July 1947; 4 July 1947, 07.00, OL.

61. To Itai [Ehud Avriel, in Palestine] from Yissar [France], 7 July 1947, HHA 14/532, 14/106.

62. Dov [Lyons] to Operations Center, 4 July 1947: "1,200 cards with photos ready. Received 300 more photos. Till evening everything will be done and sent to Rudi. We talk about 4,000."; 5 July 1947 and 9 July 1947, OL.

63. 27 March 1947, 28 March 1947, 29 March 1947, 30 March 1947, OL.

64. Bevin to Bidault, 27 June 1947, P.R.O. FO371/61811. In his letter to Bidault, Bevin stressed especially the ship *President Warfield* and asserted that it would serve as a test case. That day Foreign Minister Bevin sent letters to nine foreign ministers asking them to assist Britain in its efforts to stop the Jewish illegal immigration.

65. "From police point of view—S [Sète] is OK." Rudi [Zameret] to Operations Center in Paris, 24 June 1947 and 25 June 1947, OL.

66. Rudi [Zameret] to Operations Center, 4 July 1947, 17.00, OL.

67. Rudi to Operations Center, 9 July 1947, 07.20, OL.

68. Rudi to Operations Center, 10 July 1947, 11.00, 13.00, OL.

69. British embassy in Paris to consulate in Marseilles, 10 July 1947, P.R.O. FO371/61815.

70. André (S.), Sète to Operations Center in Paris, 13.00, 10 July 1947, OL; "The Haganah's Part in the *Exodus* Affair," Kramer Report, November 1947 (at the second conference of Haganah, Bricha, and Mossad activists in Europe).

71. Rudi to Operations Center, 10 July 1947, 13.15, OL; permit for the sailing of the *President Warfield*, 7 July 1947, signed by Mourard, Blumel Archive.

72. André [Avi Schwartz] to Paris, 10 July 1947, 15.30, OL.

73. Ra'anan (S) [Ra'anan Rubinstein, port of Sète], 10 July 1947, 17.00, OL. Zameret sent the same item from Marseilles.

74. Rudi (Marseilles) Ra'anan (Sète) to Operations Center, 10 July 1947, 19.00 and 19.15, OL.

75. Rudi to Operations Center, 10 July 1947, OL; André [Avi Schwartz] and Yossi [Hamburger], Sète, transcript of conversation of Ben-Yehuda [Shaul Meirov] to Sète, 10 July 1947, 21.15. OL.

76. André to Operations Center, 10 July 1947, 20.00, OL; to Rudi from Amnon [Yossi Hamburger, on the ship], 11 July 1947, 07.30, no. 5, HHA 14/702.

77. André to Operations Center, 07.30, 11 July 1947, OL; Rudi to Operations Center, 11 July 1947, OL.

78. Head of the General Intelligence Services in Sète to the director-general of General Intelligence in Paris, Sète, 11 July 1947, no. I.649 (copy in Blumel Archive, Paris). The signature on the document is not clear. The name of the head of the intelligence service in Sète is mentioned in the investigative report of 6 August 1947 by the general judicial supervisor in Montpellier, who conducted an investigation on the sailing of the ship without a safety permit (copy in the Blumel Archive, Paris).

79. Inspector-general, head of the General Intelligence Services (*Renseignements généraux*) in Sète, to the director-general of the General Intelligence Services in Paris, no. I.660, 12 July 1947, re: The sailing of Jews whose destination is Colombia. Reference: report no. I.649 of 11 July.

80. Head of Herault district to the Minister of the Interior, the bureau in Paris, 12 July 1947, RD/YS (copies in Blumel Archive).

81. On Rammadier's promise to Bevin of 12 July 1947, see the summary of the contacts between Britain and France on the *President Warfield* affair of 5 August 1947, signed by Crossley, P.R.O. FO371/61822 (hereinafter Crossley memo).

82. See, for example, the report of policemen Fernand Cortez and Charles Fleury to the police chief and the head of the brigade of the Territorial Surveillance (D.S.T.) in Perpignian from 12 July, in response to his cable from 11 July 1947, no. 836, N.311. ANT; see also Rousseau's cable from the Ministry of the Interior to the head of the Montpellier district, undated, FR/CD/4, S.N./R.E. 2. Rousseau was a liaison man of the Mossad in the French Ministry of the Interior.

83. From Bevin to Bidault, summary of conversation between them, 12 July 1947, P.R.O. FO371/61815.

84. Embassy in Paris to Foreign Office, 13 July 1947, P.R.O. FO371/61816; see also Crossley memo, P.R.O. FO371/61822.

85. To Arnon from Yanai [Hagever], 12 December 1947, HHA 14/234b.

86. Rudi to Operations Center, 13 July 1947, 15 July 1947, OL.

87. Georges Bernanos, *Français, si vous saviez* (Paris, 1961), p. 251.

88. Rioux, *La France,* p. 28.

89. All the figures are taken from Rioux, *La France,* p. 33–48.

90. This is the name of Roger Priouret's book: *La république des partis.*

91. Depreux, *Souvenirs,* p. 253.

92. Roger Quilliot, *La S.F.I.O. et l'exercise du pouvoir 1944–1958* (Paris, 1972), pp. 778–79.

93. From Pino [Ginsburg] to the Mossad Center, Genf, 16 November 1945, HHA 14/160.

94. Dobkin's report to the Mapai Secretariat, 24 September 1944, LPA 24/44; Jefroykin's testimony to the author, Paris, August 1983; see also Annie Latour, *La resistance juive en France 1940–1943* (Paris, 1970), p. 240.

95. Ruth Klieger's report to the Histadrut Executive Committee, 17 August 1943, LA; to Meir from Artzi, 10 January 1945, HHA 14/671; Hanum [Klieger] to Palestine, Cairo, 9 April 1945, HHA 14/176.

96. To Hanum [Klieger] and Kassuta [Shaltiel], 25 May 1945, HHA 14/176; Ya'akobi to the Mossad, Paris, 5 June 1945, HHA 14/176 and 14/144a.

97. Ben-Gurion to the Mapai Central Committee, 15 March 1945, LPA 23/45.

98. Ben-Gurion Diary, 14 May 1945, BGA.

99. Ibid, 15 May 1945.

100. Ibid, 18 May 1945

101. Ben-Gurion eight-point document, 1 October 1945, BGA.

102. Letters of Shimon [Yitzhak Levi] to Palestine, 11 May 1945, HHA 14/144a; to Eliahu Dobkin from Ruth and David (translated from French), 22 May 1945, HHA 14/144a; to the Political Department from Ruth and David, 11 June 1945, HHA 14/144; to the Immigration (*aliya*) Department from David (French), 30 November 1945, 14/144, see also the series of letters to Pol [Avraham Polonski] from the Palestine Office in Paris (unclear signature, apparently Ruth Klieger's) from March, April, May, and June 1945 on the matter of care for children and their transfer to Palestine, Avraham Polonski Archives, Paris, (AAP), D10-V/6,8ff.

103. See letter from Pol to one of the *Armée juive* (AJ) men (French), 14 December 1945, AAP D10-XXX/6; another letter on this matter, from Pol to Leonard, 31 December 1945, AAP D10-XXX/9.

104. Ya'akobi report on actions in France and western Europe, Paris, 8 January 1946, HHA 14/100.

105. Gelber, *Flag Bearers,* pp. 641–62.

106. War log of Company 178 for the month of January 1946, WO 171/9785, quoted in Gelber, *Flag Bearers,* p. 644; to Artzi from Sidney, 4 March 1946, HHA 14/299.

107. From Sidney to Artzi, 18 March 1946, HHA 14/100a.

108. On the seizure of the ship, from Artzi to Kassuta, Alon, Zaken, and Berman, 27 March 1946, HHA 14/299; on the entry to the port, to Michael [Moshe Chervinsky, the Mossad's Secretary] from Hovav, 28 March 1946, HHA 14/299; to Michael from Hofshi [David Nameri, the Mossad official responsible for activities at the port], 28 March 1946, HHA 14/299.

109. To Bina (report of the Revisionists from Paris), 24 March 1946, copy in HHA 14/100.

110. To Artzi from Mathieu, 18 April 1946, HHA 14/100; from Kassuta to Artzi, 12 April 1946, HHA 14/100.

111. Ze'ev Vanya Hadari, *Refugees Beat an Empire* (in Hebrew) (Tel Aviv, 1985), pp. 144–45.

112. Biriah report, by Tzidkiyahu, 3 July 1946, HHA 14/101.

113. HHA, files 14/100–14/104, and the Mossad's operations log.

114. Series of cables from France to Palestine, beginning of October 1946, HHA 14/103.

115. "The Formal Arrangements in Kassuta," from Lulu, 6 November 1946, HHA 14/103.

116. See Aviva Halamish, *Exodus: The True Story* (in Hebrew) (Tel Aviv, 1990), pp. 75–96.

117. See, for example, Idith Zertal, "Lost Souls—The *Ma'apilim* and the Mossad in the Struggle for the Establishment of the State and Thereafter" (in Hebrew), *Ha'Zionut* 14 (1989): 107–26; Yehoshua Freundlich, "The Affair of the Investigation of UNSCOP" (in Hebrew), *Ha'Zionut* 13 (1988): 27–51; Michael Cohen, *Palestine and the Great Powers 1945–1948* (Princeton, 1982), pp. 250–59.

118. "Doing our best with the help of our friends," was the Mossad report from Paris to Palestine, 22 July 1947, HHA 14/533; from Yissar to Arnon, 23 July 1947, HHA 14/533: "Local government decision not to impose disembarkation. We will be watching and hope that nobody wants to disembark"; Jewish Agency cables on this matter, CZA S25/1695.

119. Shertok at the Jewish Agency Executive, 28 July 1947, minutes of JAE, CZA: "It is clear that this is a serious test, if the people disembark or not."

120. Mossad operations log, items from 21–22 July 1947.

121. From Paris to Foreign Office, 18 July 1947, P.R.O. FO371/61816.

122. Summary of meeting in the Colonial Office, 24 July 1947, CZA S25/7567; summary of meeting in the Colonial Office, 25 July 1947, P.R.O. CO 733/491/1.

123. Cables from the British embassy in Paris and the Foreign Office in London, 20–21 July, P.R.O. FO371/61817; between Palestine and the Colonial Office, 23 and 30 July, 22 August 1947, P.R.O. FO371/61819/61821; also the Crossley memo, 5 August 1947, P.R.O. FO371/61822.

124. The phrasing is that of the British ambassador in Bogota. From embassy in Bogota to Foreign Office in London, 22 July 1947, P.R.O. FO371/61817.

125. Announcement by François Mitterand, French government spokesman, 23 July 1947, Blumel Archive.

126. Depreux, *Souvenirs*, p. 300.

127. Minister of the Interior to acting commissioner of the district, François Collaveri, 25 July 1947 (copy in Blumel Archive).

128. From embassy in Paris to Foreign Office, 23 July 1947, P.R.O. FO371/61818; see also other, previous documents of the Foreign Office which state bluntly that the French government has a definitely pro-Jewish tendency or that the socialist ministers have a "pro-Jewish complex," 28 May 1947, P.R.O. FO371/61808.

129. *Le Populaire*, 6 July 1947.

130. *Le Populaire,* 16, 23, 28 August 1947.

131. From Paris to Foreign Office in London, 25 July 1947, P.R.O. FO371/61818; from Foreign Office to embassy in Paris, 26 July 1947, P.R.O. FO371, files 61818 and 61819; Shertok at the JAE, 28 July 1947, CZA Executive minutes; from Yosef Fisher, a Jewish Agency man in Paris, to Shertok, 27 July 1947, CZA S25/1695; from the British embassy in Paris to Foreign Office, 28 July 1947, P.R.O. FO371/61819; meeting of the JAE, 28 July 1947.

132. Letter from Pagès to the head of national security, 1 August 1947 (copy in the Blumel Archive).

133. From the Minister of the Interior to the Minister of Foreign Affairs, 4 August, no. 1534, Blumel Archive.

134. From the Minister of Foreign Affairs to the Minister of the Interior, 5 August 1947, letter no. 3724, Blumel Archive.

135. By custom, minutes are not taken at meetings of the French government. The report from the meeting is from a record made by Vincent Auriol, president of France (who is the *pro forma* chairman of the meetings), in his diary on the evening of that day. See Vincent Auriol, *Journal d'un septennat,* 6 August 1947, vol. 1947, p. 387.

136. Rudi to the Operations Center in Paris, 29 July 1947, 14.00, OL.

137. From Marseilles to the Foreign Office, 29 July 1947, P.R.O. FO371/61820; from Marseilles to Jerusalem, 29 July 1947, P.R.O. FO371/61846.

138. The Hehalutz operative called them "deserters" (letter from Hanan Reichman, 26 August 1947, CZA S25/2630); the Colonial Office reported to Bevin on the disembarkment of the ill and handicapped (Colonial Office to Bevin, 14 August 1947, P.R.O. FO371/61822); that day's issue of *Ha'Olam* wrote that 129 people had left the ship. See also: From Arnon to Yissar, 23 August 1947, HHA 14/535.

139. From Rudi to Paris, 3 August 1947, 15 August 1947, OL; *Runnymede Park* log, 2, 5, 16 August 1947.

140. *Runnymede Park* log, 12 and 13 August 1947; the order for the strike, sent from shore on 17 August said that it was meant to "reawaken the world from its silence" (OL).

141. Rudi to the Operations Center in Paris, 17 August 1947, 07.45, OL.

142. Rudi to Paris, 17 August 1947, 18.30, OL.

143. "Bogus Jewish Hunger Strike," notation in a British log, 18 August 1947, P.R.O. ADM 1/20684.

144. "Hunger Strike Started by Jews of *Exodus 47,*" *New York Herald Tribune,* 19 August 1947; report of Moshe Perlman from Marseilles, 19 August 1947, 07.30: "Everything was ok. The people are good and strong. All took part in the strike. Moshe reported to the agencies: Reuter, A.P., U.P., A.F.P., Daily Herald. NY Herald T correspondent wrote a nice piece. Journalists were forbidden from embarking on the ships. The ships will request UNSC [sic] to visit them." *Mishmar,* 21 August 1947.

145. Operations log as well as an unpublished text by André Blumel on the *Exodus* affair and his role in it, Blumel Archive; Pierro report on the *Exodus,* August 1947, AAP Paris, D14-VII/3.

146. Hanan Reichman, 26 August 1947, CZA S25/2630.

147. The *New York Herald Tribune* wrote of the refugees who "joined the hunger strike against what they consider the apathy of a world which has conveniently forgotten them" (19 August 1947); for comments by Zionist leaders, see Sneh at the convention of the General Zionists in Europe on the *Exodus ma'apilim,* quoted in *Mishmar,* 22 August 1947.

148. Ben-Aharon at a meeting of the Zionist Executive Committee, 26 August 1947, CZA S5/320.

149. Léon Blum, *Le Populaire,* 26 August 1947.

150. Cooper to Foreign Office, no. 830, 21 August 1947, P.R.O. FO371/61823.

151. From the embassy in Paris to the Foreign Office in London, 28 July 1947, P.R.O. FO371/61819.

152. *Reports,* HHA 2751.

153. Kay to Clarke, 10 October 1947, E9869, P.R.O. FO371/61850.

CHAPTER 3

1. Kay to Clarke, 10 October 1947, E9869, P.R.O. FO371/61850.

2. *Reports,* HHA 2751.

3. Hugh Seton-Watson, *The East European Revolution* (New York, 1956), pp. 161–67, 202–11; Robert R. King, *History of the Romanian Communist Party* (Stanford, 1980), pp. 39–58.

4. In the resulting national assembly, 346 out of 382 deputies were communists, 33 were members of the National Peasants Party, and 3 were Liberals.

5. Seton-Watson, *Revolution;* King, *History;* see also Ghita Ionescu, *Communism in Rumania, 1944–1962* (London, 1956), pp. 71–156.

6. Ambassador Harriman, Moscow, to the Secretary of State, Washington, 15 September 1944, Foreign Relations of the United States (FRUS) 1944, vol. 4, pp. 234–35.

7. See, e.g., Bruce R. Kuniholm, *The Origins of the Cold War in the Near East: Great Power Conflict and Diplomacy in Iran, Turkey, and Greece* (New Jersey, 1980), pp. 109–29; Ionescu, *Communism,* pp. 92–93; Winston Churchill, *Triumph and Tragedy,* vol. 6 (London, 1953), pp. 72–81, 226–35.

8. Quoted in Kuniholm, *Origins,* p. 247.

9. Allied Control Commission, FRUS 1944, vol. 4, Document 3443 and FRUS 1945, vol. 5, document 151.

10. Documents 2232, 3422, 3423, FRUS 1944, vol. 4.

11. See Arieh Y. Kochavi, "The British Struggle against Illegal Sailings from the Ports of the Balkan Countries after World War II," in Anita Shapira, ed., *Ha'apalah: A Collection on the History of the Rescue, Bricha, Ha'apalah, and the Survivors* (in Hebrew) (Tel Aviv, 1990), p. 231. Kochavi assumes that the formal Western recognition of the Groza government led the Soviets, who until then had made an effort not to provoke the British and the Americans unnecessarily, to let the *Smirni* sail.

12. The chargé d'affaires in Bucharest to the Foreign Office in London, 13 April 1946, P.R.O. FO371/52515.

13. From Agami [Averbuch] to Artzi, 11, 21, and 26 April 1946 and 5 May 1946, HHA 14/68; *Reports,* HHA 2751.

14. Memo of the High Commissioner, "Russia and Palestine," 20 December 1945, P.R.O. FO181/1019.

15. Cunningham to Colonial Secretary Hall, 30 May 1946, P.R.O. FO181/1019.

16. Holman to Foreign Office, 8 May 1946, P.R.O. FO371/52522.

17. Kendall memorandum, 18 July 1946, P.R.O. FO371/59178.

18. Minutes of meeting number 27 of the Allied Control Committee in Romania, 20 June 1946, P.R.O. WO178/71.

19. Raphael Vago, "The Communization of Jewish Political Life in Romania, 1944–1949," *Slavic and Soviet Series* 1 (1977): 50–51.

20. Report on the status of Romanian Jewry, 20 July 1945, Yad Vashem Archive (YVA), P-6/29.

21. Letter of a member of Ha'Ihud, from Bucharest to Palestine, HHA 14/151.

22. Letter from Zissu to Richard Lichtheim, Geneva, 15 August 1944, CZA L22/88.

23. *Scanteia* (Communist Party newspaper), 18 December 1944, quoted in Vago, "Communization."

24. From Agami to Venya, Bucharest, 26 March 1945, HHA 14/397, 14/61a.

25. See Vago, "Communization," pp. 38, 54.

26. Ibid., pp. 53–54; Raphael Vago, "The Jews under the Communist Regime in Romania" (in Hebrew), in Benyamin Pinkus, ed., *East European Jewry between Holocaust and Rebirth 1944–1948*, (Sde Boker, 1987), p. 137.

27. Report on the status of Romanian Jewry, YVA, P-6/29, pp. 174–75.

28. Report of the British delegation in Romania on the status of the Jews, 5 November 1945, P.R.O. FO770/85.

29. Kendall memorandum, 18 July 1946, R11692, P.R.O. FO371/59178.

30. Kendall report on the status of the Jews, 3 November 1947, P.R.O. FO371/61831; Evelyn Shakborough to the Prime Minister's office, 19 June 1952, P.R.O. FO371/100776.

31. On the departure of the agents from Istanbul to Sofia and Bucharest, 13 September 1944, HHA 14/62; Pomerantz letters in CZA S25/3879.

32. From Averbuch to Ehud [Avriel], Bucharest, 5 November 1944, HHA 14/61a, 14/397.

33. Dalia Ofer, *Road in the Sea* (in Hebrew) (Tel Aviv, 1990), pp. 342–85.

34. From Averbuch to Ehud and Hannah, 5 November 1944, HHA 14/61a, 14/397.

35. From Averbuch to Ehud, Bucharest, 23 October 1944, HHA 14/61a.

36. Ibid.

37. From Agami to Ehud and Hannah, 5 November 1944, HHA 14/397, 14/61a; from Agami to Ehud, Bucharest, 23 October 1944, HHA 14/397, 14/61a.

38. 23 October 1944, 5 November 1944, HHA 14/61a, 14/397.

39. From Agami to Artzi, 25 November 1944, HHA 14/63b.

40 Meir, Istanbul, to Artzi, 5 November 1944, HHA 14/62.

41. Ehud to Ben-Gurion, 27 January 1945, HHA 14/63b.

42. To Venya, Sofia, from Agami, Bucharest, 11 March 1945, HHA 14/63a; to Moshe [Agami], Dov [Berger-Harari], David [Zimend] from Venya, Sofia, 18 March 1945, HHA 14/61a.

43. Report on immigration from Romania to the end of 1944, no. 271, HHA 14/67a.

44. Ibid.; Bauer, *Flight and Rescue,* pp. 15–17.

45. *Reports,* HHA 2751; from Meir to Artzi, 19 May 1944, HHA 14/60, 14/397; from Meir to comrades, 27 May 1944, HHA 14/62, 14/397.

46. Accounting of "cavaliers" (Swiss francs) to 1 August 1944, Istanbul, HHA 14/62a.

47. Cable (English) no. 6, from Istanbul to Palestine, received 17 September 1944, HHA 14/62a.

48. To Meir from Agami, Bucharest, 27 February 1945, HHA 14/61a/63a/397.

49. Bauer, *Flight and Rescue,* p. 32; see also Chapter 1.

50. Agami to Meir, 4 March 1945 (received in Istanbul on 8 June 1945), HHA 14/61a, 14/397.

51. Ibid.

52. To Venya, Sofia, from Tzvi, Moshe Pat, Ben Asaf, Peretz, Sofie, Budapest, 1 March 1945 (received in Istanbul on 8 June 1945), HHA 14/63a.

53. To Moshe [Averbuch], Dov [Berger-Harari], David [Zimend] from Venya, Sofia, 18 March 1945, HHA 14/397.

54. To Agami from Meir, Istanbul, 23 March 1945, HHA 14/61a, 14/63a, 14/397.

55. To Venya from Agami, Bucharest, 13 April 1945, HHA 14/61a, 14/63a, 14/397; see also from Agami to Meir, 9 April 1945, HHA 14/61a, 14/63, 14/397.

56. To Meir from Agami, Bucharest, 30 May 1945, HHA 14/61a, 14/397.

57. From Meir to Artzi, Istanbul, 27 May 1945, HHA 14/63a; from Meir to Artzi, Istanbul, 2 June 1945, HHA 14/63a.

58. Foreign Office memorandum to the Cabinet, 11 June 1945, P.R.O. FO371/45377; Le Rougtel to Bevin, 2 August 1945, P.R.O. FO371/51121.

59. To Meir from Agami, Bucharest, 24 June 1945, HHA 14/61a.

60. To Artzi from Agami, Bucharest, 1 August 1945, HHA 14/61a, 14/64, 14/397.

61. To Meir from Agami, 19 July 1945, HHA 14/61a, 14/397.

62. To comrades from Itaï [Avriel], Prague, 11 January 1946, HHA 14/65.

63. Ehud Avriel, *Open the Gates* (in Hebrew) (Tel Aviv, 1976), pp. 189–90.

64. *Reports,* HHA 2751.

65. To Meir from A. Bucharest, 14 October 1945, HHA 14/64, 14/397.

66. See Arieh L. Kochavi, *Displaced Persons and International Politics* (in Hebrew) (Tel Aviv, 1992), pp. 115–22.

67. To Meir from A [Agami], Bucharest, HHA 14/64, 14/397. On 19 October Agami reported on the intention to transfer the ships to Yugoslavia or Italy if the sailing from Romania were not possible. Artzi from Agami, Bucharest, 19 October 1945, HHA 14/61a, 14/64, 14/397; also from Itaï [Avriel] to comrades, Prague, 11 November 1946, HHA 14/65.

68. From Artzi to Eliahu, 20 November 1945, HHA 14/64.

69. To Agami from Eliahu, 18 November 1945, HHA 14/61a.

70. To Artzi from Rudolph-Morris [Romania], Bucharest, 3 December 1945, HHA 14/397.

71. This is the claim of the author of the relevant chapter in Yehuda Slutzki, ed., *The History of the Haganah* (in Hebrew) (Tel Aviv, 1973).

72. To Agami from Hofshi [David Nameri], 28 January 1946, HHA 14/397.

73. To Artzi from Agami, 5 February 1946, HHA 14/61a, 14/65, 14/397.

74. From Agami to Artzi, 9 April 1946, HHA 14/253; Musia-Daniel report on the *Max Nordau* [the *Smirni*], 23 May 1946, HHA 14/253.

75. Foreign Office to Bucharest, 5 April 1946, P.R.O. ADM 116/5561.

76. To Agami from Artzi (via Alon), 13 April 1946, 19.00, HHA 14/253.

77. To Artzi from Agami, Bucharest, 21 April 1946, HHA 14/253.

78. On the occurrences on the eve of the sailing, see Musia-Daniel report, 23 May 1946, HHA 14/253; from Rimon to Zvi Yehieli, 24 May 1946, HHA 14/397. On Joseph Schreier, see Vago, "Jews," p. 137.

79. To comrades from Artzi, 16 May 1946, HHA 14/65; Musia-Daniel report, 23 May 1946, HHA 14/253.

80. To comrades from Artzi, 16 May 1946, HHA 14/65. "Heart is full and almost no regrets on their being caught," said the cable to Romania from Mossad headqaurters in Palestine.

81. Holman to Foreign Office, no. 576, 4 May 1946, ADM 116/5561; Holman to Foreign Office, 11 June 1946, 12 June 1946, ADM 116/5561. All in P.R.O.

82. From the High Commissioner to the Colonial Secretary, 20 May 1946, P.R.O. FO371/52525.

83. Holman to Foreign Office, 26 July 1946, P.R.O. FO371/52544.

84. Billy to Rohl, 29 July 1946, P.R.O. FO371/52548.

85. Peterson to Dekanozov, 31 July 1946, P.R.O. FO371/52549.

86. Kendall report, Holman to Bevin, 11 November 1946, P.R.O. FO371/52629.

87. Holman to Foreign Office, 8 August 1946, P.R.O. FO371/52627.

88. Acting director of the second European department to the First Secretary in the British embassy, 25 October 1946, P.R.O. FO371/52632.

89. To Artzi from Agami, Bucharest, 10 October 1946, HHA 14/61a, 14/65, 14/397.

90. Haganah ship file, HHA 14/210; to Neter, Artzi from Agami, 20 July 1946; to Nur, Neter, Nesin from Artzi, 21 July 1946, 11.40; to Neter, Artzi from Agami, 21 July 1946, 23.00, HHA 14/101; from Yoram [Yugoslavia] to Artzi, 22 July 1946, HHA 14/75; to friends from Rico, 26 July 1946, HHA 14/73; Foreign Office to Athens, 21 December 1946, P.R.O. CO537/2391.

91. Charles Peake, British ambassador to Yugoslavia, to Foreign Office, 16 November 1946, E11377, P.R.O. FO371/52571.

92. First secretary in the British embassy, Clutton, to Foreign Office, no. 1178, 10 August 1946, E7926, P.R.O. FO371/52528.

93. 31 October 1946, P.R.O. FO371/52636.

94. Clutton to Tito, 31 December 1946, P.R.O. FO371/61838; Clutton to Foreign Office, 4 January 1947, P.R.O. CO537/2391.

95. Micha [Efraim Shilo-Schultz] report of 9 January 1947, OL; to Artzi from Felix, 17 January 1947, HHA 14/104; meeting of Bricha operatives, 12 December 1946, Basel, HHA, Bricha files III (copy in Polonsky Archive in Paris); Avriel to Mapai Central Committee, 24 June 1947, LPA 23/47.

96. King, *History*, pp. 41–42, 43, 44.

97. See note 86.

98. Yosef Klarman, "The Truth about the Organization of the Mass Immigration from Romania—The Two Pans" (in Hebrew), *Ha'Uma* 57, no. 2 (May 1979): 236–41; see also note 86.

99. Ibid.

100. Mereminsky report, 1 January 1947, HHA 14/104.

101. From Michael [the Mossad's secretary], Ofri [Czechoslovakia], 1 February 1947, OL.

102. To Neter from Max, no. 2, 2 February 1947, HHA 14/702b.

103. For example, from Rimon [Makaresku] to Neter [France], Bucharest, 10 April 1947, HHA 14/528.

104. From Rimon to Artzi, Bucharest, 5 May 1947, HHA 14/70, 14/528.

105. UNSCOP report, vol. II, appendix 18, 20 August 1947, Creech-Jones documents, (quoted in Kochavi, "British Struggle," p. 164); Mack to Foreign Office, 8 August 1947, P.R.O. FO371/66668; memorandum on meeting of the Allied Control Commission in Austria on 17 November 1947, 3 December 1947, appendix C, P.R.O. FO371/61831.

106. From Neter to all stations, Paris 23 June 1947, HHA 14/89.

107. Rico, Agami, to Paris, 25 February 1947, OL.

108. Rico, Agami, to Paris, 27 February 1947, OL.

109. Danny [Ze'ev Schind] to Paris, 24 March 1947, 14.00, OL.

110. Danny to Paris, 2 April 1947, 13.00, OL; to Neter from Danny, 15 April 1947, HHA, Tel Hashomer, Kargal files 27.

111. Danny to Paris, 5 May 1947, 12 May 1947, 15 May 1947, 19 May 1947; Danny and Pino [Ginsburg] to Paris, 23 May 1947, OL; Ze'ev Schind report, *Pan* files, HHA 14/275, 14/277.

112. Peake to Foreign Office, 21 March 1947, P.R.O. FO371/61839.

113. Foreign Office to Bucharest and Sofia, 18 August 1947, P.R.O. FO371/61847.

114. Brigadier Greer to Susaikov, 25 August 1947, P.R.O. FO371/61848; chargé d'affaires in Moscow to Foreign Office, 26 August 1947, 27 August 1947, P.R.O. FO371/61824.

115. Rico [Agami] to Paris, 19 August 1947, 10.00, OL.

116. Agami to Paris, 23 August 1947, 09.30, OL.

117. Dan (Trachtenberg)—Micha [Efraim Shilo] from Baruch [Bulgaria] to Paris, 29 August 1947, 17.30, OL; Ben-Yehuda [Meirov] from Berg [Switzerland] to Paris, 26 August 1947, 08.00, OL.

118. Micha (Baruch) [Efraim Shilo from Bulgaria] to Paris, 2 September 1947, 16.00, OL; Agami to Paris, 3 September 1947, 09.30, OL.

119. British Chargé d'Affaires in Bulgaria Strandale-Bennet to Foreign Office, 2 September 1947, 24 September 1947, P.R.O. FO371/61848 and FO371/61828, respectively.

120. See first item in note 117.

121. *Ge'ula* file, HHA 14/197, (northern) *Medinat Ha'Yehudim* file, HHA 14/248; *Reports,* HHA 2751.

122. To Arnon from Or [Meirov], Italy, 30 September 1947, HHA 14/538.

123. Weekly intelligence summary of the Sixth Airborne Division, 11 October 1947, P.R.O. WO275/60.

124. Mossad OL, 30 August 1947 and afterward.

125. From Agami to Arnon, 21 November 1947, HHA 14/275, 14/277.

126. Preliminary report on the debarking of the immigrants from the *Pan York* and the *Pan Crescent* written by Captain Linkletter, 8 January 1948, top secret. Translation may be found in HHA 14/544; the last remark is related to the British claim that the Soviets intended to inundate the Middle East with communist agents through Jewish immigration. See Ambassador Inverchapel to Marshall, 18 October 1947, P.R.O. FO115/4334; Inverchapel to Foreign Office, 1 November 1947, P.R.O. FO371/61851.

127. S. [Shaul] from Yissar [Paris] to stations, 3 November 1947, HHA 14/540.

128. See Kochavi, "British Struggle," pp. 109–12, 167–70.

129. Ambassador Inverchapel to Marshall, 18 October 1947, P.R.O. FO115/4334; Ambassador Inverchapel to Foreign Office, 1 November 1947, P.R.O. FO371/61851.

130. Marshall to Bevin, FRUS, vol. 5, pp. 1247–48.

131. Ibid.

132. Marshall to Inverchapel, 10 November 1947, P.R.O. FO115/4334.

133. Ben-Gurion to Shertok, 1 December 1947, CZA S44/647.

134. To Ben-Yehuda [Meirov] from Ovadiah [Sneh], Tel Aviv, 1 December 1947, HHA 14/71.

135. To Or from Arnon, Berg [Ginsburg], Tel Aviv 1 December 1947; to Or from Arnon, Berg, 1 December 1947, HHA 14/71.

136. To Agami from Or, Paris, 4 December 1947, HHA 14/71.

137. To "Mossad" from Romania, 4 December 1947, urgent-secret, HHA 14/71.

138. This is the explicit claim of Ze'ev Venya Hadari and Ze'ev Tzahor in their book *Ships or a State* (in Hebrew) (Tel Aviv, no date).

139. On 22 and 23 December 1947 ships with no passengers sailed from Constanta, and simultaneously more than twelve thousand Jews were sent in eight trains from Romania to the port of Burgas, from which they sailed on 27 December. According to an agreement between the British, the Jewish Agency, and the Mossad, the ships sailed straight to Cyprus.

140. From Shaul Meirov, Paris, to Moshe Shertok in Washington, 4 December 1947, quoted in Slutzki, ed., *History of the Haganah*, vol. C-2, pp. 1184–85.

CHAPTER 4

1. See Léon Blum, *Souvenirs sur l'affaire* (Paris, 1935). I owe the reference to Blum and the insight it provides to Adi Ofir, "The Dreyfus Affair and other Political Schools," lecture at the conference on the 100-year anniversary of the Dreyfus affair, Tel Aviv University, March 1994.

2. Arazi testimony, 18 August 1949, 4 September 1949, HHA, division 106, various files.

3. Compare Ben-Gurion's statement during his visit to Bulgaria before the end of the war, that the only redemption for what remained of the Jewish Diaspora

was in Eretz-Israel, and otherwise its fate would be devastation. See Chapter 7, "The Bearers and the Burdens," which is devoted to Ben-Gurion's positions.

4. Arazi testimony, HHA, Y.A. files, 37/2090.

5. Alon to Artzi, 13 April 1946, HHA 14/86.

6. *Ha'aretz,* 7 May 1946.

7. Susan Sontag, *On Photography* (New York, 1978), p. 19.

8. Ibid., p. 17.

9. The *Briah* report by Zidkihau, 3 July 1946, HHA 14/101; I. F. Stone, *Underground to Palestine* (New York, 1946).

10. To Neter, Artzi, from Alon, 23 August 1946, HHA 14/186; Claire Naikind, *Davar,* 21 October 1946.

11. Perlman published his articles in the British press, especially in the weekly magazine *Illustrated London News* (his piece on the sailing of the *Theodor Herzl* appeared on 25 May 1947); see also P.R.O. FO371/61808.

12. For his series "Terre promise, terre interdite" ("Promised Land, Forbidden Land"), on the journeys of Jewish refugees to Palestine, he received in June 1947 the prize for the best reportage in the French press.

13. François-Jean Armorin, *Des juifs quittent l'Europe* (Paris, 1990), pp. 20–23.

14. Ibid., pp. 27–28, 41.

15. Ibid, p. 117.

16. Ibid., pp. 130–31.

17. As early as the end of 1938 Ben-Gurion formulated the major points of the concept of "militant Zionism," in which demonstrations of clandestine immigration for publicity purposes held a central place. This concept was fully realized after the war.

18. Bracha Habas, recorder and ed., *The Ship That Won: The Chronicle of the Exodus 1947* (in Hebrew) (Tel Aviv, 1949), p. 48.

19. See, e.g., David Horowitz, *A State in the Making* (New York, 1953), chapter on the committee and the *Exodus;* George Garcia Granados, *So the State of Israel Was Born* (in Hebrew) (Jerusalem, 1950), p. 175.

20. 22 July 1947, 19.15 and 21.00, OL.

21. *Le Monde,* 23 July 1947.

22. 1 August 1947, OL.

23. From Rudi to Paris, 30 July 1947, 12.00, OL.

24. *Rouge Midi,* 31 July 1947.

25. *Combat,* 30 July 1947.

26. From Rudi to Paris, 29 July 1947, 18.25, OL.

27. Berl L. [Loker, London] to Paris, 18 August 1947, OL.

28. The *New York Herald Tribune* published an article about the despair of the *Exodus* passengers because of the world's apathy. See Chapter 2.

29. Rudi to Paris, 17 August 1947, 07.45, OL; 18 August 1947, 15.00, 18.30, OL; 19 August 1947, 07.30, OL; *Runnymede Park* log, 20 August 1947.

30. Nicholas Bethel, *Palestine Triangle* (London, 1979), p. 343.

31. Hugh Dalton, *High Tide and After* (London, 1962), pp. 189–90.

32. Quoted in Aviva Halamish, *Exodus: The True Story* (in Hebrew) (Tel Aviv, 1990), pp. 195–99. On the explosion, see the final chapter of the present book, "The Bearers and the Burdens."

33. Halamish, *Exodus*, pp. 199–202.

34. *Ha'aretz*, 19 September 1947; see also Halamish, *Exodus*, p. 200.

35. Quoted in Halamish, *Exodus*, p. 201.

36. From Agami, Bucharest, to Meir, Istanbul, 27 February 1945, HHA 14/61a, 14/63a, 14/397.

37. To Arnon from Or [Meirov], Italy, 30 September 1947, HHA 14/538.

38. *Davar*, 12 February 1947.

39. Arazi testimony, Arazi files, HHA 37/2090.

40. Armorin, *Des juifs*, p. 23.

41. *The Ship of Rebellion* (pamphlet, in Hebrew) (Tel Aviv, 1947), p. 24; *Chaim Arlosorov* report, submitted by Miri, HHA 14/226; *Chaim Arlosorov* log, *Ma'arachot* 44, November 1947.

42. To Catriel [the *Catriel Yaffe*] from Artzi, 7 August 1946, HHA 14/239; to Henrietta [the *Henrietta Szold*] from Artzi, 8 August 1946, HHA 14/217.

43. From Hofshi to Artzi, 12 August 1946, HHA 14/231; to Neter by Azariahu, 17 August 1946, HHA 14/412.

44. Yigal Elam, *The Followers of Orders* (in Hebrew) (Jerusalem, 1990), chapter on the *Patria* affair.

45. To Artzi from Alon, 30 August 1946, HHA 14/186.

46. To Artzi and Neter, from Alon, 30 August 1946, HHA 14/186.

47. To Artzi from AH [*Arba Heruyot*], 1 September 1946; to AH from Artzi, same day, HHA, 14/186; *Arba Heruyot* report, Akiva, 16 September 1946, HHA 14/186; testimony of Fabi Gever, HHA 4141; *Davar*, 21 October 1946.

48. Report of *Szold* team printed on 20 August 1946, HHA 14/217, and see entire *Henrietta Szold* file, HHA 14/217.

49. *Bracha Fuld* file, HHA 14/191; also *Bracha Fuld* report, 27 November 1946, HHA 14/88.

50. To Neter from Artzi, 1 September 1946, HHA 14/102.

51. Report on the *Palmach* from Amos, 12 November 1946, HHA 14/274; see also Chapter 7 of this book.

52. Ehud Avriel, *Open the Gates* (in Hebrew) (Tel Aviv, 1976), p. 239; see also Yehudah Braginsky, *A Nation Rowing to the Shore* (in Hebrew) (Tel Aviv, 1965), pp. 344–45.

53. From *Latrun* to Artzi, 31 November 1946, ship log, HHA 14/243; to *Latrun*, 31 November 1946, ship log, HHA 14/243; Uri Goren testimony, HHA/4659; reports of the British capture of the ship, P.R.O. files ADM 20595/20621.

54. Yossi Hamburger report on the *Knesset Yisrael*, November 1946, HHA 14/99, 14/629.

55. Giora Yoseftal on the *Knesset Yisrael* passengers at the Va'ad Le'umi Executive, 23 December 1946, CZA J1/6945.

56. To Hannah [*Knesset Yisrael*] from Artzi, 18 November 1946, HHA 14/237.

57. Hamburger report, op. cit.

58. To Artzi, Haganah headquarters and Palmach headquarters from Hannah [the *Knesset Yisrael*], 22 November 1946, HHA 14/237.

59. To Hannah from Artzi, 25 November 1946, HHA 14/237.

60. Hamburger report, op. cit.; report on capture of the ship, 2 December 1946, P.R.O. ADM 20589.

61. Nathan Alterman, *The Seventh Column*, vol. 1 (in Hebrew) (Tel Aviv, 1975), p. 104 (from *Davar*, 13 December 1946).

62. Nathan Alterman, "The People and Its Delegate," *The Seventh Column*, p. 87 (from *Davar* 5 September 1947).

63. Hamburger report, op. cit.

64. Armorin, *Des juifs*, p. 129.

65. From the British report on the capture of the *Guardian* [*Theodor Herzl*], 15 April 1947, P.R.O. WO 275/87.

66. Bar-Rav-Hai at the Va'ad Le'umi Executive, 21 April 1947, CZA, J1/6945.

67. Nahum Bogner, *The Ships of Rebellion: Ha'apala 1945–1948* (in Hebrew) (Tel Aviv, 1993), p. 180.

68. Ben-Gurion at the Histadrut Executive Committee, 6 August 1947, and at the Mapai Council, 8 August 1947, Labor Archive (LA) and LPA, respectively.

69. To Zehava [Golda Meyerson], 15 April 1947, HHA 14/296.

70. See, for example, Ben-Gurion to Abba Hillel Silver, 1 October 1946, BGA. See also Chapter 7 of this book.

71. *Davar*, 12 February 1947.

72. Hamburger report on the *Knesset Yisrael*, op. cit.; Alterman, "The People and Its Delegate," "Division of Roles," "Bracha Fuld," *The Seventh Column*, pp. 105–6, 85–87, 102–4, respectively; Haim Ben-Asher, "After Rafiah" (in Hebrew), *Mibefnim* 12 (1946).

73. Letter from a Palmach young man in jail to his comrades, 25 October 1946, HHA, Galili files, no. 5; Johnny, "Letter from the Jailer," *Alon Ha'Palmach*, no. 48, December 1946. There is a certain difference between the two versions, the one in the archive and the one in *Alon Ha'Palmach*. The version presented here is a merging of the two.

74. Robert Weltch, *Ha'aretz*, 11 September 1947.

75. *Ha'aretz*, 26 May 1947.

76. To Yissar and Leonard from Arnon, report on the *Mordei Ha'Getaot*, 29 May 1947, HHA 14/252; report on the *Ha'Tikvah*, 20 May 1947, HHA 14/189; to all our emissaries from Yiftah [Yigal Alon], 21 June 1947, cited in *The Palmach Book*, vol. 1 (Tel Aviv, 1956), p. 840.

77. *Mordei Ha'Getaot* report, HHA 14/252; David Sha'ari, *The Deportation to Cyprus, 1946–1948* (in Hebrew) (Jerusalem, 1981), pp. 85, 115–16.

78. Ship report, HHA 14/233; Sha'ari, *Deportation*, p. 85.

79. See interview with Shaul Biber, Ha'apala Project, Information Center, general testimonies/135 (interviewer: Bracha Eshel).

80. Log of the *She'ar Yishuv*, 22–23 April 1947, HHA 14/292.

81. Ibid.

82. To Ben-Gurion from Artzi, 24 May 1946, HHA 14/101; Ben-Gurion, *War Diary, 1948–1949*, 17 December 1947, vol. 1 (in Hebrew) (Tel Aviv, 1982), p. 51.

83. Braginsky, *A Nation*, pp. 344–45; Biber interview, op. cit.

84. Yigal Allon, *The Battles of Palmach* (in Hebrew) (Tel Aviv, 1965), p. 156; Braginsky, *A Nation*, pp. 344–45.

85. From Yiftah to all our emissaries [Palmach emissaries], 21 June 1947, p. 839 (see note 76).

86. *Alon Ha'Palmach*, no. 49, January 1947.

87. *The Palmach Book,* vol. 1, p. 839; see also Braginsky, *A Nation,* pp. 344–45.

88. See note 77.

89. From Yiftah to the members of the division in Sidney (Marseilles), 27 May 1947, KMA, 1/6/15.

90. *The Palmach Book,* vol. 1, p. 839.

91. Ibid., pp. 839–41.

92. Ibid., pp. 839–40.

93. An official report from 23 July 1947—that is, after the *Exodus* battle near the Palestinian shore—speaks of twelve dead. HHA 14/533; HHA III, pt. 2, 1135–79; ship files, HHA.

94. *Reports,* HHA 2751; see also the discussion of the names given to Mossad ships in Halamish, op. cit., p. 69.

95. *The Palmach Book,* vol. 1, p. 562.

96. Slutzki, ed., *History of the Haganah,* C-2, p. 1143.

CHAPTER 5

1. "The illegal immigration embodied the deepest rebellion against our dependence on a foreign ruler, a direct and undeterred provocation against its laws, and the ultimate proof that Jews indeed decided once and for all to take their fate in their hands," wrote the head of the Mossad. See Shaul Meirov, "Introduction," in Bracha Habas, *The Ship That Won: The History of Exodus 1947* (in Hebrew) (Tel Aviv, 1949).

2. Tabenking attacked the tendencies of "passivity," "restraint," and "cooperation" within the central leadership. See Ha'Kibbutz Ha'Meuhad Archives (KMA), Book of the 11th Council, pp. 137–38.

3. See Baruch Kanari, *To Carry Their People: The Achievement, Mission, and Self-Image of Ha'Kibbutz Ha'Meuhad* (in Hebrew) (Tel Aviv, 1989), pp. 92–94.

4. On the distress of HeHalutz at the restrictive immigration quotas, see Report of the Zionist Organization Executive and the Jewish Agency to the Twentieth Zionist Congress, p. 267; and the Twenty-first Zionist Congress, pp. 235–39, quoted in Levi Sarid, *HeHalutz in Poland 1917–1939* (in Hebrew), (Tel Aviv, 1979), pp. 351, 553ff; Huma Hayut, "In Days of Depression," in M. Basok, ed. and comp., *The Young HeHalutz* (in Hebrew) (Ein Harod, 1944), pp. 301–4.

5. For example, see Gerscht to Zvi Rosenstein (head of the Immigration Department of the Histadrut), Labor Party Archive (LPA), copy in KMA, Emissary Letters, container D, file 14; discussions in the meeting of *hakvutza,* a group of emissaries from Palestine in Poland, 15 September 1936, KMA, meeting minutes; Yehuda Braginsky, *A Nation Rowing to Shore* (in Hebrew) (Tel Aviv, 1965), pp. 50, 51, 59; Ze'ev Schind, "Labor Pains of the Beginning," in M. Basok, ed., *The Book of the Ma'apilim* (in Hebrew) (Tel Aviv, 1947), p. 35.

6. Sixty-two thousand immigrants arrived in 1935, compared with only 10,500 in 1937. See also Shabtai Teveth, *Ben Gurion and the Palestinian Arabs* (in Hebrew) (Tel Aviv, 1985), p. 306.

7. Uri Ben Eliezer, *Through the Rifle's Sight: The Creation of Israeli Militarism* (in Hebrew) (Tel Aviv, 1995), pp. 37–46.

8. Tabenkin in the Kibbutz seminar in Ein Harod, 28 August 1937, KMA, Department 25a, series d, container 2, files 1–4.

9. Braginsky was one of the founders of HeHalutz and belonged to Tabenkin's inner circle. The Kibbutz secretariat decided to send Braginsky to Poland to check "whatever needs checking" (KMA, book 17, file 2), but he actually went only after the Kibbutz defeat at the Zionist congress. See also Matityahu Mintz, *Those Who Promise and Those Who Accomplish* (in Hebrew) (Tel Aviv, 1983), pp. 53, 86, 118–19, 181ff; Kanari, *To Carry Their People*, p. 94.

10. On the struggle of the Kibbutz for political power in the Yishuv, see Henri Nir, *Kibbutz and Society 1923–1933* (in Hebrew) (Tel Aviv, 1983), pp. 285–95; Aharon Keidar, "The Political and Ideological Development of Ha'Kibbutz Ha'Meuhad 1933–1942" (in Hebrew), (Ph.D. diss., Hebrew University of Jerusalem, 1984), pp. 162–70; Kanari, *To Carry Their People*, pp. 75–82, 125–43ff.

11. Literature on the relationship between ideology and political practice is extensive. Scholars today agree that ideology serves to instill mechanisms of domination and to conceal power relationships and power struggles in society. See, for example, J. B. Thompson, *Studies in Theories of Ideology* (Cambridge, England, 1984), especially chapters 2 and 5. For a critical study of ideological-idealistic rhetoric used as a cover for power-driven motivations in political struggles, see Yonatahn Shapira, *The Historical Ahdut Ha'Avoda: The Power of a Political Organization* (in Hebrew) (Tel Aviv, 1975).

12. See Tabenkin Notebooks, no. 51, 9 February 1938; no. 52, 24 and 25 July and 21 and 25 August 1938, KMA. Not all the notebooks are open to researchers.

13. On the sailings in 1938, see e.g., Arye L. Avneri, *From Velos to Taurus: One Decade of Clandestine Immigration* (in Hebrew) (Tel Aviv, 1985), pp. 36–60.

14. Ibid.

15. The revisionists' contribution to the clandestine immigration effort is often cited by those from the Kibbutz and the Labor movement as an important catalyst of their activity. From Bendori to Braginsky, 8 December 1938, KMA, Department 2, container 4, file 17. See also Idith Zertal, "Between Ethics and Politics," in Anita Shapira, ed., *Ha'apala* (in Hebrew) (Tel Aviv, 1990), pp. 89, 368.

16. Meir Avizohar, *Militant Zionism* (in Hebrew) (Sde Boker, 1985), p. 86.

17. Ben-Gurion's direct reaction to the Nazi pogrom is unknown, since in the ten critical days between 10 and 21 November 1938 he did not write a word in his diary. On 21 November he wrote, "Publication of Woodhead report; the pogrom in Germany (11.10); Zionist Executive inauguration (11.11)." See also Shabtai Teveth, *The Burning Ground* (in Hebrew) (Tel Aviv, 1987), p. 257.

18. "A great and courageous act [is to be undertaken]. . . . The immigration revolt, waging war against Britain, not with guns and bombs, not in terror and Arabs killing, but in organizing a mass immigration into the country, in moving thousands of refugees despite the government's restrictions . . . something that will connect again the refugees question to Palestine." Ben-Gurion, *Diary,*

10 December 1938, Ben-Gurion Archives (BGA); Ben-Gurion in the Jewish Agency Executive, 11 December 1938, CZA, Minutes of the Jewish Agency Executive.

19. Minutes of these three meetings are in CZA S25/99/7; BGA.

20. Ibid.

21. Ben-Gurion in Mapai Central Committee, 28 May 1939, LPA 23/39.

22. Ben-Gurion, *Diary*, 1 May 1939 and 3 May 1939.

23. Ben-Gurion in Mapai Central Committee, 15 December 1938, LPA 23/38; Ben-Gurion at the first meeting of "Clarification of the Situation," 16 April 1939, CZA S25/99/7.

24. See History of Haganah Archives (HHA), Headquarters Files, Supreme Command.

25. Both Berl Katzenelson and Ben-Gurion in their public speeches and committee statements put their weight behind the idea of a large, organized clandestine immigration, allocating 100,000 Palestine pounds for this work. See Yitzhak Avneri, "The Immigration Revolt" (in Hebrew), *Cathedra*, no. 44, June 1987, pp. 153–57; Avneri, *From Velos to Taurus*, pp. 145–51; Habas, *The Ship That Won*, pp. 224–37.

26. Shmaryah Zameret, *Diary* (in Hebrew), 26 August 1939, Beit HaShita.

27. Ibid., 5 and 9 September 1939.

28. Katzenelson in the Histadrut Executive Secretariat, 29 November 1939, Labor Archive (LA); Katzenelson diary, 29 November 1939, LPA.

29. Interview with Pino Ginsburg; see also Ruth Zariz, "The Rescue of German Jewry by Immigration 1938–1945" (in Hebrew) (Ph.D. diss., Hebrew University of Jerusalem, 1986), pp. 256–57; Dalia Ofer, *A Road in the Sea: Aliya Bet During the Holocaust* (in Hebrew) (Tel Aviv, 1990), pp. 164–67ff, 184.

30. On the *Hilda*, see letters from Moshe (Averbuch) to Eliahu (Golomb), December 1939 to January 1940, HHA, Shamir Files, 14/4195 1. On the *Darian*, see Ofer, *A Road in the Sea*, pp. 77–113.

31. Ben-Gurion in the Jewish Agency Executive, 14 April 1940, Minutes, Jewish Agency Executive, CZA.

32. Moshe Sharett, *Political Diary D* (in Hebrew) (Tel Aviv, 1974,) p. 487. "I did not agree with this attitude," Shertok wrote in his diary. "I do not accept this contradiction between our political future and the bringing of thousands of Jews, which means their rescue."

33. From Moshe (Averbuch) to Eliahu (Golomb), 14 December 1939, HHA, Shamir Files 14/4195 1.

34. See Ruth Klieger Report, HHA 14/60; Kleiger in the Histadrut Executive Secretariat, 17 August 1943, LA; see also *B.Y. Diary* [Ben-Yehuda, Meirov], HHA 14/718.

35. Mossad diaries, 1943–44, HHA 14/489–490; Zameret, *Diary*, 20 September 1941.

36. Zerubavel Gilad, ed., *The Palmach Book, A* (in Hebrew) (Tel Aviv, 1955), pp. 399–404.

37. Eliahu Golomb, 16 March 1942, HHA, Golomb Archive, file 34.

38. Ben-Gurion, Meetings, 5 October 1942, BGA.

39. Ben-Gurion in Mapai Central Committee, 7 December 1938, LPA and BGA.

40. Meeting of "faction B" activists, 7 November 1942, KMA, Department 13, container 1, file 4.

41. Yael Yishai, *Factionalism in the Labor Movement* (in Hebrew) (Tel Aviv, 1978), pp. 122–23.

42. Ha'Kibbutz Secretariat, 4 and 5 April 1943, and Active Secretariat, 19 September 1943, Secretariat Minutes, KMA.

43. To Ben-Yehuda [Meirov] from Uri [Zameret], 26 January 1945, HHA 14/671.

44. On Meirov's meetings with new recruits, see *B.Y. Diary*, October, November, December 1944, HHA 14/490 and 14/491; see also Mossad's File of Emissaries from late 1944, early 1945, HHA 14/176 (also 14/176A and 14/176B).

45. Yonatan Shapira, *An Elite without Heirs* (in Hebrew) (Tel Aviv, 1985), especially pp. 54–65; Dan Horowitz and Moshe Lissak, *From Yishuv to State: The Jews of Palestine During the Mandate Period as a Political Community* (in Hebrew) (Tel Aviv, 1985), p. 152.

46. In response, Sereni said that she would "think about it and give her answer." *B.Y. Diary*, 15 October 1944, HHA 14/490.

47. Enzo Sereni's letter to the Mossad was written on 21 April, 1944 and is located along with other communications with him in HHA 14/488; also quoted in Ruth Bondi, *The Emissary* (in Hebrew) (Tel Aviv, 1974), pp. 391, 397–98.

48. To Hanum [Ruth Klieger] and Kassuta [Shaltiel] from Artzi, 25 May 1945, HHA 14/176; Mossad's file of operatives, 1944–45, 14/176.

49. To Meir [Kushta Istanbul] from Artzi, 14 February 1945, HHA 14/63b.

50. To Avi-Amos [Ben-Gurion] and Danny [Schind] from Ben-Yehuda [Meirov], 31 July 1945, HHA 14/81b.

51. To Alon from Artzi, 8 September 1945, and 14 September 1945, HHA 14/174.

52. Artzi Report, 19 September 1945, HHA 14/176b.

53. List of Mossad envoys in Europe, 2 October 1945, HHA 14/74, 14/489a. For some reason, this list did not include key people such as Yehuda Arazi, Ada Sereni, and Ruth Klieger.

54. On 12 April 1946, Meirov flew to Egypt on his way to France to coordinate the Mossad activity there. The communications station in France also began to operate at this time. To Kassuta from Artzi, April 11 and 12, 1946, HHA 14/100.

55. List of Kotzer [code name for Palmach] envoys in Italy, 11 December 1947, HHA 14/544.

56. "The clandestine immigration and its auxiliary operations were considered in the division [Palmach] to be of first order importance," wrote Yigal Allon. See *The Palmach Book*, vol. 1, p. 543.

57. From Yiftach [Allon] to Palmach members on a Haganah mission, 12 December 1947. Ibid, pp. 838–41.

58. Ibid, p. 20.

59. *Palmach Newsletter*, no. 40 (March 1946).

60. Yigal Allon in a seminar to envoys of Ha'Kibbutz, 29 May 1945, KMA, Security Committee, container 6, file 105, quoted in *The Palmach Book*, p. 460.

61. The possession of weapons, said Israel Galili, a Kibbutz leader, allowed the Palmach "to recognize its value and sense its power"; see Israel Galili in *The Palmach Book,* p. 13. On the Palmach spirit, see Ben Eliezer, *Through the Rifle's Sight,* pp. 117–21.

62. Yigal Allon, "Trends and Deeds," in *The Palmach Book,* p. 563.

63. Ben-Gurion, *Diary,* 17 April 1947.

64. Ben-Gurion, *War Diary, A,* 17 December 1947, p. 51; Yigal Allon, *Palmach Battles* (in Hebrew) (Tel Aviv, 1965), p. 170; Aviva Halamish, *Exodus: The True Story* (in Hebrew) (Tel Aviv, 1990), pp. 183–84, 195–99.

65. To Michael from Hofshi, 26 August 1946, HHA 14/513; to Neter from Artzi, 1 September 1946, HHA 14/513.

66. From Eliezer, 19 August 1946, HHA 14/239.

67. Yosef Report, *La Negev* (*Merika*), 20 February 1947, HHA 14/104.

68. Allon, "Trends and Deeds," p. 578.

69. Nahum Bogner, *The Ships of Revolt: The Clandestine Immigration 1945–1948* (in Hebrew) (Tel Aviv, 1993), p. 283.

70. *The Palmach Book,* pp. 681–727.

71. Montesquieu, *L'Esprit des lois,* pp. 3, 8, ["l'on obéit et l'on commande à des égaux et l'on a que des égaux pour maitres"].

72. See Paris discussion of the Ziesling affair, January 1947, LA 4–32–3, Illegal Immigration; see also Braginsky files, KMA.

73. The data here are from a databank of Mossad activists (hereinafter referred to as Databank) that I compiled based on questionnaires given to over 100 people who had worked in the Mossad, or the survivors of those no longer alive when this research was conducted, as well as books of memoirs, autobiographies of Mossad people, later testimonies, and documents from the Mossad archive (located in the Haganah Historical Archives, Code 14). The only citation I found for Ruth Klieger's year of birth was in Peggy Mann, *The Last Refuge* (in Hebrew) (Tel Aviv, 1973).

74. On the evolution of a "service aristocracy" in the Yishuv, see Gabriel Sheffer, *Ha'Zionut 8* (in Hebrew) (Tel Aviv, 1983).

75. Letters from Zameret, Marseilles, 7 December 1939, in *Morning Forever: Letters and Writings* (in Hebrew) (Beit HaShita, 1965–66), pp. 72–73.

76. Ibid; Zameret Diaries, Shmarya Zameret Archives (SZA); Zvi Yehieli on Shmarya Zameret, Zim Archive; testimony from Pino Ginsburg, Ha'apala Project, Tel Aviv University.

77. On Namier's thoughts about biographies of secondary elite members, see Ved Mehta, *Fly and the Fly Bottle* (London, 1965), pp. 184–85.

78. Jacob Burckhardt, *Force and Freedom* (New York, 1943), p. 303, quoted in C. W. Mills, *The Power Elite* (New York, 1963), p. 3.

79. Tabenkin Notebooks, no. 50, 9 February 1938, KMA. The recruitment of Yehieli was decided upon in a meeting with Tabenkin in which Braginsky and Yisrael Idelson (eventually Bar-Yehuda), the secretary general of the Kibbutz, participated.

80. Ibid.

81. See also Avneri, *From Velos to Taurus,* p. 53.

82. Yehieli Report, HHA 14/153; Agami [Averbuch] Letters 1939–40, HHA 14/4195.

83. Testimony of Yehieli's daughter, Nira Yehieli Faran, Databank.

84. Testimony of the paratrooper Baruch Kaminer, Zim Archive.

85. Yehieli Report, HHA 14/153; Agami Letters, HHA, Shamir Files 14/4195.

86. See Yehieli's letter of resignation from the Mossad to the Mapai Executive, August 1947, Minutes of the Mapai Executive, LPA 25/47; see also Chapter 3 in this book.

87. "Davidka Talks," in Avraham Yavin and Shlomo Derekh, eds., *The Story of Davidka* (in Hebrew) (Tel Aviv, 1973–74), p. 31.

88. Harat [Nameri] Letters, fall 1947–early 1948, HHA 14/132.

89. Yavin and Derekh, eds., *The Story of Davidka,* pp. 98–101.

90. Ibid., p. 26.

91. Ibid., p. 40.

92. Giron testimony, ibid., p. 9.

93. Yehuda to Tuvia, Warsaw, 10 September 1938, HHA 41/3134.

94. Shaul Avigur [Meirov], *With the Haganah Generation,* vol. 2 (in Hebrew) (Tel Aviv, 1977), p. 146.

95. Ibid., p. 144.

96. Shabtai Teveth, *The Assassination of Arlosorov* (in Hebrew) (Tel Aviv, 1982), pp. 23, 154, 159.

97. Avigur, *With the Haganah Generation,* vol. 2, pp. 150, 154.

98. Ibid., pp. 154, 157, 158, 175.

99. Pino Ginsburg testimony, Ha'apala Project, Tel Aviv University.

100. Michel de Certeau, *Heterologies: Discourses on the Other* (Minneapolis, 1986), pp. 47–48.

101. Avigur, *With the Haganah Generation,* p. 20; Pino Ginsburg testimony, op. cit.

102. Braginsky, *A Nation Rowing to Shore,* pp. 336–50; interviews with Ginsburg and Sereni.

103. Leo Tolstoy, *War and Peace,* trans. Louise and Aylmer Maude (Chicago, 1952), p. 426.

104. Ibid., pp. 425–26.

105. Avigur, *With the Haganah Generation,* vol. 2, p. 159.

106. Avigur, *With the Haganah Generation,* vol. 1 (Tel Aviv, 1970), p. 208.

107. Ibid., p. 215.

108. Ibid.

109. Avigur, *With the Haganah Generation,* vol. 2 (Tel Aviv, 1977), pp. 13–14.

110. Yehuda Slutzki, ed., *The History of the Haganah, A,* vol. 2 (in Hebrew) (Tel Aviv, 1973–74), p. 585; see also Idith Zertal, "The Sacrificed and the Sanctified: The Constitution of a National Martyrology" (in Hebrew), *Zmanim* 48 (Spring 1994): 16–34.

111. Gabriel Sheffer, "The Creation of a Service Aristocracy" (in Hebrew), *Ha'Zionut 8,* pp. 166, 171.

112. Ibid., pp. 151–54; Eliahu Golomb, *Hidden Power* (in Hebrew) (Tel Aviv, 1950), pp. 88, 100; Avigur, *With the Haganah Generation,* vol. 1, p. 211; Moshe Sharett, *Political Diary, B* (in Hebrew) (Tel Aviv, 1971), p. 237.

113. Teveth, *The Assassination of Arlosorov,* p. 160.

114. Avigur to Mardor, 13 January 1959, quoted in Slutzki, ed., *History of the Haganah, C,* pt. 1, p. 155.

115. Yehieli to Mapai Executive, August 1947, LPA 25/47.

116. Isaiah Berlin, *The Hedgehog and the Fox: An Essay on Tolstoy's View of History* (New York, 1953).

117. Avigur, *With the Haganah Generation,* vol. 2, p. 20.

CHAPTER 6

1. *Weekly Digest* (October 1944); quoted in Yehuda Bauer, *American Jewry and the Holocaust* (Detroit, 1981), p. 451.

2. Natan Reich, *JDC Primer Principles* (New York, 1945), p. 1; quoted in Bauer, *American Jewry,* p. 182.

3. Bauer, *American Jewry,* p. 451–52.

4. Letter, Moses Leavitt, 16 March 1946, Poland file, General, JDC Archive.

5. See notes 1, 2, and 4.

6. The JDC leadership took pride in the fact that throughout their years of overseas activity, they never acted in opposition to an order or request of the U.S. State Department, and thus had earned the confidence of Washington and special status among all the private American agencies. See Herbert Agar, *The Saving Remnant: An Account of Jewish Survival* (New York, 1960), p. 65; see also Bauer, *American Jewry,* pp. 182–83.

7. Minutes of the Administrative Committee, 30 March 1943, JDC Archive, quoted in Bauer, *American Jewry,* pp. 184–85.

8. Minutes of the Executive Committee, 21 February 1945, JDC Archive, quoted in Bauer, *American Jewry,* p. 185.

9. Notes of a conversation between Bauer and Moses Leavitt, 1962, quoted in Yehuda Bauer, *Bricha: Flight and Rescue* (New York, 1970), p. 300.

10. Letter, Yoseph Bankover, 16 November 1944, CZA S25/6606.

11. B. Hoffman, *Daily Forward,* 27 February 1943; quoted in Bauer, *American Jewry,* p. 184.

12. Ze'ev Schind in the Kibbutz Council, Beit HaShita, 2 September 1944, HHA 14/59.

13. Ibid.

14. Eliahu Dobkin to the Jewish Agency Executive, 21 September 1944, Minutes of the Jewish Agency Executive, CZA.

15. Ben-Gurion in the Jewish Agency Executive, 25 February 1945, Minutes of the Jewish Agency Executive, CZA.

16. Minutes of the Rescue Commission, (?) September 1944, 3 October 1944, 9 May 1945, and 3 October 1945, CZA S26/1238.

17. Ben-Gurion, *Diary,* 3 November 1945, BGA.

18. Ibid., 24 October 1945.

19. Zerah Wahrhaftig, *Refugee and Survivor During the Holocaust* (in Hebrew) (Jerusalem, 1984), pp. 339–40.

20. See Jewish Agency Executive meetings, 16 July 1944 and 27 October 1944, Minutes of the Jewish Agency Executive, CZA.

21. Eliezer Kaplan in a meeting of the Jewish Agency Executive, 25 February 1945, Minutes of the Jewish Agency Executive, CZA. Although the minutes indicate that the agreement is an appendix, it is not extant. I did, however, find draft versions of the agreement between the Agency and the JDC from 9 and 13 February 1945, ibid.

22. Ruth Klieger to Eliahu Dobkin, 9 April 1945, HHA 14/176.

23. Ibid.

24. Ben-Gurion, *Diary*, 14 May 1945.

25. Yoseph Bankover to Eliahu Dobkin, 23 July 1944, CZA S6/4654.

26. Bankover to Dobkin, 24 October 1944, CZA S6/4654.

27. Testimony by Misha Noktin for the project of a book on the Ha'apala from Italy, 6 February 1956. This was the only time a senior Mossad official spoke negatively of Joseph Schwartz, either in testimony at the time or in later testimony such as this.

28. Letter from Yehiel Duvdevani, 1 August 1945, CZA S25/5243.

29. "Passman has brought a revolution here. Attitude has changed . . . Succeeded in many important things." Yehiel Duvdevani from Rome to Palestine, 2 March 1946, HHA 14/502.

30. JDC–Diaspora Center agreement, CZA S6/4654.

31. A control report from December 1945 on six Bricha stations asserted that "money comes from the Diaspora Center and Moshe A[verbuch]." HHA 14/176a.

32. "Joint behaves well, helps mostly when operations fail in documents, cars, pays for whatever needed for the road: alcohol, cigarettes, chocolate, bribe" Report, Gershon Hirsch, December 1945, HHA 14/176a.

33. Letter from Erich Frank in Vienna to Artzi, 12 January 1946, and Frank's letter to the Diaspora Center, 3 January 1946, HHA 14/176b and 14/502 respectively.

34. "Schwartz gave explicit orders to give maximum help. He promised $70,000. $10,000 was paid immediately." Report, Gerschon Hirsch, December 1945, HHA 14/176a. See also letter from Yitzhak [Steiner] in Prague to Artzi, 29 November 1945, HHA 14/176b and 14/502.

35. Letter, Erich Frank in Vienna to Diaspora Center, 3 January 1946, HHA 14/176b, 14/502.

36. Ibid.

37. From Yitzhak [Steiner], Prague, to Artzi, 29 November 1945, HHA 14/176a.

38. Ibid.; see also "Information Brochure No. 2 for *Bricha* Activists," HHA.

39. Parenta, letter from 29 November 1945, HHA 14/176a.

40. Letter, Yashek, Levi and Parenta, from Prague to Artzi, 24 October 1945, HHA 14/176a.

41. To Artzi from Parenta, 11 January 1946; see also cable from Palestine to Ben-Yehuda in Paris, HHA 14/506.

42. Ben-Gurion in the Political Executive of Mapai, 22 November 1945, LPA 26/45.

43. Ben-Gurion, *Diary,* 28 October 1945.

44. Ibid., 29 October 1945.

45. Ibid., 3 November 1945.

46 Letter, Ben-Kedem [Shertok] to Palestine, 31 October 1945, HHA 14/160.

47. Ibid.

48. "I had long talks with Schwartz from the JDC, and I don't think we should despair. I'll meet him again in Paris and Genf" (Danny [Schind] from London to Palestine, 14 August 1945, HHA 14/160a).

49. For example, cable from Danny to Pino in Genf (through Alon), 27 October 1945, HHA 14/160a.

50. "Avi-Amos is willing to give us only a hundred thousand Stephens [dollars]," cable, Pino to Artzi, 4 November 1945, HHA 14/175.

51. Cable from Artzi to Berg [Pino Ginsburg], 3 December 1945, HHA 14/175. From mid-November 1945, the Marseilles office also began to press for large sums of money to purchase ships (one for 800 people and another for 1,300). See cables from 13 and 16 November 1945, HHA 14/175.

52. From Pino [Ginsburg] to Artzi, 16 December 1945, HHA 14/160.

53. From Leavitt to Passman, 22 January 1946, file 122 (Immigration to Palestine 46–48), Joint Distribution Committee Archives (JDCA).

54. See Bauer, *American Jewry,* pp. 41–42, 178–86, 220, 450–51.

55. See, for example, cable from Ben-Yehuda and Berg to Artzi and Kadmon, 13 May 1946, HHA 14/507.

56. See news item from Cairo published in *Davar,* 9 November 1943; see also meetings of Schwartz with generals Clarke and Tate and meeting of Schwartz and Leavitt with General Hildering, Bauer's interviews with Schwartz, and Schwartz Report, General File 1945, JDCA (in Bauer, *American Jewry,* pp. 90–91.)

57. Bauer, *Flight and Rescue,* p. 78.

58. See, e.g., cable, Kaplan, August 1945, about the Schwartz mission, CZA.

59. Amitzur Ilan, *America, Britain, and Palestine* (in Hebrew) (Jerusalem, 1979), p. 189.

60. Briefings of the president concerning Palestine prior to the Potsdam Conference, FRUS, The Berlin Conference, vol. 2, p. 318.

61. Meir Avizohar, ed., *Ben-Gurion: Toward the End of the Mandate: Memoirs* (in Hebrew) (Tel Aviv, 1993), p. 44.

62. Report, Kaplan meeting of the Jewish Agency Executive, 10 February 1945, CZA.

63. Following the conference Edward Warburg, JDC president, also admitted that the displaced persons have no refuge except Palestine, and his colleague Paul Baerwald agreed with this view. Interviews with Herbert Friedman, executive vice-president of the United Jewish Appeal, January–May 1976, Oral Documentation Department (ODD) 14:128; Report on the Emergency Conference, *The New Palestine,* 31 December 1945, quoted in Menahem Kaufman, *Non-Zionists in America in the Struggle for the State 1939–1948* (in Hebrew) (Jerusalem, 1984), p. 145.

64. Testimony, Schwartz to the Anglo-American Committee, 7 January 1946, CZA S25/6381.

65. Report, Kaplan to the Jewish Agency Executive, 10 February 1945, CZA S25/6381.

66. Ibid.

67. The Mossad gradually moved its center of operations from Palestine to Paris (see Chapter 2), improved its communication channels, and began to function as one organic unit.

68. *Reports*, HHA 2751.

69. To Yossifon [Dobkin] c/o Berg from Artzi, 3 March 1946, HHA 14/78, 14/501.

70. First the JDC promised to fund half the costs of transferring 4,400 refugees from the ports of Europe to Palestine: later it agreed to increase the quota to 6,600 without committing itself to further amounts. The JDC also required that the Mossad submit all its work plans for prior approval. See cables to Eliezer [Kaplan] and Artzi from Yossifon, 9 March 1946, HHA 14/503.

71. See for example, from Giora [Mossad treasurer in France] to Arnon [the Mossad office in Palestine], 19 May 1947, HHA 14/530; to Yissar [France], Or [Meirov], and Berg [Ginsburg] from Arnon, 27 June 1947, HHA 14/551; see also the letters of the Bricha activists, (notes 33–41).

72. Cable from Artzi to Berg through Alon, 12 March 1946, HHA 14/503.

73. To Yossifon through Berg from Artzi, 3 March 1946, HHA 14/78, 14/501.

74. To Artzi from Berg, no. 22, 8 March 1946, HHA 14/78.

75. Ibid.

76. To Artzi from Berg through Alon, 2 March 1946, HHA 14/503; also Berg to Artzi, 8 March 1946, HHA 14/78; to Eliezer [Kaplan] and Artzi from Yossifon [Dobkin], 8 March 1946, HHA 14/78.

77. See Mossad files, HHA 14/505a; see also summary of the conversation between Schwartz and Leavitt, 17 May 1946, file 122 (Immigration to Palestine 46–48), JDCA.

78. To Artzi from Kassuta, 14 April 1946, HHA 14/505; letter, Zameret to Artzi, 14 April 1946, HHA 14/509; see also from Kadmon [Barpal, head of Palestine Headquarters], to Ben-Yehuda, 23 April 1946, HHA 14/100.

79. On the La Spezia affair, see a fuller discussion in Chapter 1; see also HHA 14/100, 14/176, 14/86.

80. See note 78. The British maneuver, in the first months of 1946, of releasing the illegal immigrants who had been caught on the Mossad ships and deducting their number from the approved immigration quotas accomplished exactly what the JDC claimed: they became immigrants at three or four times the cost of regular immigrants.

81. To Artzi and Kadmon from Ben-Yehuda and Berg, 13 May 1946, HHA 14/101, 14/507.

82. Ibid: see also the conversation between Schwartz and Leavitt, 17 May 1946, file 122, JDCA.

83. See note 65.

84. "The mishap in Alon places us in a catastrophic situation, because we have already paid for the two vessels related to the failure. The money is lost or at least frozen for a long time" (to Artzi from Berg, 8 April 1946, HHA 14/505).

85. The delay in departure of the *Smirni* (*Max Nordau*) from Constanta was caused by, among other factors, the lack of proper visas and deliberate delays

by the Romanian government, not by the immediate financial crisis. To Artzi from Berg, 26 April 1946, HHA 14/505a. See also Chapter 3 in this book.

86. Cables from 26 April 1946, HHA 14/505a, and from 13 May 1946, HHA 14/507.

87. "Demands to stop all negotiations with Passman [Palestine]. Negotiations will be held only in America and Paris," was Meirov's order. To Artzi from Ben-Yehuda, 7 May 1946, HHA 14/506.

88. For an extensive discussion of the *Smirni* (*Max Nordau*) affair, see Chapter 3.

89. *Reports,* HHA 2751.

90. To Artzi from Berg and Ben-Yehuda, 13 May 1946, nos. 66, 67, 68, 69, HHA 14/507; see also to Danny from Artzi, 14 May 1946, HHA 14/507.

91. Ibid.

92. Interviews with Pino Ginsburg, Mossad treasurer in Europe, and Zecharia Kikayon, Mossad comptroller.

93. To Artzi from Berg, 6 June 1946, HHA 14/509.

94. See, for example, cable from Meirov, 13 May 1946, HHA 14/507, about the "transactions" made by the Jewish Agency officials.

95. To Neter from Artzi, 3 June 1946, HHA 14/101.

96. To Artzi from Neter, 20 August 1946, HHA 14/102, 14/503.

97. Ibid.; to Artzi from Neter, 20 August 1946, HHA 14/102, 14/503; minutes of meeting between Louis Sobel and Ze'ev Schind, 6 July 1946, file 122, JDCA. In a letter to Pino Ginsburg from 23 July 1946, Schind wrote, "Leavitt told me yesterday that, at Eliezer's request, they sent an advance of 800,000 until a new agreement is reached." IDF Archive (Tel HaShomer), Mossad files in Paris, box 27, no. 1559/85.

98. To Artzi from Berg, 15 October 1946, HHA 14/518; to Artzi from Neter-Or [France-Meirov], 25 October 1946, HHA 14/519.

99. Report by Mereminski about the congress decisions and the Mossad plans for 1947, 1 January 1947, HHA 14/78.

100. Ibid.

101. To Artzi from Kadmon [Barpal], 8 January 1947, HHA 14/523; to Neter from Artzi, 31 January 1947, HHA 14/104.

102. To Arnon from Shulamit, 24 February 1947, no. 91, HHA 14/529; to Arnon from Shulamit, 19 March 1947, no. 18, HHA 14/529.

103. To Arnon from Or and Berg, 29 March 1947 [date apparently erroneous], no. 11, HHA 14/527; to Palestine from Neter, 18 May 1947, HHA 14/530.

104. To Arnon from Berg, 17 April 1947, no. 61, HHA 14/527; to Arnon from Yissar [France], 4 May 1947, no. 11, HHA 14/78, 14/528.

105. Correspondence in file 14/78, HHA.

106. The meeting was recorded by the JDC, apparently in great detail, and classified "top secret." JDCA, New York, microfilm 1/29. Schind and Ginsburg gave a very brief telephone report of the conversation to their colleagues in Paris. 26 May 1947, OL.

107. See, for example, "Report from July, August, and September 1947 in Italy," intended for Dr. Schwartz in Paris, 20 October 1947, file 137 ("Italy 47"), JDCA; report of the Executive Committee, July 1947, file 122, JDCA.

108. Files 122 and 137, JDCA.

109. Report on north Africa, 8 June 1947, HHA 14/530; to Arnon from Yissar, 18 June 1947, HHA 14/531; from Neter to Palestine, 19 June 1947, HHA 14/533.

110. From Neter to Palestine, 19 June 1947, HHA 14/533.

111. JDC Annual Reports for the years 1947–48.

112. *Reports,* HHA 2751.

113. "Pessimistic about *Shachor's* [Schwartz]. Even though Danny knows that they received money, they have paid nothing yet. I fear that the payments may be delayed" (telephone conversation from Danny [Schind], 20 June 1947), OL. See also Louis Sobel's words from his New York meeting with Mossad representatives. Schind and Ginsburg, 26 May 1947, OL.

114. Telephone transcripts of Rudi [Shmarya Zameret] from Marseilles at the time that the deportation ships were moored opposite Port de Bouc, OL; see also Agar, *The Saving Remnant,* p. 212.

115. See Aviva Halamish, "The United States Position Regarding the Illegal Immigration Ship 'Exodus 1947'" (in Hebrew), *Contemporary Jewry Annual,* no. 3 (1985).

116. From Ben-Yehuda to Artzi, 12 August 1947, HHA 14/158; to Alon from Yissar, 30 October 1947, HHA 14/78; letters of Harat [Davidka Nameri] from the United States, October–December 1947, HHA 14/132. See also note 113.

117. From Neter to Palestine, 19 June 1947, HHA 14/533.

118. To Arnon from Yissar, 31 October 1947, HHA 14/78.

119. Letters of Harat, December 1947, HHA 14/132; cable, Ginsburg on the Harat report, 14 December 1947; to Arnon from Berg, 14 December 1947, HHA 14/132; from Arnon to Yissar, 13 January 1948, HHA 14/79; from Yissar to Arnon, 17 January 1948, HHA 14/79.

120. See David Sha'ari, *The Deportation to Cyprus 1946–1949, the Illegal Immigration, the Camps, and the Organization of Illegal Immigrants* (in Hebrew) (Jerusalem, 1981), especially pp. 190–96; Nahum Bogner, *Island of Deportation: Illegal Immigrant Camps in Cyprus 1946–48* (in Hebrew) (Tel Aviv, 1991), especially pp. 80–95.

121. On 21 August Passman left to investigate the possibility of providing JDC relief services to the camps. Passman testimony, ODD, file 71/4.

122. Commission Report, HHA 14/520.

123. Minutes, Jewish Agency Executive, 15 May 1947, CZA. On Morris Laub, see Bogner, *Island of Deportation,* pp. 80–95; Sha'ari, *Deportation,* p. 192.

124. Letter, Barlas, 10 September 1946, CZA S6/4312.

125. This matter was deliberated in the Jewish Agency Executive, 15 May 1947, minutes, CZA; statements of Moshe Kolodny in the Jewish Agency Executive, CZA.

126. Sha'ari, *Deportation,* p. 193.

127. According to various testimonies, the firm of Kesselman and Kesselman did the Mossad accounts for the years 1945–48 (they signed the CPA reports during the war years). The balance sheet was apparently lost or destroyed in a fire in their offices. The CPA report does not exist in the Mossad files in the HHA.

128. The calculation is as follows. For the first 2,100 passengers after the war ended, the JDC paid PP50 per person, which is $200 (i.e., a total of $420,000).

For the next 4,500 passengers, the JDC paid PP40 per person (i.e., $720,000). For the remaining (approximately) 63,000 refugees brought into Palestine by the Mossad in those years, the JDC paid $100 per person (i.e., $6,300,000). The total: $7,440,000.

129. See information newsletter no. 2 for Bricha activists, HHA 14/176.

130. Bauer, *Flight and Rescue*, p. 320.

131. Ephraim Dekel, *In the Routes of Bricha* (in Hebrew) (Tel Aviv, 1959), p. 450.

132. In the report from Italy covering July through September 1947, Dr. Schwartz was informed that in July 726 people left Italy "without certificates," and in September 632 did so (although the accurate numbers were 658 and 438, respectively) (from Traub to Dr. Schwartz, 20 October 1947, file 137 ["Italy 47"], JDCA). In a letter by Schind to Sobel, this Mossad official reports 1,290 passengers on board the *Josiah Wedgewood* (the accurate number was 1,257), 1,060 people on board the *Biriya* (999 in actuality), and 2,700 on the *Hagana* (versus 2,678).

133. Conversation with Mossad treasurer Pino Ginsburg, October 1990.

CHAPTER 7

1. See previous chapters. See also Ben-Gurion, *Diary,* 15 October 1945, BGA; "Amos's Father" [Ben-Gurion], letter to the Executive in Jersualem, 7 October 1945, BGA; Ben-Gurion in Mapai Secretariat, 22 November 1945, LPA 24/25; Ben-Gurion in the Jewish Agency Executive, 21 November 1945, Protocols, Agency Executive, CZA.

2. Talks about transforming Jewish suffering into Zionist redemption reverberate in Ben-Gurion's statements throughout the 1930s and 1940s. The strength of Zionism emanates from Jewish tragedy, "and the force of Jewish trouble has increased Zionism's force," he said in the Jewish Agency Executive in May 1941. In the Mapai Council on 25 October 1942, Ben-Gurion explained his entire "Zionist view": "to forge Jewish catastrophe into redemption matrix. . . . We have power . . . and there is a great disaster—this is power. If there is an idea, one can transform catastrophe into redemption. Catastrophe of millions into redemption of millions" (LPA 23/42). For a comprehensive analysis of Ben-Gurion's "exploiting the tragedy," see Shabtai Teveth, *The Burning Ground* (in Hebrew) (Tel Aviv, 1987), pp. 423–24.

3. Minutes, Jewish Agency Executive, 24 February 1946, CZA.

4. Ben-Gurion to the Mapai Executive, 22–23 July 1949, LPA 24/49.

5. Ruth [Klieger] and David [Shaltiel] to Shertok and Dobkin, 11 June 1945, S25/5241, CZA.

6. David Shaltiel to the Mapai Executive, 11 September 1945, LPA 24/45.

7. Ben-Asher to Nehama and Elik, 3 Tammuz 1945; quoted in Yoav Gelber, *Flag Bearers* (in Hebrew) (Jerusalem, 1984), p. 328.

8. Letter from the soldier Hofesh, Afikim, 8 December 1944; quoted in Gelber, *Flag Bearers,* pp. 257–59.

9. Letter from Italy, *Letter to Soldiers,* 27 June 1945; quoted in Gelber, *Flag Bearers,* p. 284.

10. Giora Yoseftal to the Va'ad Le'umi (National Council) Executive, 3 December 1946, CZA J 1/6945.

11. Cited in Shabtai Teveth, *The Road to Iyyar* (in Hebrew) (Tel Aviv, 1986), p. 226.

12. Avi-Amos [Ben-Gurion], letter from London to the Executive in Jerusalem, 7 October 1945, BGA.

13. Ben-Gurion, 24 February 1946, minutes of the Jewish Agency Executive, CZA.

14. Ben-Gurion's notes from meetings with soldiers and envoys, Münich, 30 January 1946; Ben-Gurion, *Diary,* October 1945; see also minutes, Jewish Agency Executive, 24 February 1946, CZA.

15. Ben-Gurion, *Diary,* 27 October 1945.

16. Ibid., 3 December 1944.

17. Ibid., 4 December 1944.

18. Cited in Teveth, *Road to Iyyar,* p. 228; see also Shabtai Teveth, "The Black Hole: Ben-Gurion between Shoah and Rebirth" (in Hebrew), *Alpayim* 10 (1994): 111–95.

19. Ben-Gurion to the Jewish Agency Executive, 24 February 1946, CZA.

20. Ben-Gurion, *In Battle,* vol. 5 (in Hebrew) (Tel Aviv, 1958), pp. 97–107.

21. Ben-Gurion to Moshav members at Kfar Vitkin, 1 November 1947, BGA.

22. Ibid.

23. Testimony of Louisa Dekalo, in Hayim Kishales, "The Revolution of September 9, 1944," *History of Bulgarian Jewry* (in Hebrew) (Tel Aviv, 1970), pp. 66–68.

24. See Dina Porat, "With Apology and Mercy" (in Hebrew), *Moreshet* 52 (1992): 14; see also Teveth, "The Black Hole."

25. Antonio Gramsci, *Selections from Cultural Writings* (Cambridge, England, 1985), pp. 27–29; Jonathan Steinberg, "The Historian and the Questione della Lingua," in Peter Burke and Roy Porter, eds., *The Social History of Language* (Cambridge, England, 1987), pp. 245–55.

26. See Aviva Halamish, *Exodus: The True Story* (in Hebrew) (Tel Aviv, 1990), pp. 68–69; see also a discussion on the naming of the ship *Knesset Israel* in Chapter 3 of this book.

27. Teveth, *The Road to Iyyar,* p. 229.

28. The text of the interview is quoted in Meir Avizohar, ed., *Ben-Gurion: Toward the End of the Mandate: Memoirs* (in Hebrew) (Tel Aviv, 1993), p. 171 (the document was not found in BGA); *Catriel Yafeh* file, HHA 14/239; see also the writings of Eliezer Klein and Aya Pinkerfeld in *The Palmach Book,* vol. 1, pp. 688–91.

29. Ben-Gurion, "European Jewry on the Eve of the Zionist Congress," Paris, 30 September 1946, BGA.

30. Ben-Gurion to the Twenty-second Congress, 10 December 1946, CZA.

31. *Palmach* ship file, HHA 14/274; testimony of a clandestine immigrant, CZA S25/4317.

32. Ben-Gurion to Abba Hillel Silver, "For a United Zionist Struggle as the Twenty-second Zionist Congress Approaches," Paris, 1 October 1946, CZA Z6/4058; and also BGA. Only the Hebrew version was found.

33. See, for example, Ben-Gurion to the Political Committee of the Congress, 18 December 1946, CZA.

34. Ben-Gurion to the annual Hadassah convention, Boston, 11 November 1946, BGA.

35. Ben-Gurion to Creech-Jones, London. Notes of the meeting made by Ben-Gurion appear in his diary (in Hebrew), 2 January 1947, BGA; also see his speech in English to UNSCOP, Jerusalem, 4 July 1947, Special Committees, UNSCOP file, BGA.

36. Ben-Gurion to the Labor group, Twenty-first Zionist Congress, 19 August 1939, *Memoirs* (in Hebrew), vol. 6, pp. 505–15.

37. Ben-Gurion to the Mapai Executive, 22 November 1945, LPA 24/45.

38. Notes by Ben-Gurion from a meeting with soldiers stationed in camps in Munich, Bavaria, 30 January 1946, BGA; see also notes 25 and 26.

39. Ben-Gurion to soldiers of the Third Battalion, Kiryat Motzkin, 23 September 1944, CZA S25/6078.

40. Ben-Gurion to the Jewish Agency Executive, 21 November 1945, minutes of the Jewish Agency Executive, CZA.

41. Ben-Gurion to the Mapai Executive, 22 November 1945, LPA 24/45.

42. Ben-Gurion to the Conference of Mapai in Eretz-Israel, Paris, 23 August 1946, BGA.

43. Ben-Gurion, *Diary,* 1 November 1945.

44. Ben-Gurion, "Letter to the Yishuv," Paris, 23 October 1946, BGA.

45. Ben-Gurion, *Diary,* March (no day cited) 1945; "For Clarification in Athens," 14 May 1945, BGA; Ben-Gurion to the Mapai Central Committee, 15 March 1945, LPA 23/45.

46. Ben-Gurion, *Diary,* March 1945, 14 May 1945, BGA.

47. Ben-Gurion, "Zionist Accounting after the War," *Diary,* 30 July 1945; summary of the World Zionist Conference in London, CZA S25/1912.

48. See, for example, Ben-Gurion at the World Union of Po'alei Zion Council, 26 April 1939, LPA.

49. Ben-Gurion, "Zionist Accounting," *Diary,* 30 July 1945.

50. Churchill to Weizmann, 9 June 1945; quoted in Michael Bar Zohar, *Ben Gurion,* vol. 1 (in Hebrew) (Tel Aviv, 1975), p. 501.

51. Ben-Gurion, *Diary,* 19 June and 21 June 1945.

52. See Chapter 5 in this book; see also Idith Zertal, "Between Ethics and Politics," (in Hebrew), in Anita Shapira, ed., *Ha'apala,* (Tel Aviv, 1990), pp. 102–5.

53. Ben-Gurion, *Diary,* 19 June and 21 June 1945.

54. Ben-Gurion, "Towards an Army and the State of Israel," article 37; Meir Weisgal, *So Far: An Autobiography* (in Hebrew) (Jerusalem, 1972), p. 180 (quoted in Bar Zohar, *Ben Gurion,* p. 515).

55. Oscar Handlin, *A Continuing Task: The AJDC 1914–1964* (New York, 1964), p. 89; see also Chapter 6 of this book.

56. See note 54; see also Ben-Gurion, *Diary,* 23 July 1945.

57. Ben-Gurion at the World Zionist Conference, London, 2 August 1945, CZA S25/1912; Ben-Gurion, *In Battle,* vol. 4, p. 216.

58. Chaim Weizmann, World Zionist Conference, London, 2 August 1945, CZA.

59. See note 57.

60. Political declaration at the Zionist Conference in London, CZA.

61. Blanche Dugdale, *Diaries,* 21 September 1945, p. 225.

62. Dov Yoseph [Bernard Joseph] to the Mapai Executive convened as the Political Committee, 25 September 1945, LPA 24/45.

63. "Amos's Father" [Ben-Gurion], letter from London to the Jewish Agency Executive in Jerusalem, 7 October 1945, BGA. Regarding the date of this letter, see Meir Avizohar, "Ben-Gurion's Visit to the Displaced Persons Camps," in Binyamin Pinkus, ed., *Eastern European Jewry between Shoah and Rebirth* (in Hebrew) (Sdeh-Boker, Jerusalem, 1987), pp. 267–68.

64. Zertal, "Between Ethics and Politics," pp. 102–6; Idith Zertal, "Lost Souls—The Clandestine Immigrants and the Mossad in the Struggle for the State and Afterwards" (in Hebrew), *Ha'zionut* 14 (1989): 107–26.

65. See Ben-Gurion's eight-point document sent to the Jewish Agency Executive, October 1945, BGA.

66. See, for example, letter from Ben-Gurion to Abba Hillel Silver, 1 October 1946, CZA z6/4058; BGA.

67. He used the term "concentration camp" extensively in relation to the British detention camps; see cable to the Jewish Agency in Washington, 2 July 1945. To Felix Frankfurter he wrote that Bevin's regime in Palestine was almost similar to a Nazi dictatorship; Paris, 17 July 1946, BGA; address to the expanded Executive, Paris, 15 August 1946, CZA.

68. Ben-Gurion's eight-point document sent to the Jewish Agency Executive in Jerusalem, 1 October 1945, BGA; see also note 63.

69. Eight-point document, op. cit.; see also Ben-Gurion, *Diary,* 3 and 6 October 1945.

70. Ben-Gurion, *Diary,* op. cit., 28–29 October 1945; see also Chapter 6 of this book, on the JDC.

71. Jewish Agency Executive decision from 6 December 1945, HHA 14/73 and 14/107.

72. Ben-Gurion, *Diary,* 13 November 1945.

73. Bar Zohar, *Ben Gurion, p.* 529.

74. Avizohar, "Introduction," *Toward the End of the Mandate.*

75. *Reports,* HHA 2751.

76. Letter to Paula Ben-Gurion, New York, 8 July 1946, BGA; David Horowitz, *A State in the Making* (New York, 1953), pp. 104–5; Cunningham to Hall, 19 August 1946, Cunningham Papers, box 1, file 1, Middle East Center (MEC), St. Antony's College, Oxford.

77. Ben-Gurion, *Diary,* 29 June 1946. In Paris Ben-Gurion claimed that the British government had miscalculated. "There will be no Jew, from right to left . . . who will participate in the Executive—Quisling or Petain" (4 July 1946, *In Battle,* vol. 5 [in Hebrew], p. 88).

78. Series of cables from Ben-Gurion in the United States to London and Jerusalem, 8–11 July 1946, BGA.

79. Cable to members of the Jewish Agency Executive, New York, 9 July 1945; letter to Paula Ben-Gurion, New York, 11 July 1945, BGA.

80. Cable from Weizmann to Ben-Gurion, 10 July 1946; cable from Ben-Gurion in New York to the Jewish Agency in Jerusalem, 11 July 1946; Weizmann

to Ben-Gurion, 15 September 1946, Weizmann Archive (WA); Weisgal, *So Far,* p. 184; Dugdale, *Diaries,* 5 August 1946, p. 239. (The two latter references are quoted in Bar Zohar, *Ben Gurion,* p. 548.)

81. Ben-Gurion to the Zionist Executive, 8 October 1945, CZA.

82. Ben-Gurion to Weizmann, 10 October 1945, WA.

83. Ben-Gurion to Weizmann, 12 October 1945, WA.

84. Ben-Gurion to Sneh, 1 October 1946, BGA.

85. Ibid.

86. Bar Zohar, *Ben Gurion,* p. 549.

87. Report of meeting between Weizmann and Hall, 2 August 1946, P.R.O. C0537/1785.

88. Report of Colonial Secretary Hall to a cabinet meeting, 11 July 1946, and further cabinet meetings, 29–30 July and 1, 7, 9, 10 August 1946, P.R.O. CAB 128/6/08546.

89. Ben-Gurion to the expanded Executive, Paris, 5 August 1946, CZA.

90. For the British announcement, see *New Judea,* 12 (July–August 1946): 172–73.

91. Yehuda Slutzki, ed., *The History of the Haganah* C-2 (in Hebrew) (Tel Aviv, 1973), p. 903.

92. "If they are deported without a proper resistance, we'll never be forgiven" (David Nameri, 12 August 1946, HHA 14/231); "The Yishuv did not resist the way everybody said it would" (Arye Kaplan, Oral Documentation Department [ODD], 40/60).

93. Ben-Gurion to the Expanded Executive, Paris, 5 August 1946, CZA.

94. Ibid., 15 August 1946.

95. Ben-Gurion to the Political Committee of the Jewish Agency Executive, 25 August 1946, CZA.

96. Avizohar, "Introduction," *Toward the End of the Mandate.*

97. Ben-Gurion to the plenary of the Twenty-second Zionist Congress, Basel, 16 September 1946, CZA.

98. Ben-Gurion to the Political Committee of the Congress, 18 September 1946, CZA; Mereminski Report, 1 January 1947, HHA 14/104; to Artzi from Neter, 22 December 1947, HHA 14/103; from Kadmon and Berg to Artzi, 27 December 1946, HHA 14/103.

99. Zertal, "Between Ethics and Politics," p. 105.

100. Ben-Gurion, *Diary,* 18 July 1947.

101. See Chapters 2 and 4 in this book; see also Idith Zertal, "The Fifth Side of the Triangle: France and the Issue of Palestine after World War II" (in Hebrew), *Yahadut Zmanenu* 5 (1989): 241–57.

102. Slutzki, ed., *The History of the Haganah* C/2, p. 957.

103. Ben-Gurion to the Histadrut General Council, 6 August 1947, BGA.

104. Ibid.

105. Ben-Gurion to the Mapai Council, 8 August 1947, LPA.

106. Ibid.

107. Ben-Gurion to the Zionist General Council, Zurich, 26 August 1947 (third session), CZA S5/320.

108. Slutzki, ed., *The History of the Haganah* C/2, p. 1326.

109. Cunningham to Foreign Secretary Bevin, 30 August 1947, Cunningham Papers, MEC 2/2.

110. See note 107; Slutzki, ed., *The History of the Haganah* C/2, pp. 1326–27.

111. Ben-Gurion, "Towards an Army and the State of Israel," article 37; statements at the Zionist General Council, 6 April 1948, *In Battle*, vol. 5, p. 291.

112. See note 107.

113. Slutzki, ed., *The History of the Haganah* C/2, pp. 1327, 1329–32.

114. Ibid.; see also note 111.

115. Ben-Gurion to the Political Committee of the Zionist Congress, 18 December 1946, CZA, *In Battle*, vol. 5, pp. 135–37.

116. Report of the High Commissioner, 17 January 1947, BGA.

117. See decisions of the Twenty-second Zionist Congress, CZA.

118. Bevin to the House of Commons, 18 February 1947; quoted in Michael Cohen, *Palestine and the Great Powers, 1945–1948* (Princeton, 1982), pp. 217–28, 223.

119. Bar Zohar, *Ben Gurion*, vol. 2, pp. 645–65.

120. Horowitz, *A State in the Making*, p. 178; conversation between Horowitz and Lissitzki, 2 August 1947, CZA S25/5991; Kennan to Lurie, 21 July 1947, CZA Z5/475.

121. See notes 103 and 105.

122. On the process of the wording of the statement, see Halamish, *Exodus*, p. 180–81.

123. Decisions of the Zionist General Council, Zurich, 25 August–2 September 1947, CZA S5/320.

124. Shertok to the Zionist General Council, Zurich, 25 August 1947, CZA S5/320.

125. See note 107.

126. Pino Ginsburg and Meirov in Zurich to the Mossad headquarters in Paris, 27 August 1947; letter from Shaul Avigur to Hayim Yahil, 22 July 1966; Yahil to Avigur, 31 July 1966; Ha'apala Project, Information Center, Temporary Marking 20.4; Daniel (Kurt) Levine to Shaul Avigur, 19 September 1966, HHA 461; testimony of Hayim Yahil (Hoffman), ODD 1(12).

127. Ibid.

128. Ibid.

129. Letter from Weizmann to the Jewish Agency Executive in London, 6 September 1947, *The Letters and Papers of Chaim Weizmann*, vol. 23 (Jerusalem, 1980), pp. 4–7.

130. Weizmann, speech in Basel, quoted in *Ha'aretz*, 2 September 1947.

131. See note 129.

132. Ibid.

133. Ibid.

134. Ben-Gurion to the Executive in London, Genf [Geneva], 7 September 1947, BGA.

135. Ibid.

136. Ibid.

137. Ibid.

138. See note 129.

139. In earlier stages of the *Exodus* affair, members of the Jewish Agency Executive in London tried to involve Weizmann. See Shertok to the Jewish Agency Executive, 28 July 1947, CZA.

140. The minutes of the Jewish Agency Executive indicate no decision.

141. As Ben-Gurion said to Meirov, Hoffman and Levine in late August in Zurich; see note 126.

142. See Chapters 2 and 4; see also Ben-Yehuda [Shaul Meirov] to Andre [Avi Schwartz] and Yossi [Hamburger, *Exodus* commander], 19 July 1947, 9:15 P.M., OL; to vessel from Arnon, 17 July 1947, 4:30 P.M. (no. 19); to Amnon from Arnon, 17 July 1947, 5 P.M. (no. 30), HHA 14/234.

143. From the Colonial Secretary to the High Commissioner, 13 July 1947, box 2, file 1, Cunningham Papers, MEC; from Bevin to French Minster of Foreign Affairs Georges Bidault, 12 July 1947, quoted in Allan Bullock, *Ernest Bevin: Foreign Secretary 1945–1951* (New York, London, 1983), pp. 449–50.

144. See note 120.

145. The British navy commanders opposed the sailing of the *Exodus* westward to France and the transfer of the refugees there, as planned by Bevin; see the High Commissioner to the Colonial Secretary, 15 July 1947, Cunningham Papers, MEC.

146. Report of the British consulate, Marseilles, to Foreign Office, 29 July 1947, P.R.O. FO371/61820; announcement by the British government, 21 August 1947, CZA S25/2630; Shmarya Zameret, *Diary*, Marseille, 5 August 1947, Beit Hashita.

147. See note 94; see also Ben-Gurion, *Diary*, 12 February 1947, BGA.

148. Bullock, *Ernest Bevin*, p. 450.

149. In a memorandum to President Truman, the American acting secretary of state mentions Bevin's extreme sensitivity about the issue: 22 July 1947, FRUS 1947, vol. 5, pp. 1138–39.

150. Arthur Koestler, *Promise and Fulfillment: Palestine 1917–1949* (New York, 1949), p. 180.

151. The high commissioner tried to prevent the deportation to Hamburg. See High Commissioner to the Colonial Secretary, 14 August 1947, P.R.O. FO371/61822; Ben-Gurion to Paula, 29 August 1947, BGA; Golda Meyerson to Alan Cunningham, 1 September 1947, CZA S25/2630.

152. Bevin to the British Ambassador to Washington, 16 August 1947, P.R.O. FO371/61822.

153. Ben-Gurion in the Histadrut General Council, 6 August 1947, BGA; Ben-Gurion in the Mapai Council, 8 August 1947, LPA.

154. Ibid.

155. Decisions of the Zionist General Council, Zurich, 3 September 1947, CZA S5/320.

156. Testimony of Hayim Yahil (Hoffman), ODD 1(12).

157. From Shertok in Geneva to Meyerson in Jerusalem, 23 August 1947, CZA S25/2630.

158. Ben-Gurion to the Histadrut General Council, 6 August 1947, BGA; Ben-Gurion in the Mapai Council, 8 August 1947, LPA.

159. Cable from the Jewish Agency Executive to the Prime Minister of Denmark, Zurich, 26 August 1947, CZA S25/2630.

160. Closing words of Ben-Gurion to the Zionist General Council, Zurich, 2 September 1947, CZA S25/2630.

161. Meyerson to Ben-Gurion, Jerusalem, 1 September 1947, CZA S25/1696.

162. "Hamburg Day," leaflet of the Va'ad Le'umi to the local authorities, community committees, and agricultural settlements, 3 September 1947, CZA S25/2630.

163. *Davar,* 22 August 1947.

164. The deportation of the *Exodus* passengers to Hamburg indeed aroused a storm in the American press. See the summary of the articles in the American press concerning the *Exodus,* Jewish Agency in America, 25 September 1947, CZA S25/2630.

165. Letter from Ben-Gurion to the Executive in London, 7 September 1947, CZA S25/2630.

166. Ibid.

167. "Today we are mounting on the ship which is the battleship of the Jewish people's survival. We will march with our head high along with the Jewish masses—be their avant-garde, beside them, with them—as did our friends in the underground, the ghettos, in the effort of saving Jews and for Israel's honor." This was the "Order of the Day" issued by HaShomer HaTzair "somewhere in Europe" to all its members on the ship. See Moreshet Archive D.1.5943; see also *HaShomer HaTzair Book,* vol. 2 (in Hebrew) (Merhavia, 1961), file 3; report of Elhanan Winhotzker (Yishai) to Mapai Council, 2 September 1947, LPA; HHA 14/234b. The operations log of the Mossad is also rich with exclamations about the *Exodus* people; see 29 July 1947, OL; Zamaret, *Diary,* 5 August 1947 and 14 August 1947.

168. Ben-Gurion in the Mapai Council, 8 August 1947, LPA.

169. Ben-Gurion to Meirov, Hoffman, and Levine; see note 126.

170. Slutzki, ed., *The History of the Haganah* C/2, p. 1163.

171. Halamish, *Exodus,* p. 195–202.

172. Cables from the Mossad in Romania, 16, 17, 18 December 1947, HHA 14/71, 14/703, 14/705b.

173. Cable from Shertok to Ben-Gurion, 13 December 1947, no. 43; see also cable no. 82 to Arnon [the Mossad in Palestine] from Yissar [the Mossad in France]: "Ben-Kedem [Shertok] reported he is considering [the ship's sailing directly to Cyprus] and will consult with Ami [Ben-Gurion]." (18 December 1947, HHA 14/705b); Ben-Gurion, *Diary,* 17 December 1947, quoted in Ben-Gurion, *War Diary 1947–1949,* vol. 1 (Tel Aviv, 1982), p. 51.

174. Ben-Gurion, *Diary,* 17 December 1947.

175. Ibid.

176. Halamish, *Exodus,* 197–99. In a cable from Marseilles to Mossad headqaurters in Paris, which warned of a violent and bloody resistance by the refugees in Hamburg, it was also stressed that "the people will resist anyhow in spite of the clear order not to do so" (22 August 1947, OL.)

177. See Ze'ev Hadari and Ze'ev Zahor, *Ships or State* (in Hebrew) (Tel Aviv, n.d.), p. 126.

178. Ben-Gurion, *Diary*, 10 December 1947, quoted in *War Diary*, p. 36.

179. Slutzki, ed., *The History of the Haganah* C/2, p. 1163.

180. The two ships were purchased in March 1947 in the United States for $500,000. Danny [Schind] to Mossad heaquarters in Paris, 24 March 1947, OL.

181. Yeshayahu Trachtenberg (Dan) in Mapai Executive, 9 December 1947, LPA 24/47. The complete minutes of this meeting are reproduced in Avizohar and Bareli, *Now or Never* (in Hebrew) (Tel Aviv, 1990), pp. 436–38.

182. Shaul Meirov to the Mapai Executive, 9 December 1947, LPA 24/47.

183. Sailings consequences "catastrophic," cabled Zelig Brodetzky and Nahum Goldman to the Jewish Agency Executive, London, 18 December 1947, quoted in Gedalya Yogev, *Documents, Policy, and Diplomacy, December 1947–May 1948* (in Hebrew) (Jerusalem, 1980).

184. See the cable received by Averbuch in Romania on the decision to let Shertok decide: to Agami from Or [Meirov], 4 December 1947, HHA 14/71.

185. Ben-Gurion to the Mapai Executive, 9 December 1947, LPA 24/47.

186. Ibid.

187. Ibid. Ben-Gurion's claim that for a year and a half he had opposed the Mossad's shift to bigger ships contradicts his words in the Zionist congress of December 1946 that the immigrants should be transported "in bigger and safer ships." Ben-Gurion to the Political Committee, 18 December 1946, BGA; also see Avriel, *Open the Gates*, pp. 239–42.

188. Ben-Gurion to the Mapai Executive, 19 December 1947, LPA 24/47.

189. Ibid.

190. On Ben-Gurion's ambivalent attitude toward clandestine immigration, see Zertal, "Between Ethics and Politics," pp. 100–105.

191. Schind to HeHalutz in Warsaw, 15 November 1937, HHA, Poseidon file.

192. See note 183.

193. See Chapter 3. See also Hadari and Zahor, *Ships or State*, pp. 129–30, 138ff; Ben-Gurion, *War Diary*, p. 70, note 17.

194. Ben-Gurion, *Diary*, 10 December 1947, 24 December 1947 (meeting with Meirov and Schind on immigration budget, where one million dollars was allocated for the next six months); Ben-Gurion, *War Diary*, pp. 146, 168, 224, and elsewhere.

195. For example, "You had many times commented on the human material we have sent on the ships, and undoubtedly you were right . . . and what is the picture: large part of the 6,500 will be a heavy burden on the Yishuv, being children, youth, and elderly not capable of doing any work. Even the pioneering part is not of the best education . . . if we have to take now 20,000, practically 13,000 of them will be without sufficient control and the human material will be much worse" (from Rimon [Romania] to Neter [France], Bucharest, 10 April 1947, HHA 14/528).

196. Ben-Gurion to the Mapai Executive, 9 December 1947, LPA 24/47.

197. Yehuda Braginsky, *A Nation Rowing to Shore* (in Hebrew) (Tel Aviv, 1964–65), pp. 337, 339–40; from Tzadi [Tzisling] to the Mossad, Paris, 14 January 1947, HHA.

198. Ben-Gurion's diaries during this period carry many references to meetings with key Mossad people (such as Ze'ev Schind, Pino Ginsburg, Ehud Avriel, and Yosef Barpal).

199. Statements by the Mossad head to the Mapai Executive, 9 December 1947, LPA 24/47.

200. See Averbuch in Romania to the Mossad, including the appeal of "David [B. G.]," 4 December 1947, HHA 14/71; see also the end of Chapter 3 in this book.

201. Elhanan Winhotzker in the Mapai Executive, 9 September 1947, LPA, HHA 14/234b.

202. Danny to the Mossad headquarters in Paris, 24 March 1947, OL.

203. See note 201.

204. Shaul Meirov, in the Mapai executive, 9 December 1947, LPA 24/47.

205. "Shaul reports that the ships moved from Varna to Burgas. Conveyed to him the Executive's decision" (Ben-Gurion, *War Diary*, 24 and 28 December 1947). The *Pan* issue occupies just a few lines in Ben-Gurion's diary, with no comments.

206. Ibid.

207. To one of the envoys who tried to tell Ben-Gurion about the *Exodus* passengers' herosim, he said, "It's over. Finished. This is the past. Now there is a future . . . there are other, severe problems" (quoted in Bar Zohar, *Ben Gurion*, p. 656).

208. Ben-Gurion to the Mapai Executive, 9 December 1947, LPA 24/47.

209. Braginsky, *A Nation Rowing*, p. 357.

EPILOGUE

1. Y. Noded [Yitzhak Sadeh], "My Sister on the Beach," in Zerubavel Gilead, ed., *The Palmach Book*, vol. 1 (in Hebrew) (Tel Aviv, 1953), p. 725.

2. Z. B. [Zerubavel Gilead], "At the Outset" (in Hebrew), in Gilead, ed., *The Palmach Book*, p. vii.

3. An Israeli historian defines this text of Yitzhak Sadeh as "a kind of order of the day," a "command" to the Palmach people and the entire Zionist community. She does a literal reading of the text—that is, "We sons of the *Yishuv*, young and healthy men, jeopardize our lives on her behalf"—and she talks about the "enormous" moral and educational effect of the text. See Aviva Halamish, "The Clandestine Immigration: Values, Myth, and Reality," in Nurit Gertz, ed., *Lookout Points: Culture and Society in Palestine* (in Hebrew) (Tel Aviv, 1988), p. 87.

4. Nathan Alterman, "Michael's Page," *City of the Dove* (in Hebrew) (Tel Aviv, 1972), pp. 25–27.

5. Moshe Dayan, "Endless Depth" (in Hebrew), *Davar*, 20 May 1980.

6. See Dan Miron, "'Around the Campfire'—Around the Point," *Facing the Silent Brother: Essays on the Poetry of the War of Independence* (in Hebrew) (Jerusalem, 1992), p. 89. See also Miron's fascinating discussion of 1948 poetry, especially his new reading of Alterman's poem "The Silver Tray," which "from a distance of forty years" allows Miron, in his words, "to expose layers in the poem that were not visible at first sight" (ibid., p. 66).

7. Haim Hoffman-Yahil, "The Work of the Palestinian Commission to the Survivors, 1945–1949" (in Hebrew), *Moreshet*, 31 April 1981, p. 175.

8. Alterman, "Michael's Page," p. 26.

9. Sigmund Freud, "The Uncanny," *On Creativity and the Unconscious* (New York, 1958). A fascinating and unsettling discussion of this article, its meaning, and the interpretive possibilities it offers can be found in Shoshana Felman, "Textuality and the Riddle of Bisexuality," *What Does a Woman Want* (Baltimore and London, 1993), pp. 62–66; see also Julia Kristeva, *Etrangers à nous-mêmes* (Paris, 1988), pp. 269–77.

10. Freud, "The Uncanny," op. cit.

11. See Miron, "'Around the Campfire,'" pp. 78–79. The literature on the possibilities of representing and understanding the historical event of the destruction of European Jewry and the "Auschwitz" phenomenon has greatly expanded in recent years, with new titles constantly appearing. Two outstanding works are: Shoshana Felman and Dori Laub, *Testimony: Crisis of Witnessing in Literature, Psychoanalysis, and History* (New York and London, 1992); and Saul Friedländer, ed., *Probing the Limits of Representation: Nazism and the "Final Solution"* (Cambridge and London, 1992). For more on the tabooing and politicization of the Holocaust in Israel, see Moshe Zuckerman, *Shoah in the Sealed Room* (in Hebrew) (Tel Aviv, 1994).

12. Siegfried Kracauer was the first to connect the myth of the Medusa with the description of that which is indescribable. He wrote that looking at the Nazi horrors through movies about the death camps redeemed "horror from its invisibility behind the veils of panic and imagination." "The experience," he added, "is liberating in as much as it removes a most powerful taboo. Perhaps Perseus' greatest achievement was not to cut off Medusa's head but to overcome his fears and look at its reflection in the shield." Kracauer, *Theory of Film: The Redemption of Physical Reality* (New York, 1960), pp. 305–6.

Abbreviations

AAP	Avraham Polonsky Archive, Paris
ADM	Admiralty
BGA	Ben-Gurion Archive, Sdeh Boker
CAB	Cabinet Offices
CO	Colonial Office
CZA	Central Zionist Archive, Jerusalem
DP	Displaced persons
FMFAA	French Ministry of Foreign Affairs Archive, Paris
FO	Foreign Office
FRUS	Foreign Relations of the United States
HHA	History of Haganah Archive, Tel Aviv
JDCA	American Jewish Joint Distribution Committee Archive, New York, Jerusalem
KMA	Ha'Kibbutz Ha'Meuhad Archive, Efal
LA	Labor Archive, Tel Aviv
LPA	Labor Party Archive, Beit Berl
MEC	Middle East Center, Oxford
ODD	Oral Documentation Department, Jerusalem
OL	(Mossad) Operations Log
ORC	Overseas Reconstructions Committee
PRO	Public Record Office, London
UNRRA	United Nations Relief and Rehabilitation Administration
UNSCOP	United Nations Special Committee on Palestine
WA	Weitzmann Archive, Rehovot
WO	War Office

Glossary

The information in this glossary pertains mostly to the roles of the individuals and organizations during the time period discussed in the book.

INDIVIDUALS

Allon, Yigal	Palmach's commander in chief (1945–48); commander of the southern front during the war of independence (1948–49); member of Knesset and senior cabinet minister.
Alterman, Nathan	The poet laureate of Labor Zionism and the state of Israel in its first two decades; close to Ben-Gurion.
Arazi, Yehuda ("Alon")	Head of Mossad operations in Italy (1945–47).
Armorin, François-Jean	French journalist; covered the Mossad operations.
Attlee, Clement	British Labour Party politician; Britain's prime minister (1945–51).
Auriol, Vincent	French socialist politician; France's president (1947–54)
Averbuch, Moshe ("Agami")	Head of Mossad operations in Romania (1944–48).
Avriel, Ehud ("Itai")	Mossad's ambassador-at-large; assistant to Mossad head in Paris (1946–47).
Barpal, Yosef ("Kadmon")	Treasurer and deputy Mossad head.

Ben-Gurion, David ("Ami")	The prominent Zionist leader of the pre-state period; chairman of the Jewish Agency Executive (1935–48); Mapai party leader since 1930; Israel's first prime minister and minister of defense (1948–53; 1955–63).
Bevin, Ernest	British Labour Party politician; foreign secretary (1945–51).
Bidault, Georges	French Catholic politician; prime minister (1946, 1949–50, 1958); foreign minister (1944, 1947, 1953–54).
Blum, Léon	French statesman (of Jewish origin); socialist prime minister (1936, Dec. 1946–Jan. 1947)
Blumel, André	French jurist; member of the Socialist Party; Zionist activist; Prime Minister Léon Blum's head of office (1938); minister of the interior's head of office (1946–47).
Bodnaras, Emil	Chief of Romanian secret police of the communist regime; secretary general of the Romanian government; war minister and member of cabinet, regarded as "Moscow's man."
Bonomi, Ivanoe	Italy's prime minister (June 1944–June 1945).
Braginsky, Yehuda	Founder of the small organization for clandestine immigration which later became the Mossad; retired for political reasons from Mossad headquarters and returned to the Mossad office in Paris (1947), but only for marginal roles.
Creech-Jones, Arthur	British politician; undersecretary in the colonial office (1945–46), colonial secretary during the *Exodus* affair.
Depreux, Edouard	French socialist; minister of the interior (1946–47); Zionist sympathizer.
Dobkin, Eliahu	Head of the Jewish Agency's immigration department.
Filderman, Wilhelm	Leader of the Federation of Jewish Communities in Romania.
Frank, Efrayim ("Ernst")	Zionist agent in Munich.
Galili, Israel	Haganah chief of staff (1947–48); leader of Achdut Ha'Avodah and senior cabinet minister (1965–77).
Gasperi, Alcide de	Italian Christian-Democratic prime minister (1946–53).

Gilead, Zerubavel	Israeli writer; member of the Palmach and editor of *The Palmach Book*.
Ginsburg, Pino ("Berg")	Mossad senior operative in Europe (1939–48); stationed in Switzerland; in charge of financial operations.
Goldmann, Nahum	Administrative chairman of the World Jewish Congress; member of the expanded Jewish Agency Executive.
Golomb, Eliahu ("Dalin")	Haganah founder and commander until his death in 1945.
Groza, Petru	Romanian prime minister; leader of the Communist Party and the National Democratic Front (NDF).
Guri, Hayim	Poet; member of the Palmach.
Hall, George	Britain's colonial secretary (1945–46).
Hamburger (Har'el), Yossi	Haganah officer; commander of the *Exodus* and *Pan* ships.
Hazaz, Hayim	A Zionist and Israeli novelist; close to Ben-Gurion.
Hefer, Hayim	Member of the Palmach; songwriter.
Hoffman (Yahil), Hayim	Head of the 1945 Zionist Palestinian commission to the DP camps; head of the Jewish Agency delegation to Europe.
Jarblum, Marc	French-Jewish socialist activist, born in Poland; served as liaison between the Zionist operatives and the French government.
Kantoni, Rafael	President of the Federation of Jewish Communities in Italy; senior member of the Italian Socialist Party; served as liaison between the Zionist operatives and the Italian government.
Kaplan, Eliezer	Treasurer of the Jewish Agency and member of the Jewish Agency Executive.
Katzenelson, Berl	Labor movement spiritual leader; founder and first editor of *Davar*, the Histadrut daily newspaper.
Klarman, Yosef	Representative of the Revisionist party and Mossad delegate to Turkey and Romania.
Klieger, Ruth ("Hanum")	First woman to serve in the Mossad before and during World War II; Mossad envoy to France, Germany, and South America after the war.

Korczak, Ruzka	Leader of the Jewish combat organization in the Vilna (Vilnius) ghetto.
Kovner, Abba	Leader of the "east European survivors brigade," founded in 1945 in Romania; member of the combat organization in the Vilna (Vilnius) ghetto; partisan during World War II; Israeli poet.
Laski, Harold	British Labour Party chairman (1945–46); played a role in the La Spezia affair.
Laub, Morris	JDC representative in Cyprus deportee camps (1946–48).
Levine, Kurt	Jewish Agency envoy to the British occupied zone in Germany.
Lupescu, Rico	Israeli paratrooper to Romania during World War II; Mossad operative in Romania (1945–47).
Margolis, Laura	JDC delegate to France, in charge of the *Exodus* refugees.
Mayer, Saly	JDC representative in Switzerland.
Meirov (Avigur), Shaul ("Ben-Yehuda")	Head of the Mossad.
Meyerson, Golda	Deputy chairman of the Jewish Agency political department; senior cabinet minister and Israel's fourth prime minister (1969–74).
Mitterand, François	French socialist leader; France's president; during the *Exodus* affair, the youngest cabinet member and French government spokesman.
Moch, Jules	French socialist; minister of transportation and public works, in charge of the ports (1946–47).
Nahon, Umberto	Jewish Agency representative in Italy.
Nameri, David ("Hofshi")	One of the founders of the Mossad; founder and senior officer of the Palmach; liaison between the Palmach and the Mossad; head of Mossad's Haifa station.
Passman, Charles	Senior JDC operative in Europe and the Middle East.
Pauker, Anna	Romanian (of Jewish origin) foreign minister and leader of the Romanian Communist Party.
Pendelis, Yanaki	Greek ship contractor; worked for the Mossad (1939–48).
Perlman, Moshe	Journalist for British papers; Mossad's foreign press liaison during the *Exodus* affair.

Piade, Moshe	Yugoslav leader of Jewish origin; one of the founders and leaders of the Yugoslavian Communist Party; aided Mossad operatives in Yugoslavia.
Ramadier, Paul	French socialist prime minister (Jan.–Nov. 1947).
Rastani, Aldo	Italian journalist from Genoa; covered the La Spezia affair.
Sadeh, Yitzhak	Founder of the Palmach; military leader in the pre-state period.
Schind, Ze'ev ("Danny")	One of the founders of the Mossad; liaison with the JDC; after the war, Mossad's representative in the United States.
Schwartz, Joseph ("Shachor")	Head of JDC operations in Europe during and after World War II; member of the 1945 Harrison Commission.
Schwartz (Shevat), Levi	Mossad operative in Greece; also in charge of training Mossad and Palmach ship crews.
Sereni, Ada ("Daniela" "Claire")	Mossad's second in command in Italy (1945–46); head of Italy station (1947–48); widow of Enzo Sereni.
Sforza, Carlo	Italy's foreign minister (1947).
Shaltiel, David ("Kassuto")	Mossad's first operative in France (1945); served as delegate of the Jewish Agency and as liaison to Jewish resistance groups.
Sharett (Shertok), Moshe ("Ben-Kedem")	Head of the Jewish Agency political department; Israel's second prime minister (1953–55).
Silver, Abba Hillel	Senior American Zionist leader.
Sneh, Moshe	Senior Haganah officer; member of the Jewish Agency Executive; smuggled out of Palestine after Britain's Operation Broadside ("Black Saturday"); served as Mossad political supervisor in Europe.
Steiner, Yitzhak ("Parenta")	Mossad and Bricha operative in charge of Central Europe.
Tabenkin, Yitzhak	One of the founding fathers of Zionist labor movement; leader of Ha'Kibbutz Ha'meuhad movement; launched the organization for clandestine immigration, which later became the Mossad.
Tito, Josip Broz	Yugoslavian anti-Nazi partisan; prime minister and president of communist Yugoslavia (1945–80).

Tixier, Adrian	French socialist minister of the interior (1946).
Trachtenberg (Dan), Yeshayahu	Yishuv paratrooper to occupied Romania (June 1944); Mossad envoy to eastern Europe.
Trumpeldor, Joseph	Jewish Russian officer who came to the rescue of the Tel-Hai settlement and died defending it (1920); became the symbol and myth of Zionist heroism.
Velebit, Vlatko	Yugoslavia's deputy foreign minister (1946–47).
Wahrhaftig, Zerah	Member of the Rescue Commission of American Rabbis to post-war Europe; senior member of Israel's National Religious Party and cabinet minister.
Weizmann, Chaim	Head of the Zionist movement until Dec. 1946, when he was ousted by Ben-Gurion; Israel's first president (1948–52).
Weltch, Robert	Correspondent for the daily *Ha'aretz;* covered the *Exodus* affair.
Yehieli, Zvi	One of the founders and senior member of the Mossad; operated in Europe, Turkey, and Egypt during World War II; organized the launching of the Yishuv paratroopers to Europe; responsible for special missions after the war.
Zameret, Shmarya ("Meyuhas")	Mossad operative (1938–47); was active in Greece, France, and Italy; Mossad head of Marseilles (France) station (1946–47); in charge of preparation of the *Exodus.*
Zissu, Abraham L.	Leader of the National Jewish Party in Romania; Zionist revisionist journalist and author; officially in charge of the Jewish immigration from Romania.

ORGANIZATIONS AND CONCEPTS

Achdut Ha'Avodah	(Hebrew, Unity of Labor) A Zionist political party founded in 1919 by Berl Katzenelson and David Ben-Gurion, later to be closely associated with Ha'Kibbutz Ha'Meuhad and the Palmach; in 1930 became part of Mapai, and in 1944 an opposition to Ben-Gurion formed within the party.
Aliya	(Hebrew, ascent) The Zionist term for immigration to Israel.
Aliya bet	Immigration to Palestine without British certificates.

Aliya gimmel	An armed, clandestine immigration of young people that Ben-Gurion attempted to initiate in the fall of 1945.
Altalena	An immigrant and arms boat brought by the Irgun during the war of 1948; it was shot and sank by the Israeli army after the Irgun refused to hand over the arms.
Anglo-American Committee (on Palestine)	Established in Nov. 1945 to examine the conditions of the Jews in the American and British occupied zones in Europe and the possibilities of their resettlement in Europe and Palestine. In its report (Apr. 1946) the committee adopted the recommendations of the Harrison Commission to allow 100,000 of the displaced Jews to emigrate to Palestine.
Biltmore Plan	Zionist "activist" program, adopted in 1942 in New York, regarding the struggle against British rule and the establishment of a Jewish state in Palestine.
Bricha	(Hebrew, flight) A clandestine campaign, initiated by Holocaust survivors, later under Zionist control, to direct Jewish refugees to Mediterranean ports and to Mossad's gathering sites for immigration to Palestine.
Davar	The Histadrut daily newspaper.
Ha'apala	(Hebrew, summit climbing) The Zionist term for Jewish illegal immigration against the British restrictions.
Haganah	(Hebrew, Defense) The Yishuv underground armed forces, founded in 1920; from 1939 in charge of the Mossad.
Ha'halutz	(Hebrew, pioneer) A Zionist youth movement in the Diaspora.
Ha'Kibbutz Ha'Meuhad	(Hebrew, United Kibbutz) One of the three major kibbutz movements; closely associated with the Palmach, Mossad in its first years, and Achdut Ha'Avodah.
Ha'mossad Le'aliya Bet	(in short, "Mossad") The Zionist organization in charge of clandestine immigration (1939–48).
Harrison Commission	Appointed in 1945 by U.S. president Harry Truman to investigate the situation of the displaced Jews in the camps. The commission, headed by Earl G. Harrison, dean of the law

<table>
<tr><td></td><td>school of the University of Pennsylvania, recommended that 100,000 displaced Jews be immediately allowed to enter Palestine.</td></tr>
<tr><td>Havlagah</td><td>(Hebrew, restraint) A policy maintained by the Haganah toward Palestinian attacks (1936–39); in favor of cooperation with the British.</td></tr>
<tr><td>Histadrut</td><td>The federation of labor founded in 1920; combination of trade unions, an owner of economic enterprises, and a provider of social services.</td></tr>
<tr><td>Irgun</td><td>(Short for irgun z'vai leu'mi; Hebrew, national military organization) An underground organization associated with the revisionist party, favoring terrorist attacks and a militaristic approach toward the British and the Palestinians.</td></tr>
<tr><td>Joint Distribution Committee (JDC)</td><td>American-Jewish philanthropic organization, created to provide international assistance to Jews in distress.</td></tr>
<tr><td>Lechi</td><td>(Acronym for lochamei herut Israel; Hebrew, Israel's freedom fighters) An underground organization that split from the Irgun, unwilling to accept the decision to stop fighting the British during WW II; led by Yair Stern (until killed by the British in 1942); known as the Stern group.</td></tr>
<tr><td>Mapai</td><td>(Hebrew acronym for Eretz Israel workers party) A social-democratic party dominant in the Yishuv since the 1930s and in the early years of Israeli state; a merger between Achdut Ha'Avodah and Ha'Poel Ha'Tzair; later the labor party of Israel.</td></tr>
<tr><td>Palmach</td><td>(Hebrew acronym for plugot mahatz, striking units) Fighting units the Yishuv formed in 1941.</td></tr>
<tr><td>Palyam</td><td>(Hebrew acronym for plugot yam, naval units) Palmach's naval division.</td></tr>
<tr><td>Stern group</td><td>see Lechi.</td></tr>
<tr><td>UNSCOP</td><td>(Acronym for United Nations Special Committee on Palestine) Appointed to inquire for the situation in Palestine. The committee report, submitted to the UN on 1 Sept. 1947,</td></tr>
</table>

recommended ending the British mandate and the partitioning of Palestine to two states.

Va'ad Le'umi   The pre-state Jewish national council in Palestine.

Yishuv   (Hebrew, settlement) The Jewish community in Palestine before the establishment of the State of Israel.

White Paper   British official policy documents, published regularly on matters such as immigration, land purchase, and settlements.

Index

Compositor:	Publication Service, Inc.
Text:	Galliard
Display:	Bernhard
Printer:	Edwards Brothers
Binder:	Edwards Brothers